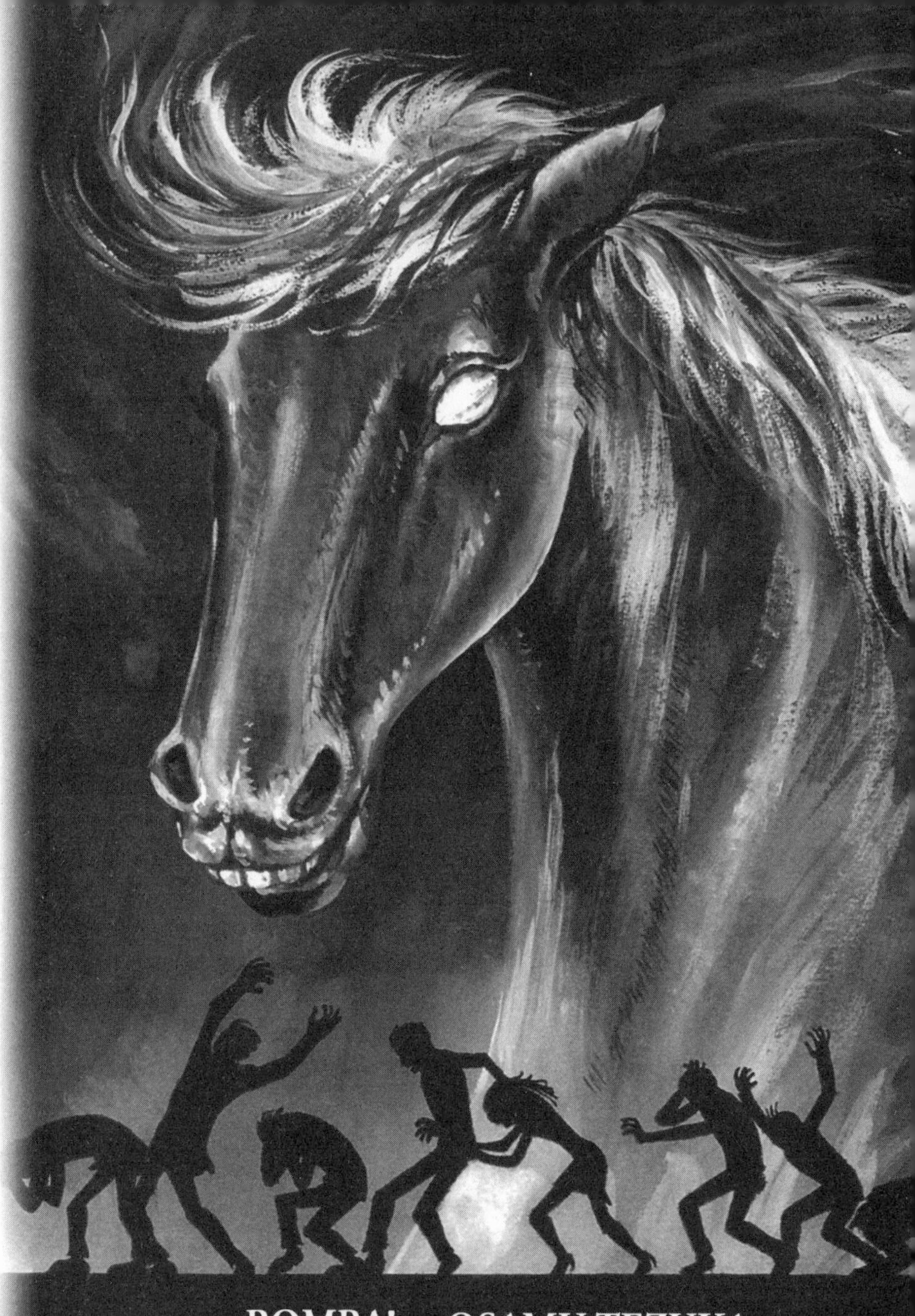

BOMBA! OSAMU TEZUKA

BOMBA!

A VERTICAL Book

Editor: Daniel Joseph
Translation: Polly Barton
Production: Risa Cho
Shirley Fang
Evan Hayden
Proofreading: Micah Q. Allen

First published in Japan in 1970
English translation rights arranged with Tezuka Productions.
English language version produced by Kodansha USA Publishing, LLC, 2022

Originally published in Japanese as *Tezuka Osamu Bunkozenshuu Bonba!* by Kodansha, Ltd.
Bonba! first serialized in *Bessatsu Shonen Magazine*, Kodansha, Ltd., 1970

ISBN: 978-1-64729-056-6

Printed in the United States of America

First Edition

Kodansha USA Publishing, LLC
451 Park Avenue South
7th Floor
New York, NY 10016
www.kodansha.us

KODANSHA

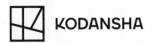

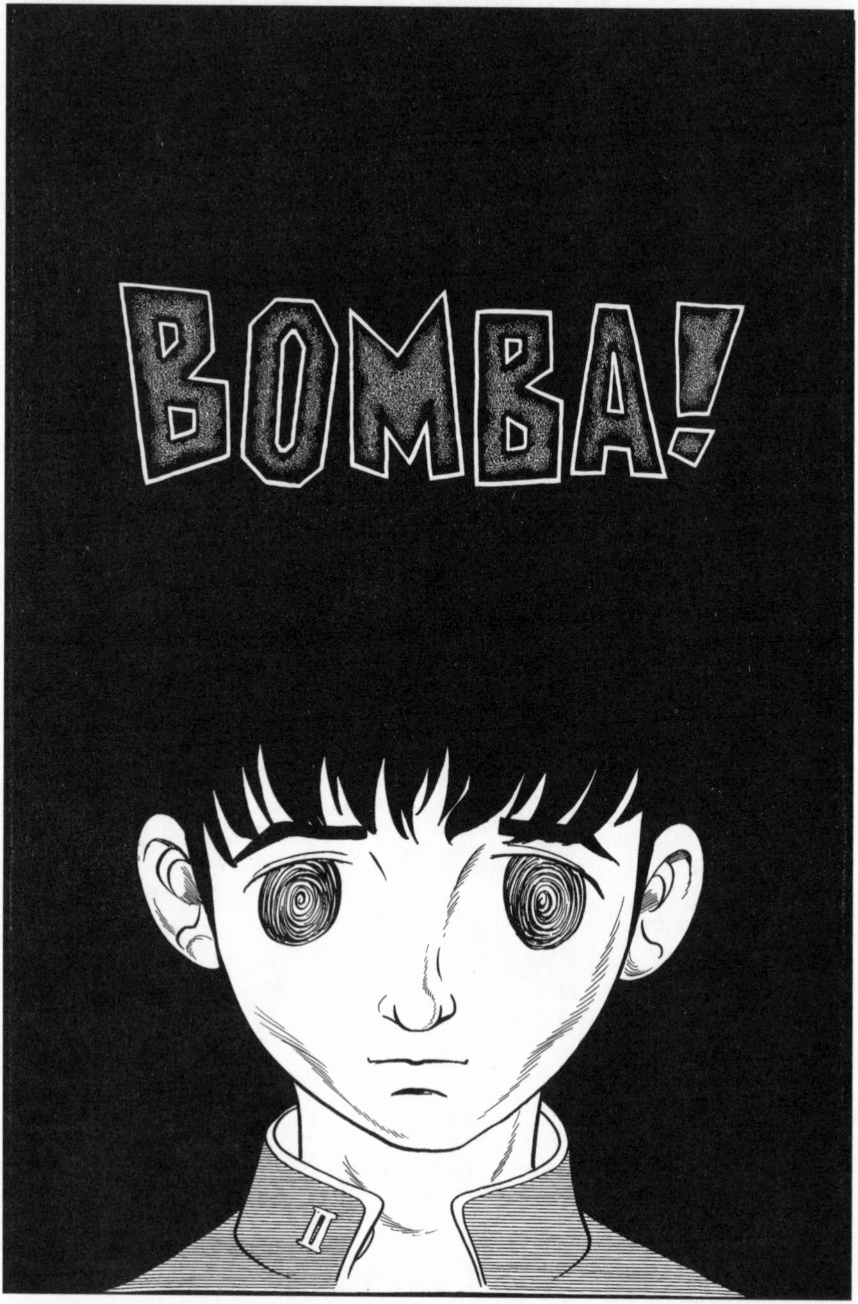
BOMBA!

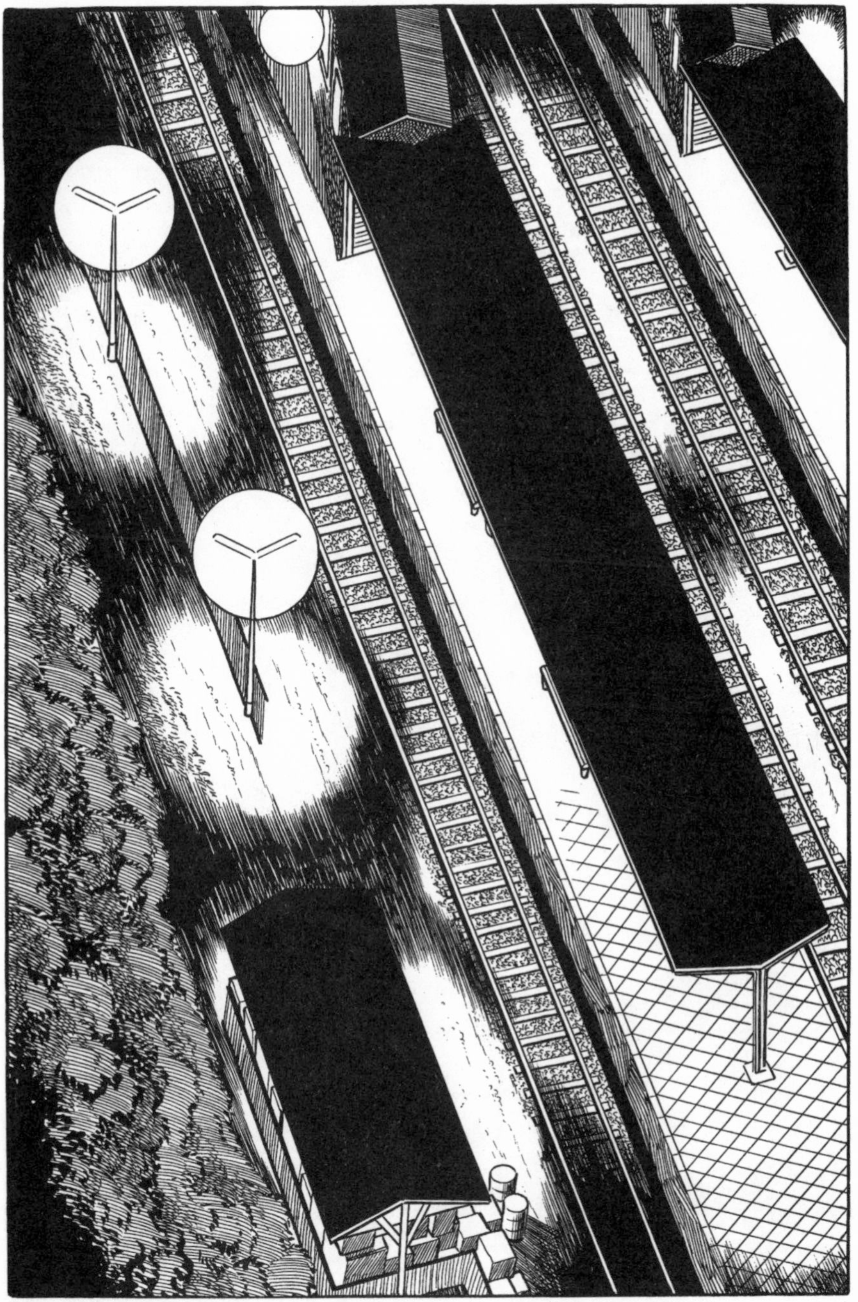

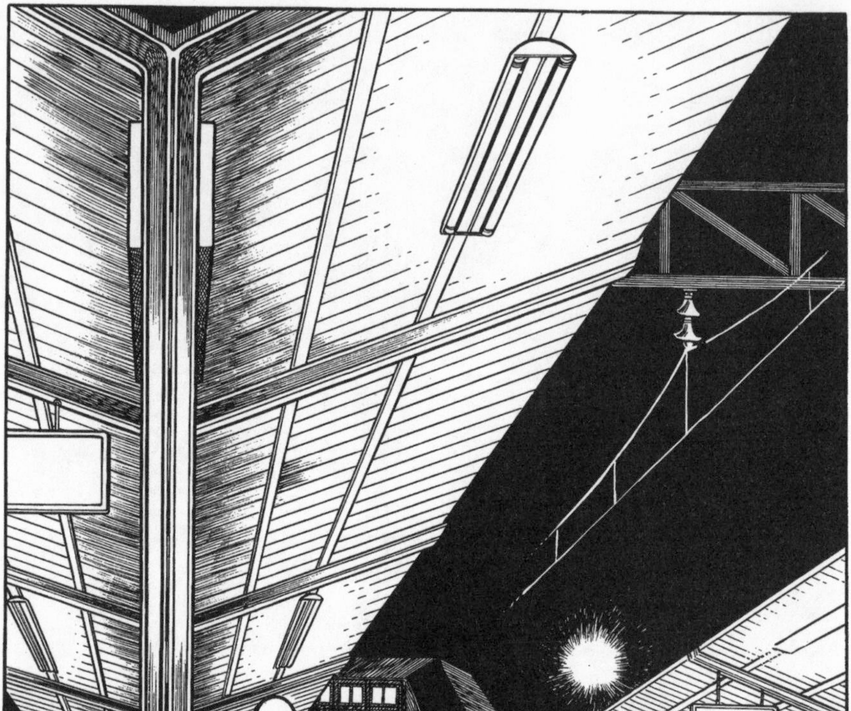
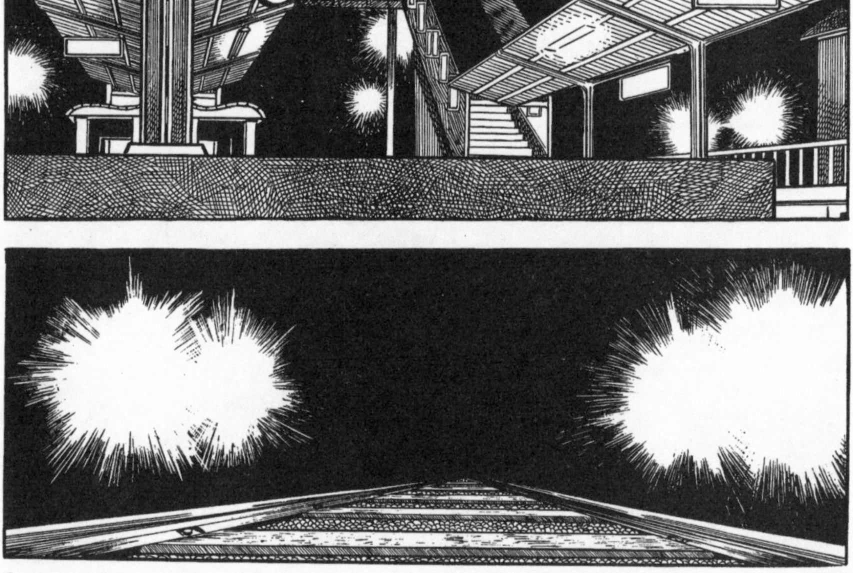

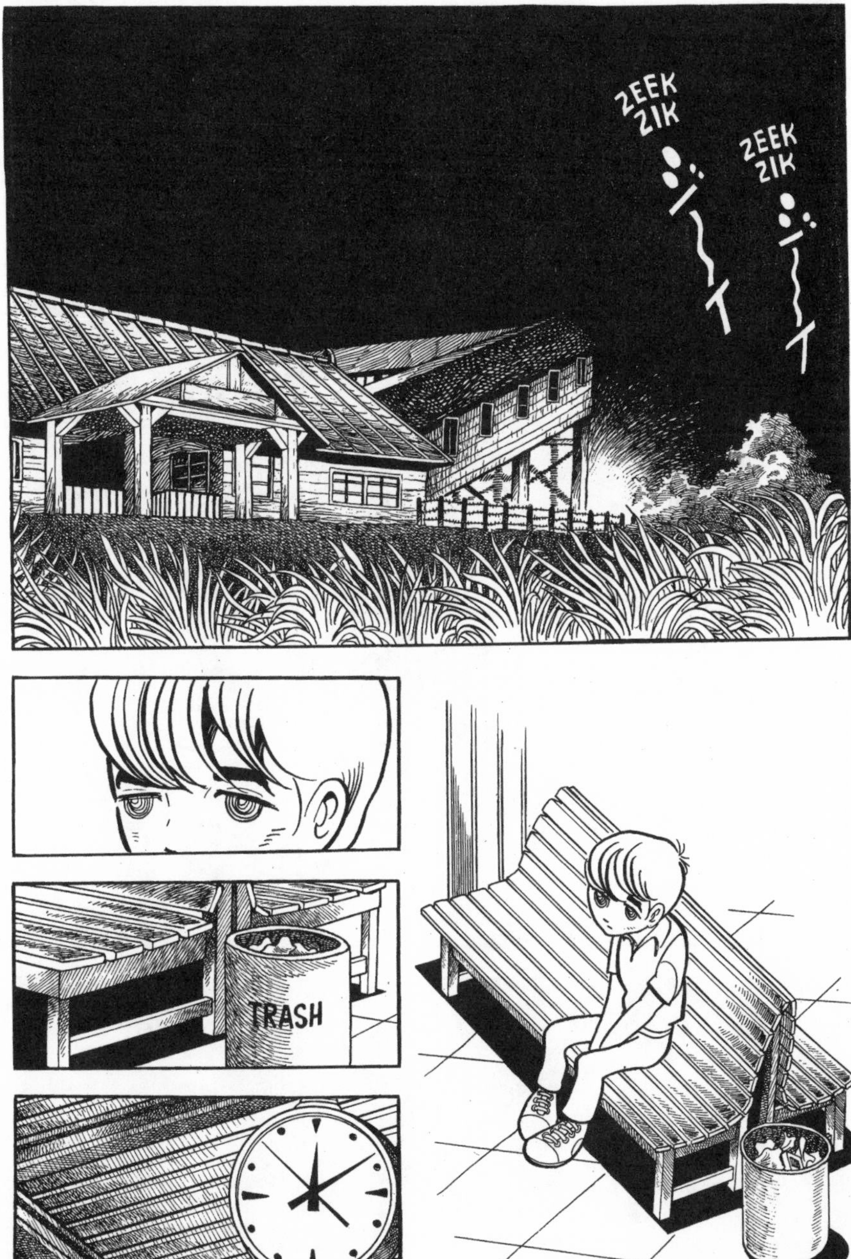
ZEEK ZIK
ジ〜イ
ZEEK ZIK
ジ〜イ
TRASH

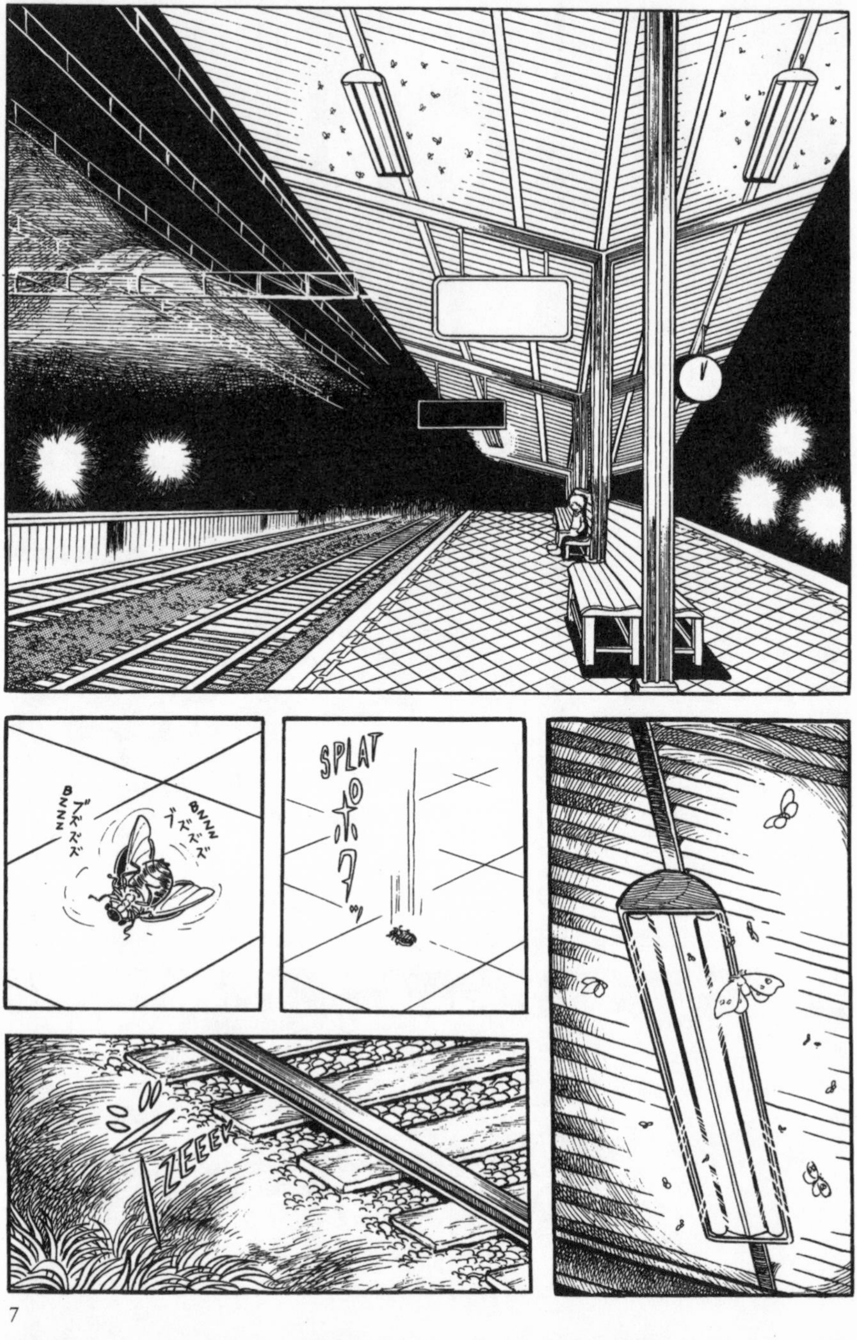
SPLAT
ポタッ
BZZZ
ブズズズ
BZZZ
ブズズズ
ZEEEK

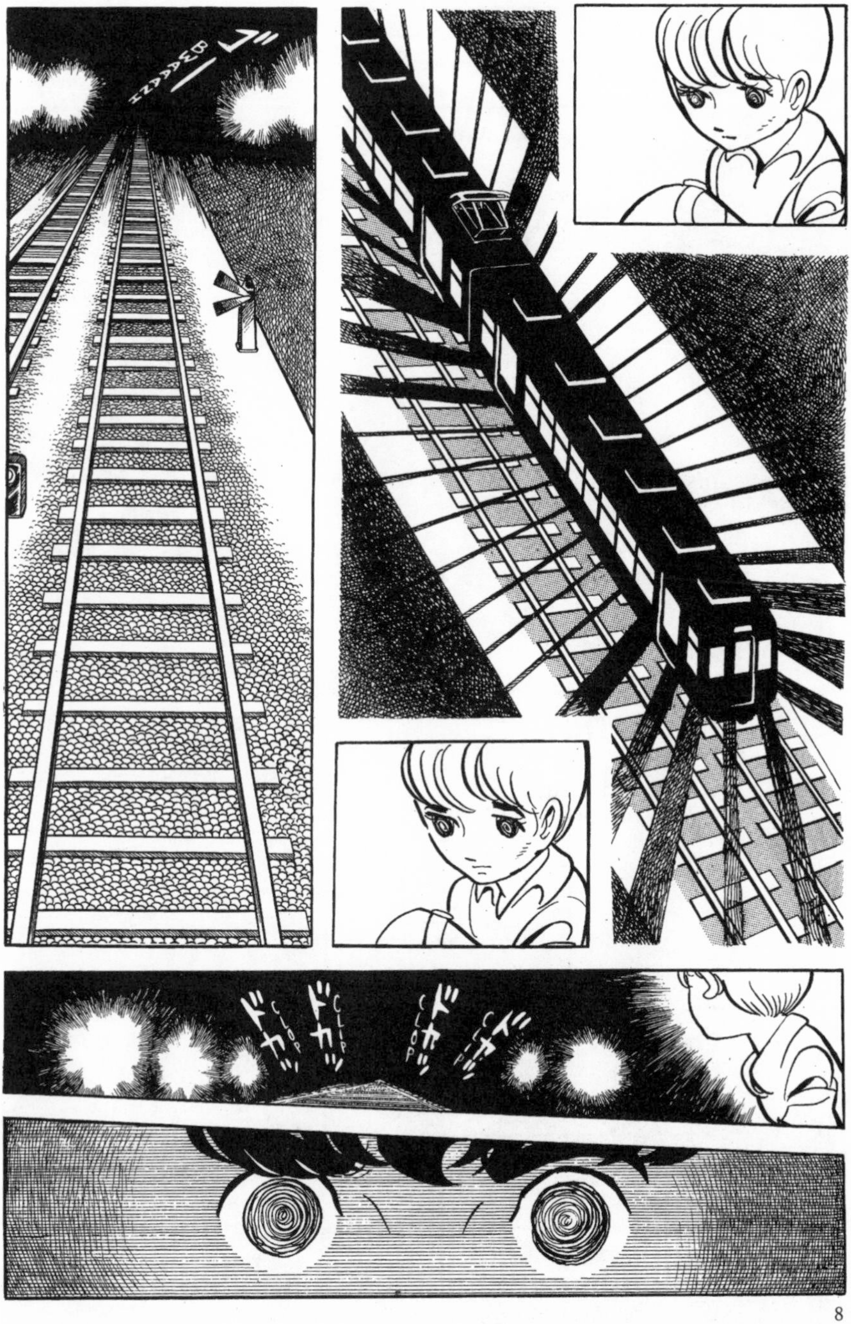
ゴー
BWAAAH
CLIP
CLOP
CLIP
CLOP

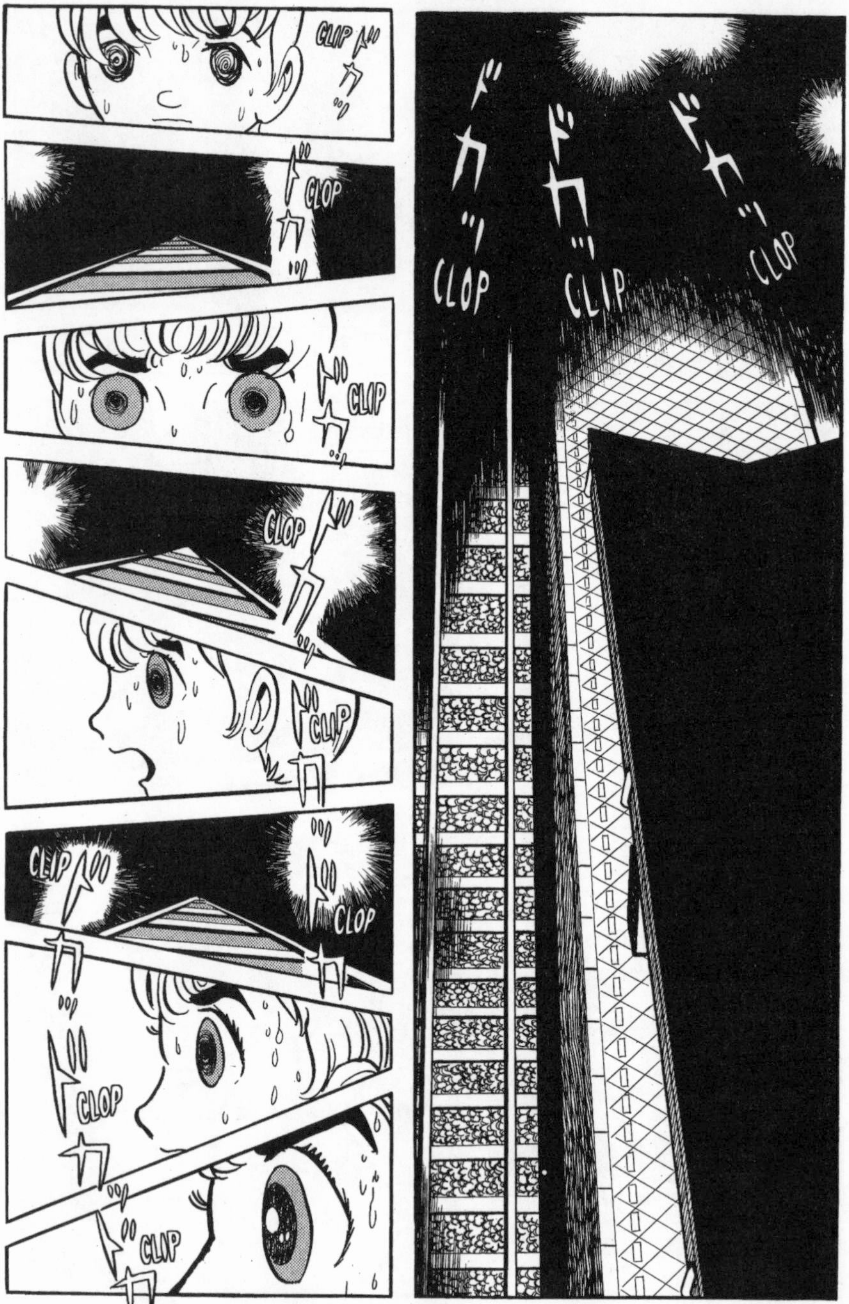
ドカッ
CLOP
ドカッ
CLIP
ドカッ
CLOP
CLIP
ドカッ
ドカッ
CLOP
ドカッ
CLIP
CLOP
ドカッ
ドカッ
CLIP
ドカッ
CLOP
CLIP
ドカッ
ドカッ
CLOP
ドカッ
CLIP
ドカッ

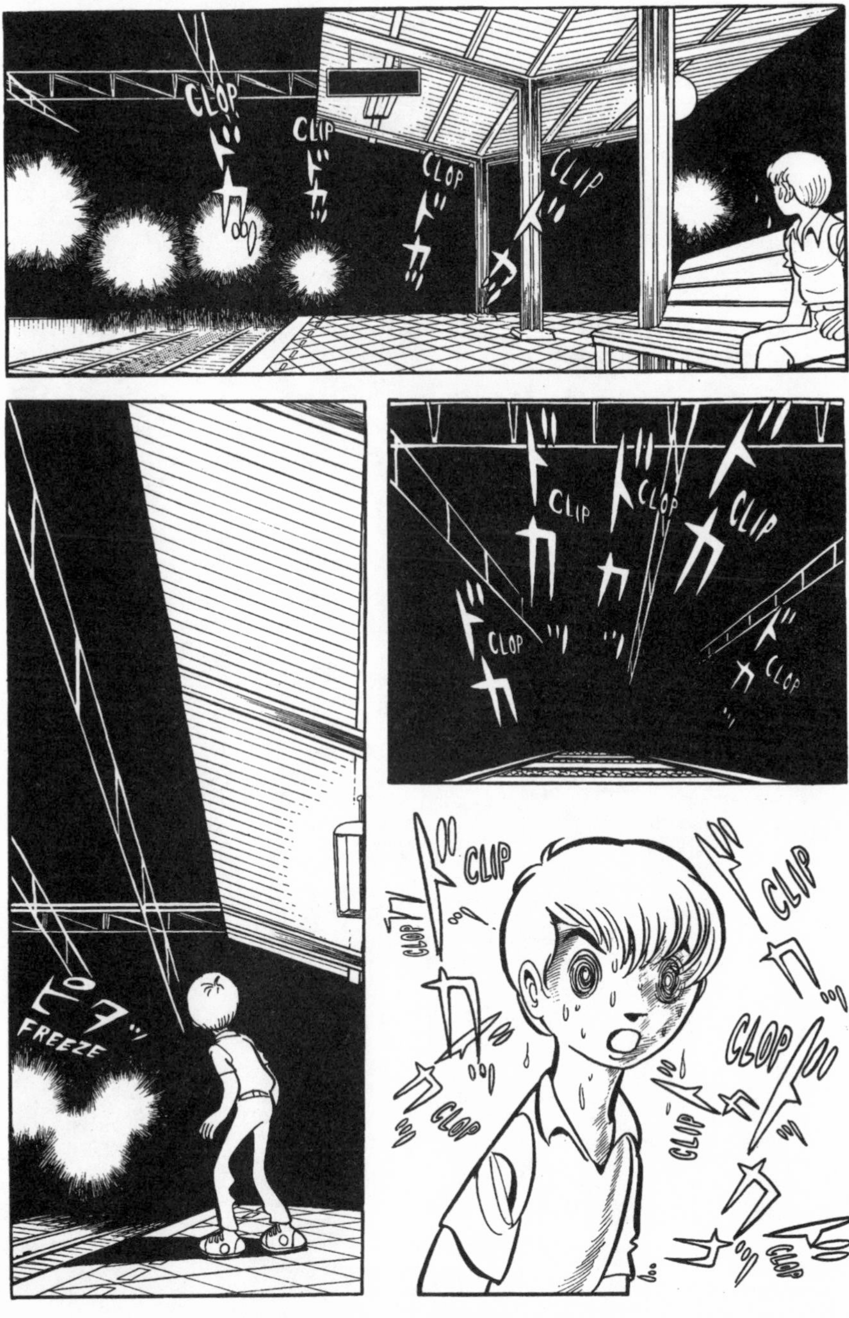
CLIP
CLOP
CLIP
CLOP
CLIP
CLOP
CLIP
CLOP
CLOP
CLIP
CLIP
CLOP
CLIP
CLOP
CLOP
CLOP
FREEZE

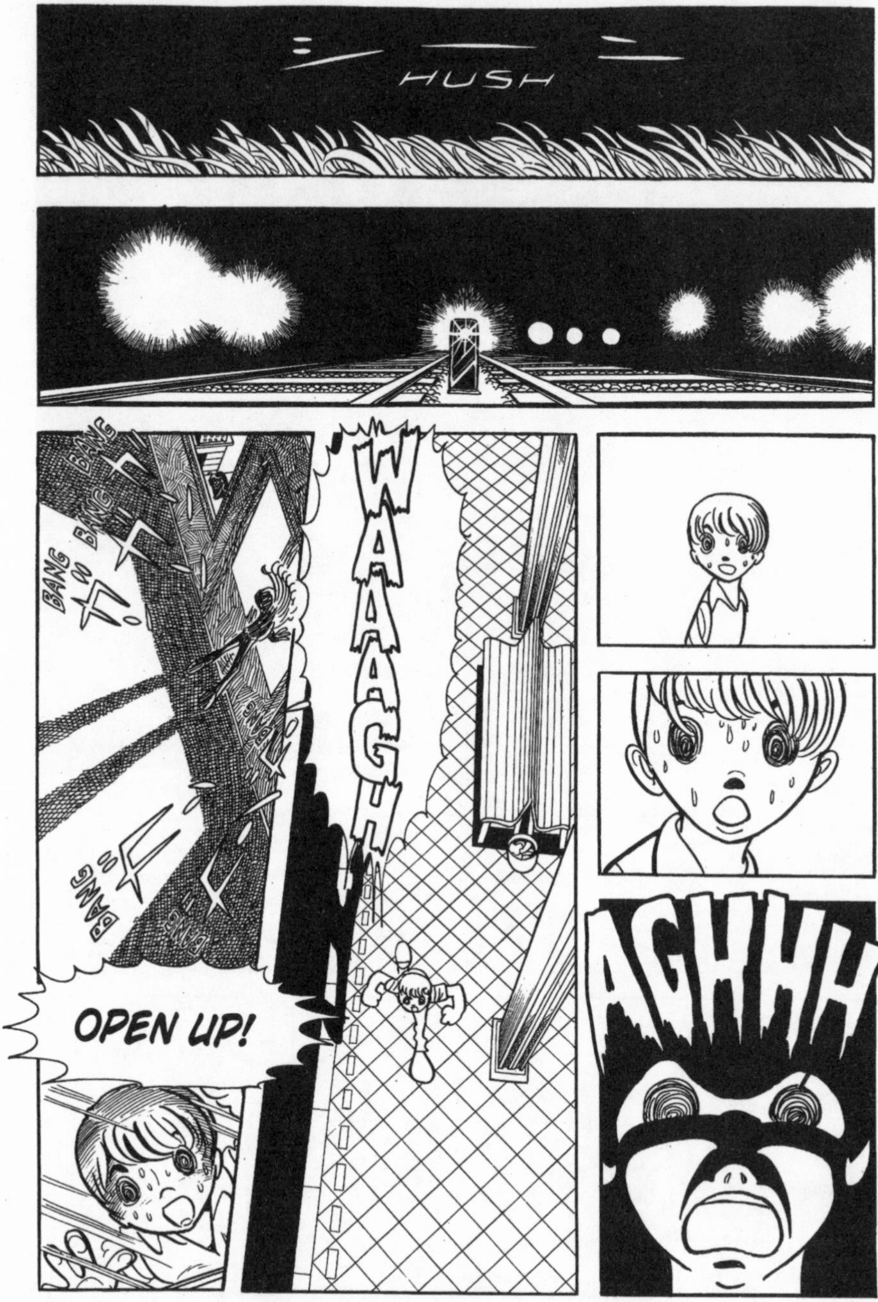
HUSH
AGHHH
WAAAAGH
BANG BANG
BANG BANG
BANG
BANG BANG
BANG
OPEN UP!

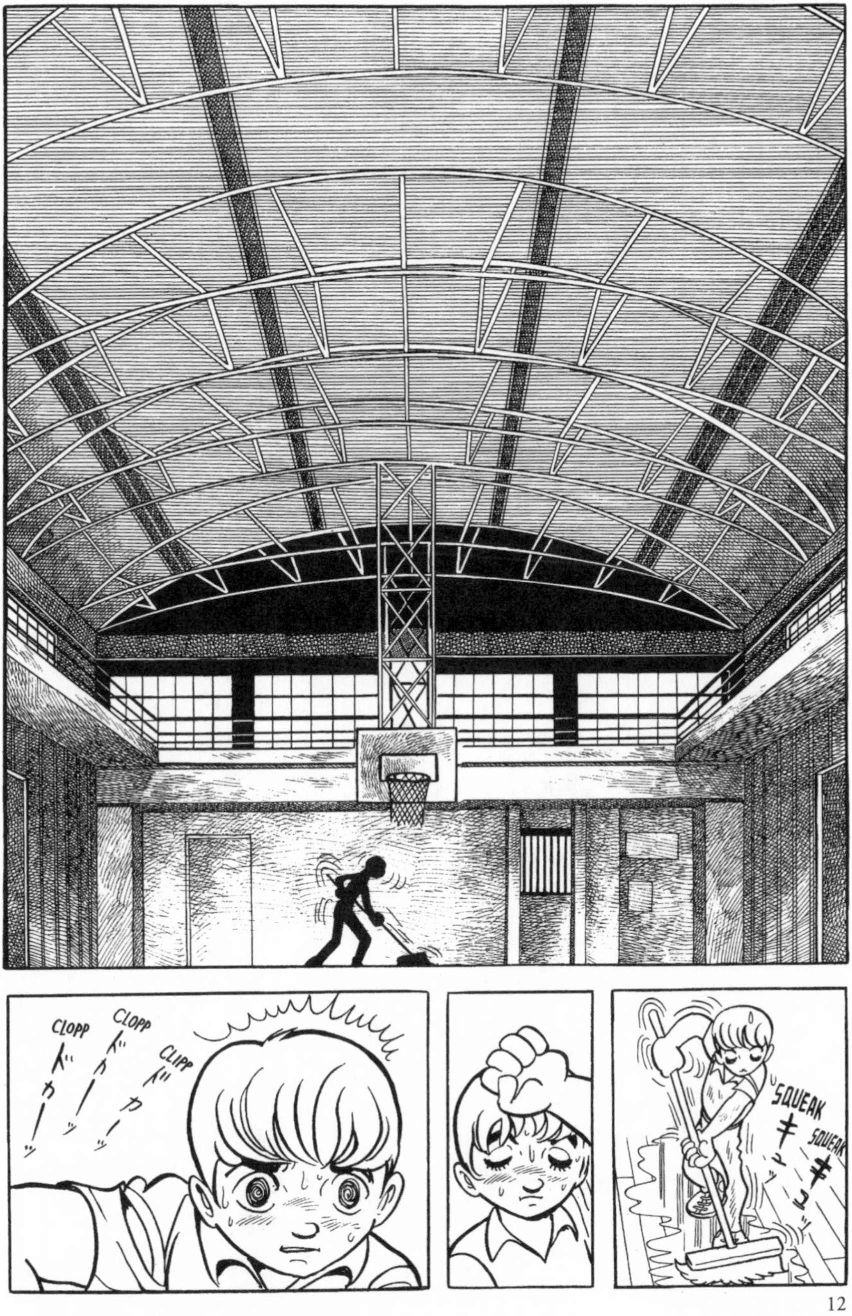
SQUEAK
キュッ
SQUEAK
キュッ
CLIPP
ドカッ!
CLOPP
ドカーッ!
CLOPP
ドカーッ!

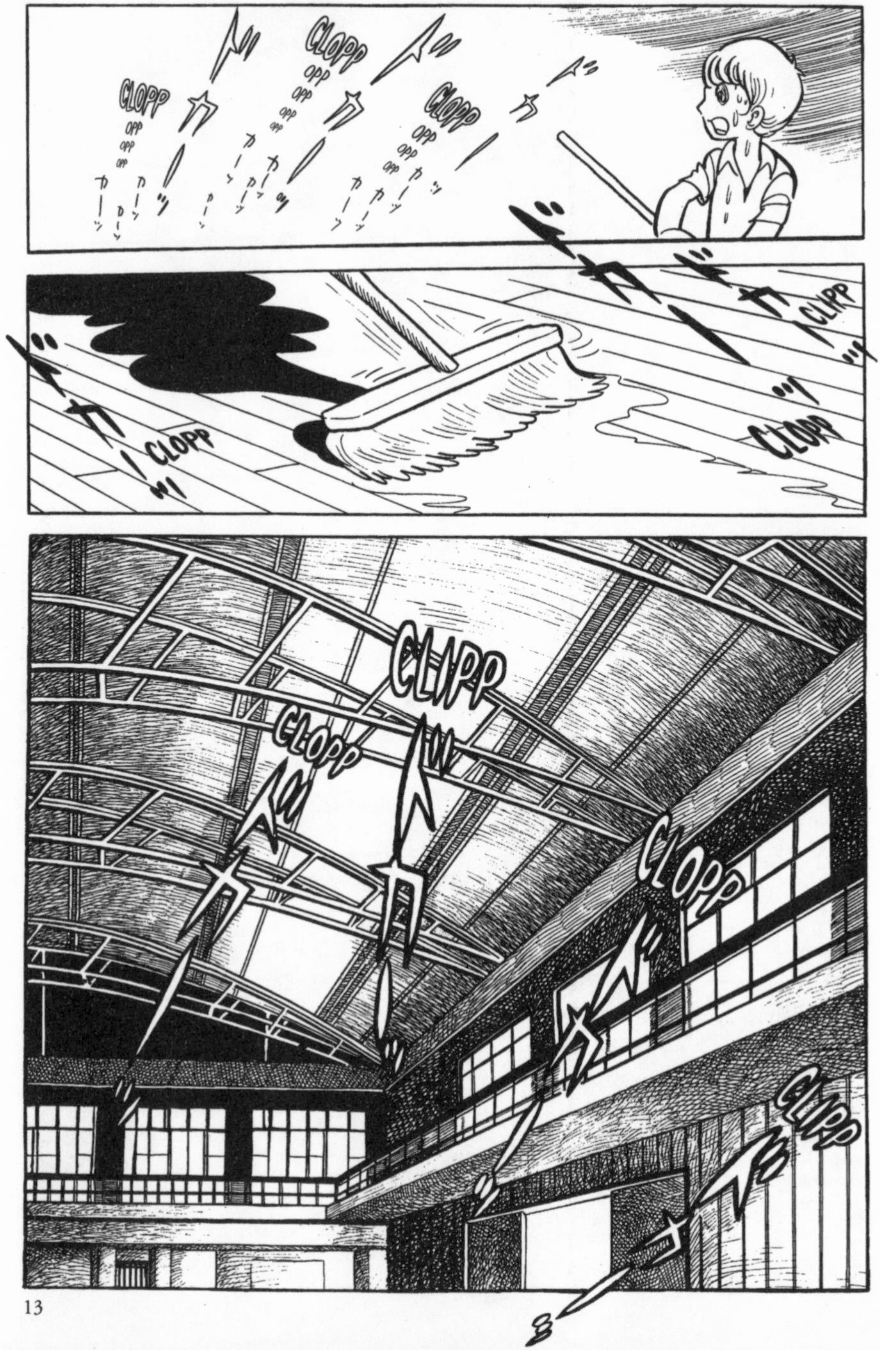
CLOPP
CLOPP OPP OPP OPP OPP
CLOPP OPP OPP OPP
CLOPP OPP OPP OPP
CLIPP
CLOPP
CLOPP
CLIPP
CLOPP
CLIPP
CLOPP

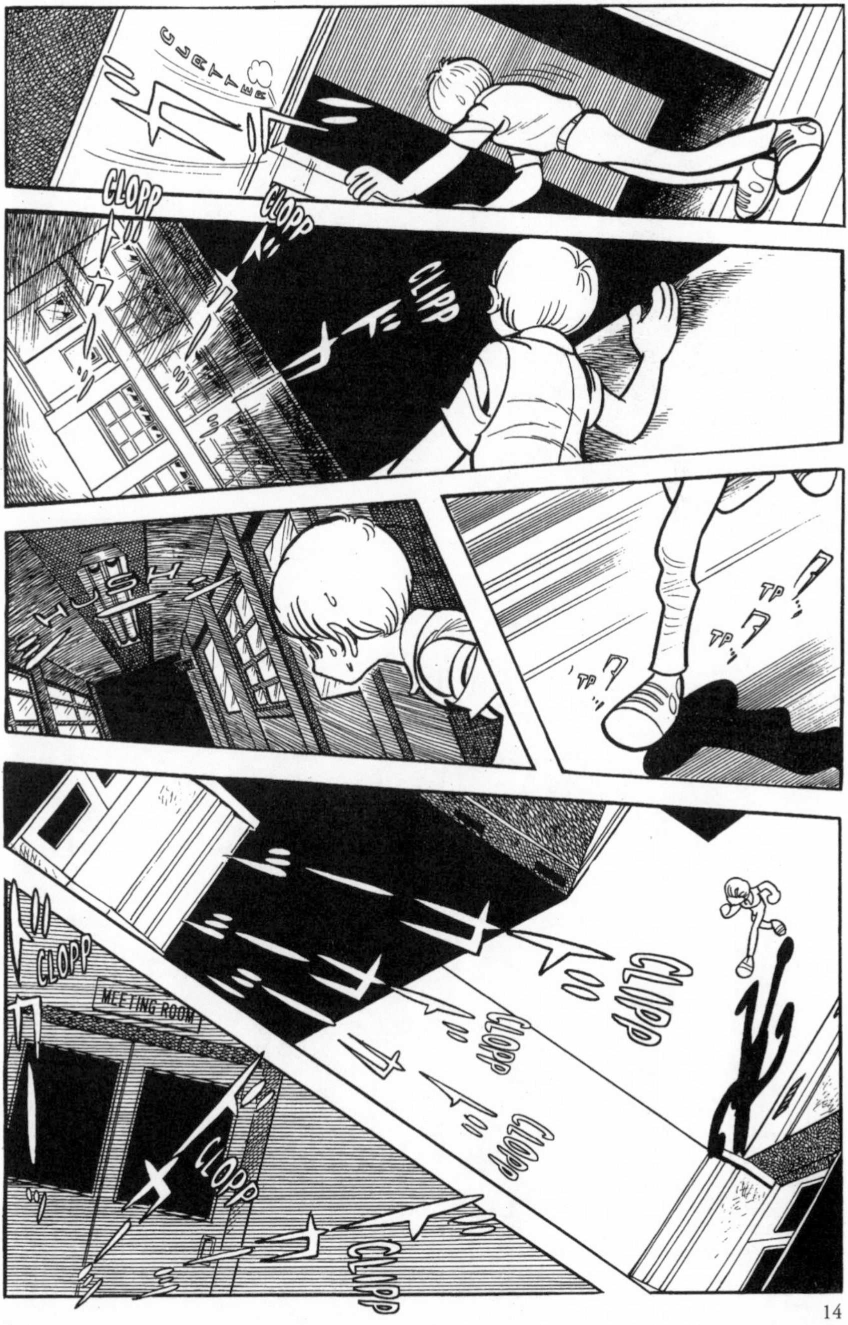
CLATTER
CLOPP
CLOPP
CLIPP
TP
TP
TP
CLIPP
CLOPP
CLOPP
CLOPP
MEETING ROOM
CLOPP
CLOPP

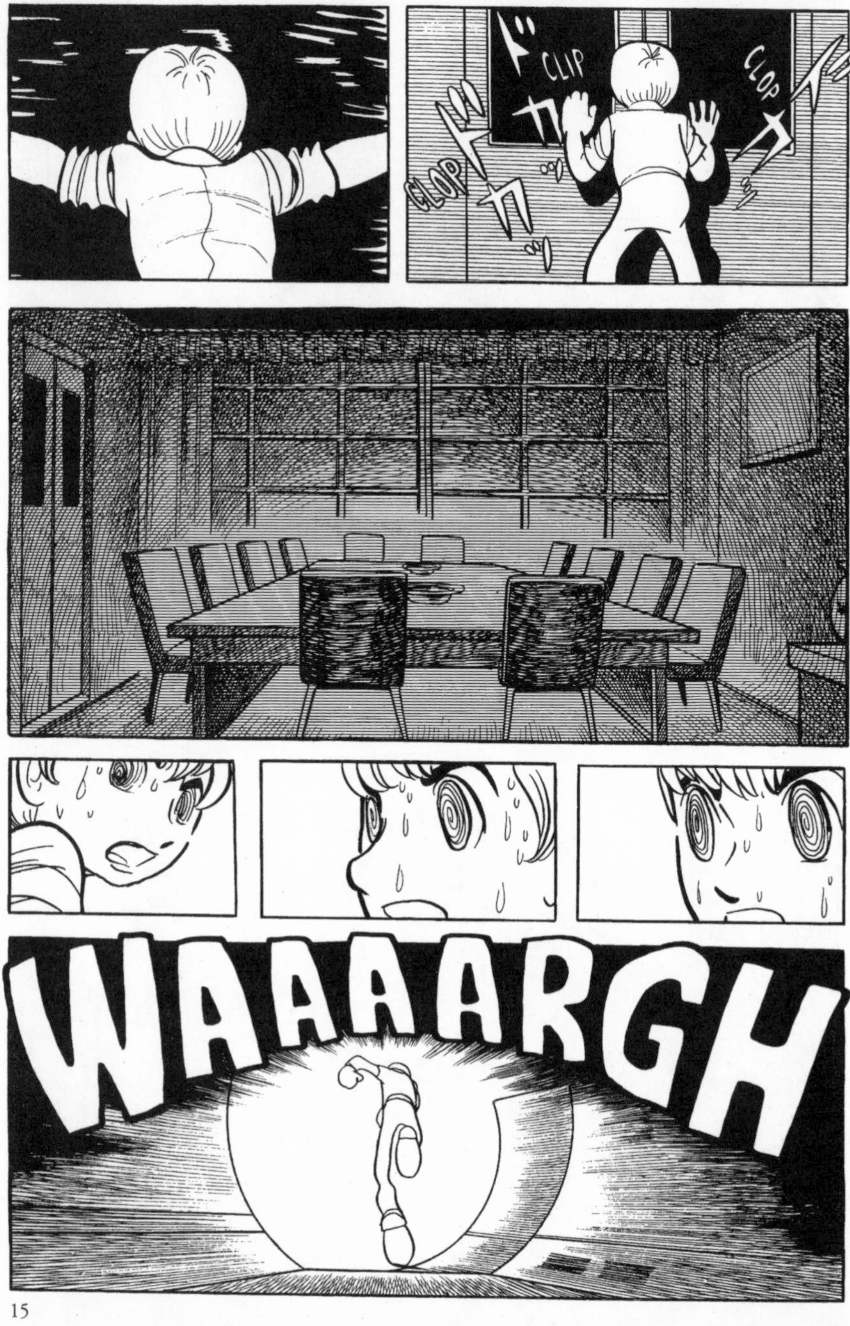
CLOP
CLIP
CLOP
WAAAARGH

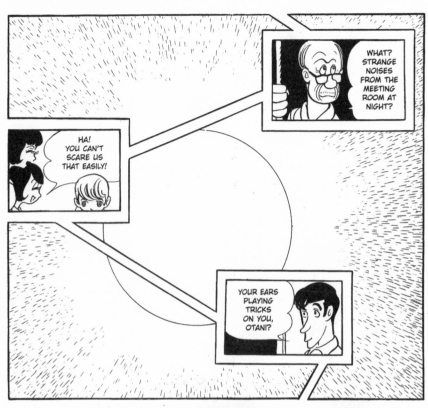

WHAT? STRANGE NOISES FROM THE MEETING ROOM AT NIGHT?

HA! YOU CAN'T SCARE US THAT EASILY!

YOUR EARS PLAYING TRICKS ON YOU, OTANI?

HEH HEH HEH

BAH HA HAH

TEE HEE HEE

HA HA

I HEARD IT! I REALLY DID!

I'M NOT MAKING IT UP!

I'VE HEARD IT A BUNCH OF TIMES!

ALWAYS WHEN I'M ALONE!

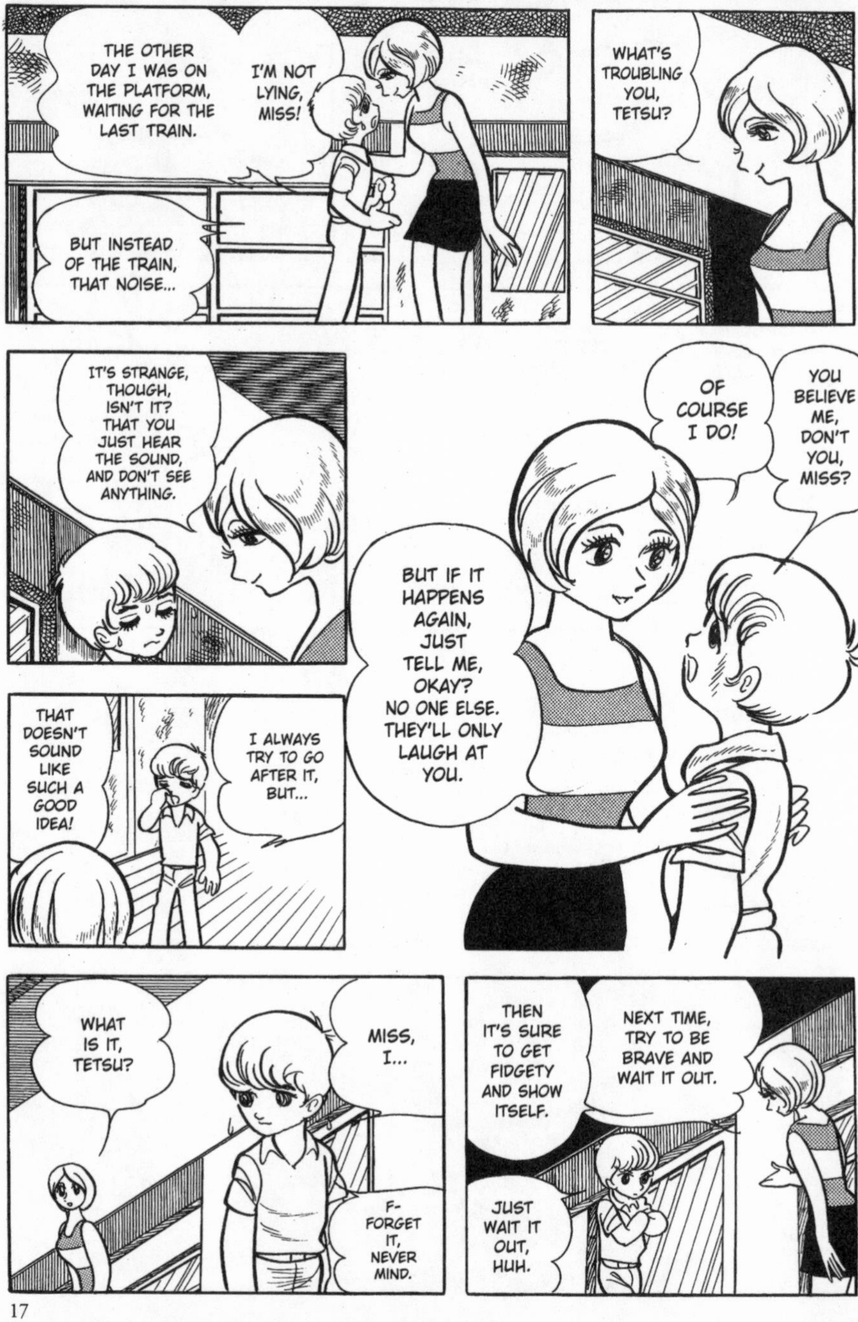
WHAT'S TROUBLING YOU, TETSU?
I'M NOT LYING, MISS!
THE OTHER DAY I WAS ON THE PLATFORM, WAITING FOR THE LAST TRAIN.
BUT INSTEAD OF THE TRAIN, THAT NOISE...
YOU BELIEVE ME, DON'T YOU, MISS?
OF COURSE I DO!
BUT IF IT HAPPENS AGAIN, JUST TELL ME, OKAY? NO ONE ELSE. THEY'LL ONLY LAUGH AT YOU.
IT'S STRANGE, THOUGH, ISN'T IT? THAT YOU JUST HEAR THE SOUND, AND DON'T SEE ANYTHING.
I ALWAYS TRY TO GO AFTER IT, BUT...
THAT DOESN'T SOUND LIKE SUCH A GOOD IDEA!
NEXT TIME, TRY TO BE BRAVE AND WAIT IT OUT.
THEN IT'S SURE TO GET FIDGETY AND SHOW ITSELF.
JUST WAIT IT OUT, HUH.
MISS, I...
WHAT IS IT, TETSU?
F-FORGET IT, NEVER MIND.

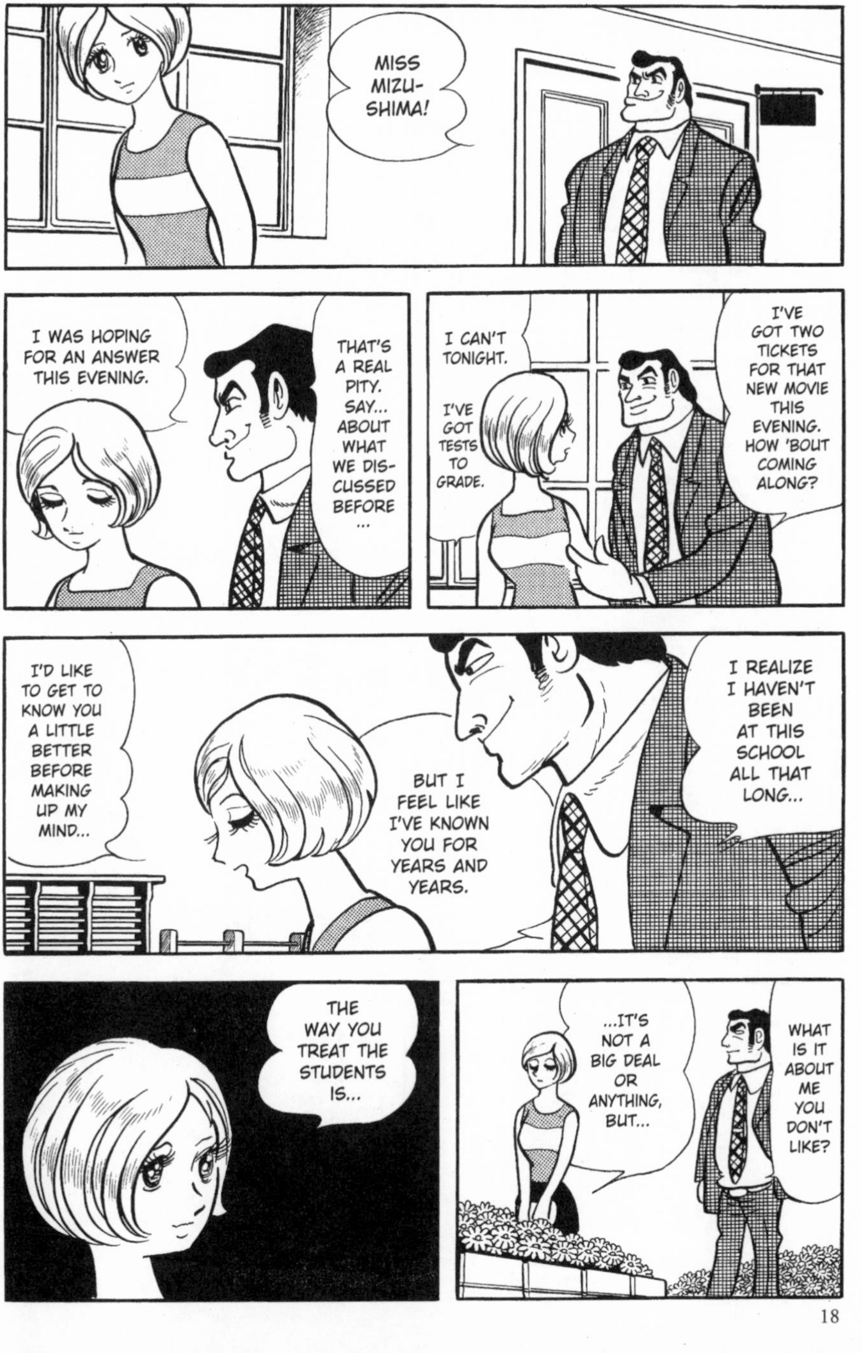
MISS MIZU-SHIMA!
I'VE GOT TWO TICKETS FOR THAT NEW MOVIE THIS EVENING. HOW 'BOUT COMING ALONG?
I CAN'T TONIGHT.
I'VE GOT TESTS TO GRADE.
THAT'S A REAL PITY. SAY... ABOUT WHAT WE DISCUSSED BEFORE...
I WAS HOPING FOR AN ANSWER THIS EVENING.
I REALIZE I HAVEN'T BEEN AT THIS SCHOOL ALL THAT LONG...
BUT I FEEL LIKE I'VE KNOWN YOU FOR YEARS AND YEARS.
I'D LIKE TO GET TO KNOW YOU A LITTLE BETTER BEFORE MAKING UP MY MIND...
WHAT IS IT ABOUT ME YOU DON'T LIKE?
...IT'S NOT A BIG DEAL OR ANYTHING, BUT...
THE WAY YOU TREAT THE STUDENTS IS...

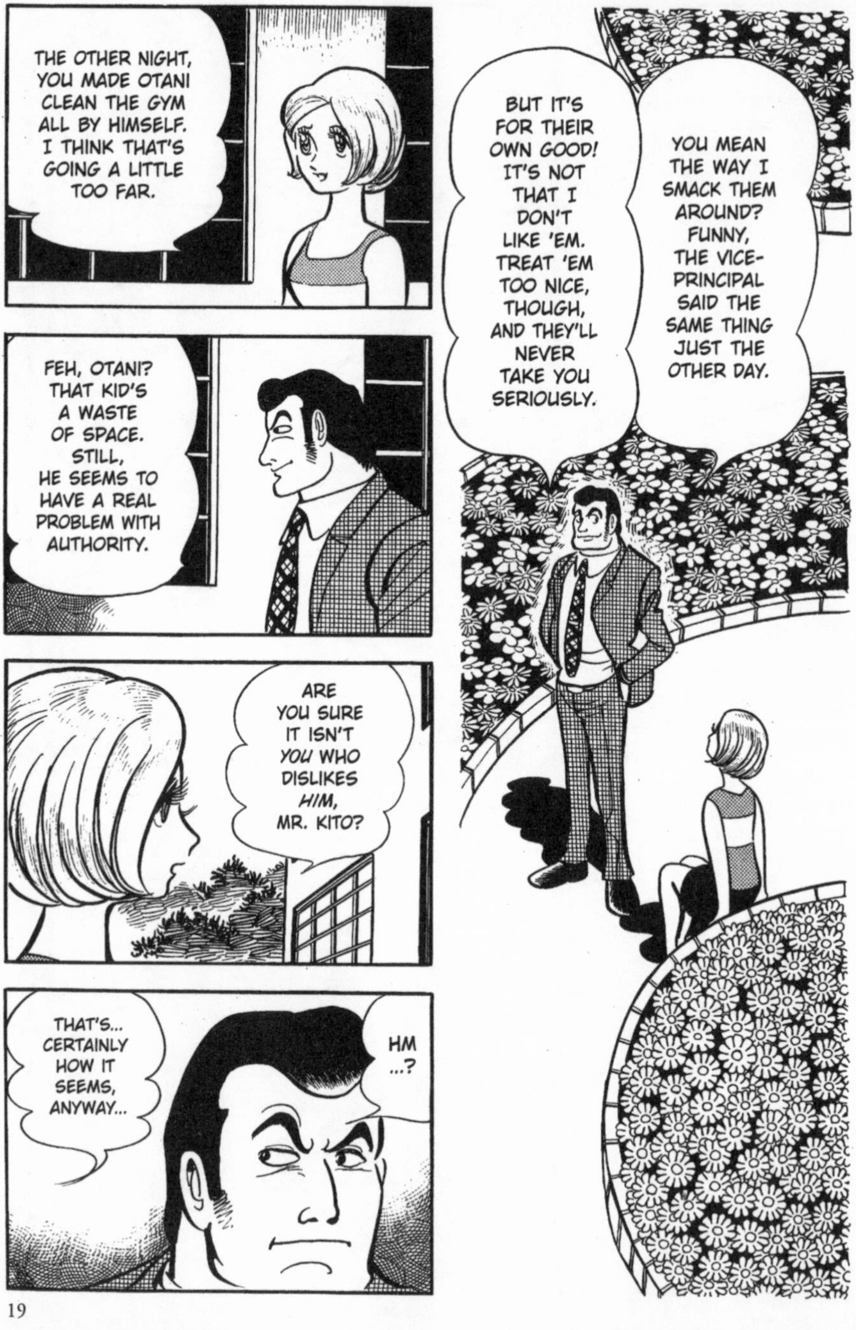
YOU MEAN THE WAY I SMACK THEM AROUND? FUNNY, THE VICE-PRINCIPAL SAID THE SAME THING JUST THE OTHER DAY.
BUT IT'S FOR THEIR OWN GOOD! IT'S NOT THAT I DON'T LIKE 'EM. TREAT 'EM TOO NICE, THOUGH, AND THEY'LL NEVER TAKE YOU SERIOUSLY.
THE OTHER NIGHT, YOU MADE OTANI CLEAN THE GYM ALL BY HIMSELF. I THINK THAT'S GOING A LITTLE TOO FAR.
FEH, OTANI? THAT KID'S A WASTE OF SPACE. STILL, HE SEEMS TO HAVE A REAL PROBLEM WITH AUTHORITY.
ARE YOU SURE IT ISN'T *YOU* WHO DISLIKES *HIM*, MR. KITO?
HM ...?
THAT'S... CERTAINLY HOW IT SEEMS, ANYWAY...

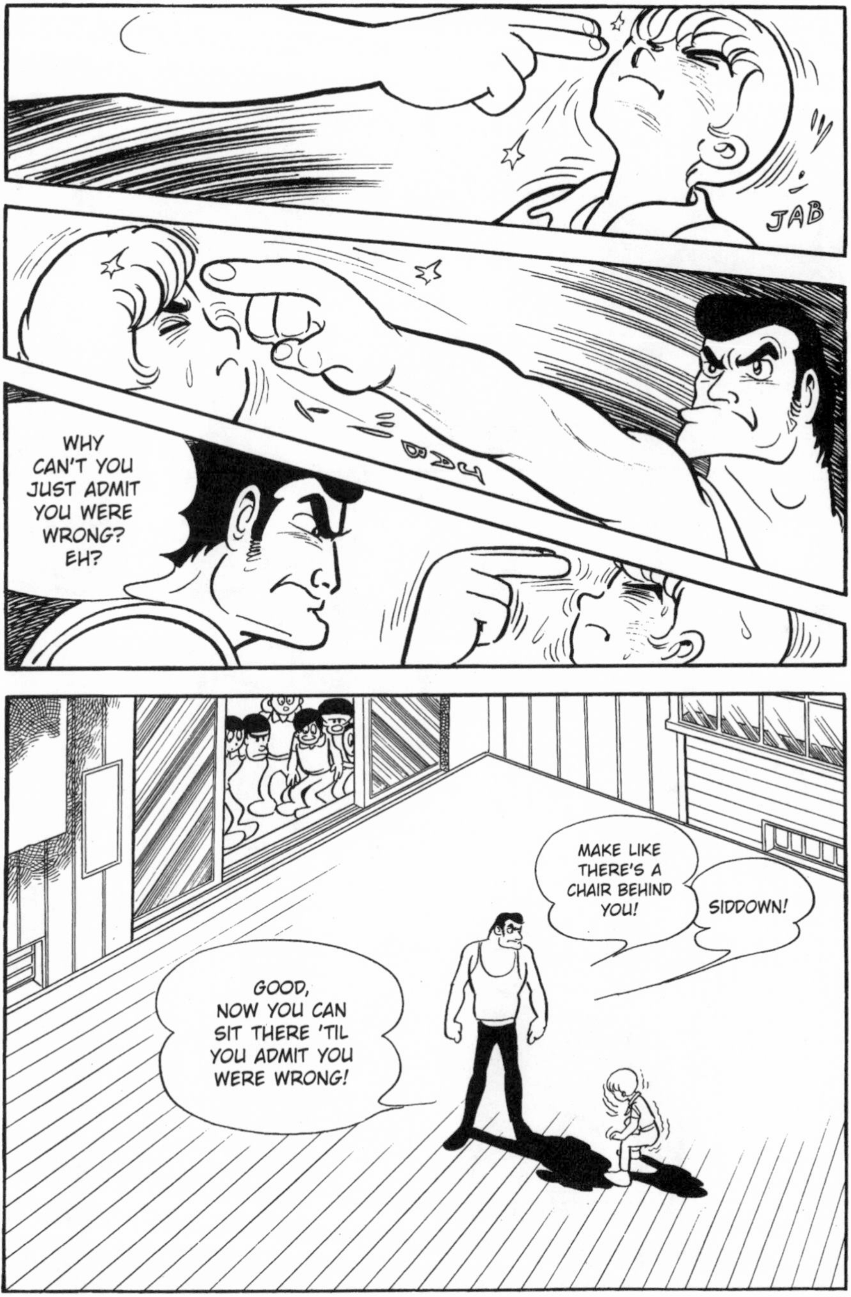
JAB
JAB
WHY CAN'T YOU JUST ADMIT YOU WERE WRONG? EH?
SIDDOWN!
MAKE LIKE THERE'S A CHAIR BEHIND YOU!
GOOD, NOW YOU CAN SIT THERE 'TIL YOU ADMIT YOU WERE WRONG!

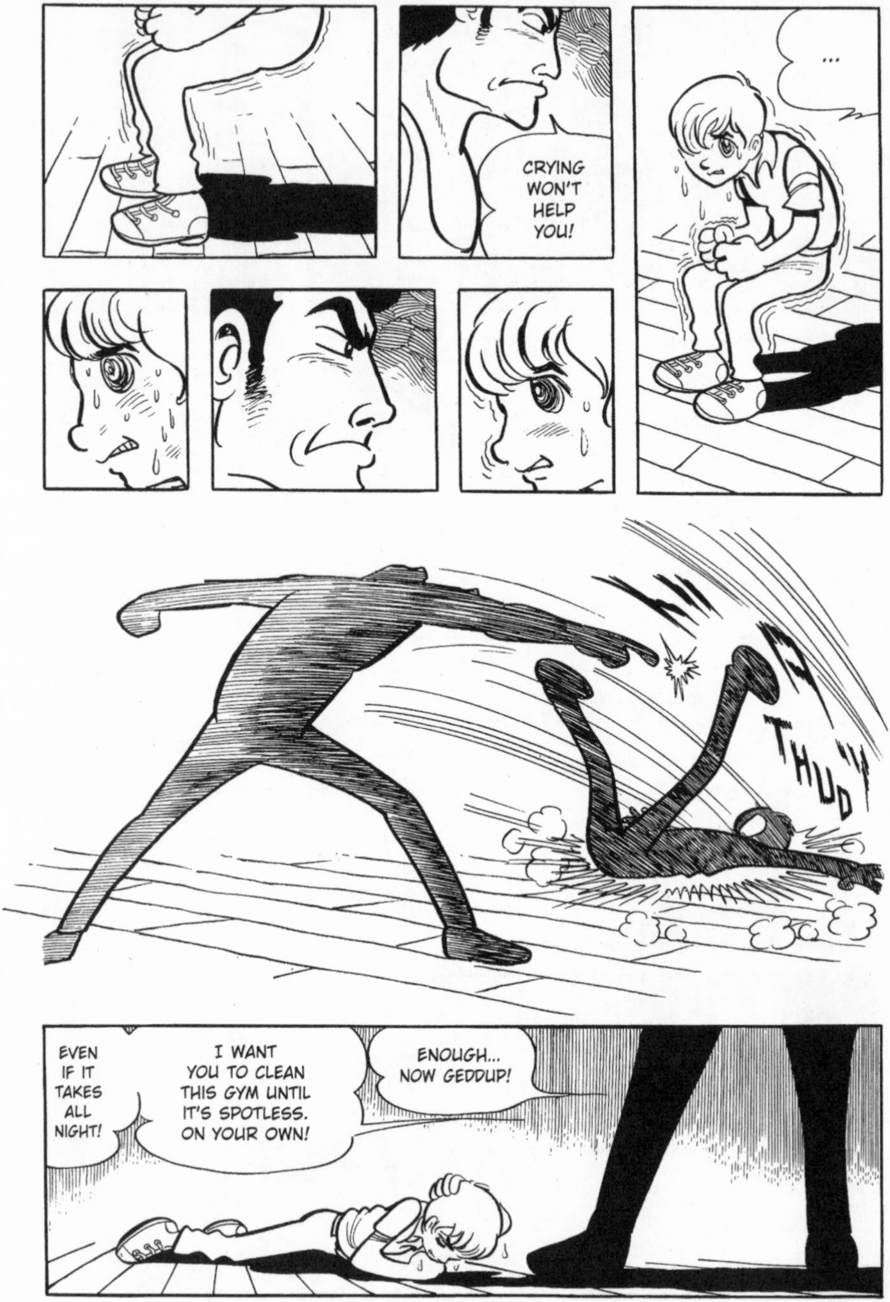
...
CRYING WON'T HELP YOU!
THUD
ENOUGH... NOW GEDDUP!
I WANT YOU TO CLEAN THIS GYM UNTIL IT'S SPOTLESS. ON YOUR OWN!
EVEN IF IT TAKES ALL NIGHT!

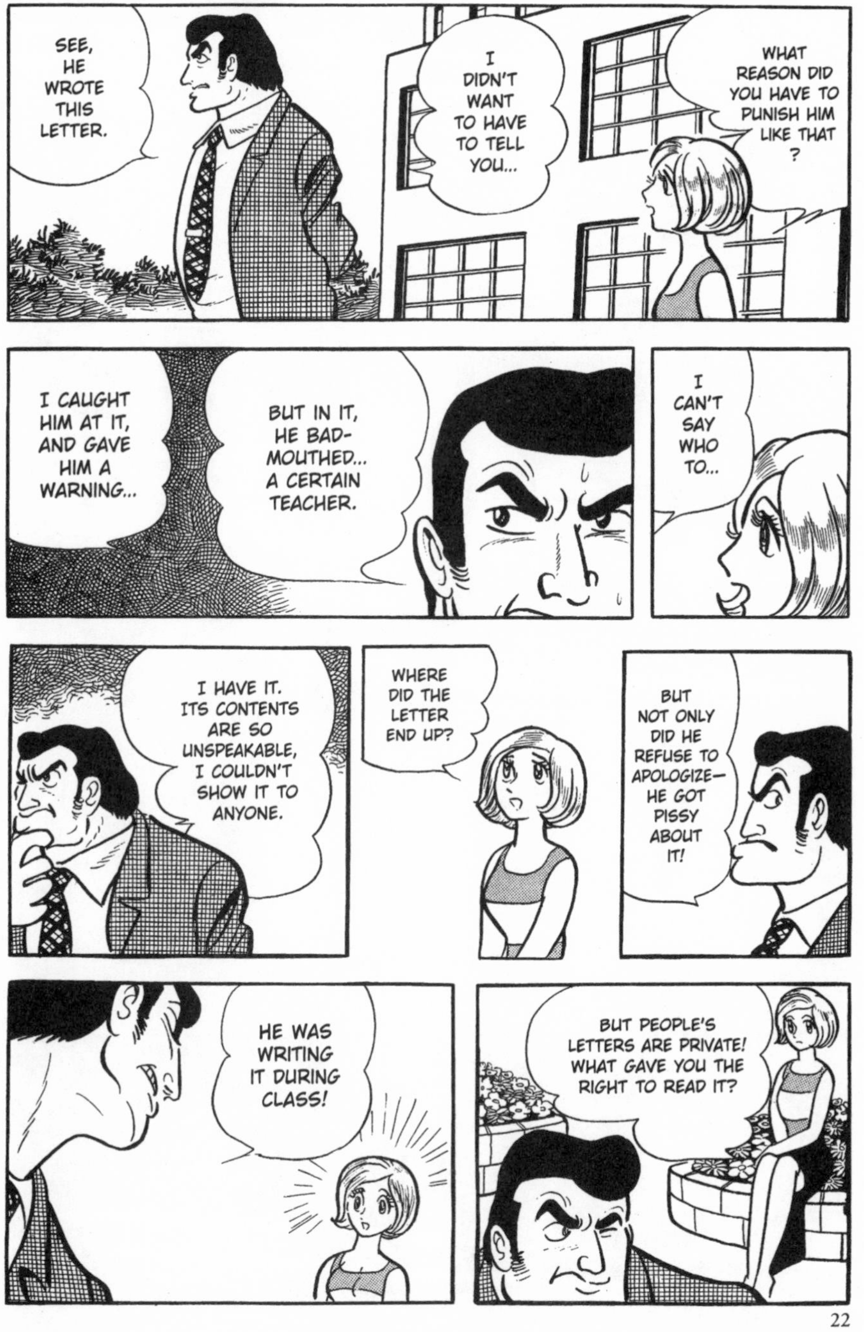
WHAT REASON DID YOU HAVE TO PUNISH HIM LIKE THAT ?
I DIDN'T WANT TO HAVE TO TELL YOU...
SEE, HE WROTE THIS LETTER.
I CAN'T SAY WHO TO...
BUT IN IT, HE BAD-MOUTHED... A CERTAIN TEACHER.
I CAUGHT HIM AT IT, AND GAVE HIM A WARNING...
BUT NOT ONLY DID HE REFUSE TO APOLOGIZE—HE GOT PISSY ABOUT IT!
WHERE DID THE LETTER END UP?
I HAVE IT. ITS CONTENTS ARE SO UNSPEAKABLE, I COULDN'T SHOW IT TO ANYONE.
BUT PEOPLE'S LETTERS ARE PRIVATE! WHAT GAVE YOU THE RIGHT TO READ IT?
HE WAS WRITING IT DURING CLASS!

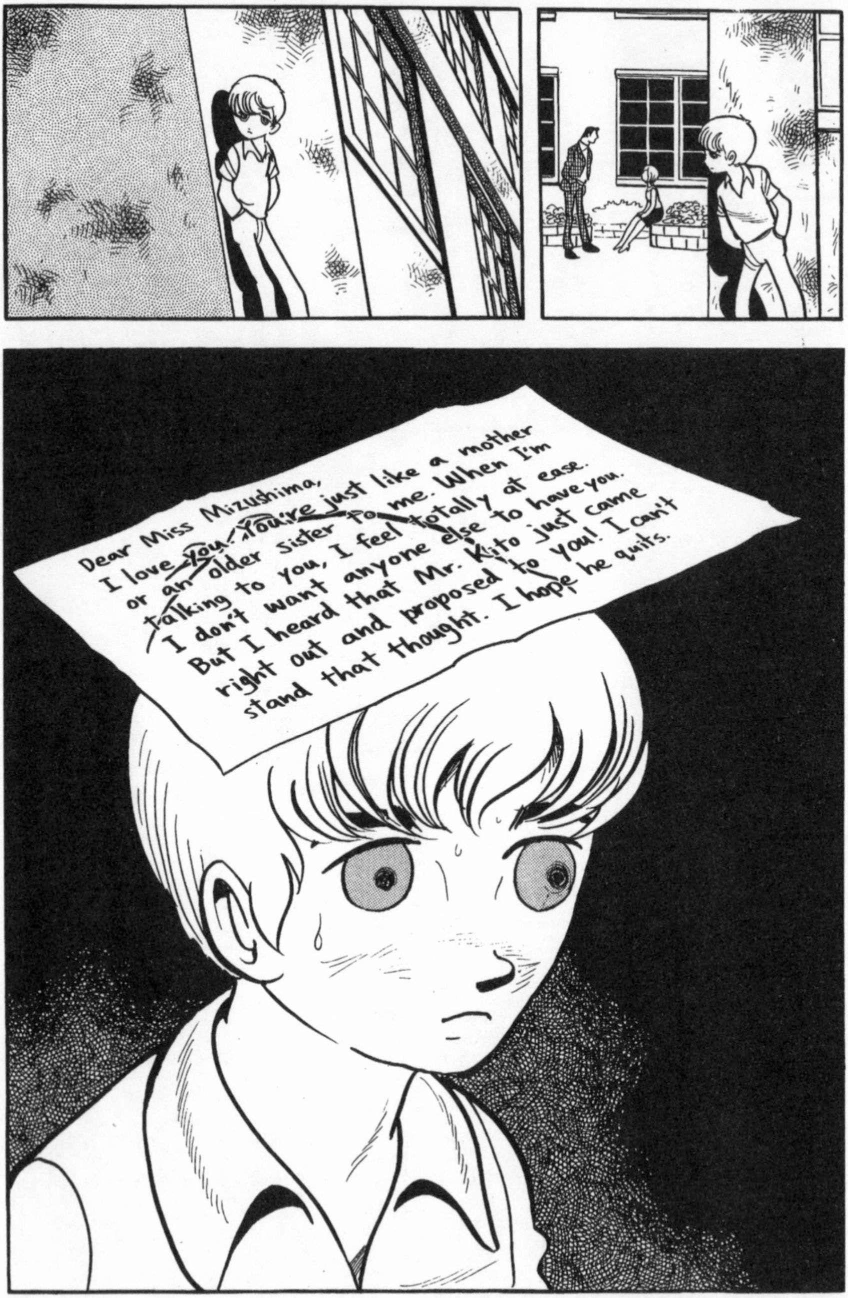
Dear Miss Mizushima,
I love you! You're just like a mother
or an older sister to me. When I'm
talking to you, I feel totally at ease.
I don't want anyone else to have you.
But I heard that Mr. Kito just came
right out and proposed to you! I can't
stand that thought. I hope he quits.

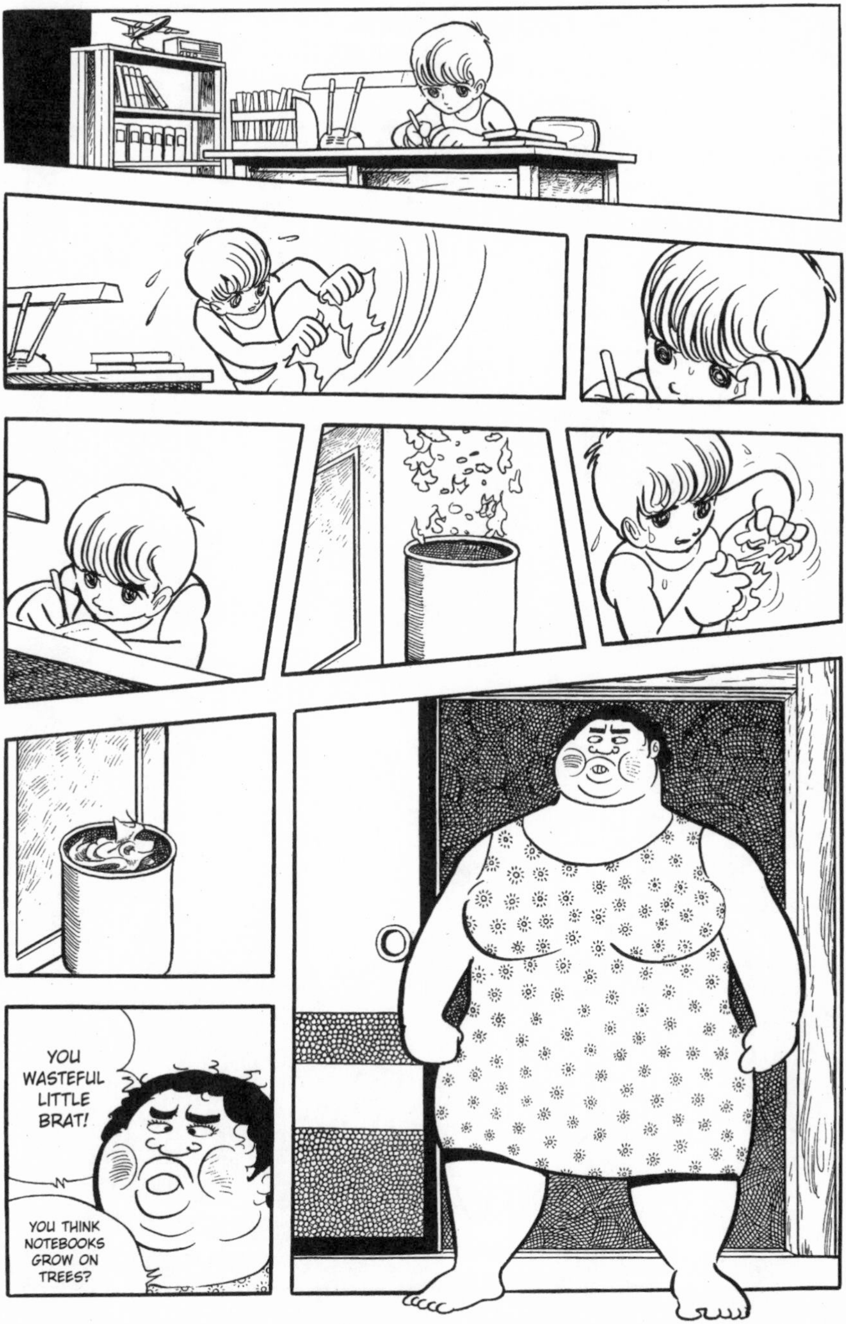
YOU WASTEFUL LITTLE BRAT!
YOU THINK NOTEBOOKS GROW ON TREES?

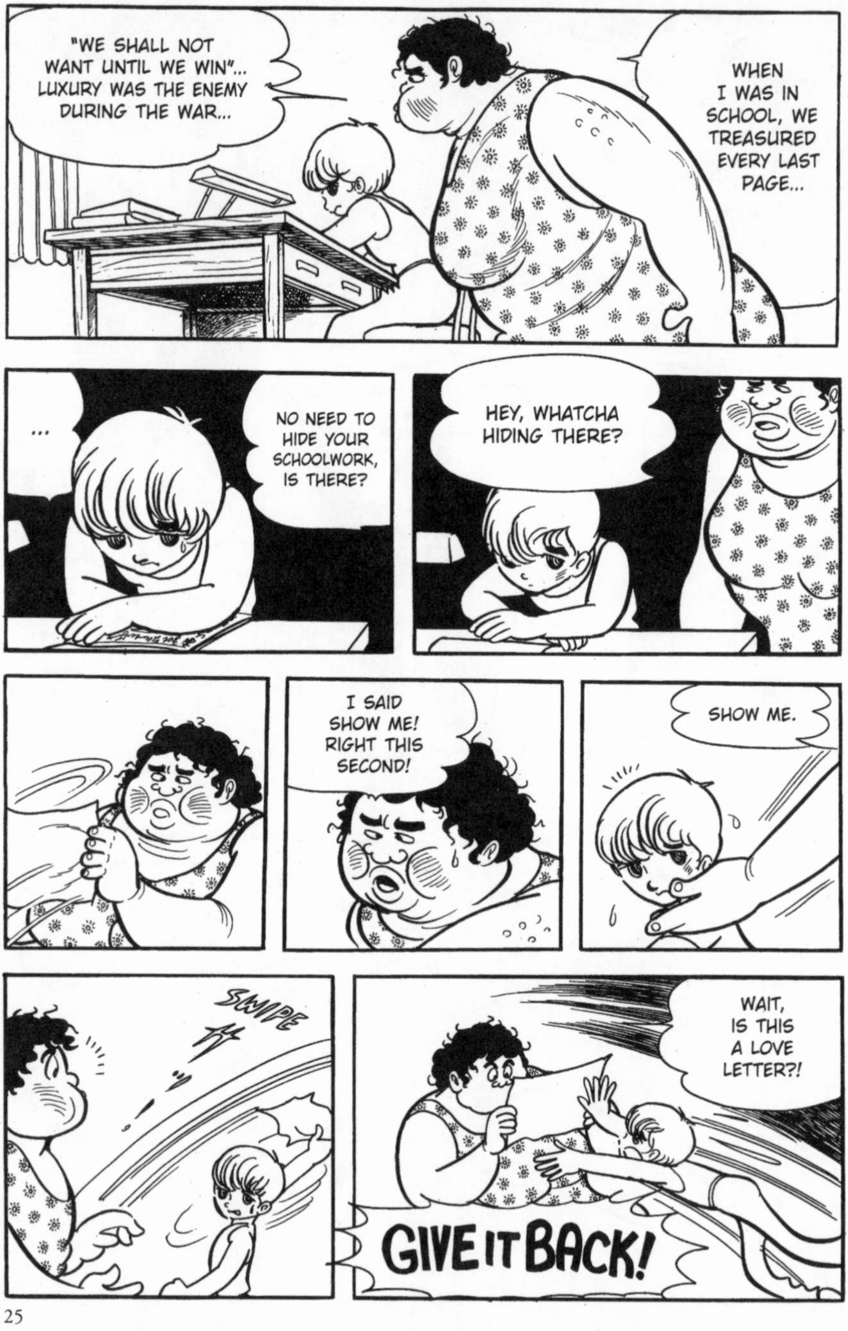
WHEN I WAS IN SCHOOL, WE TREASURED EVERY LAST PAGE...
"WE SHALL NOT WANT UNTIL WE WIN"... LUXURY WAS THE ENEMY DURING THE WAR...
HEY, WHATCHA HIDING THERE?
NO NEED TO HIDE YOUR SCHOOLWORK, IS THERE?
...
SHOW ME.
I SAID SHOW ME! RIGHT THIS SECOND!
WAIT, IS THIS A LOVE LETTER?!
GIVE IT BACK!
SWIPE

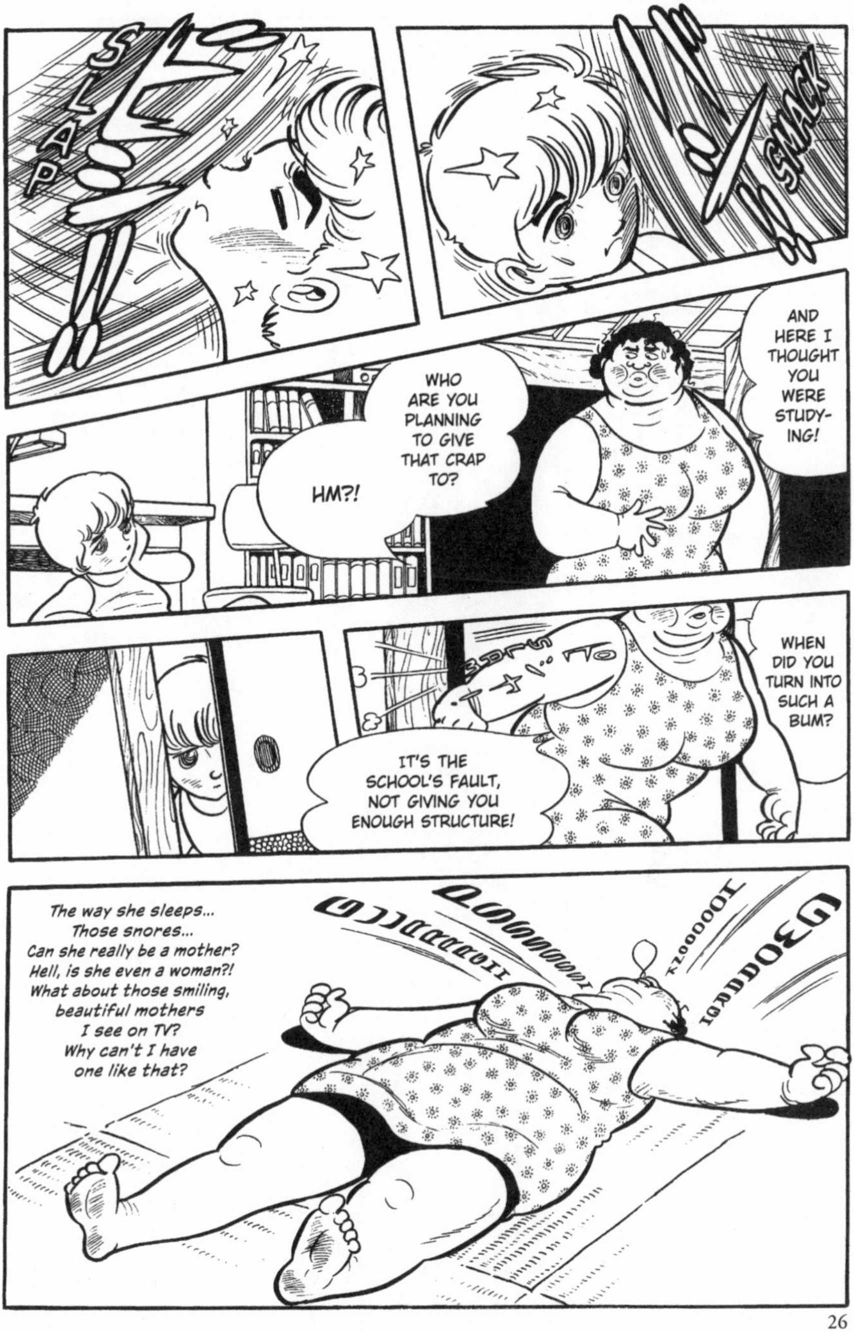
SMACK
SLAP
AND HERE I THOUGHT YOU WERE STUDY-ING!
WHO ARE YOU PLANNING TO GIVE THAT CRAP TO?
HM?!
WHEN DID YOU TURN INTO SUCH A BUM?
IT'S THE SCHOOL'S FAULT, NOT GIVING YOU ENOUGH STRUCTURE!
The way she sleeps... Those snores... Can she really be a mother? Hell, is she even a woman?! What about those smiling, beautiful mothers I see on TV? Why can't I have one like that?

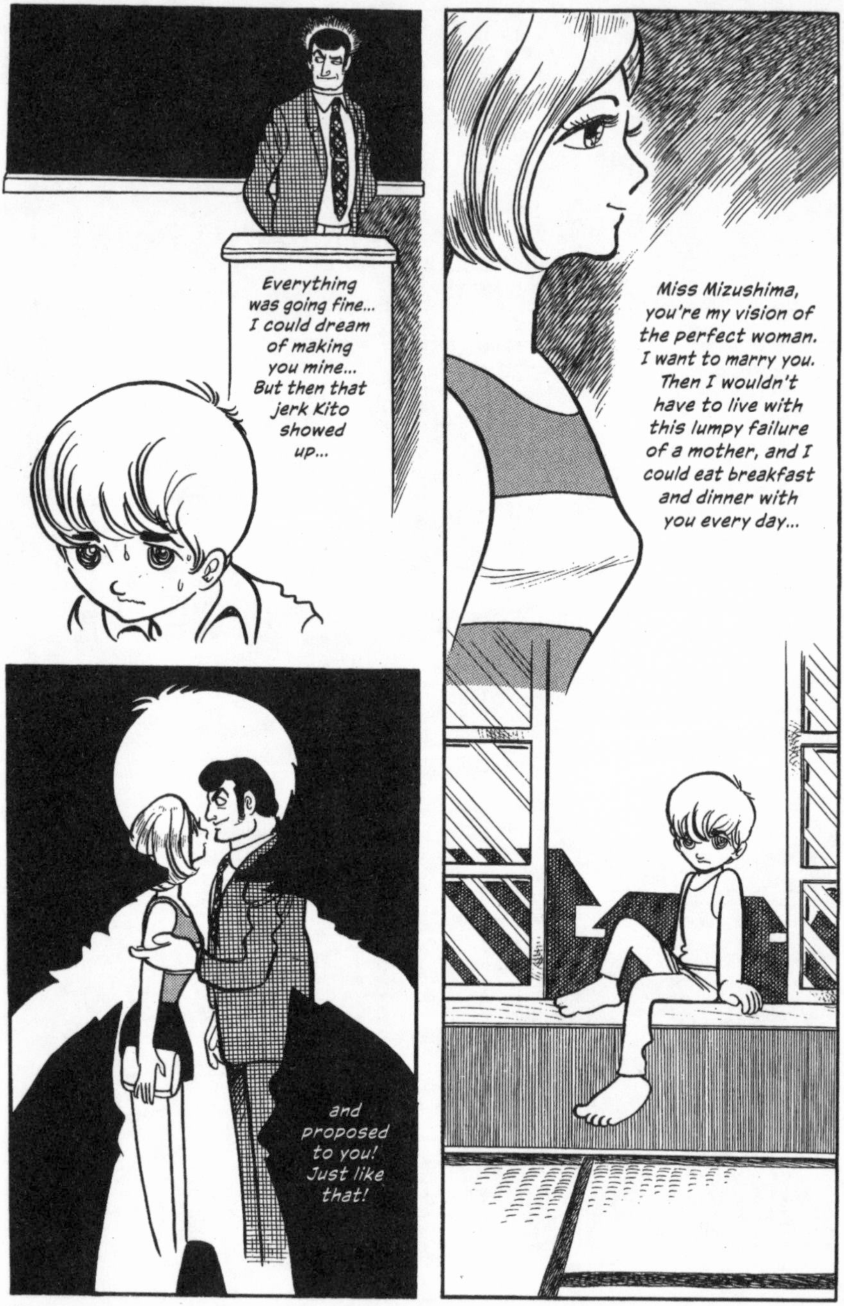
Miss Mizushima, you're my vision of the perfect woman. I want to marry you. Then I wouldn't have to live with this lumpy failure of a mother, and I could eat breakfast and dinner with you every day...
Everything was going fine... I could dream of making you mine... But then that jerk Kito showed up...
and proposed to you! Just like that!

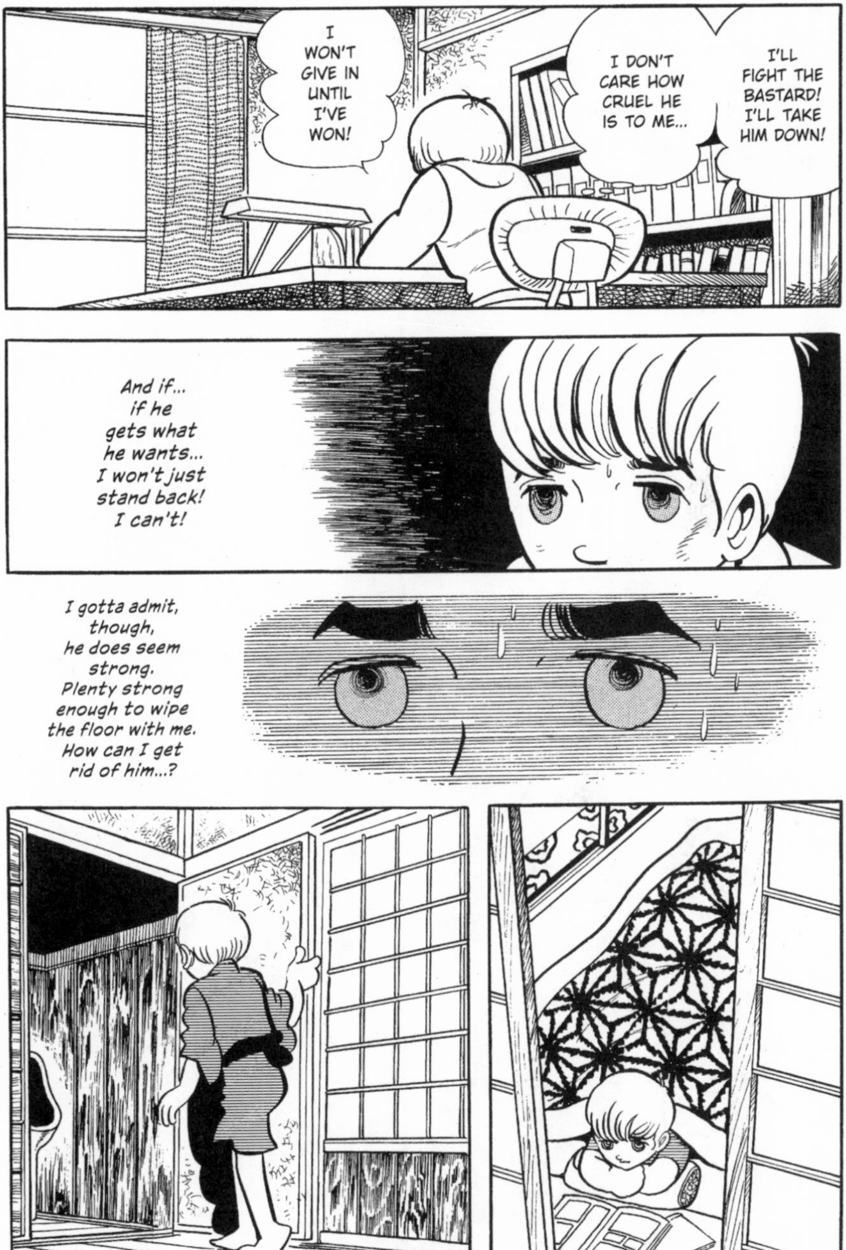
I'LL FIGHT THE BASTARD! I'LL TAKE HIM DOWN!
I DON'T CARE HOW CRUEL HE IS TO ME...
I WON'T GIVE IN UNTIL I'VE WON!
And if... if he gets what he wants... I won't just stand back! I can't!
I gotta admit, though, he does seem strong. Plenty strong enough to wipe the floor with me. How can I get rid of him...?

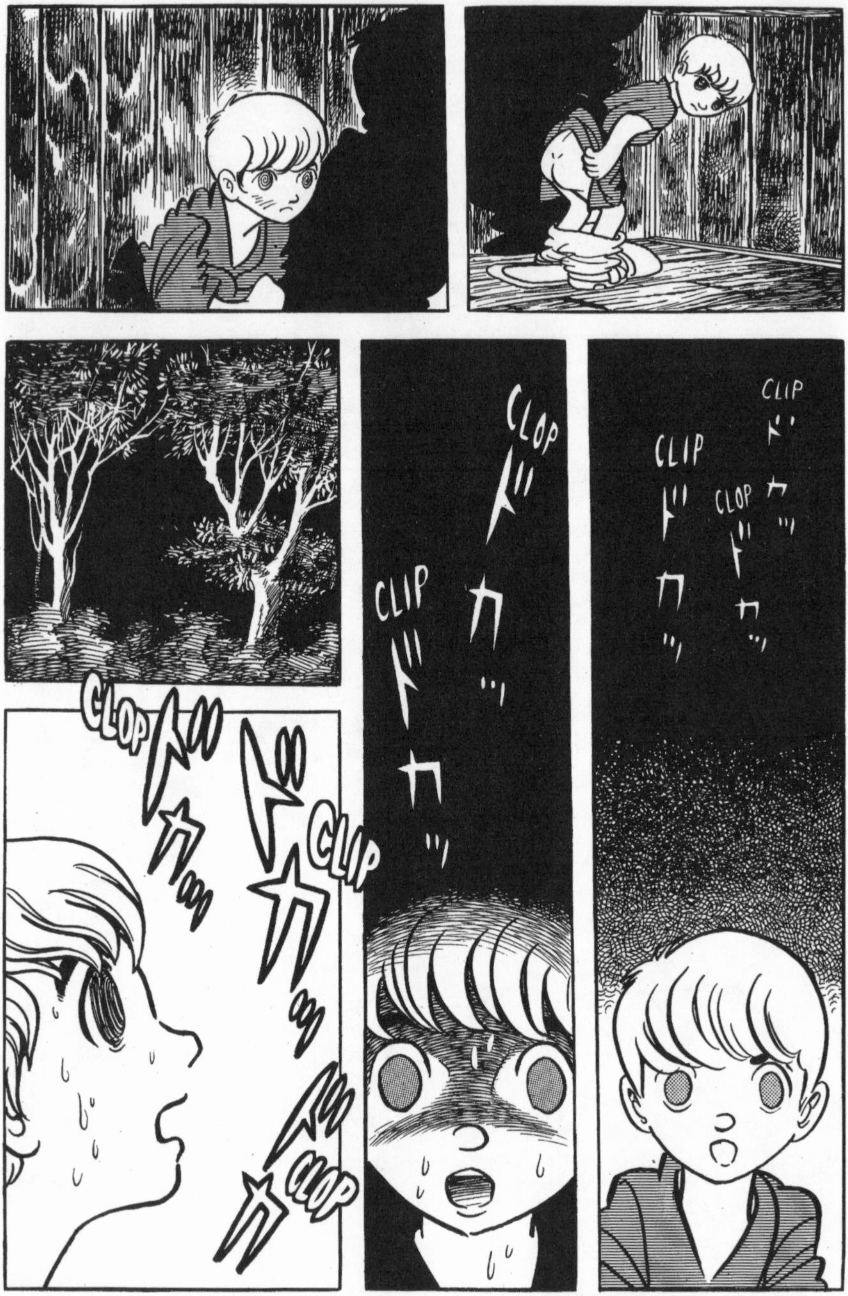
CLIP
ドカッ
CLIP
ドカッ
CLOP
ドカッ
CLOP
ドカッ
CLIP
ドカッ
CLOP
ドカッ
CLIP
ドカッ
CLOP
ドカッ

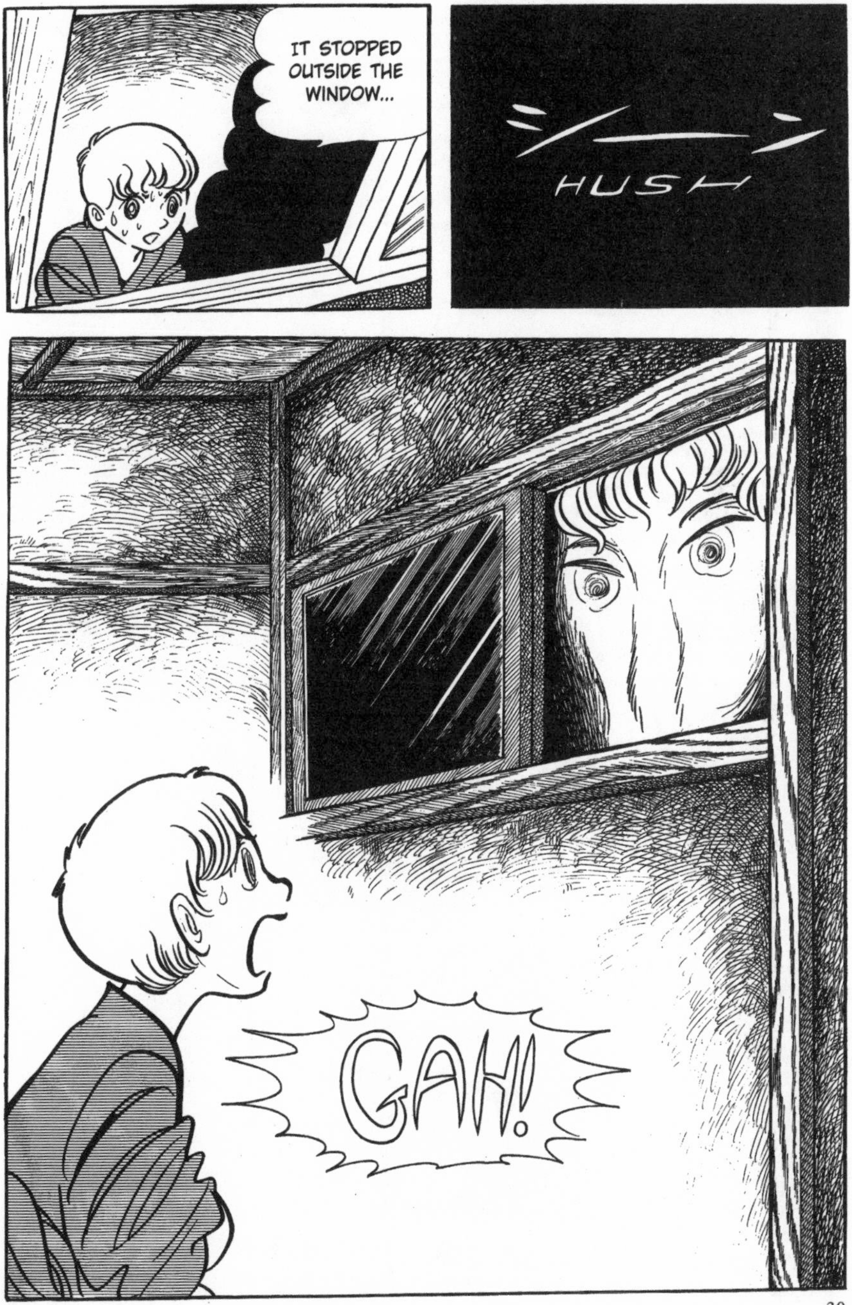
HUSH
IT STOPPED OUTSIDE THE WINDOW...
GAH!

TUP
TUP
TUP
SWOOSH
I S-SAW IT!
IT WAS A HORSE!

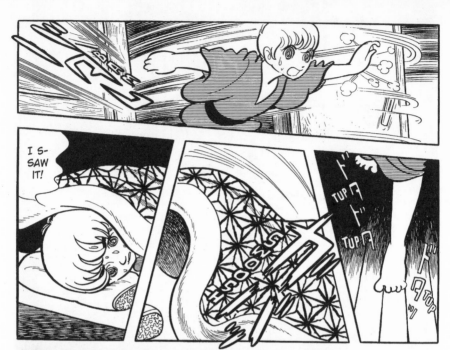

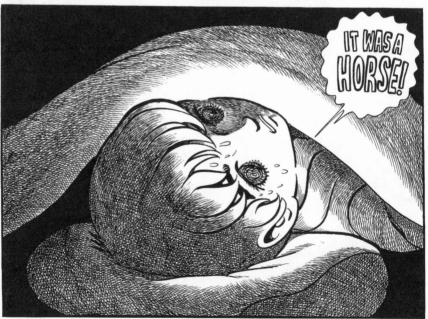

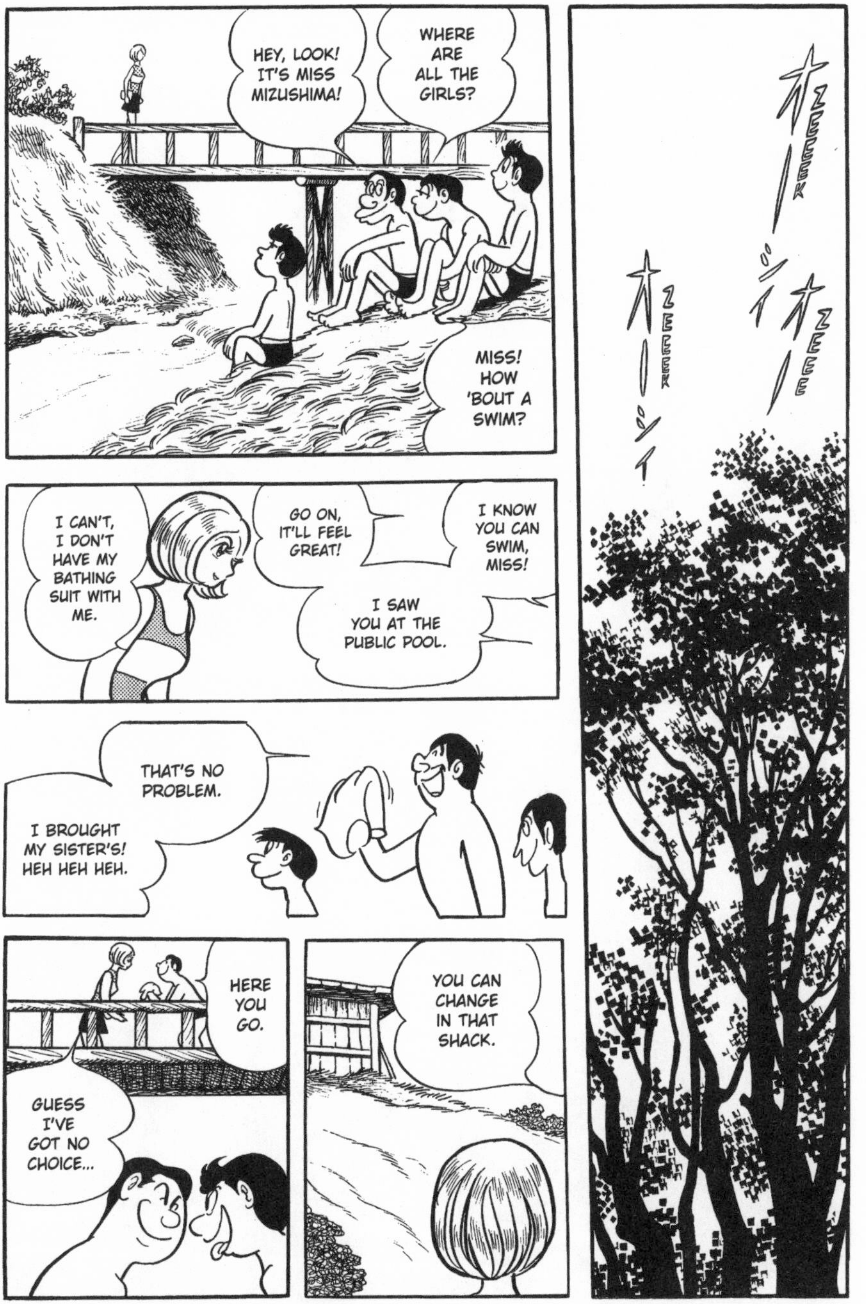
ZEEEEK
ZEEEE
ZEEEK
WHERE ARE ALL THE GIRLS?
HEY, LOOK! IT'S MISS MIZUSHIMA!
MISS! HOW 'BOUT A SWIM?
I KNOW YOU CAN SWIM, MISS!
GO ON, IT'LL FEEL GREAT!
I SAW YOU AT THE PUBLIC POOL.
I CAN'T, I DON'T HAVE MY BATHING SUIT WITH ME.
THAT'S NO PROBLEM.
I BROUGHT MY SISTER'S! HEH HEH HEH.
YOU CAN CHANGE IN THAT SHACK.
HERE YOU GO.
GUESS I'VE GOT NO CHOICE...

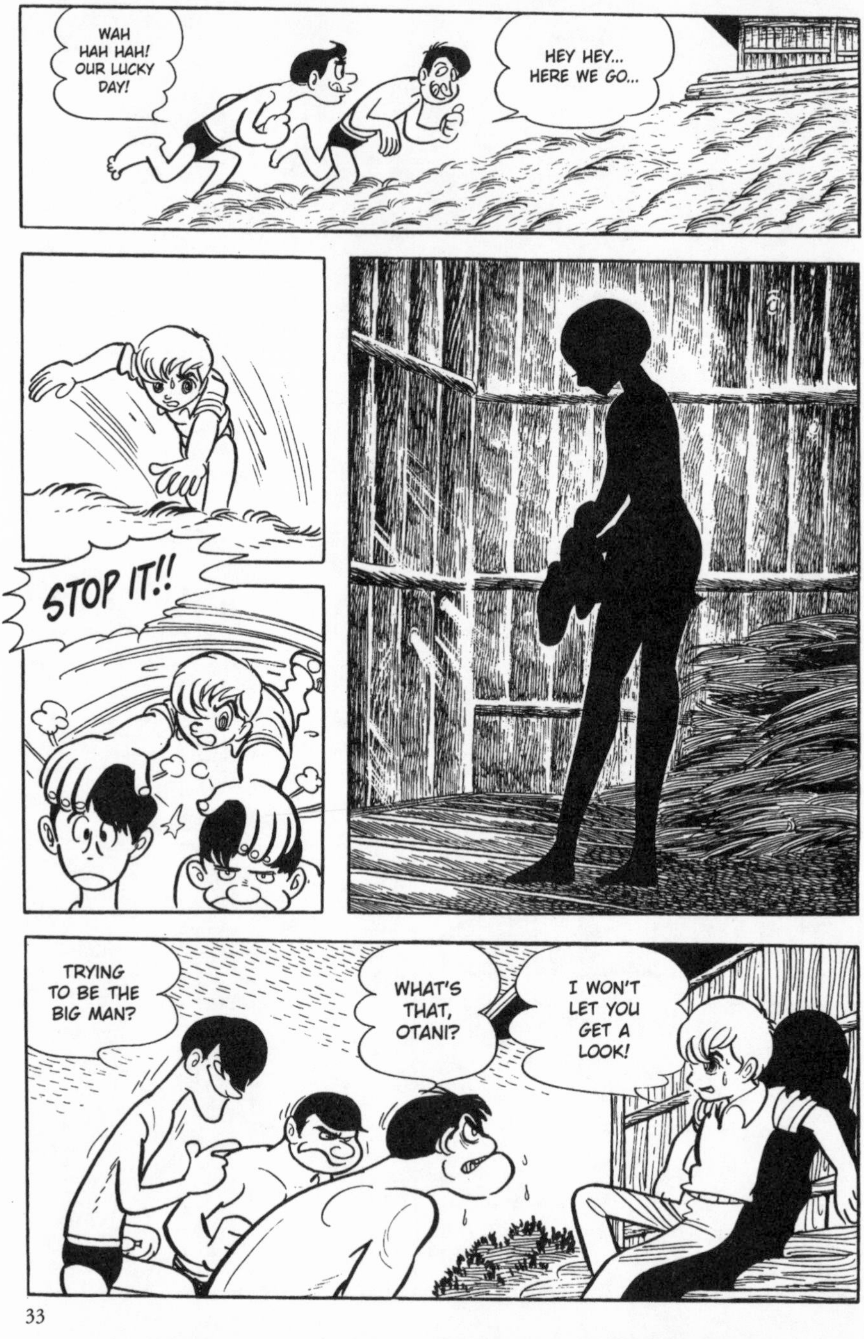
HEY HEY... HERE WE GO...
WAH HAH HAH! OUR LUCKY DAY!
STOP IT!!
I WON'T LET YOU GET A LOOK!
WHAT'S THAT, OTANI?
TRYING TO BE THE BIG MAN?

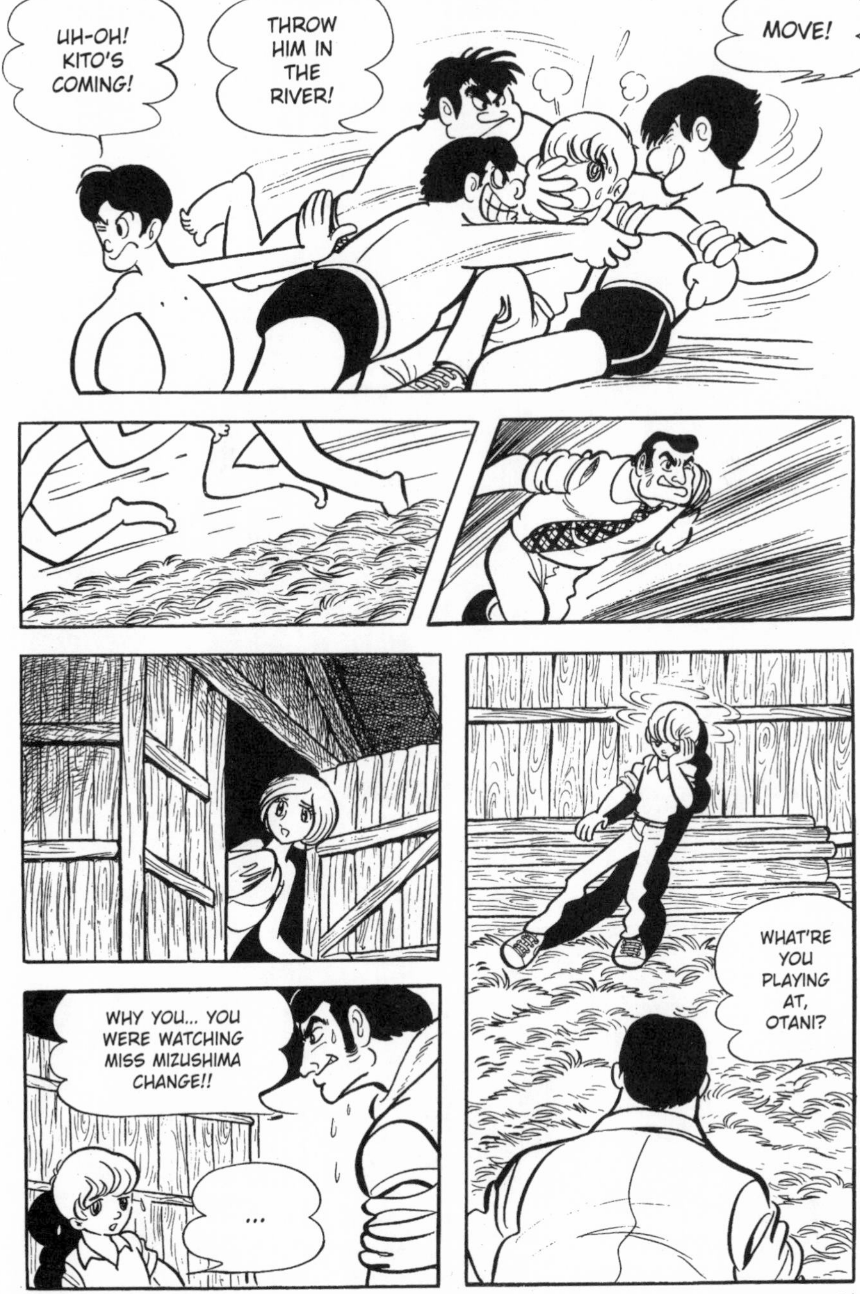
MOVE!
THROW HIM IN THE RIVER!
UH-OH! KITO'S COMING!
WHAT'RE YOU PLAYING AT, OTANI?
WHY YOU... YOU WERE WATCHING MISS MIZUSHIMA CHANGE!!
...

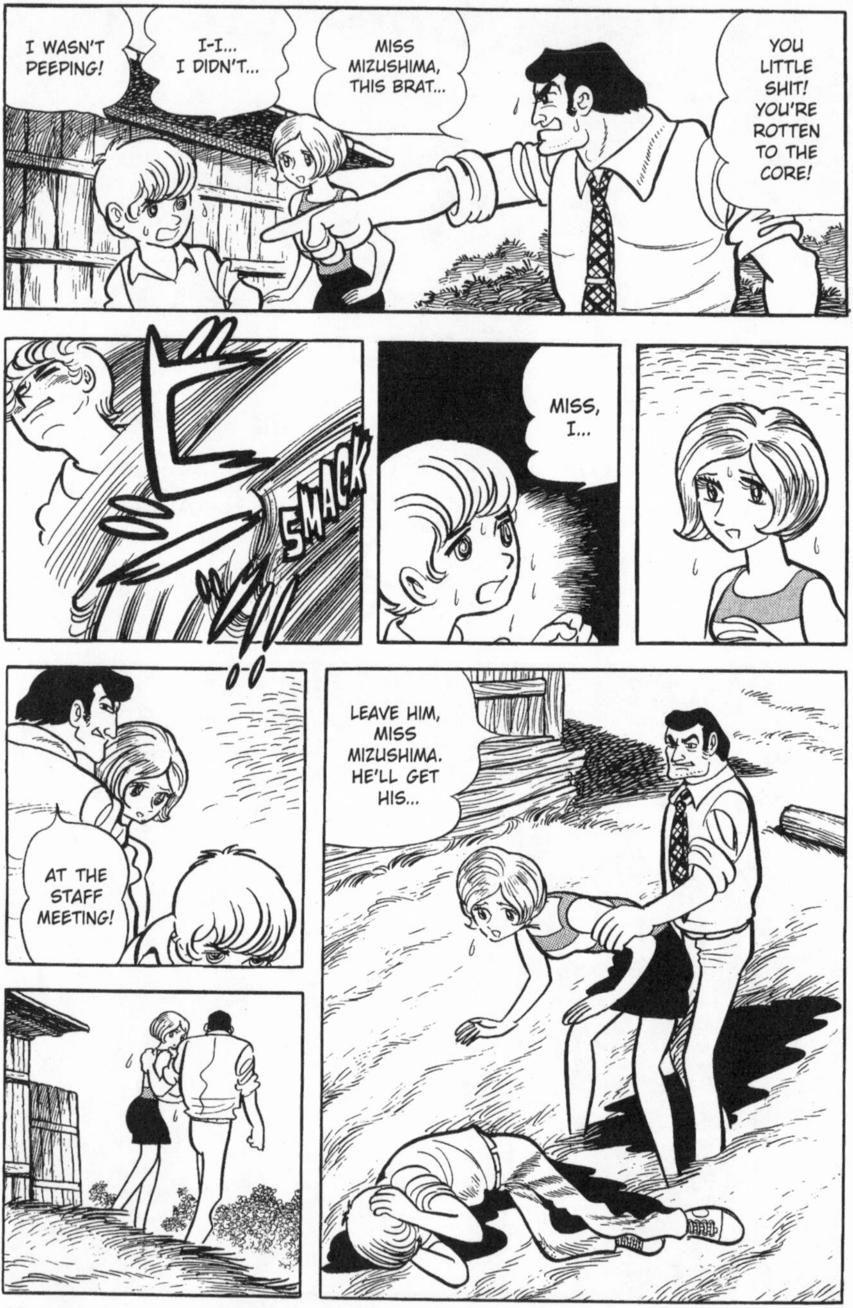
YOU LITTLE SHIT! YOU'RE ROTTEN TO THE CORE!
MISS MIZUSHIMA, THIS BRAT...
I-I... I DIDN'T...
I WASN'T PEEPING!
MISS, I...
SMACK
LEAVE HIM, MISS MIZUSHIMA. HE'LL GET HIS...
AT THE STAFF MEETING!

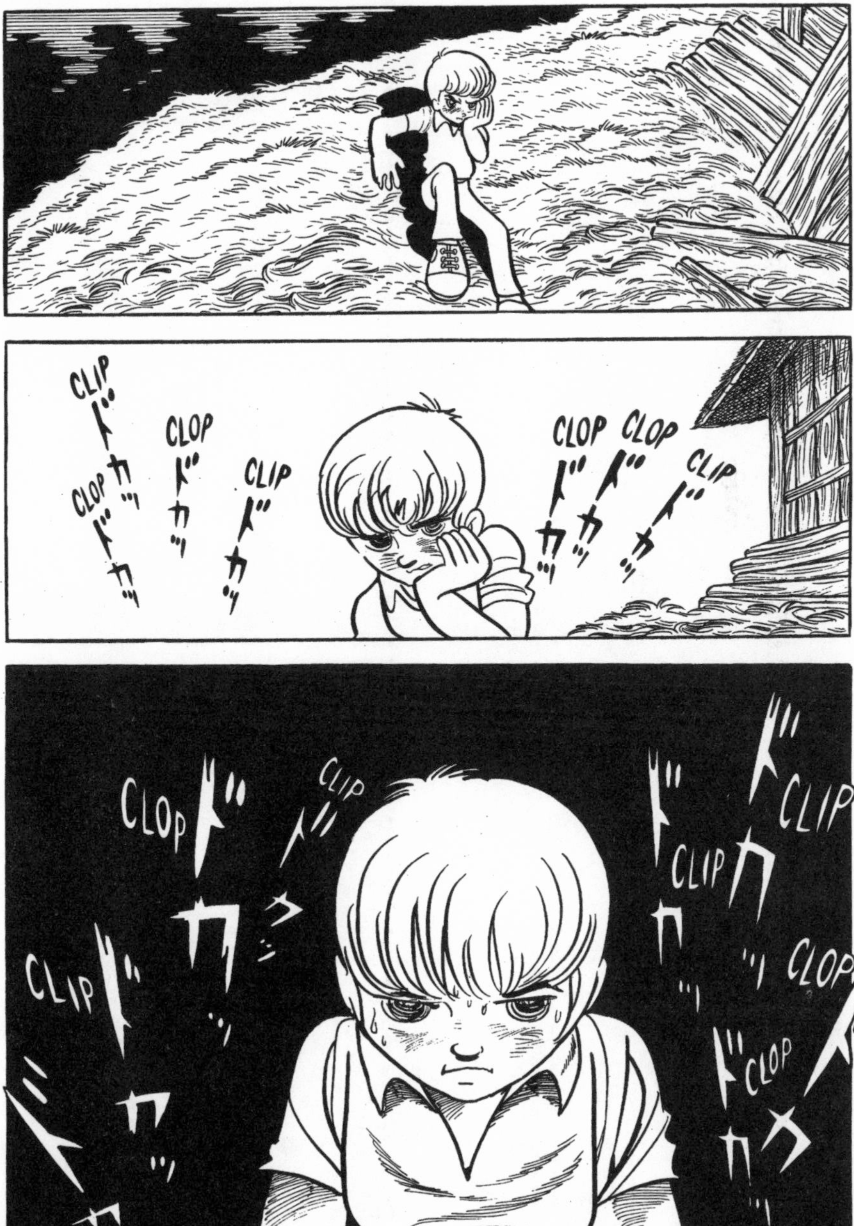

CLIP
CLOP
CLOP
CLIP
CLOP
CLOP
CLIP
CLIP
CLIP
CLOP
CLOP
CLIP
CLOP
CLIP
CLOP

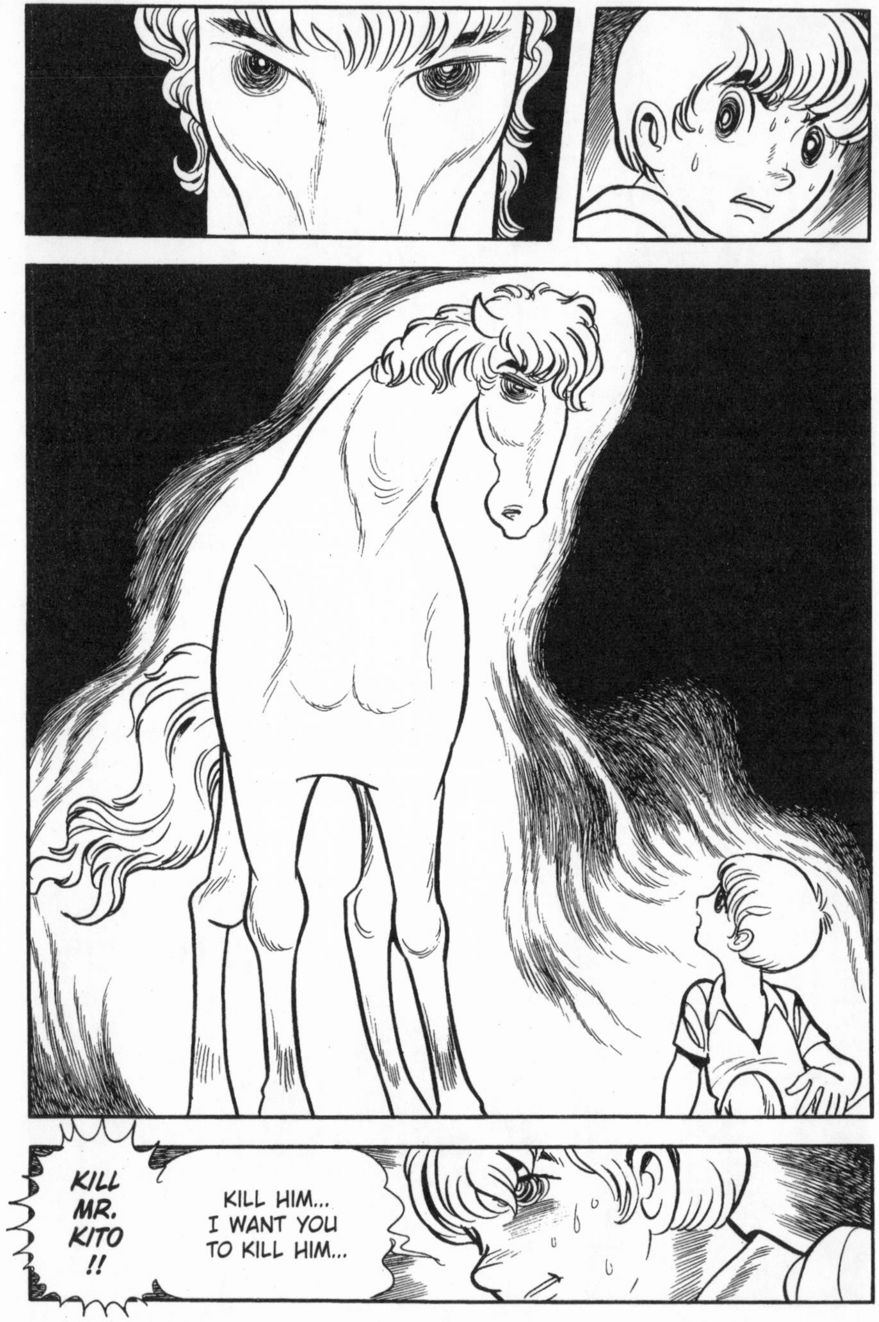
KILL HIM... I WANT YOU TO KILL HIM...
KILL MR. KITO !!

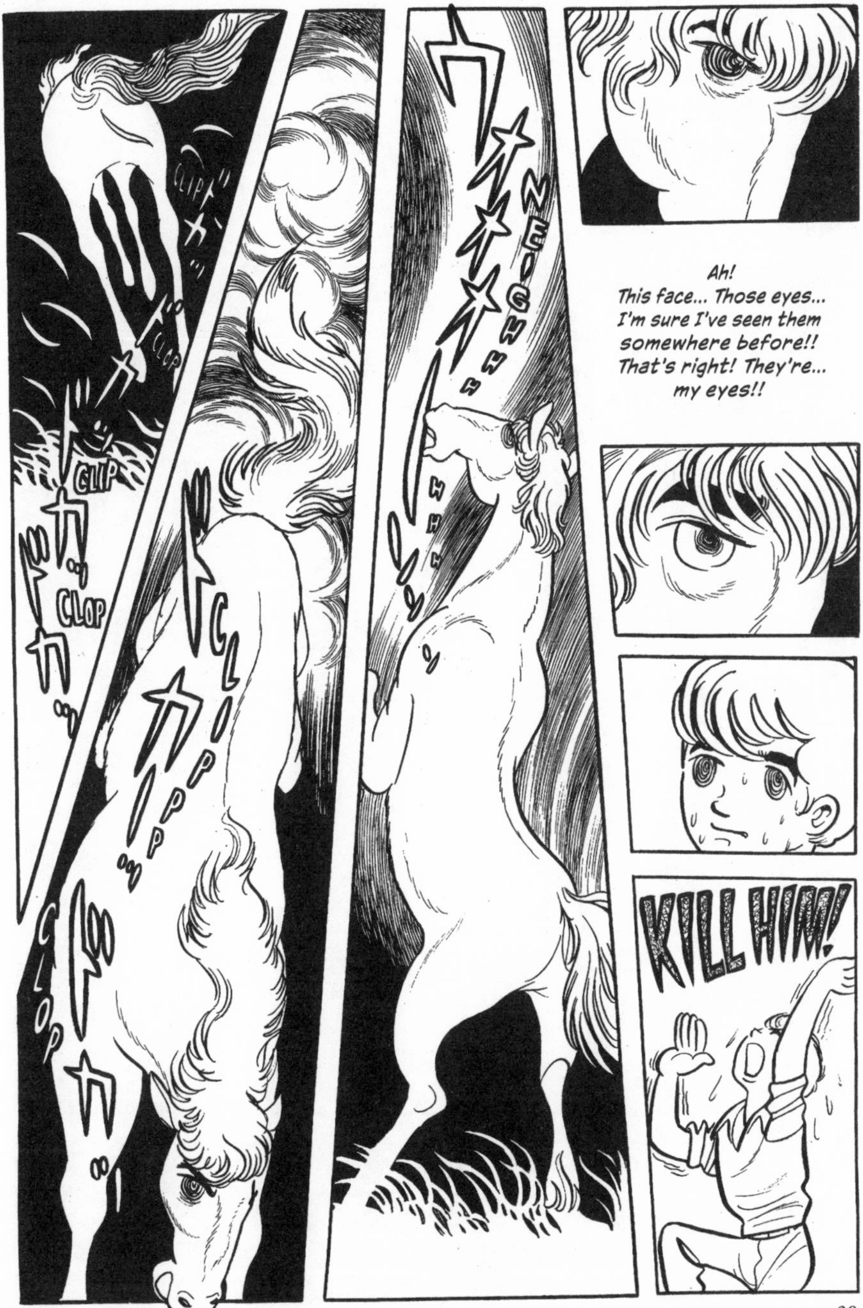
Ah!
This face... Those eyes...
I'm sure I've seen them
somewhere before!!
That's right! They're...
my eyes!!
KILL HIM!
NEIGHHHH
CLIPPP
CLOP
CLIP
CLOP
CLIP
CLOP

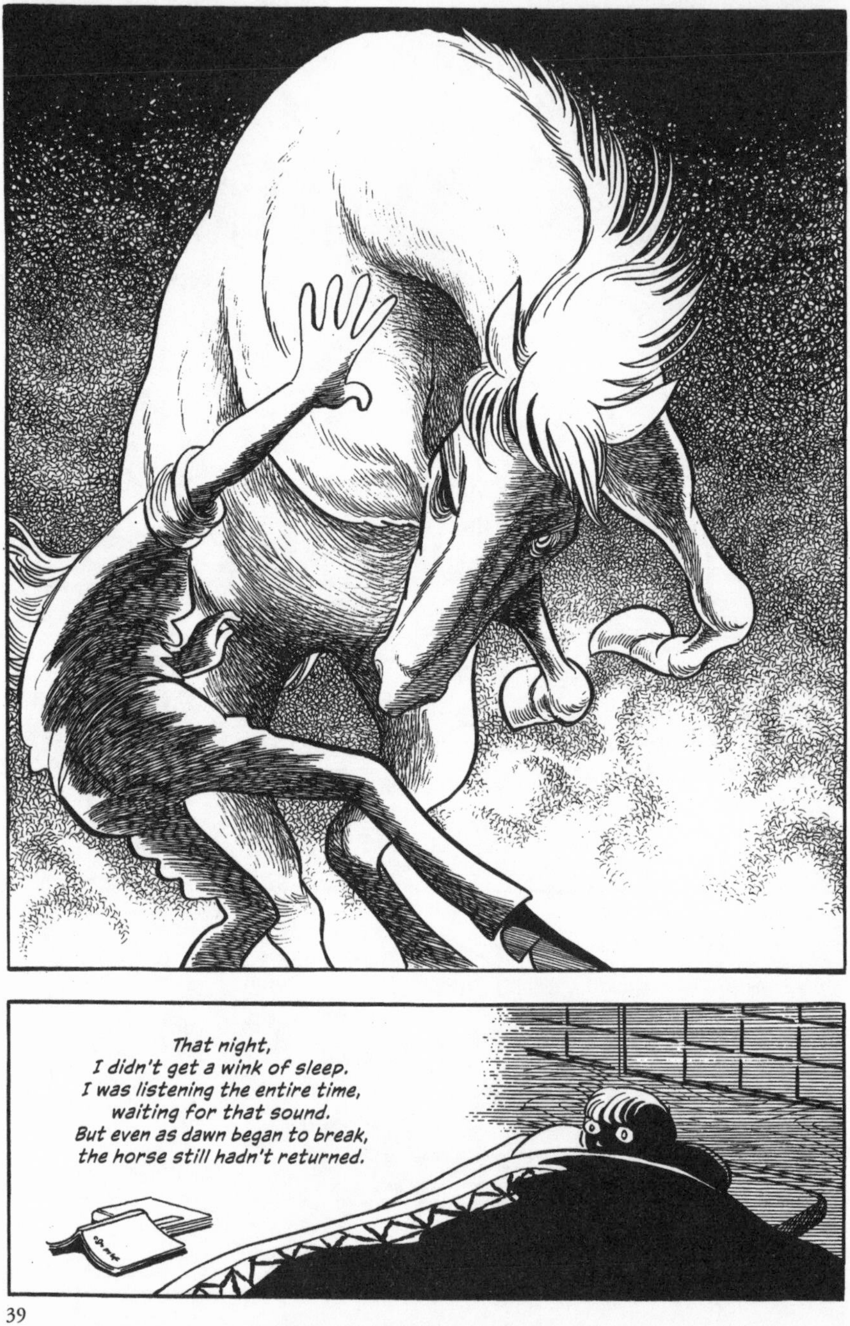
That night,
I didn't get a wink of sleep.
I was listening the entire time,
waiting for that sound.
But even as dawn began to break,
the horse still hadn't returned.

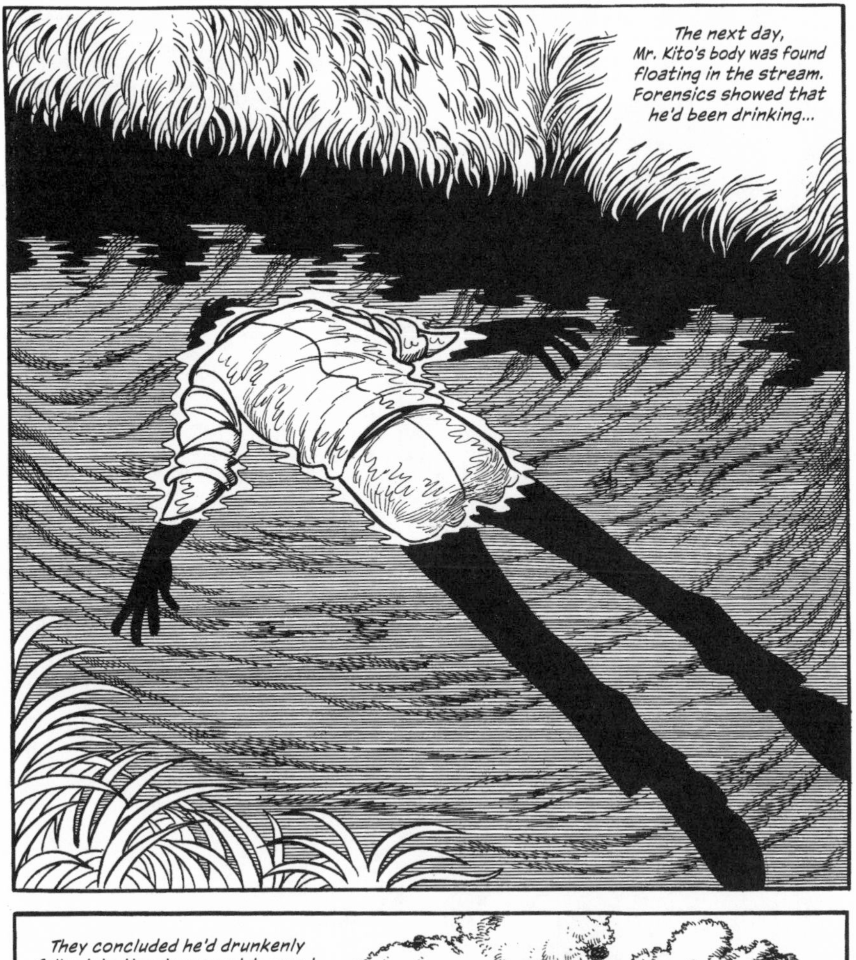
The next day, Mr. Kito's body was found floating in the stream. Forensics showed that he'd been drinking...
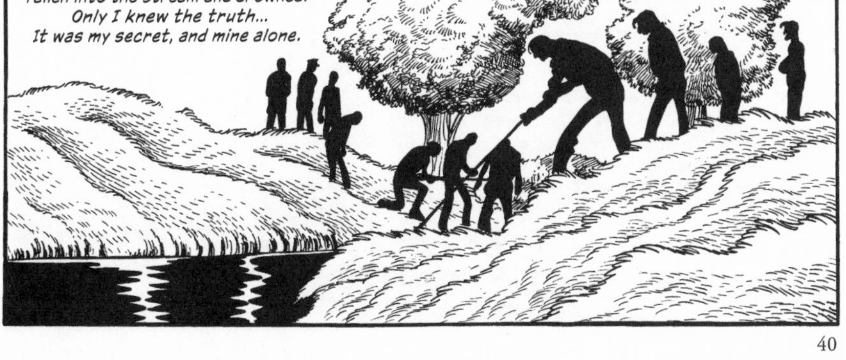
They concluded he'd drunkenly fallen into the stream and drowned. Only I knew the truth... It was my secret, and mine alone.

I started high school, and I stopped hearing the sound of those hooves.

Miss Mizushima still taught at my old school.

She was mine—that much I knew. I wouldn't let anyone else have her.
If anyone tried to go near her, I'd show no mercy.

I would marry Miss Mizushima—I had to!

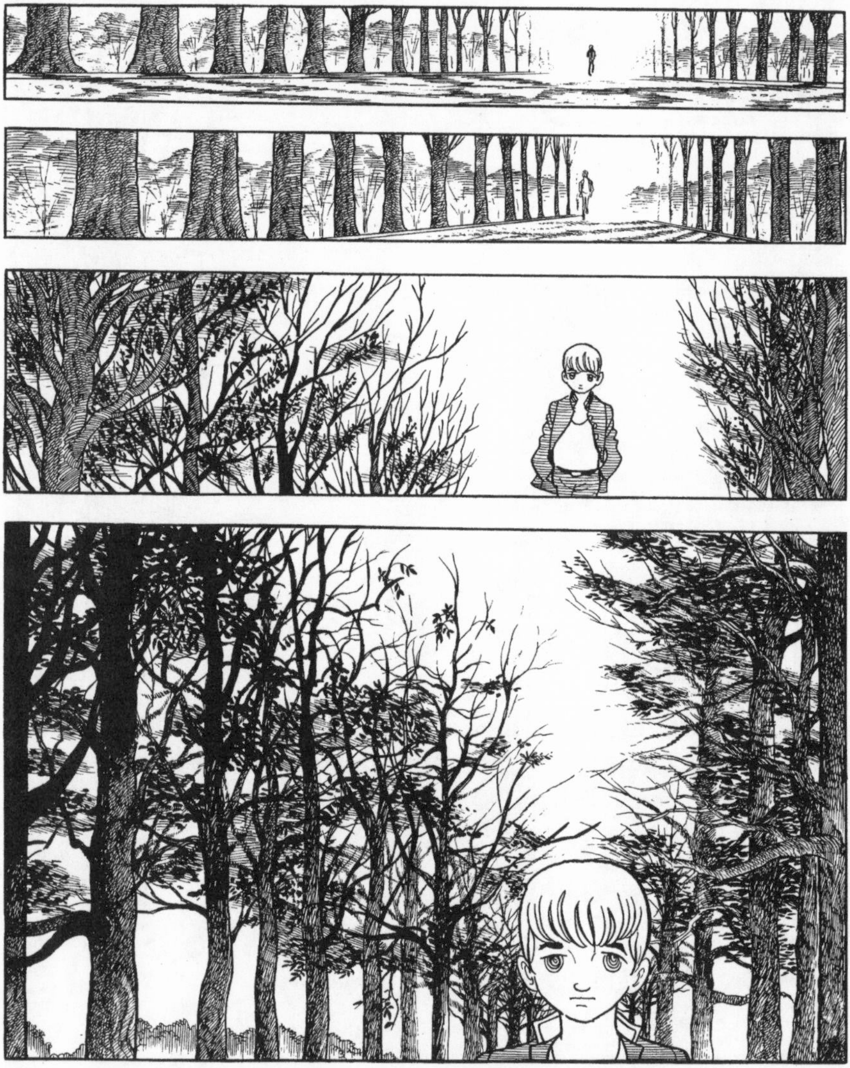

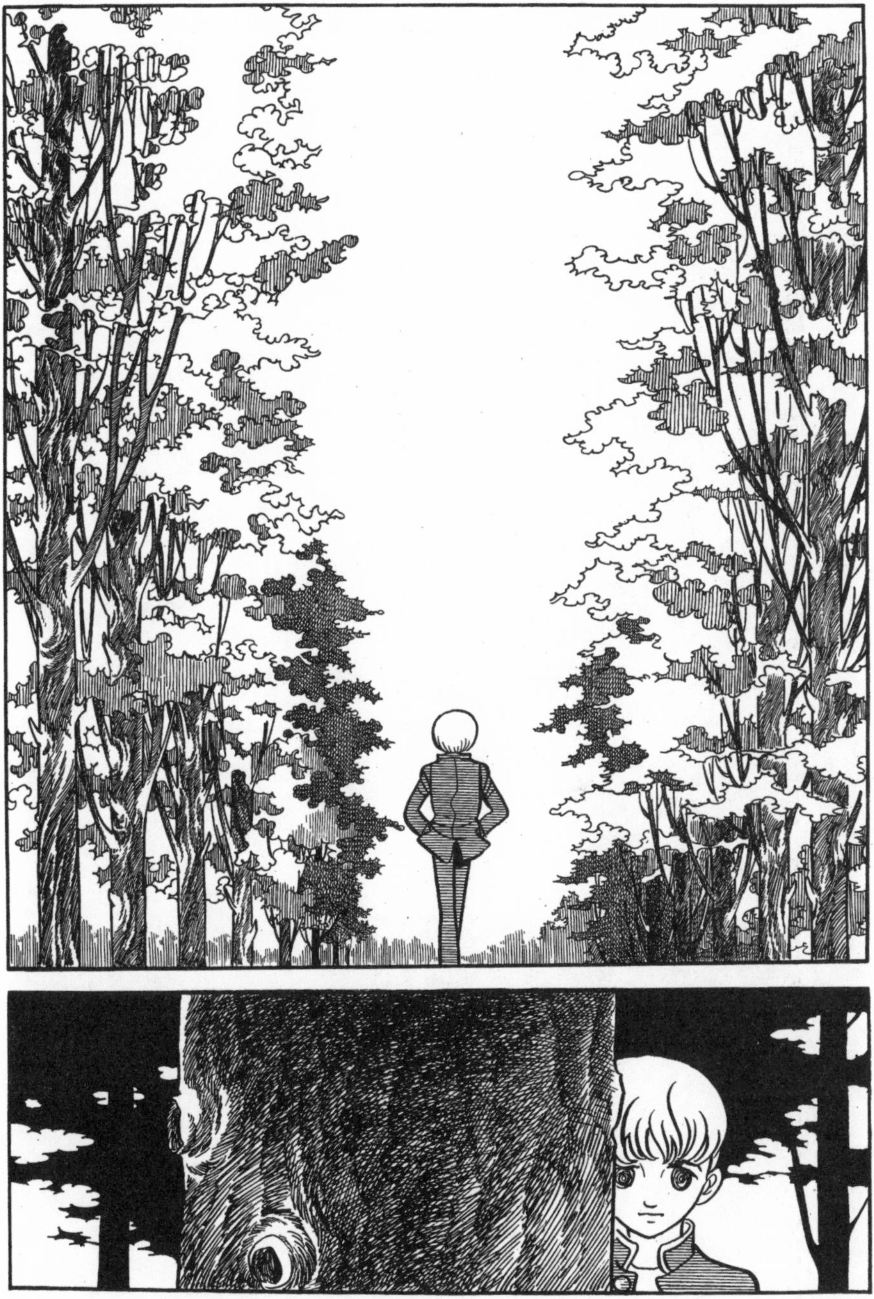

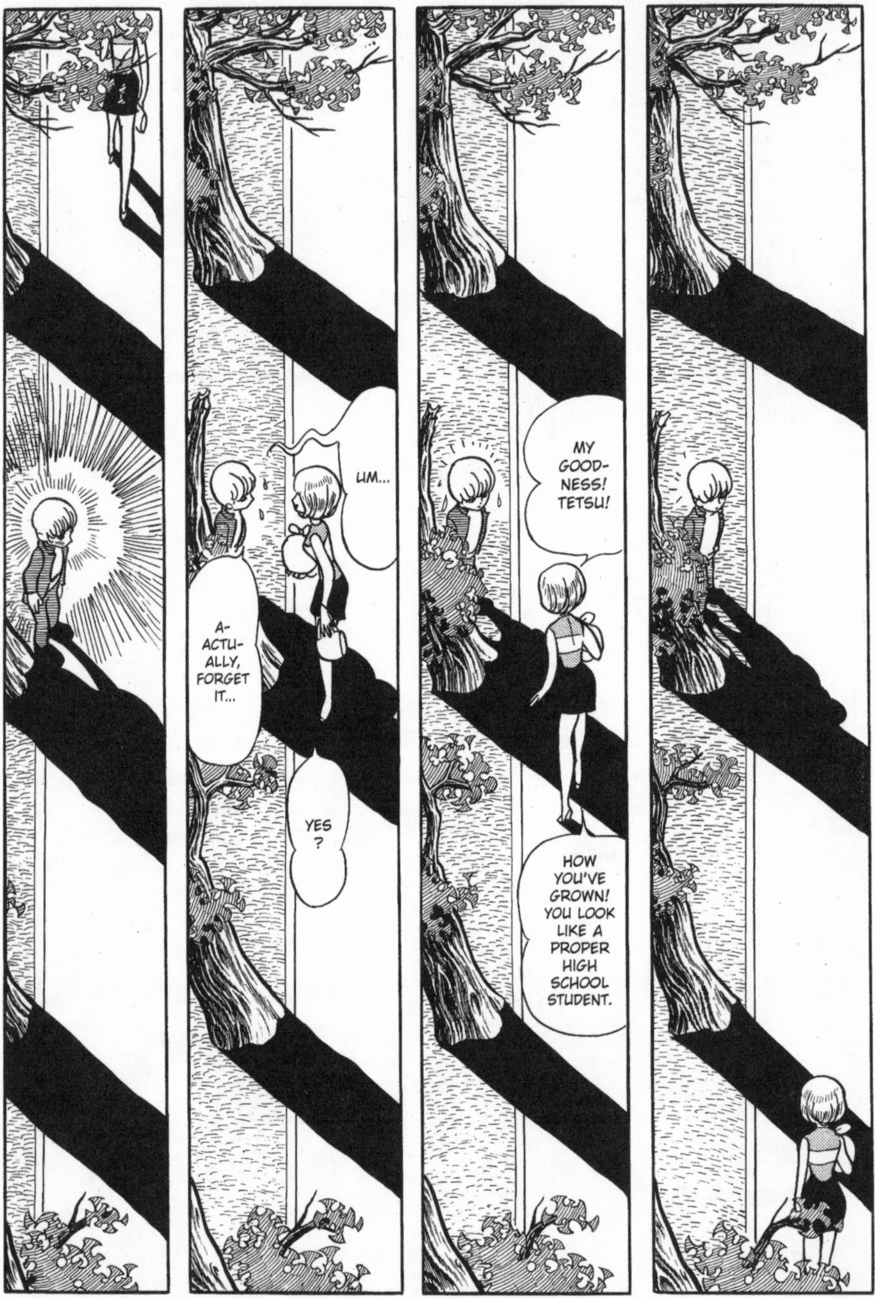
MY GOODNESS! TETSU!
HOW YOU'VE GROWN! YOU LOOK LIKE A PROPER HIGH SCHOOL STUDENT.
UM...
A-ACTUALLY, FORGET IT...
YES?

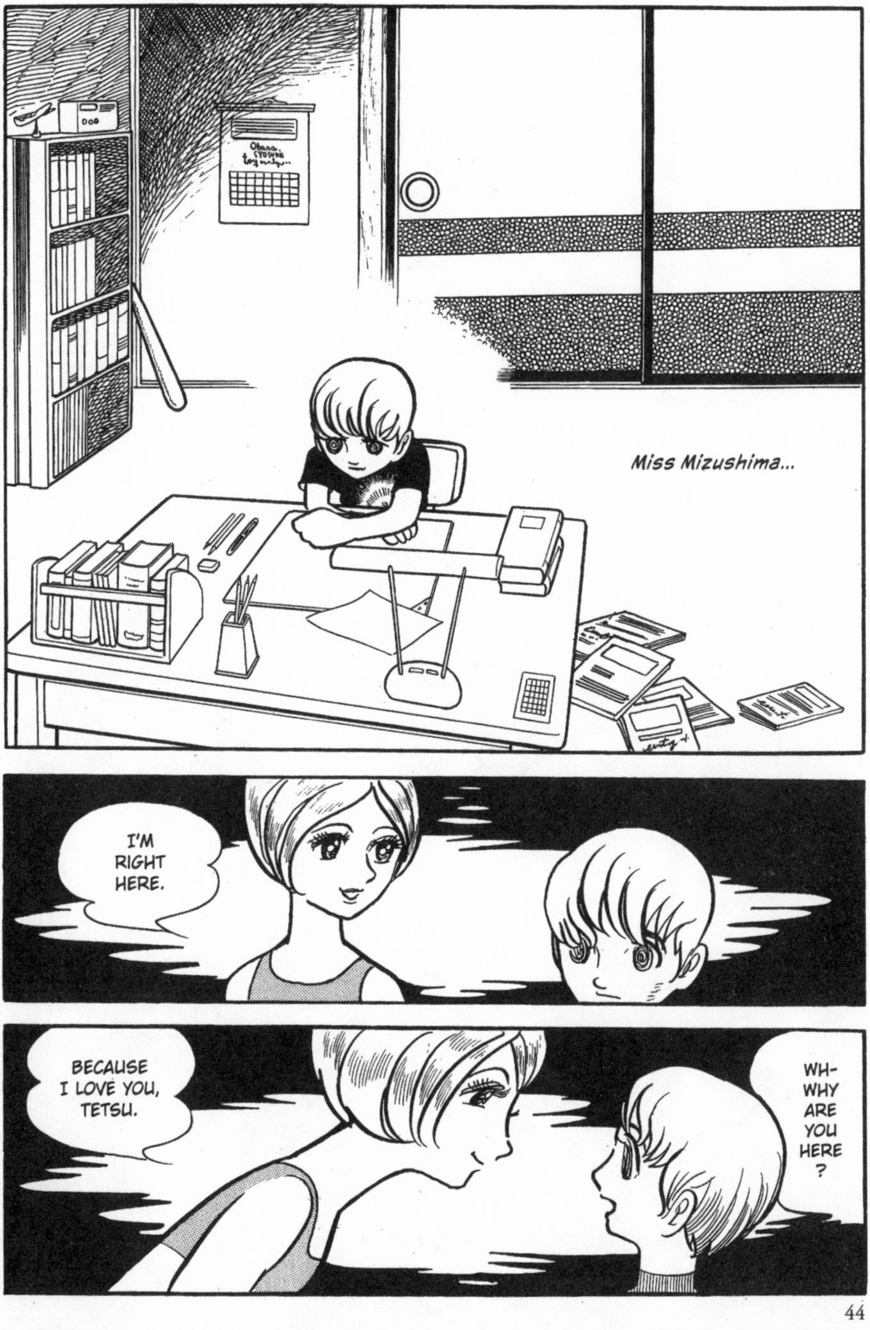
Miss Mizushima...
I'M RIGHT HERE.
WH- WHY ARE YOU HERE ?
BECAUSE I LOVE YOU, TETSU.

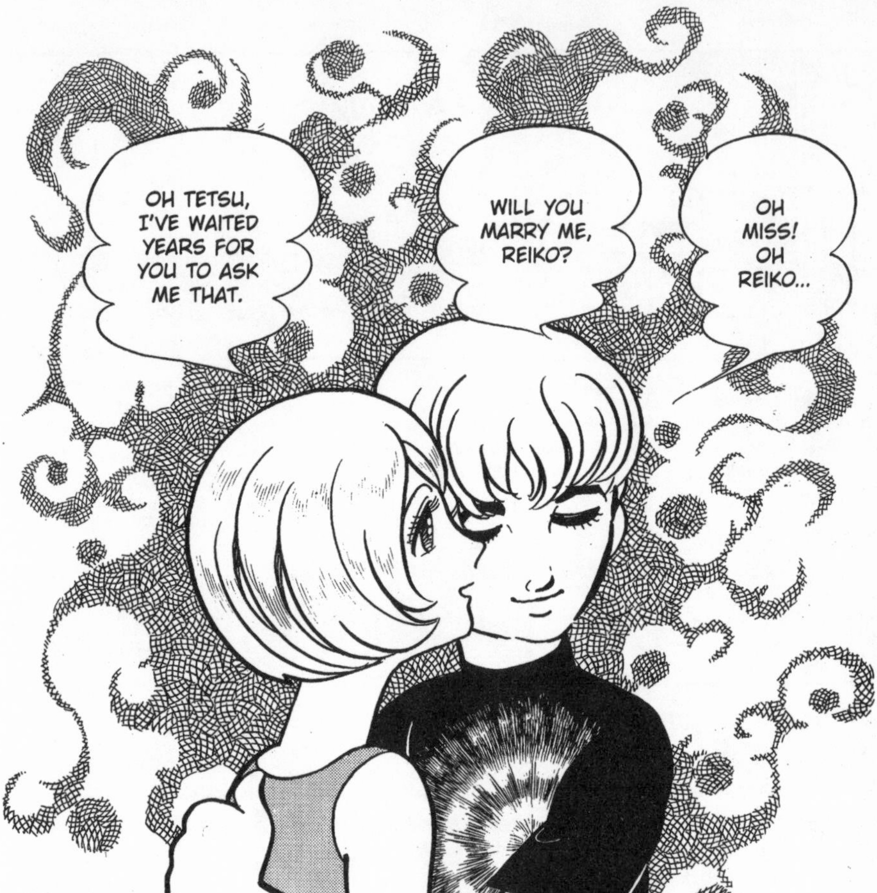
OH MISS! OH REIKO...
WILL YOU MARRY ME, REIKO?
OH TETSU, I'VE WAITED YEARS FOR YOU TO ASK ME THAT.
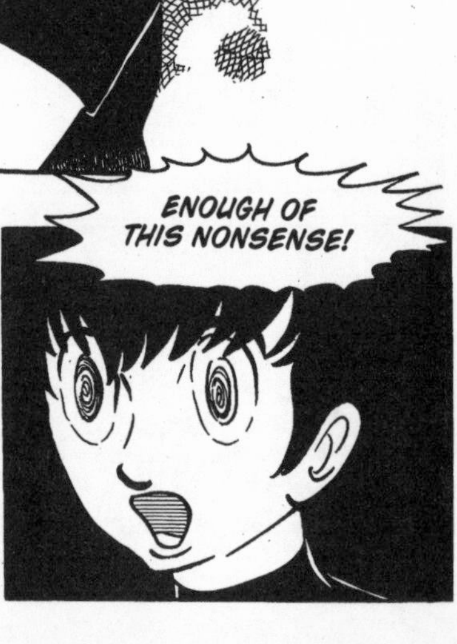
ENOUGH OF THIS NONSENSE!
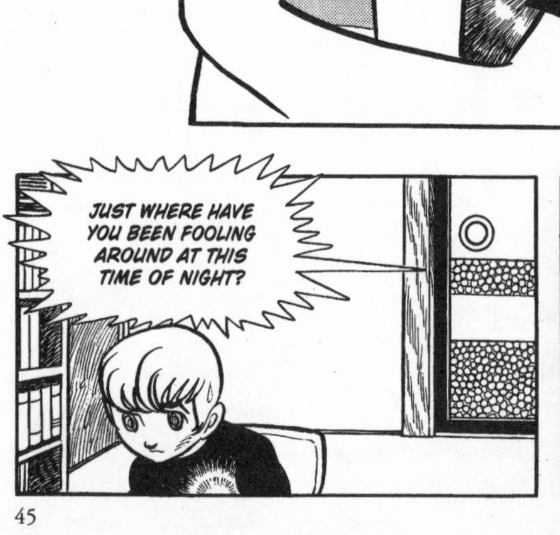
JUST WHERE HAVE YOU BEEN FOOLING AROUND AT THIS TIME OF NIGHT?

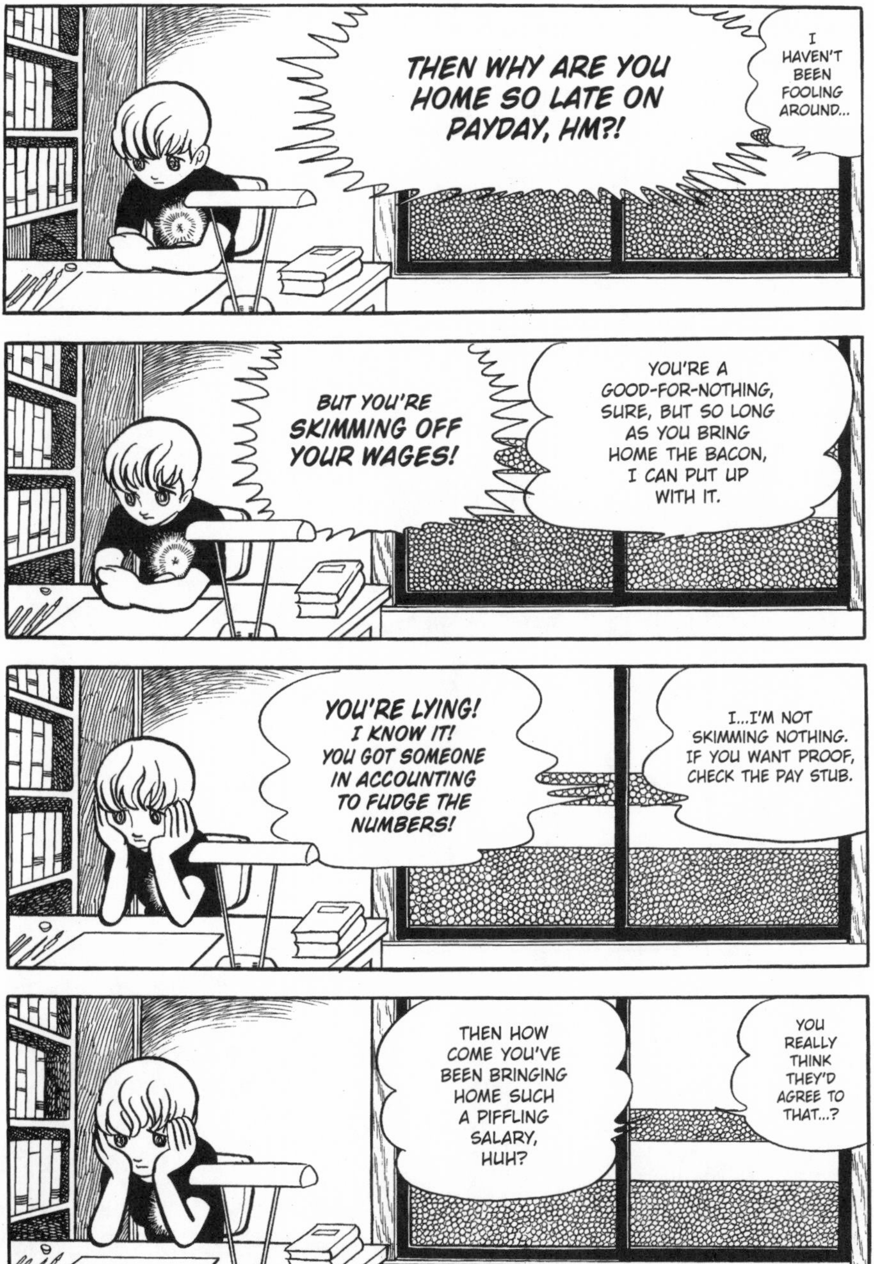
I HAVEN'T BEEN FOOLING AROUND...
THEN WHY ARE YOU HOME SO LATE ON PAYDAY, HM?!
YOU'RE A GOOD-FOR-NOTHING, SURE, BUT SO LONG AS YOU BRING HOME THE BACON, I CAN PUT UP WITH IT.
BUT YOU'RE SKIMMING OFF YOUR WAGES!
I...I'M NOT SKIMMING NOTHING. IF YOU WANT PROOF, CHECK THE PAY STUB.
YOU'RE LYING! I KNOW IT! YOU GOT SOMEONE IN ACCOUNTING TO FUDGE THE NUMBERS!
YOU REALLY THINK THEY'D AGREE TO THAT...?
THEN HOW COME YOU'VE BEEN BRINGING HOME SUCH A PIFFLING SALARY, HUH?

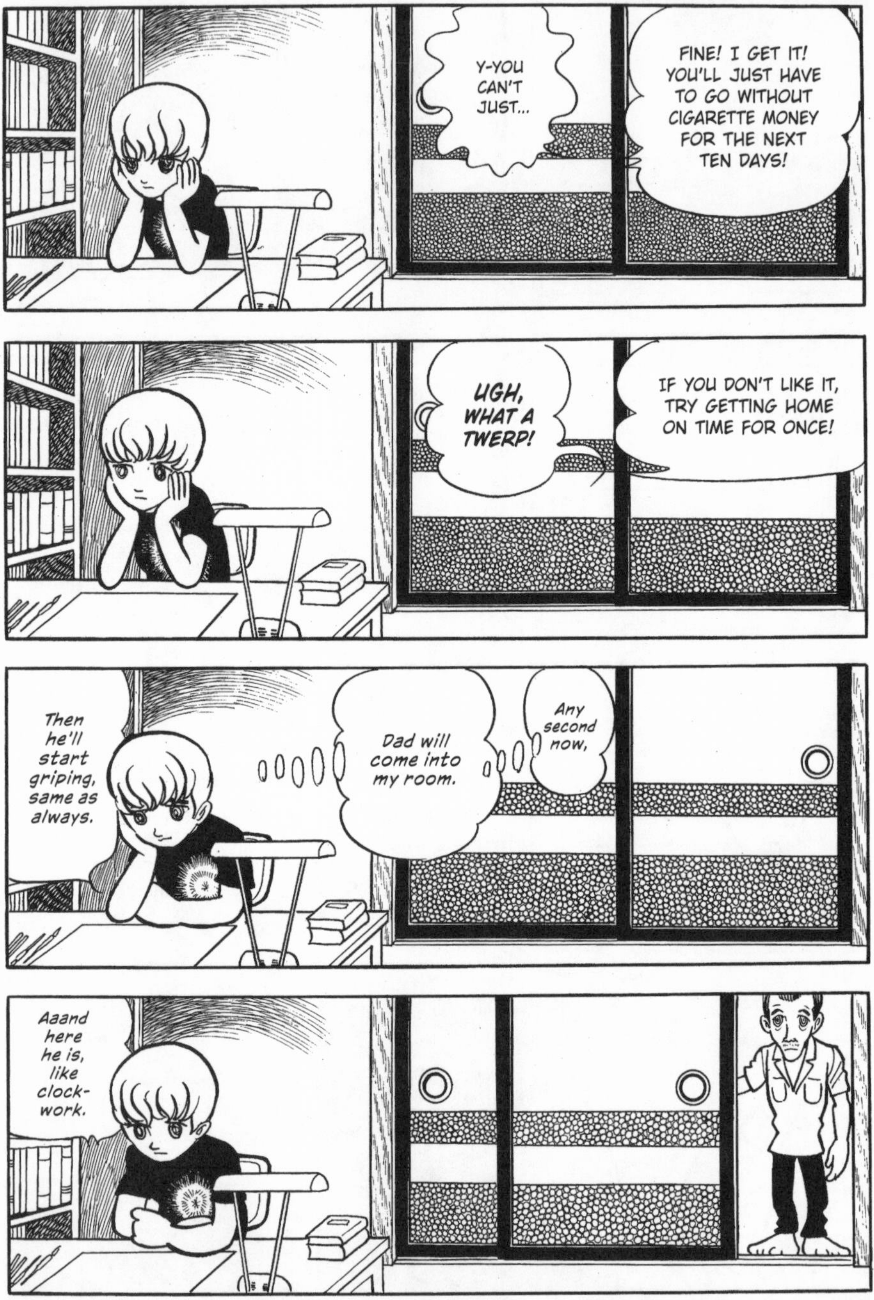
FINE! I GET IT! YOU'LL JUST HAVE TO GO WITHOUT CIGARETTE MONEY FOR THE NEXT TEN DAYS!
Y-YOU CAN'T JUST...
IF YOU DON'T LIKE IT, TRY GETTING HOME ON TIME FOR ONCE!
UGH, WHAT A TWERP!
Any second now,
Dad will come into my room.
Then he'll start griping, same as always.
Aaand here he is, like clockwork.

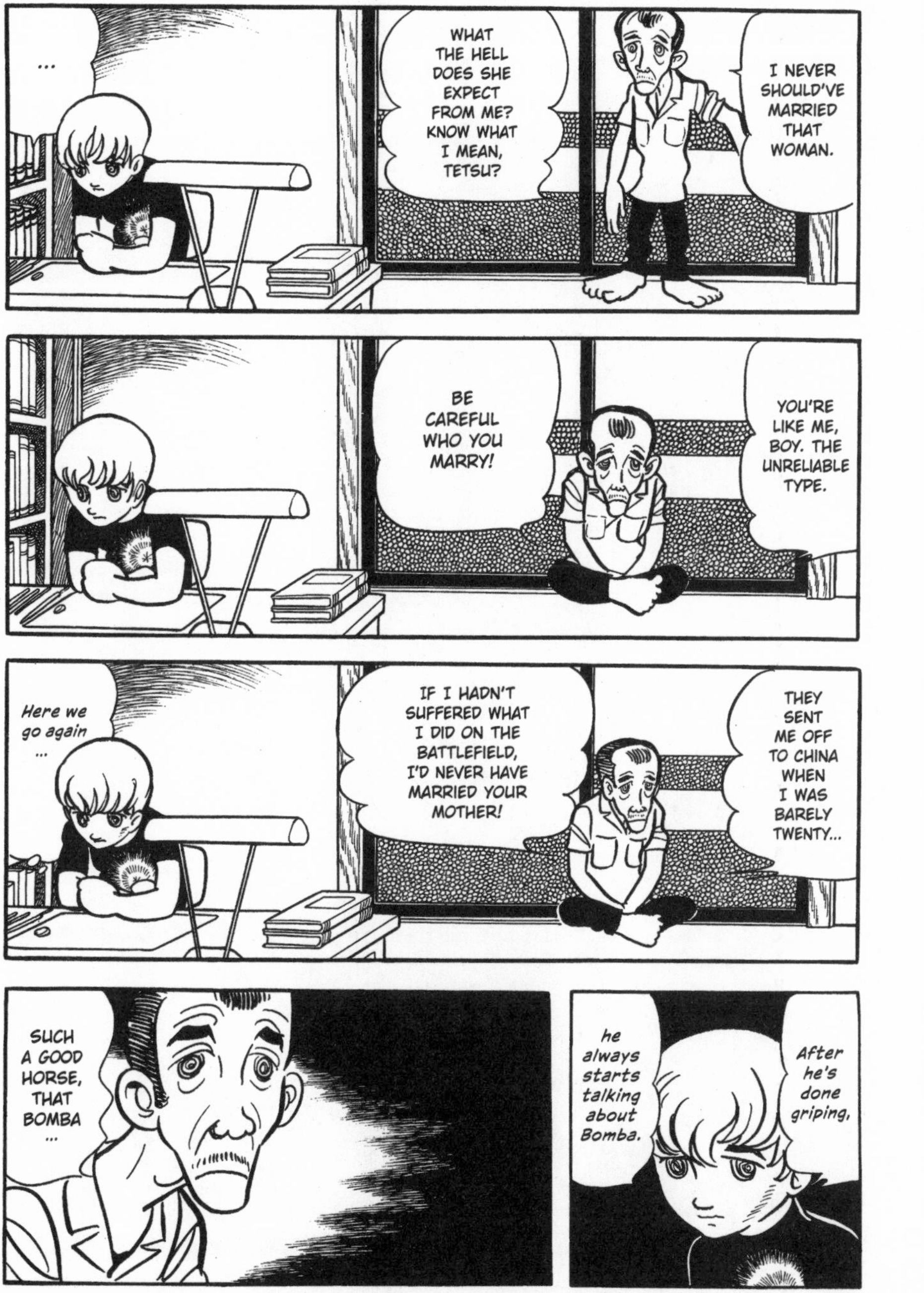
I NEVER SHOULD'VE MARRIED THAT WOMAN.
WHAT THE HELL DOES SHE EXPECT FROM ME? KNOW WHAT I MEAN, TETSU?
...
YOU'RE LIKE ME, BOY. THE UNRELIABLE TYPE.
BE CAREFUL WHO YOU MARRY!
THEY SENT ME OFF TO CHINA WHEN I WAS BARELY TWENTY...
IF I HADN'T SUFFERED WHAT I DID ON THE BATTLEFIELD, I'D NEVER HAVE MARRIED YOUR MOTHER!
Here we go again ...
After he's done griping,
he always starts talking about Bomba.
SUCH A GOOD HORSE, THAT BOMBA ...

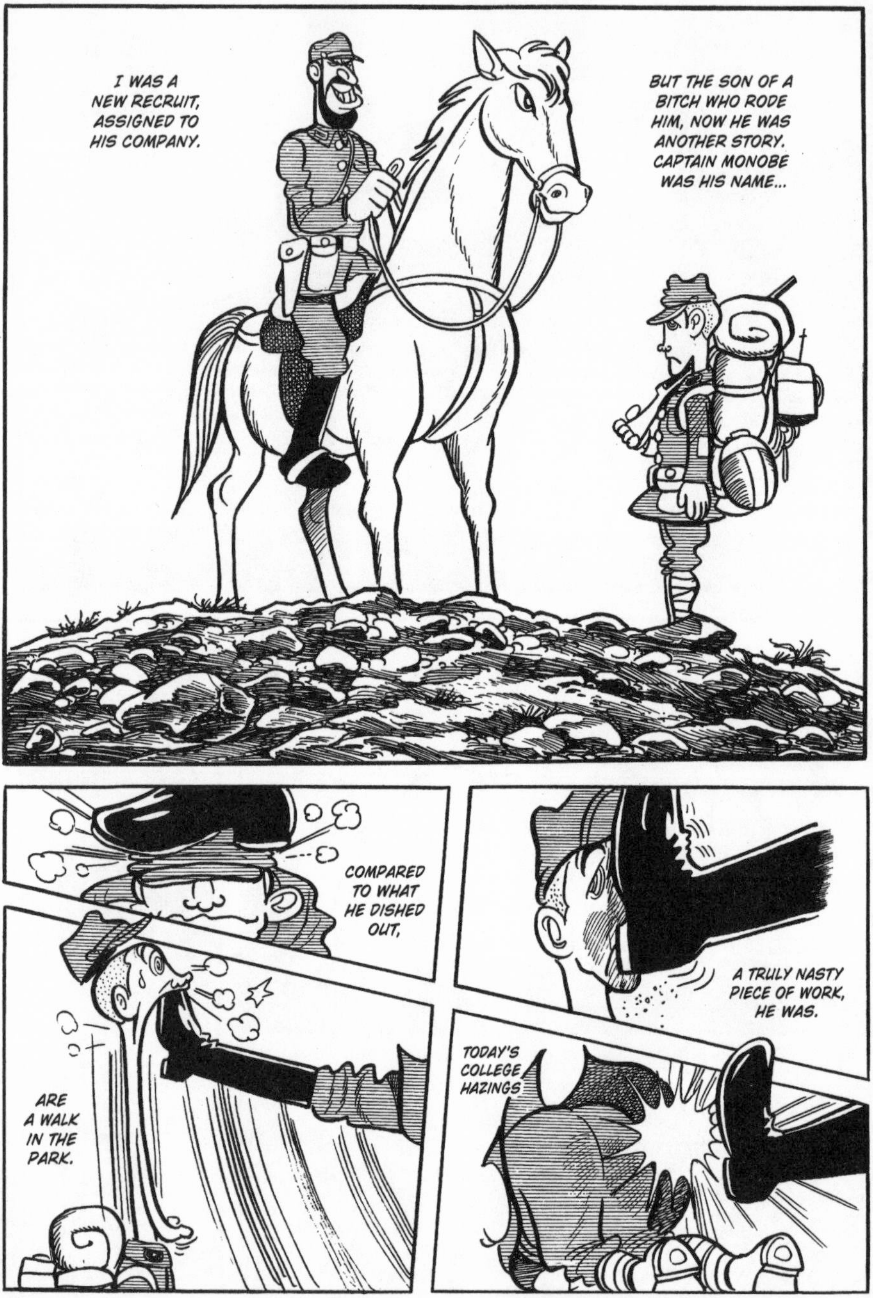
BUT THE SON OF A BITCH WHO RODE HIM, NOW HE WAS ANOTHER STORY. CAPTAIN MONOBE WAS HIS NAME...
I WAS A NEW RECRUIT, ASSIGNED TO HIS COMPANY.
A TRULY NASTY PIECE OF WORK, HE WAS.
COMPARED TO WHAT HE DISHED OUT,
TODAY'S COLLEGE HAZINGS
ARE A WALK IN THE PARK.

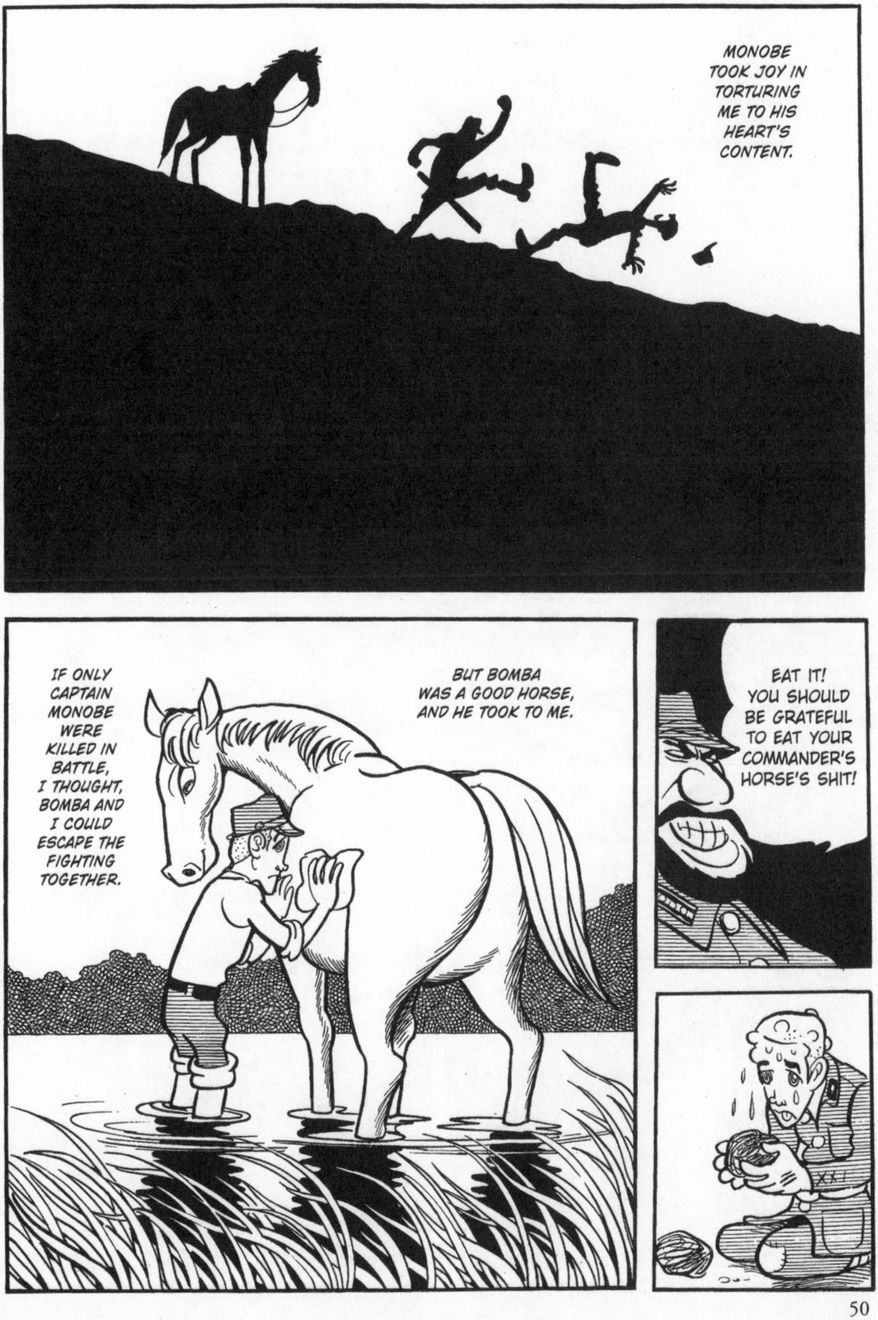
MONOBE TOOK JOY IN TORTURING ME TO HIS HEART'S CONTENT.
EAT IT! YOU SHOULD BE GRATEFUL TO EAT YOUR COMMANDER'S HORSE'S SHIT!
BUT BOMBA WAS A GOOD HORSE, AND HE TOOK TO ME.
IF ONLY CAPTAIN MONOBE WERE KILLED IN BATTLE, I THOUGHT, BOMBA AND I COULD ESCAPE THE FIGHTING TOGETHER.

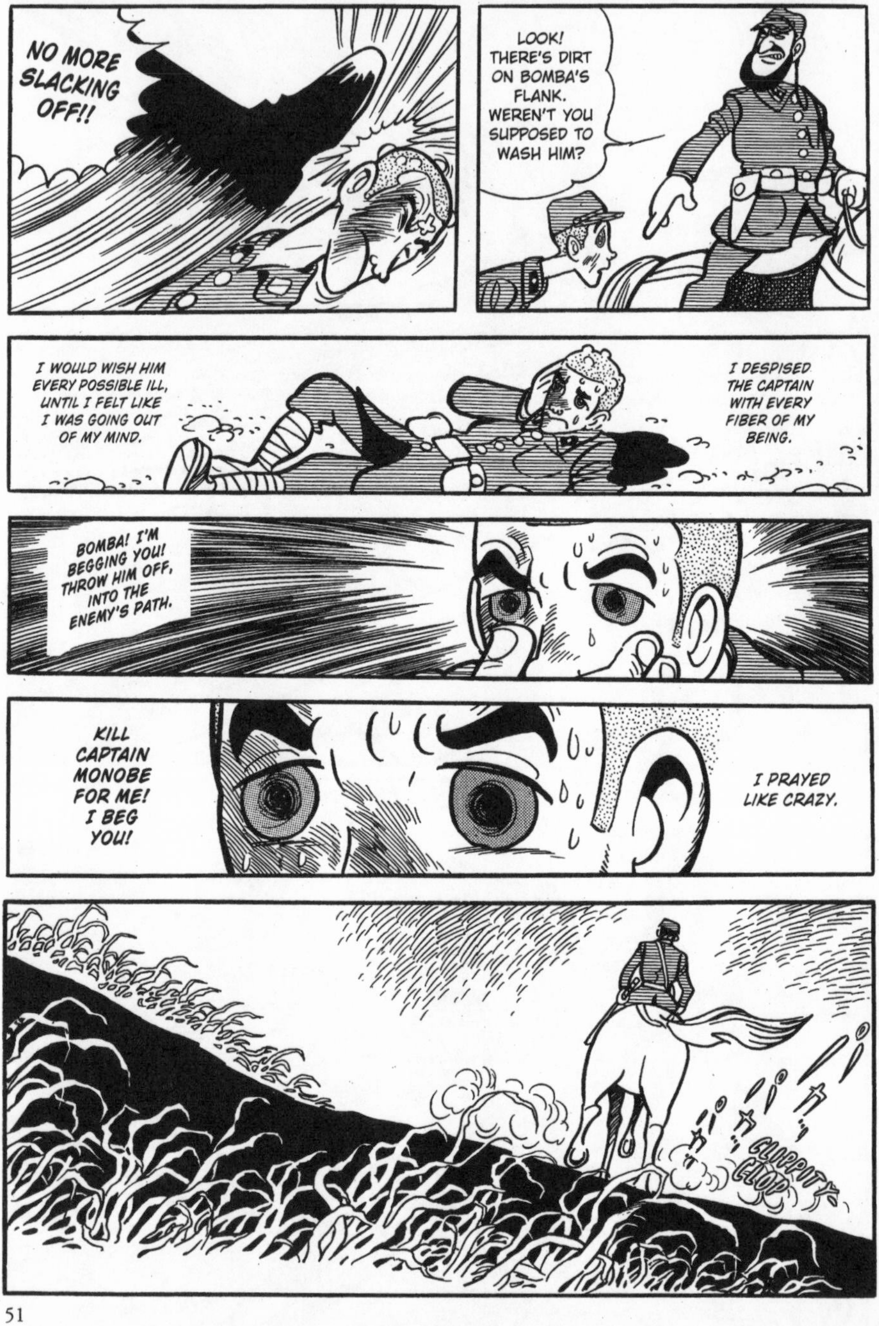
LOOK! THERE'S DIRT ON BOMBA'S FLANK. WEREN'T YOU SUPPOSED TO WASH HIM?
NO MORE SLACKING OFF!!
I DESPISED THE CAPTAIN WITH EVERY FIBER OF MY BEING.
I WOULD WISH HIM EVERY POSSIBLE ILL, UNTIL I FELT LIKE I WAS GOING OUT OF MY MIND.
BOMBA! I'M BEGGING YOU! THROW HIM OFF, INTO THE ENEMY'S PATH.
I PRAYED LIKE CRAZY.
KILL CAPTAIN MONOBE FOR ME! I BEG YOU!
CLIPPITY CLOP

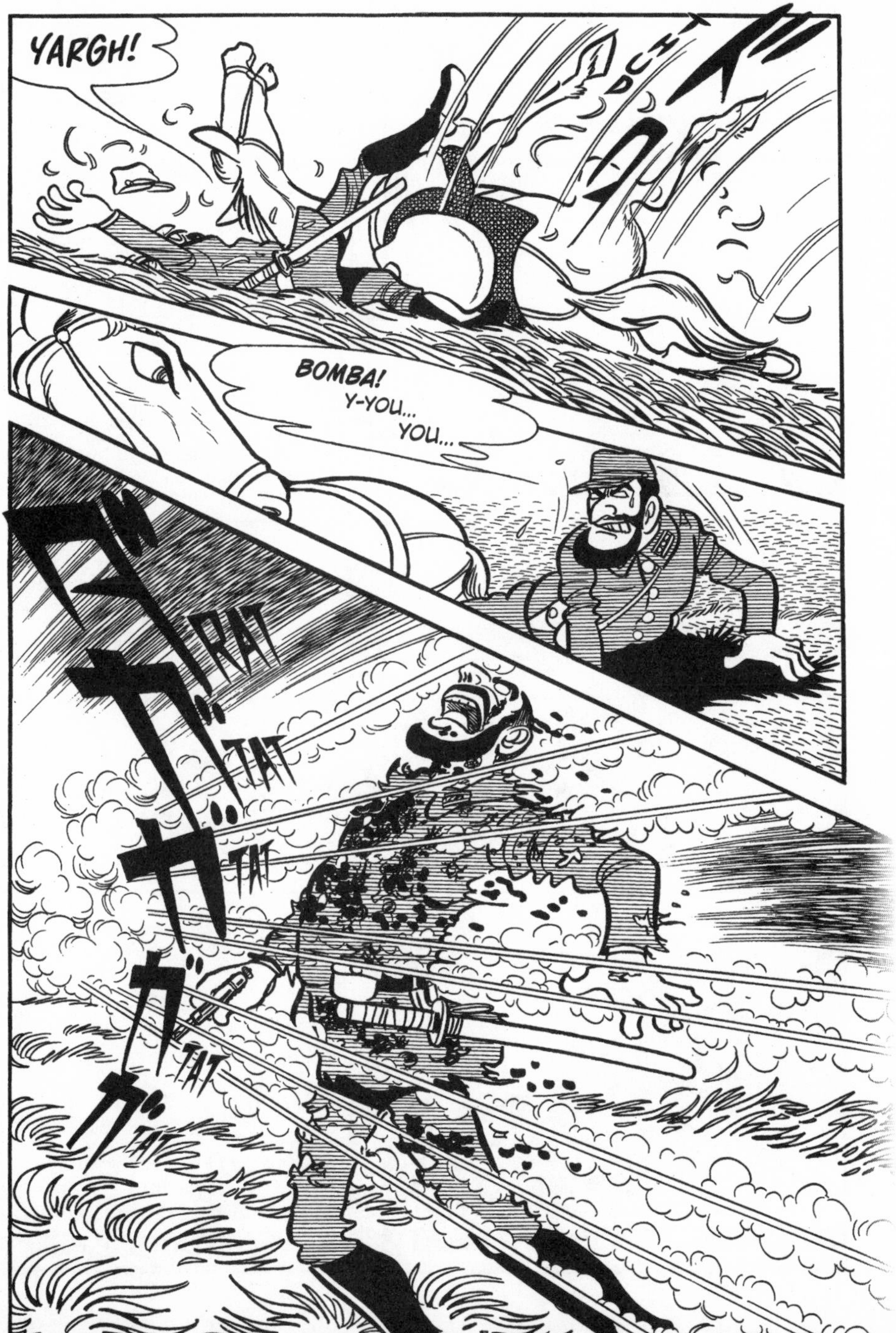
DCHT
YARGH!
BOMBA! Y-YOU... YOU...
RAT TAT TAT TAT TAT

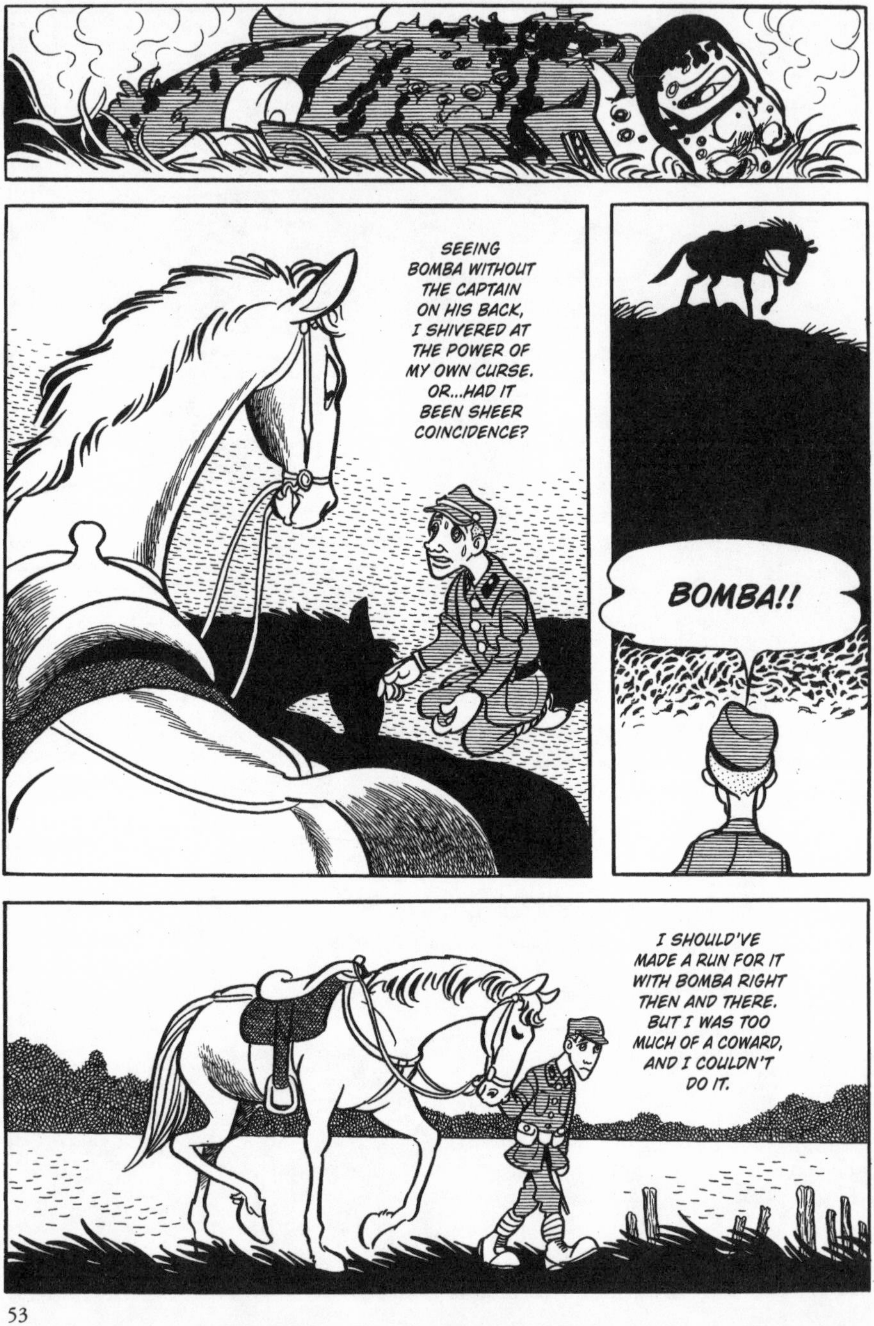
BOMBA!!
SEEING BOMBA WITHOUT THE CAPTAIN ON HIS BACK, I SHIVERED AT THE POWER OF MY OWN CURSE. OR...HAD IT BEEN SHEER COINCIDENCE?
I SHOULD'VE MADE A RUN FOR IT WITH BOMBA RIGHT THEN AND THERE. BUT I WAS TOO MUCH OF A COWARD, AND I COULDN'T DO IT.

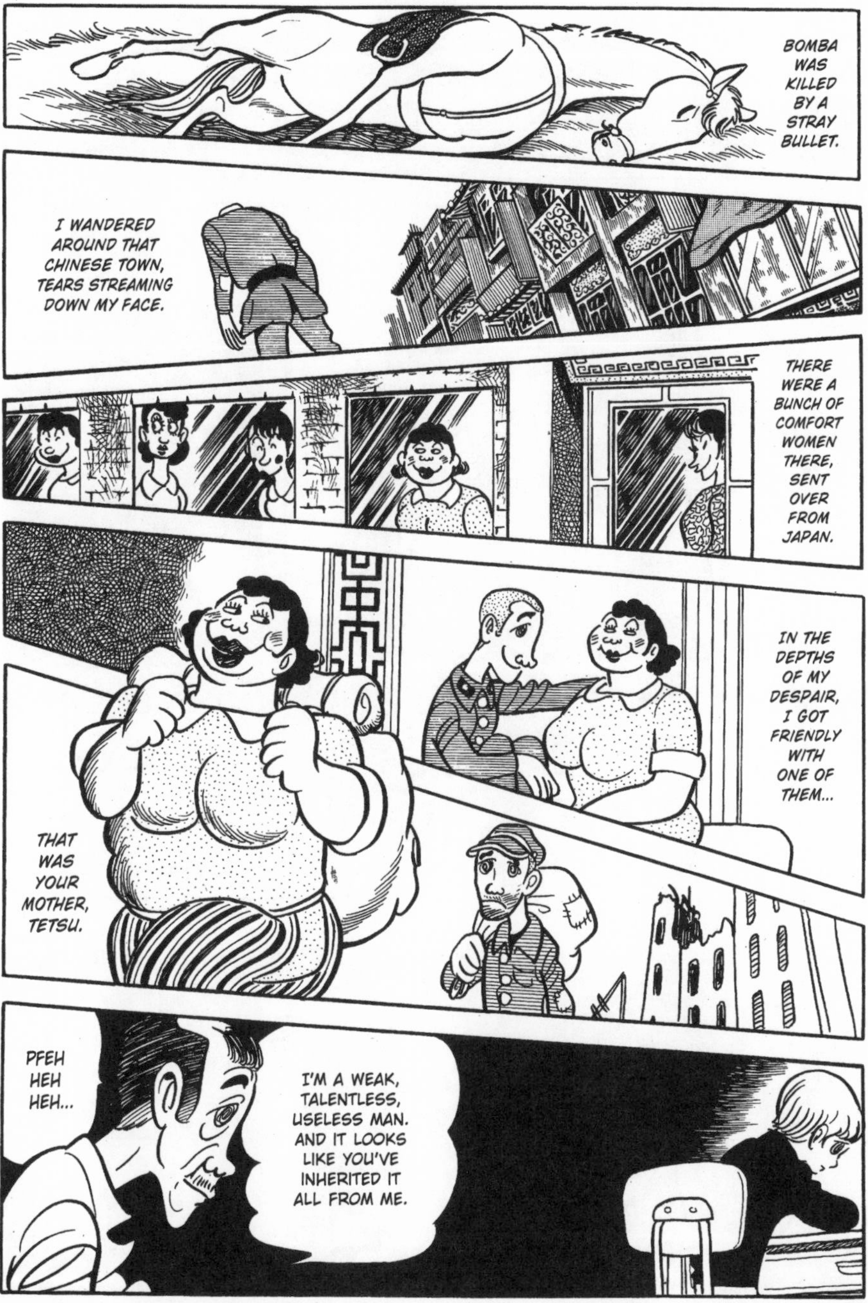
BOMBA WAS KILLED BY A STRAY BULLET.
I WANDERED AROUND THAT CHINESE TOWN, TEARS STREAMING DOWN MY FACE.
THERE WERE A BUNCH OF COMFORT WOMEN THERE, SENT OVER FROM JAPAN.
IN THE DEPTHS OF MY DESPAIR, I GOT FRIENDLY WITH ONE OF THEM...
THAT WAS YOUR MOTHER, TETSU.
PFEH HEH HEH...
I'M A WEAK, TALENTLESS, USELESS MAN. AND IT LOOKS LIKE YOU'VE INHERITED IT ALL FROM ME.

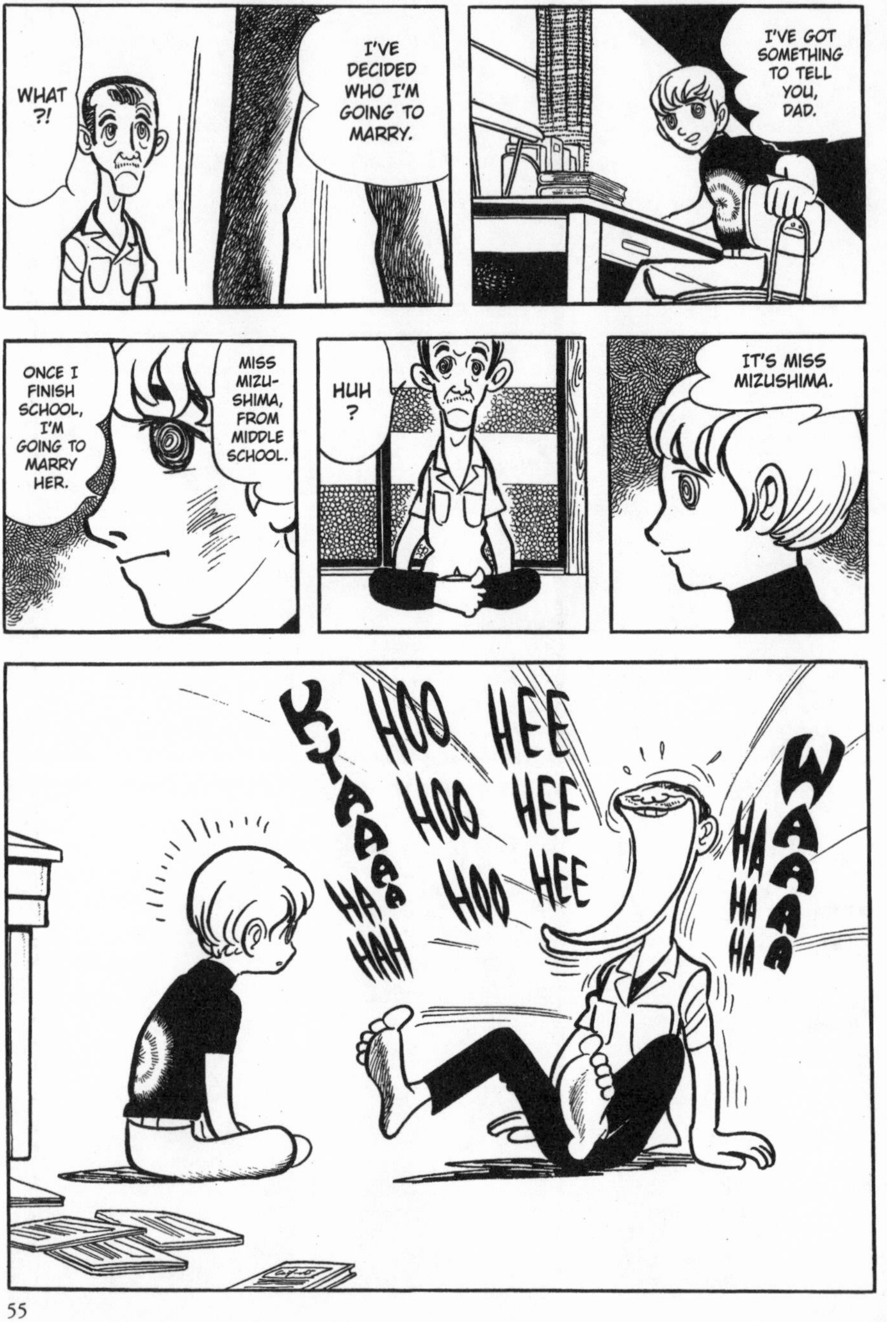
I'VE GOT SOMETHING TO TELL YOU, DAD.
I'VE DECIDED WHO I'M GOING TO MARRY.
WHAT ?!
IT'S MISS MIZUSHIMA.
HUH ?
MISS MIZU-SHIMA, FROM MIDDLE SCHOOL.
ONCE I FINISH SCHOOL, I'M GOING TO MARRY HER.
WAAAAA
HA HA HA HA
HOO HEE
HOO HEE
HOO HEE
KYAAAA
HA HAH

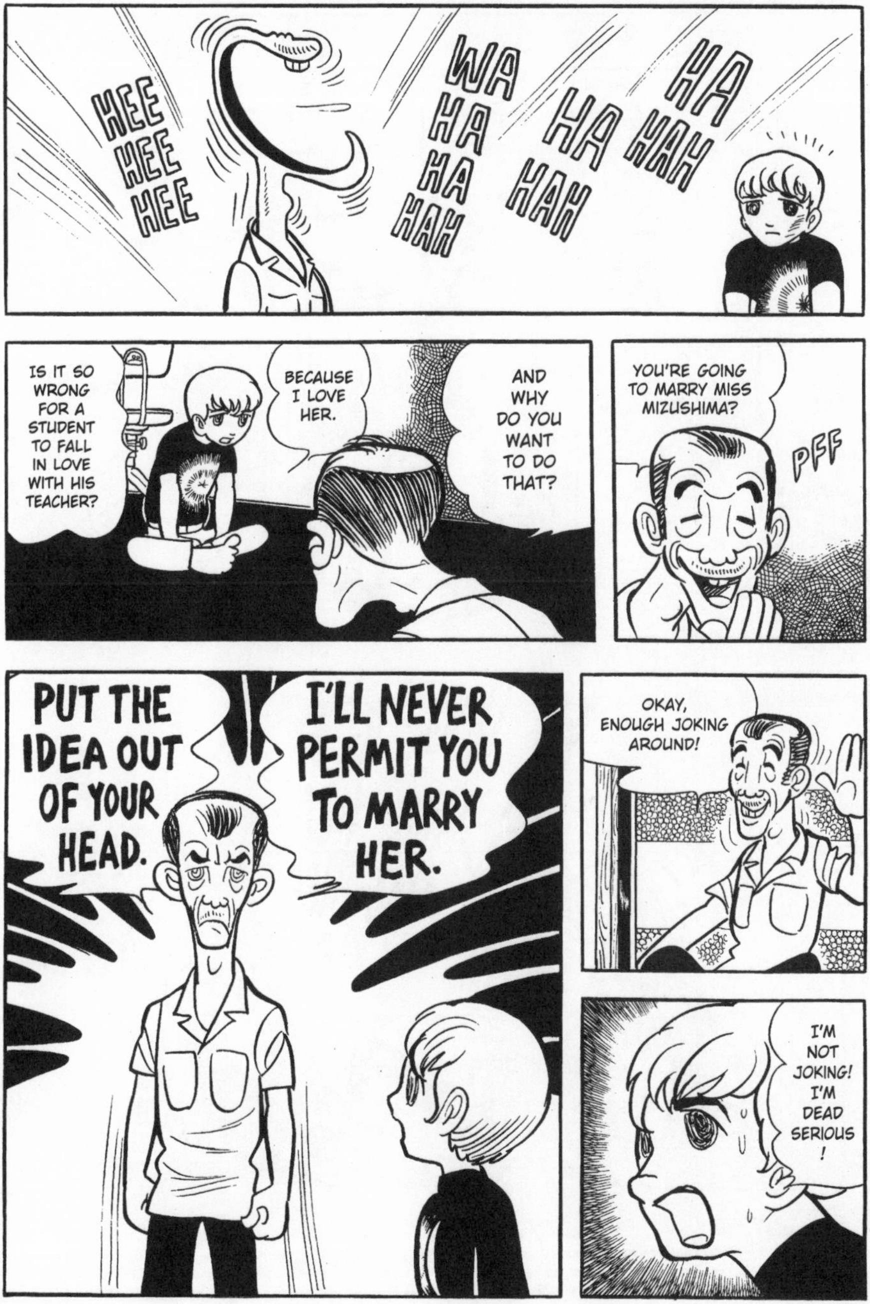
HA HAH
HA HAH
WA HA HA HAH
HEE HEE HEE
YOU'RE GOING TO MARRY MISS MIZUSHIMA?
PFF
AND WHY DO YOU WANT TO DO THAT?
BECAUSE I LOVE HER.
IS IT SO WRONG FOR A STUDENT TO FALL IN LOVE WITH HIS TEACHER?
OKAY, ENOUGH JOKING AROUND!
I'M NOT JOKING! I'M DEAD SERIOUS!
I'LL NEVER PERMIT YOU TO MARRY HER.
PUT THE IDEA OUT OF YOUR HEAD.

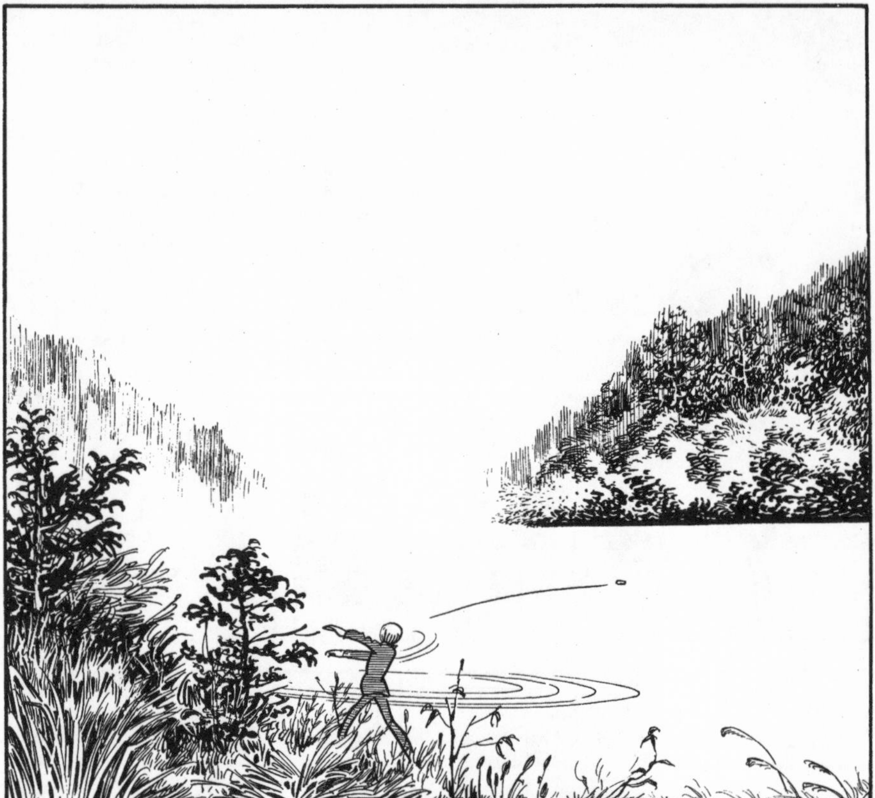

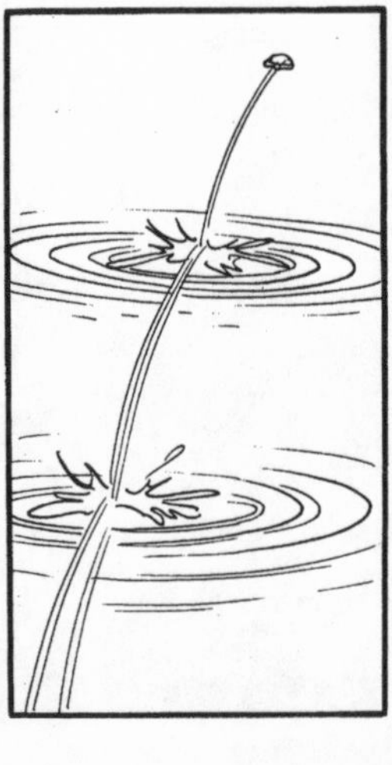

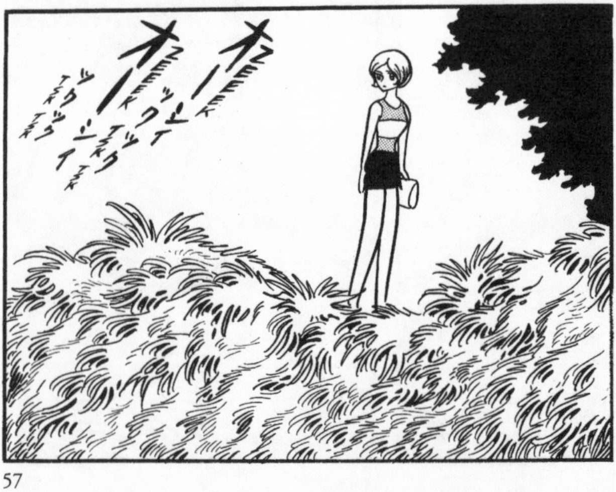
ZEEEK
ZEEEK

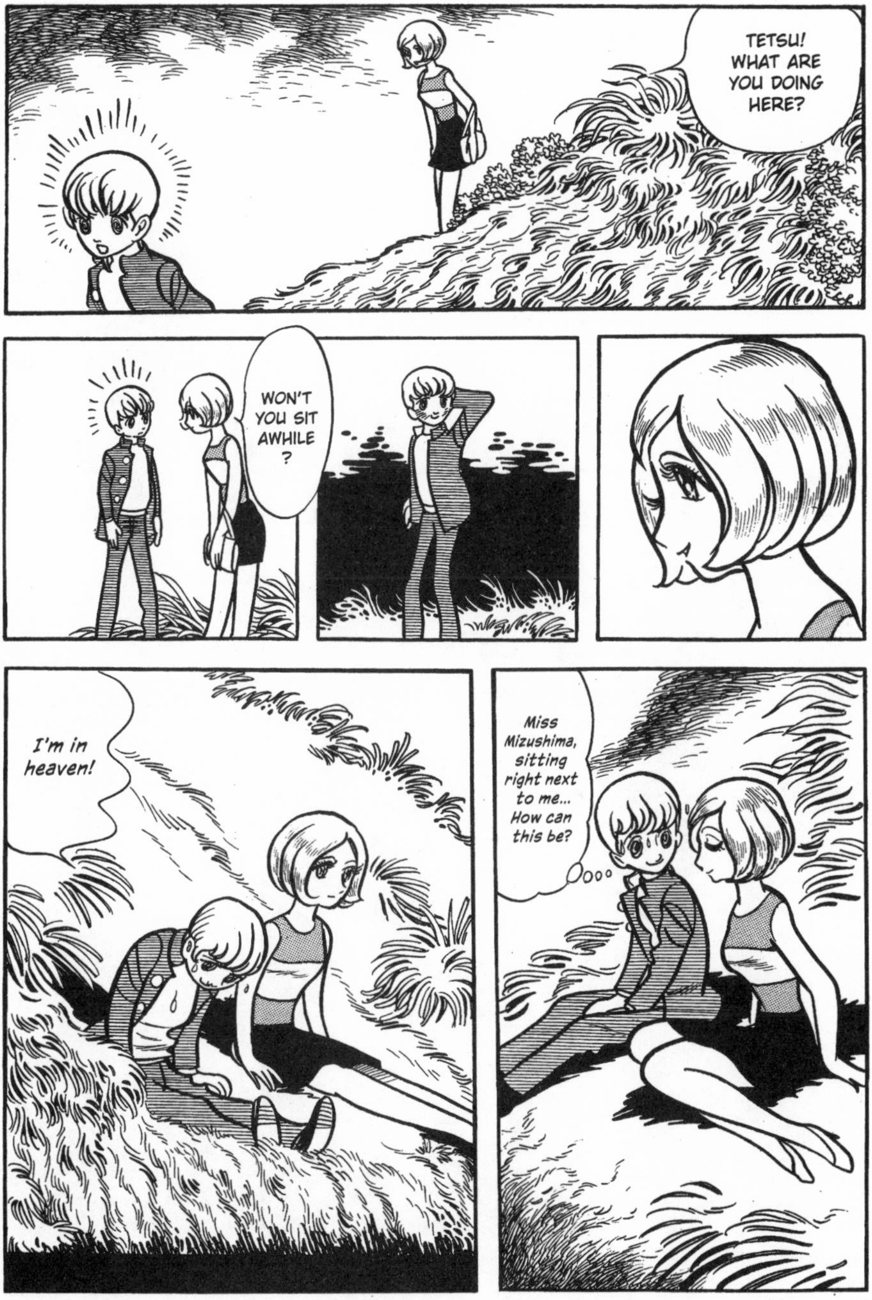
TETSU! WHAT ARE YOU DOING HERE?
WON'T YOU SIT AWHILE ?
Miss Mizushima, sitting right next to me... How can this be?
I'm in heaven!

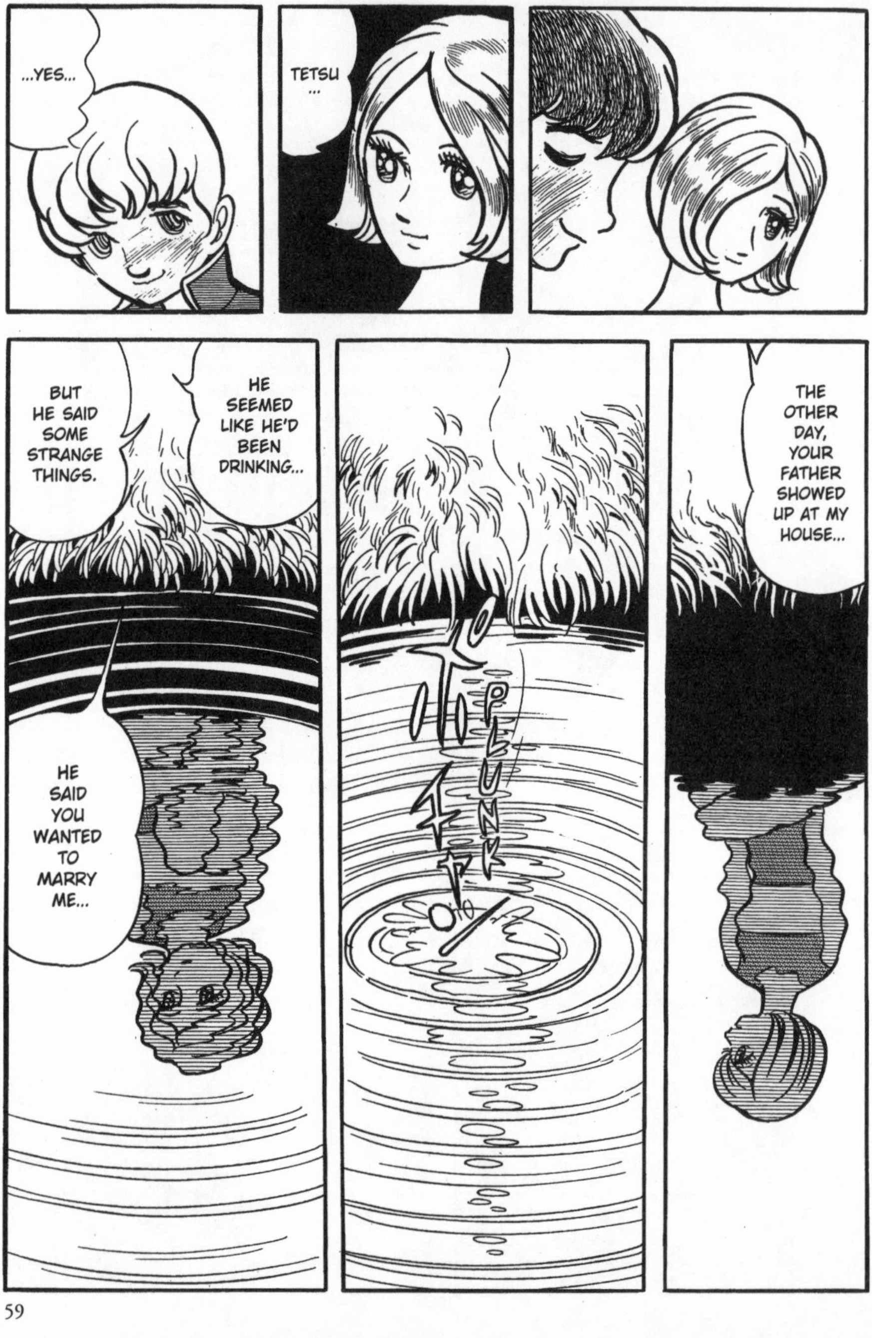
TETSU ...
...YES...
THE OTHER DAY, YOUR FATHER SHOWED UP AT MY HOUSE...
PLUNK
HE SEEMED LIKE HE'D BEEN DRINKING...
BUT HE SAID SOME STRANGE THINGS.
HE SAID YOU WANTED TO MARRY ME...

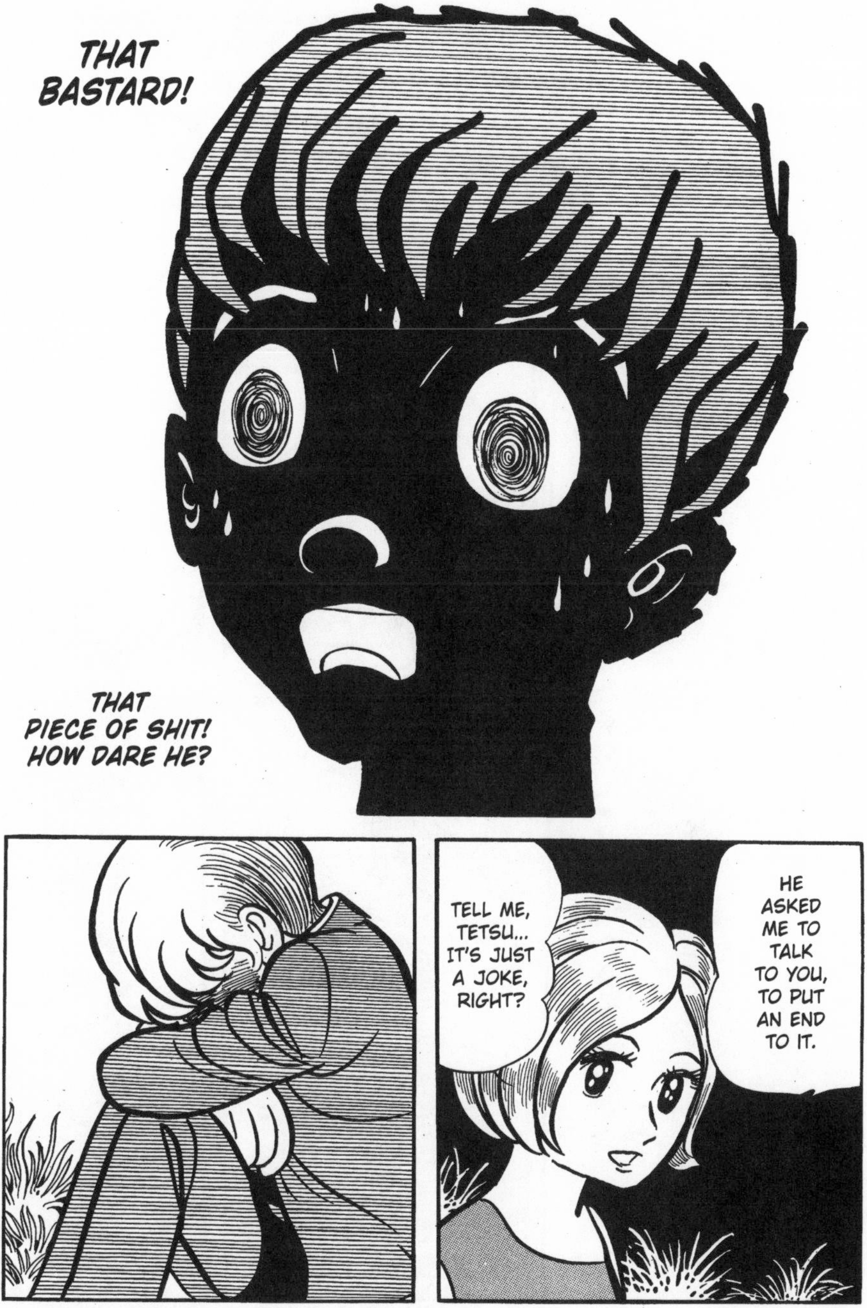
THAT BASTARD!
THAT PIECE OF SHIT! HOW DARE HE?
HE ASKED ME TO TALK TO YOU, TO PUT AN END TO IT.
TELL ME, TETSU... IT'S JUST A JOKE, RIGHT?

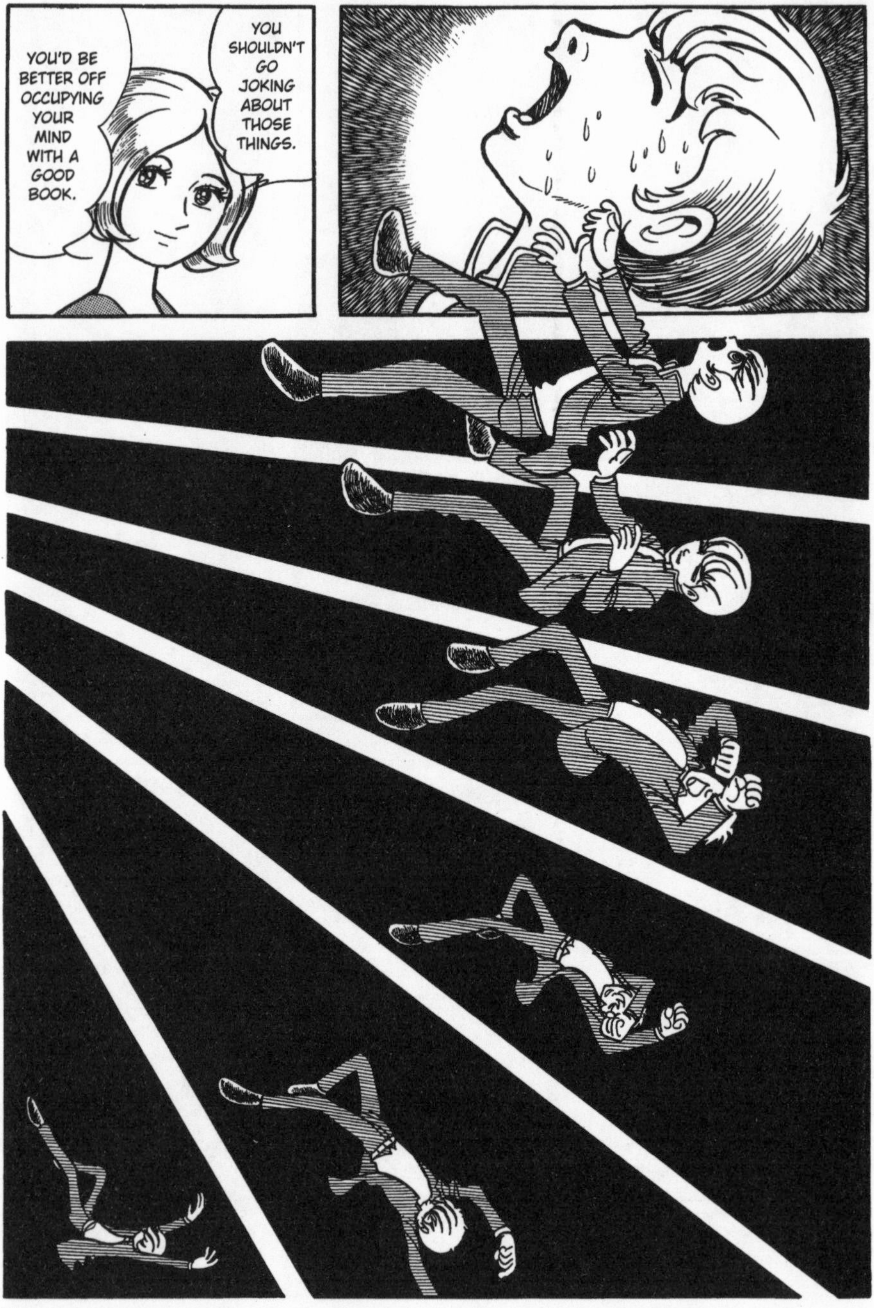
YOU SHOULDN'T GO JOKING ABOUT THOSE THINGS.
YOU'D BE BETTER OFF OCCUPYING YOUR MIND WITH A GOOD BOOK.

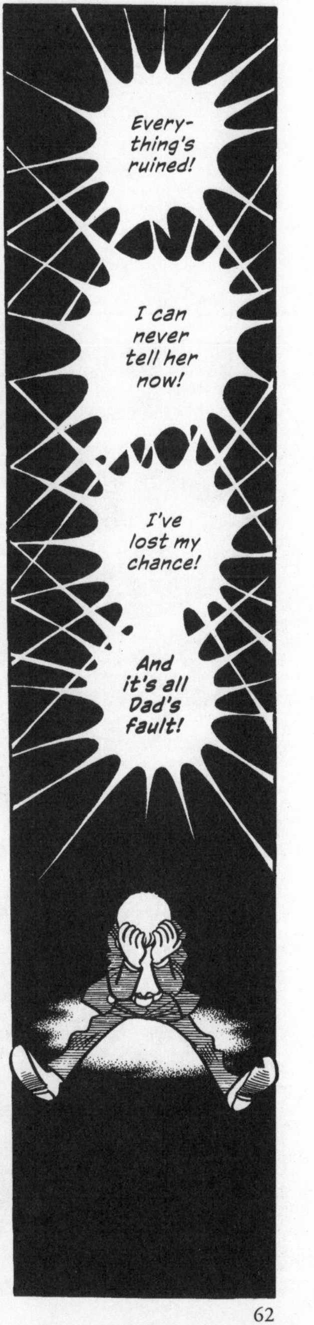
Every-thing's ruined!
I can never tell her now!
I've lost my chance!
And it's all Dad's fault!

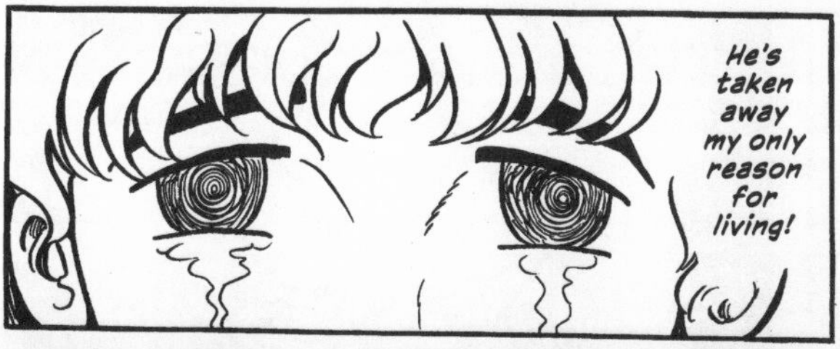
He's taken away my only reason for living!

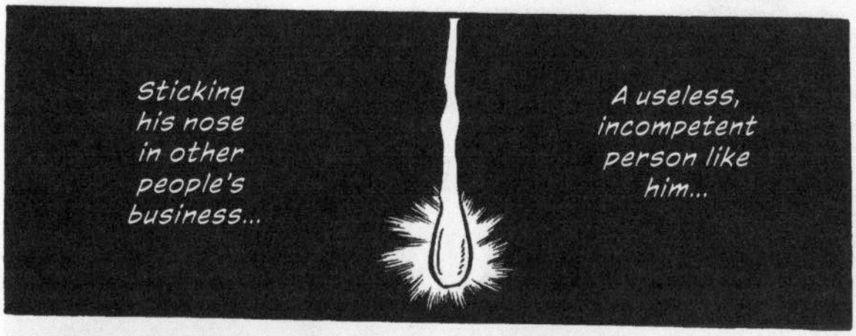
A useless, incompetent person like him...
Sticking his nose in other people's business...

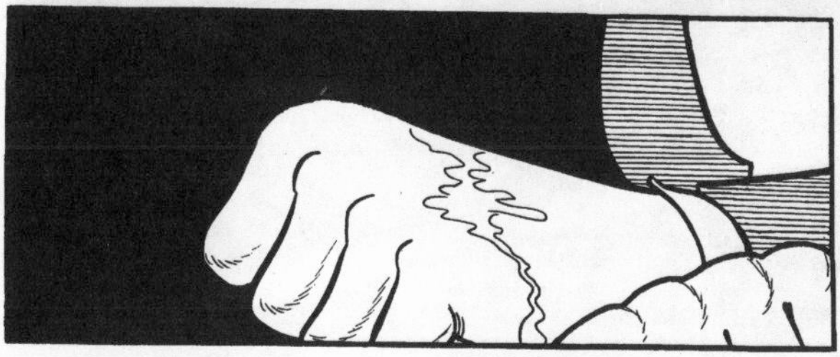

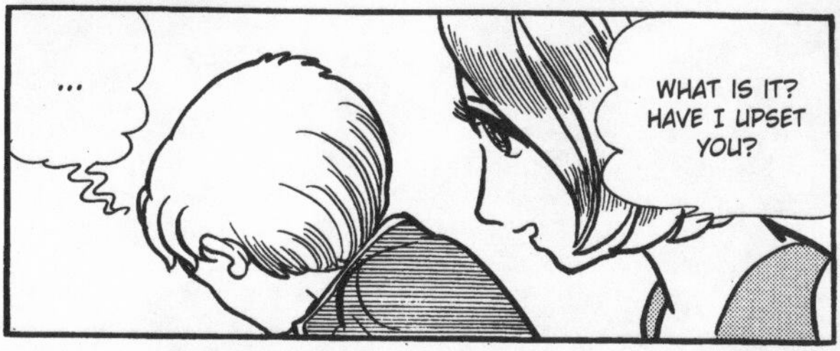
WHAT IS IT? HAVE I UPSET YOU?
...

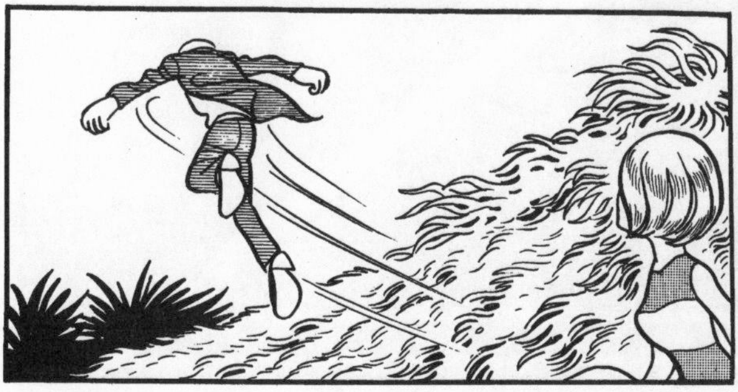

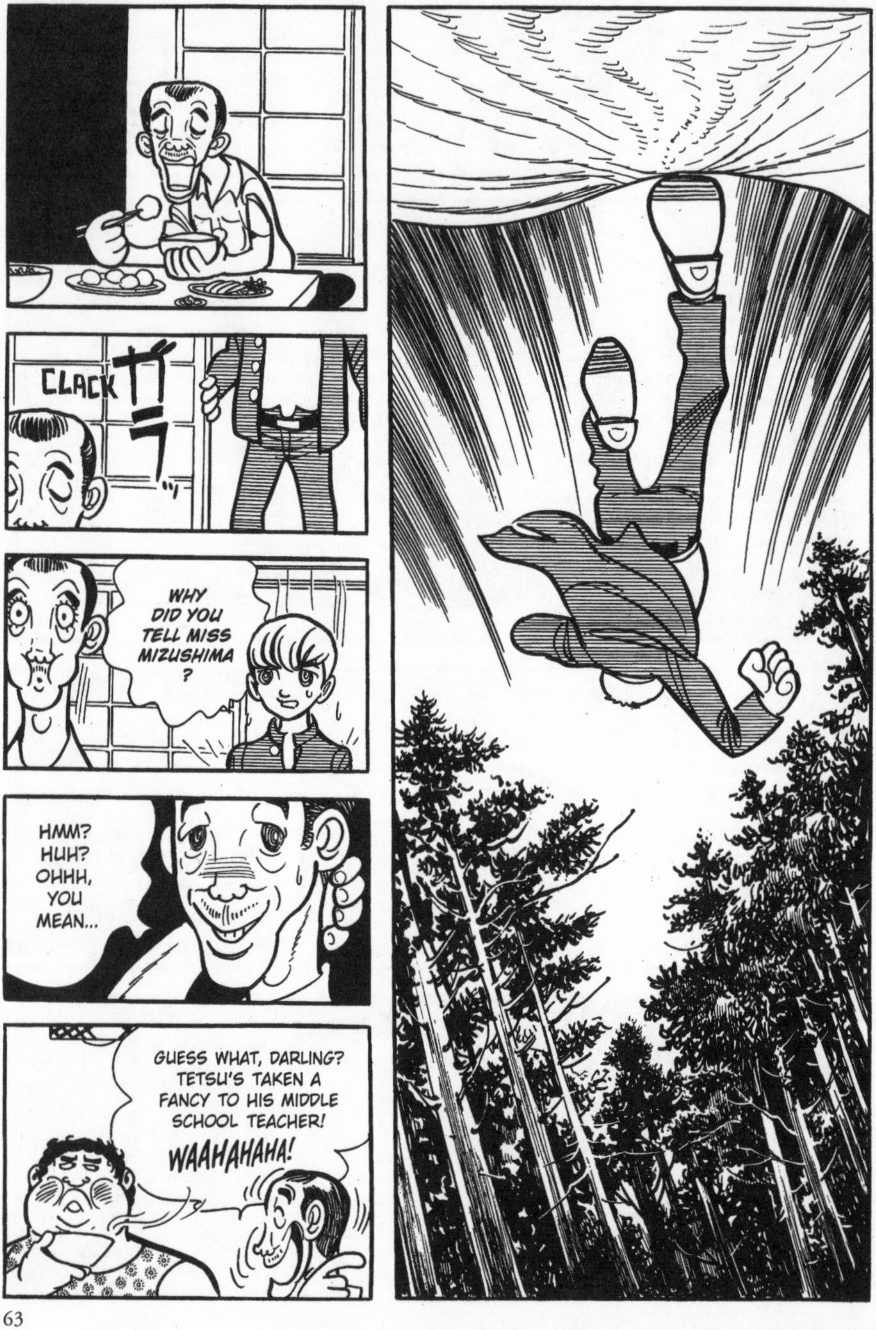
CLACK
ガラ
WHY DID YOU TELL MISS MIZUSHIMA?
HMM? HUH? OHHH, YOU MEAN...
GUESS WHAT, DARLING? TETSU'S TAKEN A FANCY TO HIS MIDDLE SCHOOL TEACHER!
WAAHAHAHA!

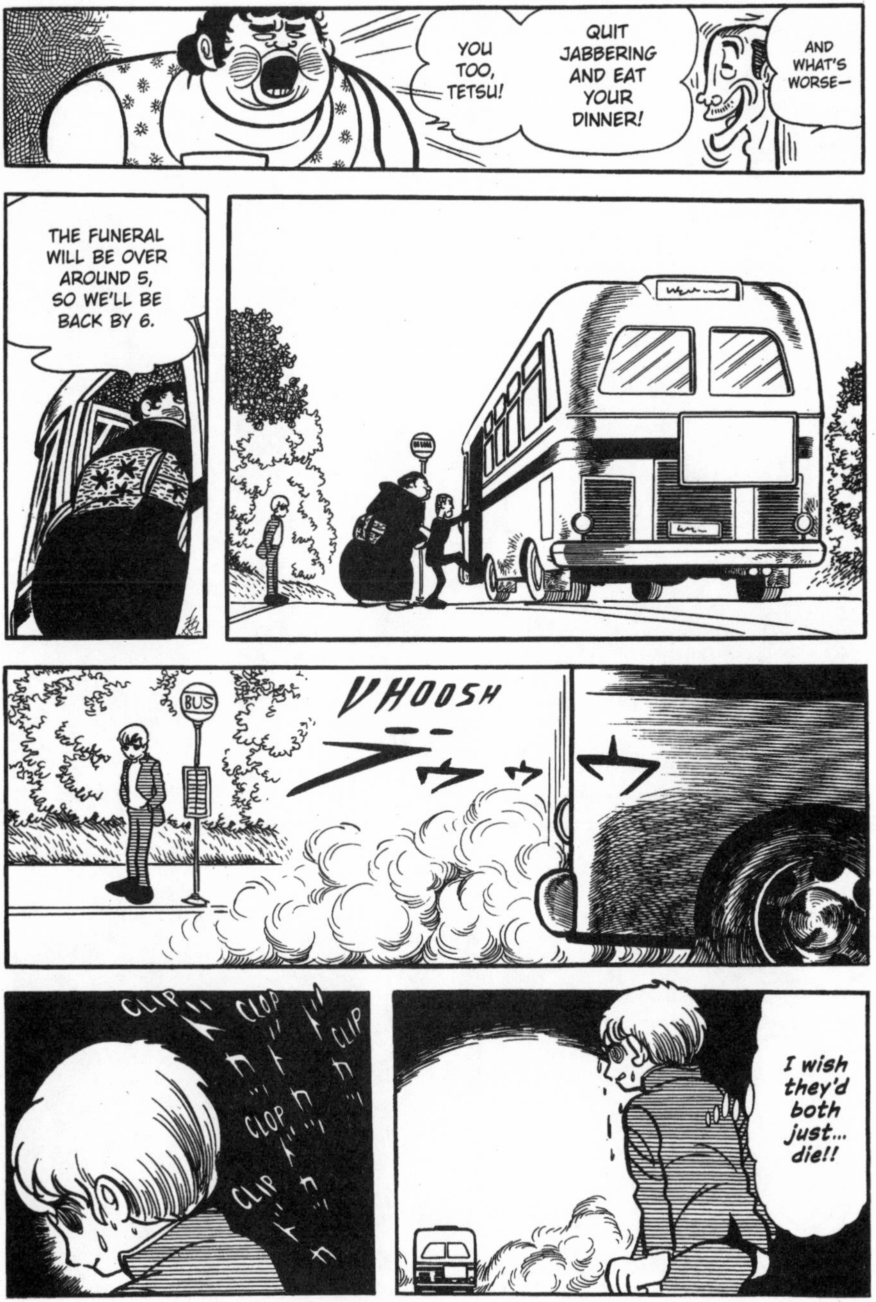
AND WHAT'S WORSE—
QUIT JABBERING AND EAT YOUR DINNER!
YOU TOO, TETSU!
THE FUNERAL WILL BE OVER AROUND 5, SO WE'LL BE BACK BY 6.
BUS
VHOOSH
I wish they'd both just... die!!
CLIP
CLOP
CLIP
CLOP
CLIP

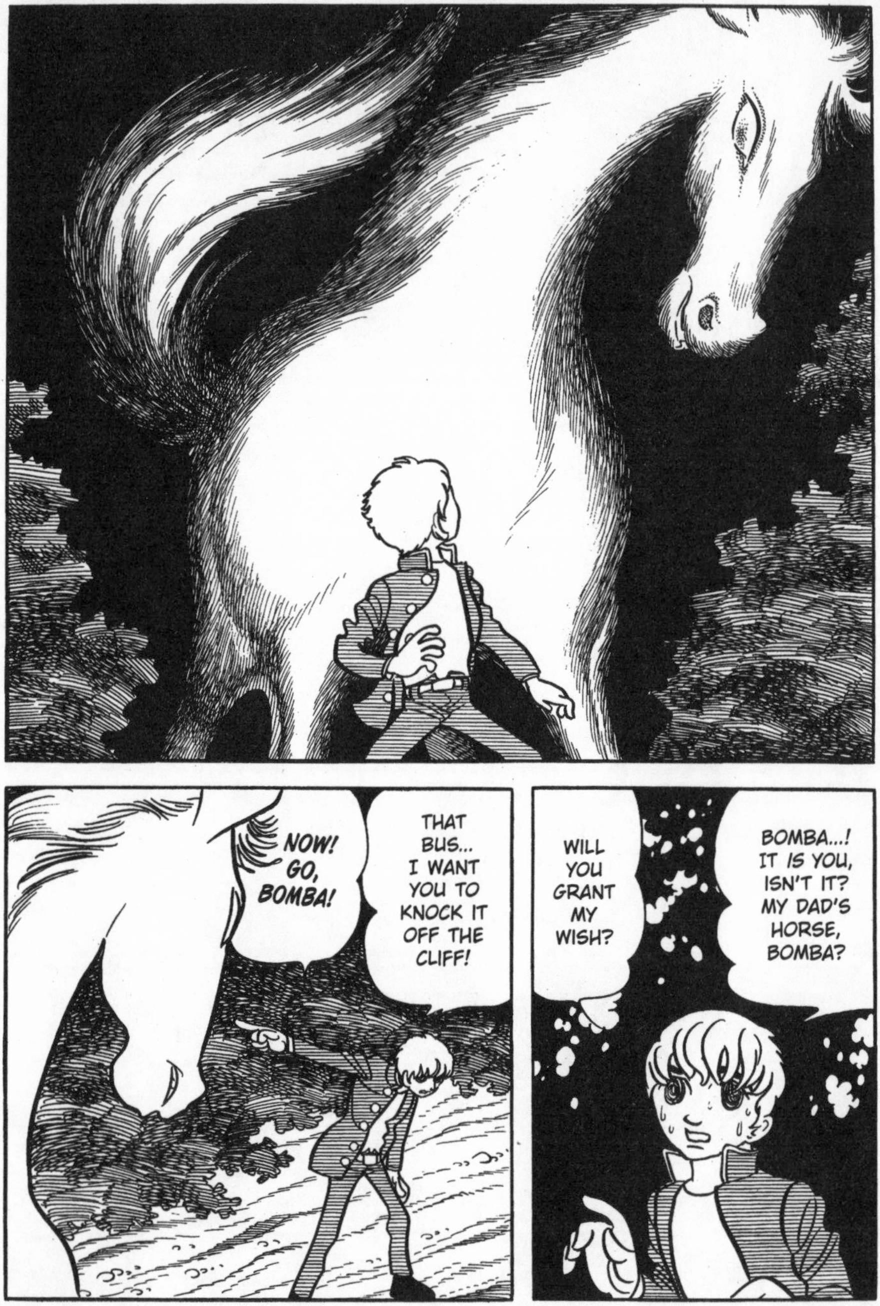
BOMBA...! IT *IS* YOU, ISN'T IT? MY DAD'S HORSE, BOMBA?
WILL YOU GRANT MY WISH?
THAT BUS... I WANT YOU TO KNOCK IT OFF THE CLIFF!
NOW! GO, BOMBA!

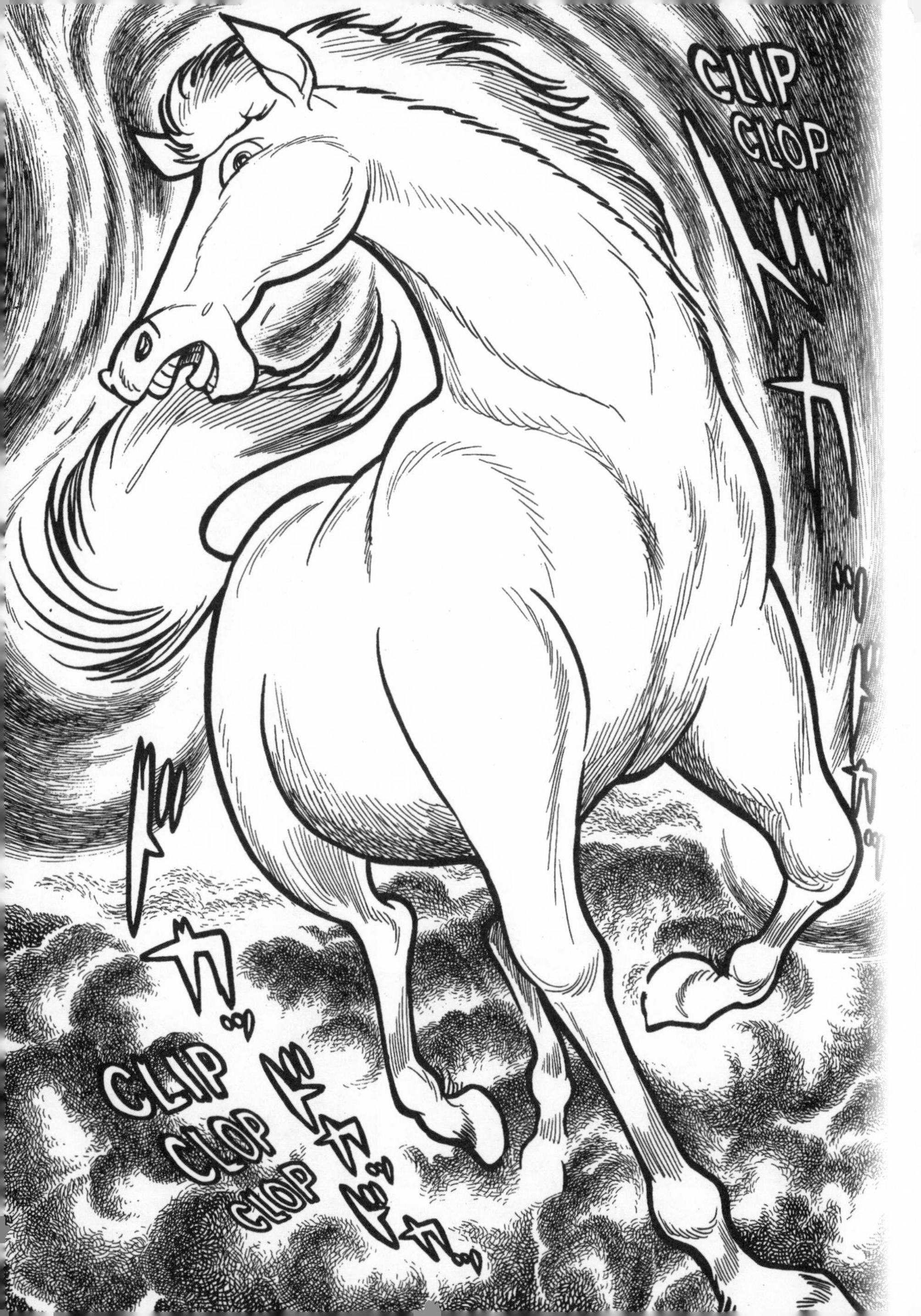
CLIP CLOP
CLIP CLOP CLOP

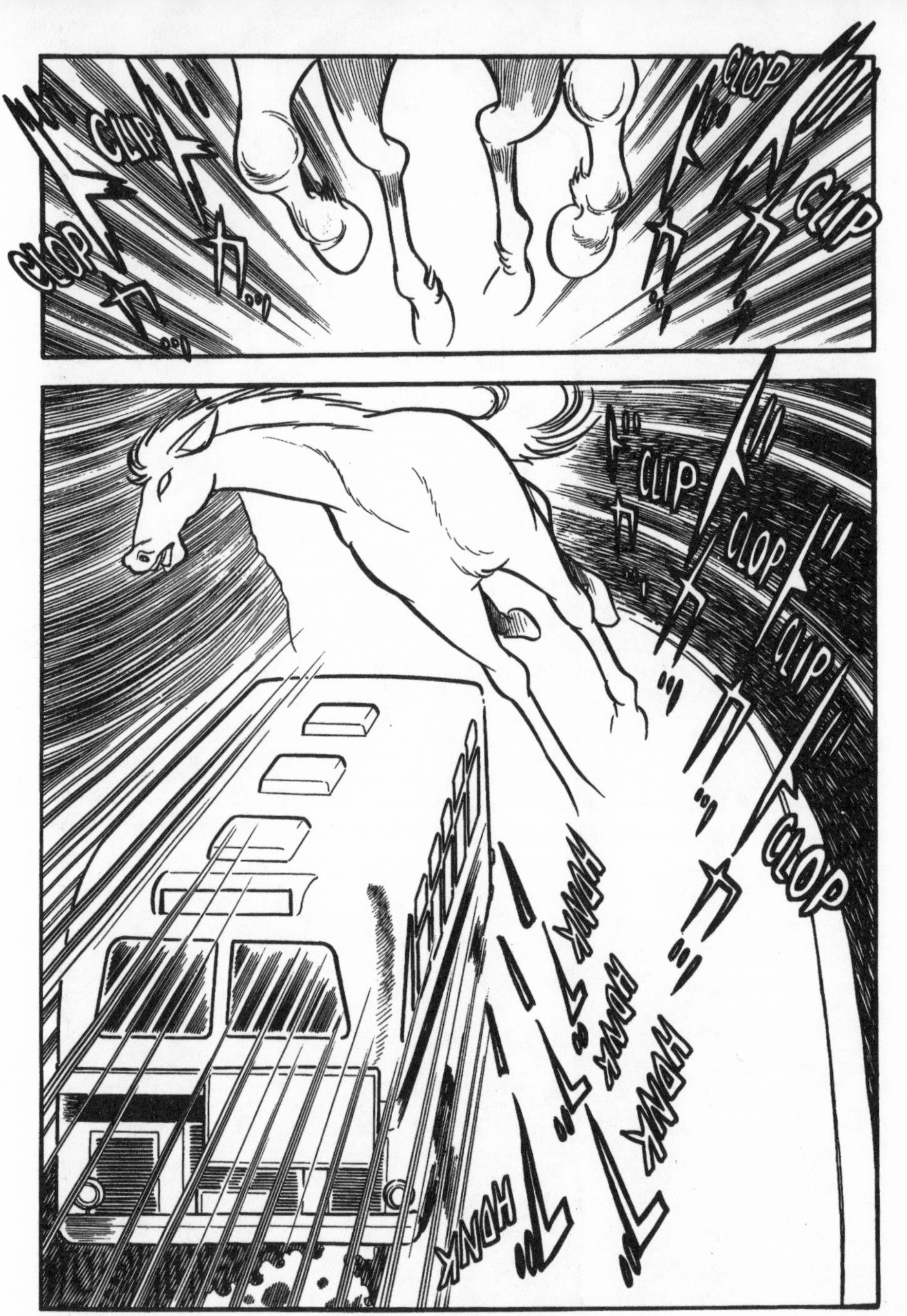
CLOP
CLIP
CLIP
CLOP
CLIP
CLOP
CLIP
CLOP
HONK
HONK
HONK
HONK
HONK

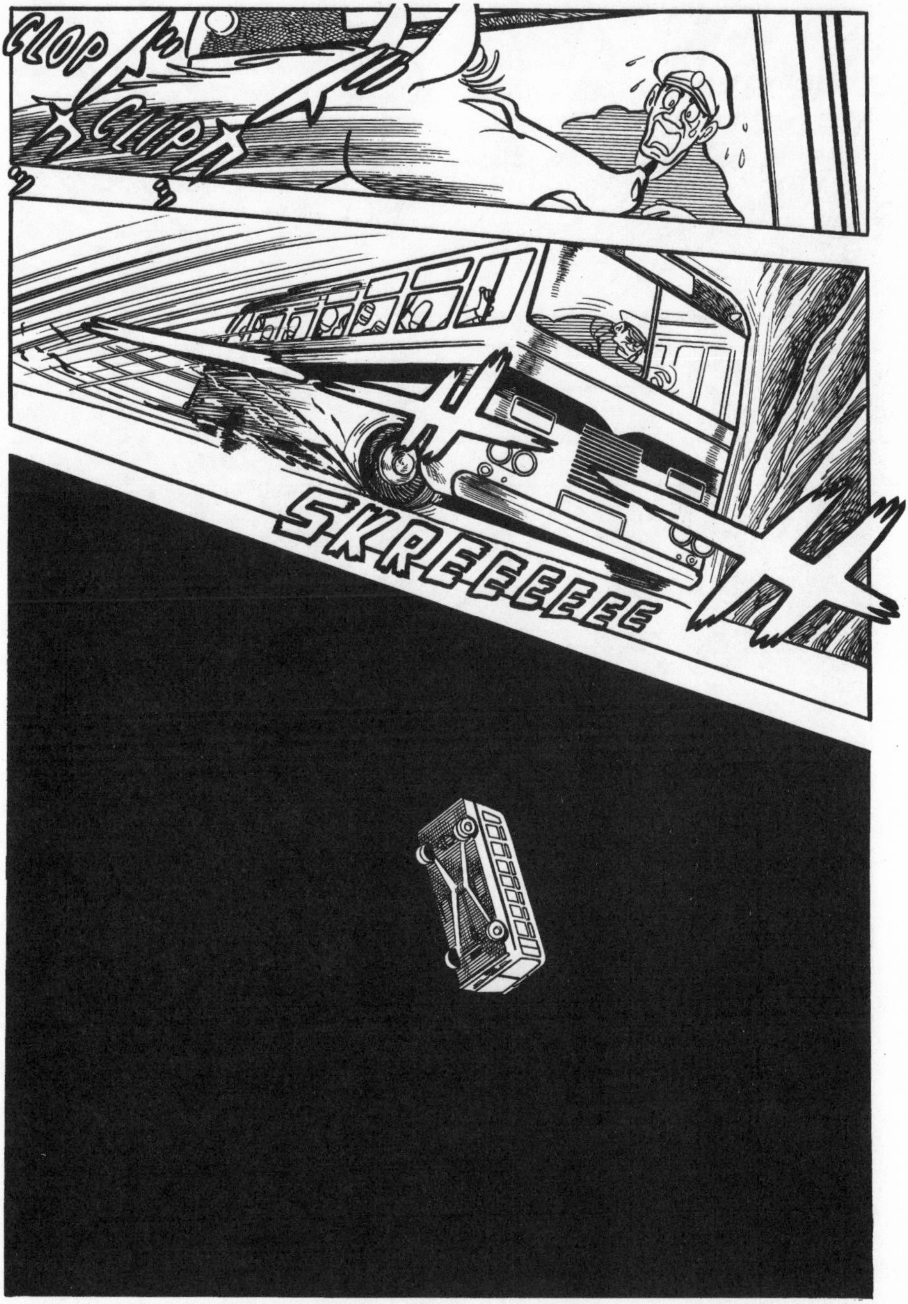
CLOP
CLIP
SKREEEEEE

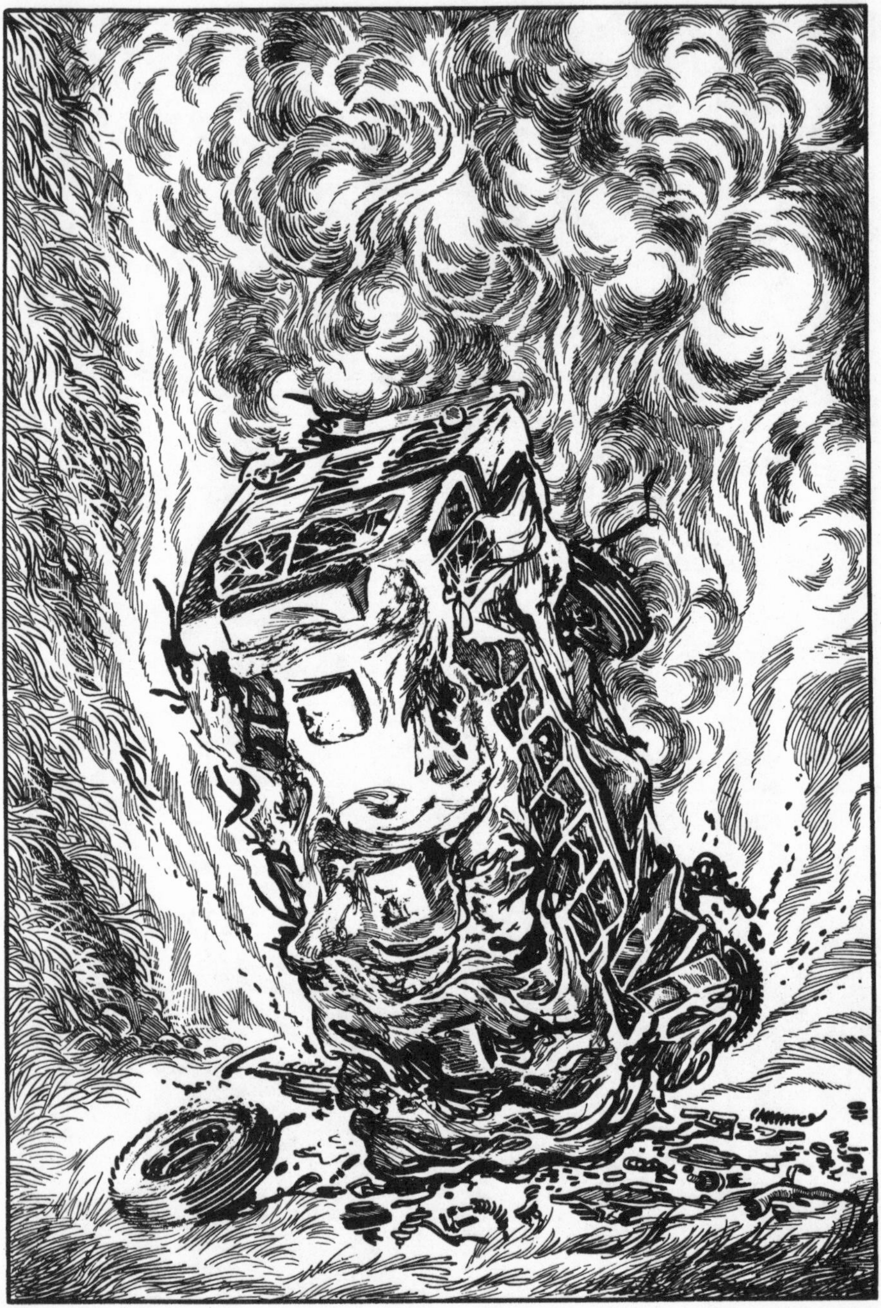

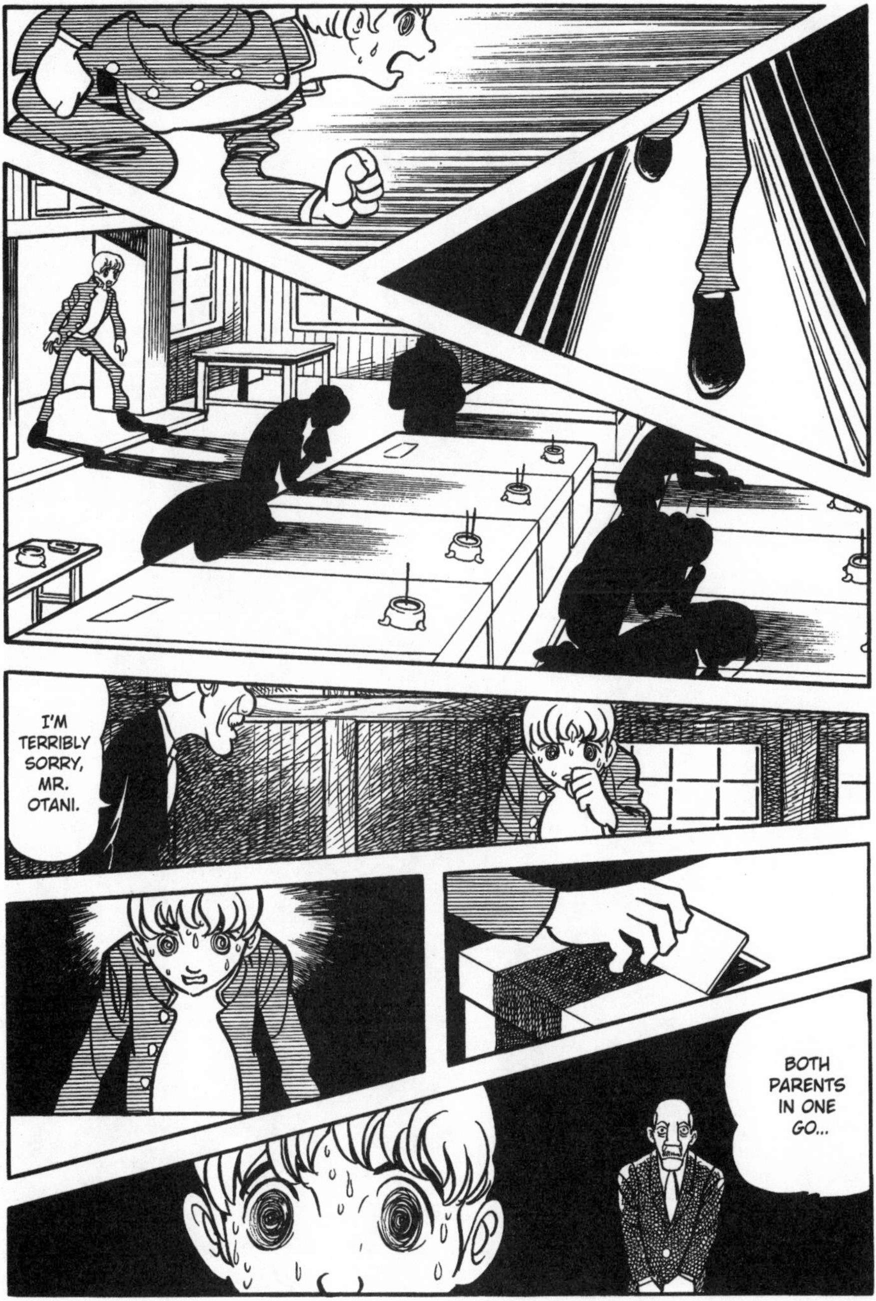
I'M TERRIBLY SORRY, MR. OTANI.
BOTH PARENTS IN ONE GO...

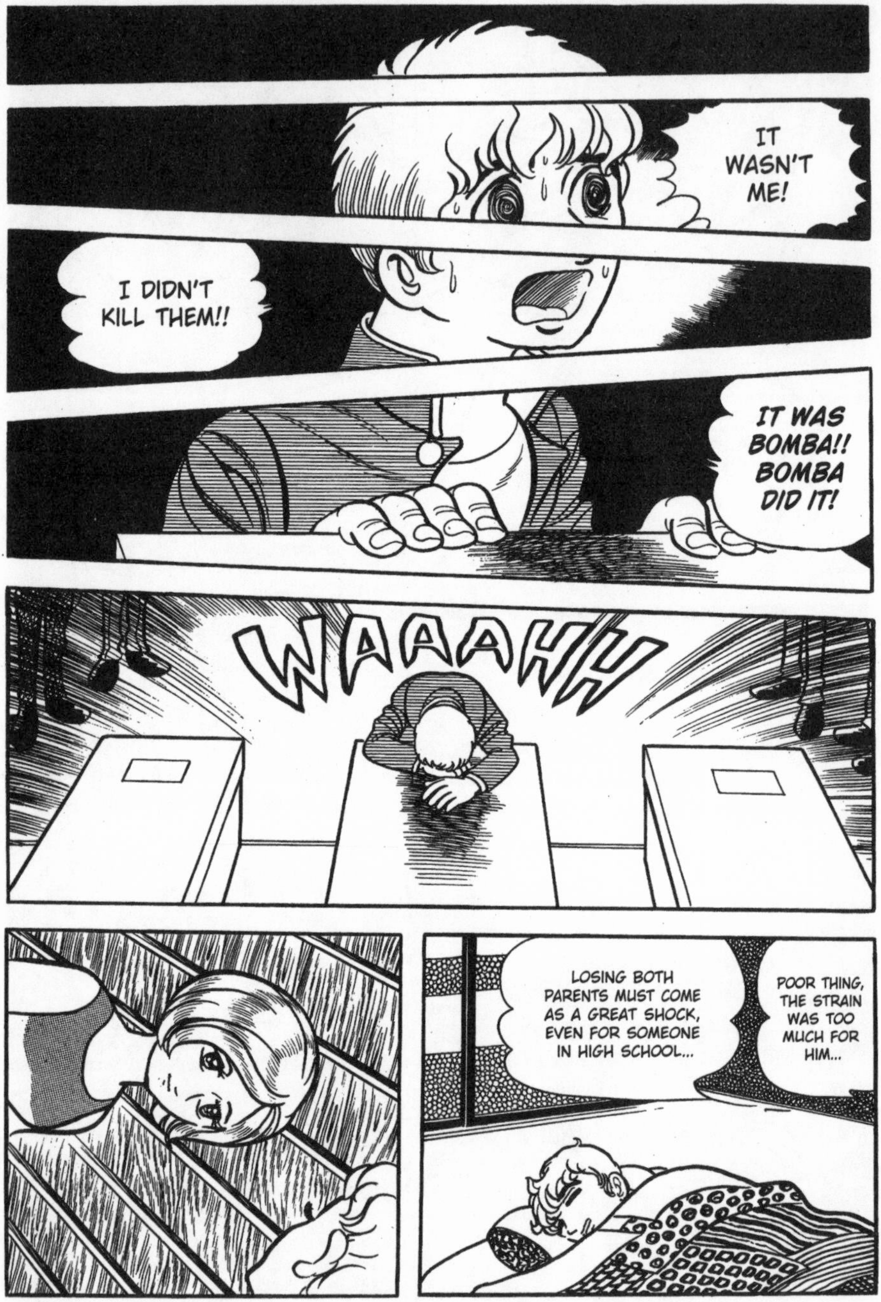
IT WASN'T ME!
I DIDN'T KILL THEM!!
IT WAS BOMBA!! BOMBA DID IT!
WAAAHH
POOR THING, THE STRAIN WAS TOO MUCH FOR HIM...
LOSING BOTH PARENTS MUST COME AS A GREAT SHOCK, EVEN FOR SOMEONE IN HIGH SCHOOL...

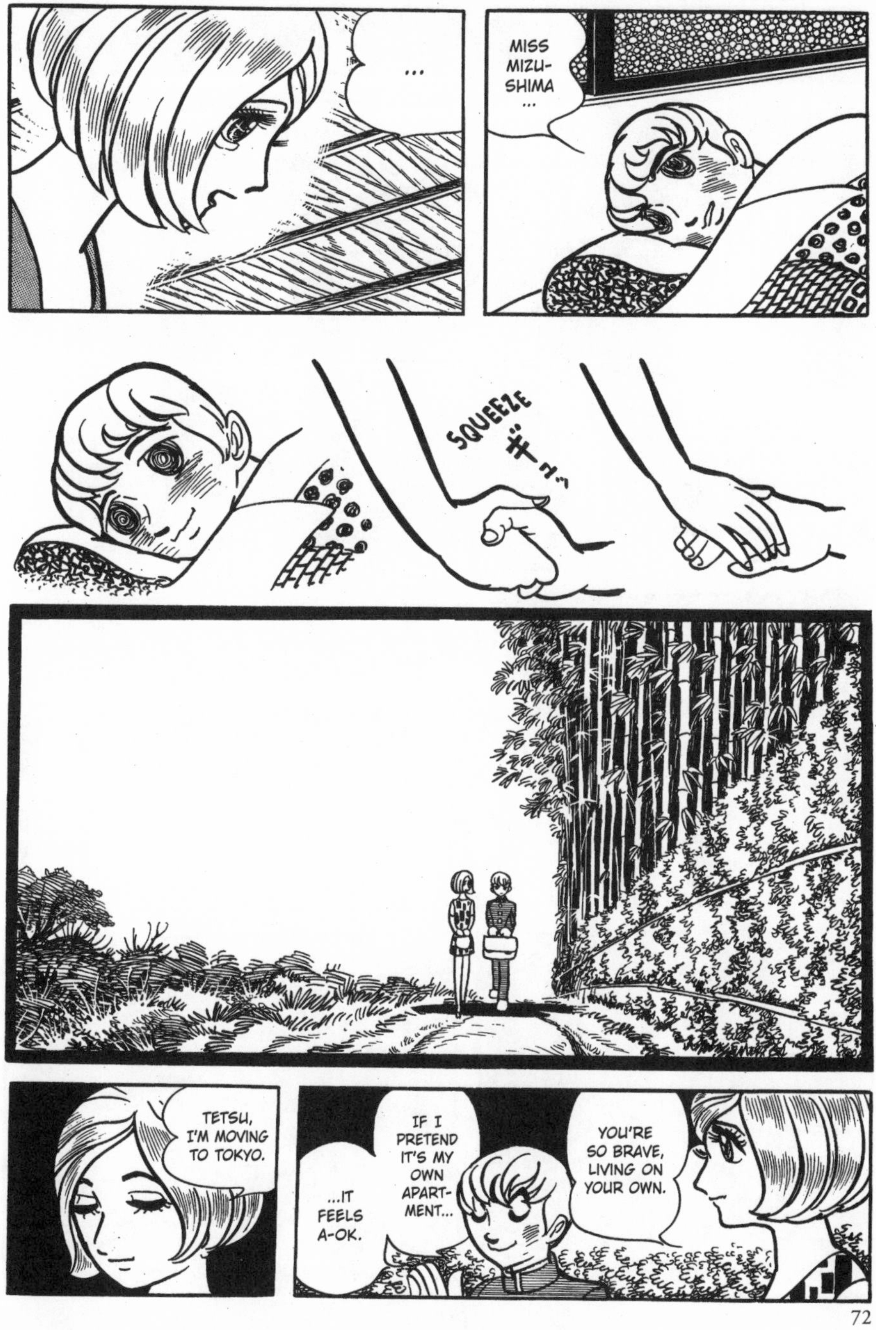
MISS MIZU-SHIMA ...
...
SQUEEZE
ギュッ
YOU'RE SO BRAVE, LIVING ON YOUR OWN.
IF I PRETEND IT'S MY OWN APART-MENT...
...IT FEELS A-OK.
TETSU, I'M MOVING TO TOKYO.

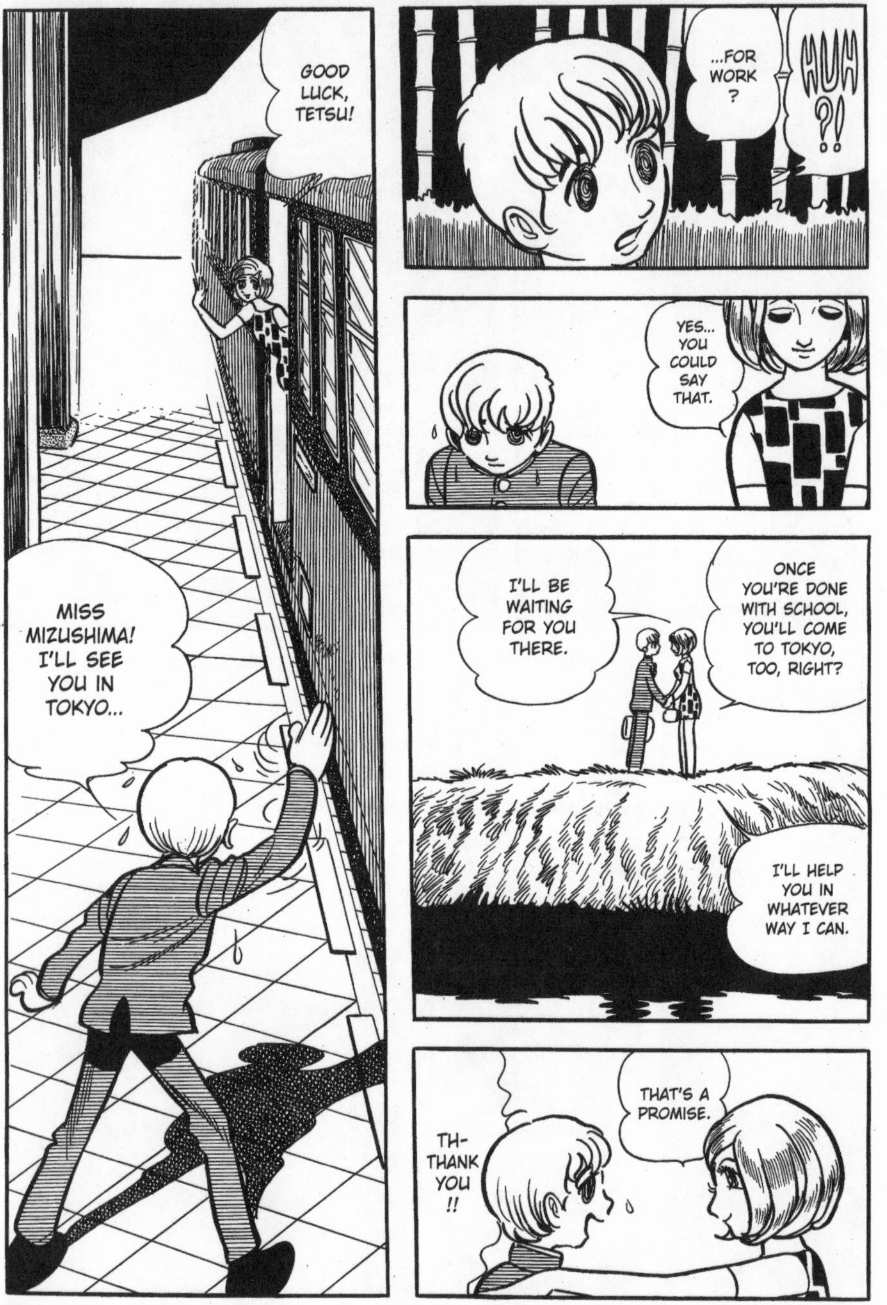
HUH ?!
...FOR WORK ?
YES... YOU COULD SAY THAT.
ONCE YOU'RE DONE WITH SCHOOL, YOU'LL COME TO TOKYO, TOO, RIGHT?
I'LL BE WAITING FOR YOU THERE.
I'LL HELP YOU IN WHATEVER WAY I CAN.
THAT'S A PROMISE.
TH-THANK YOU !!
GOOD LUCK, TETSU!
MISS MIZUSHIMA! I'LL SEE YOU IN TOKYO...

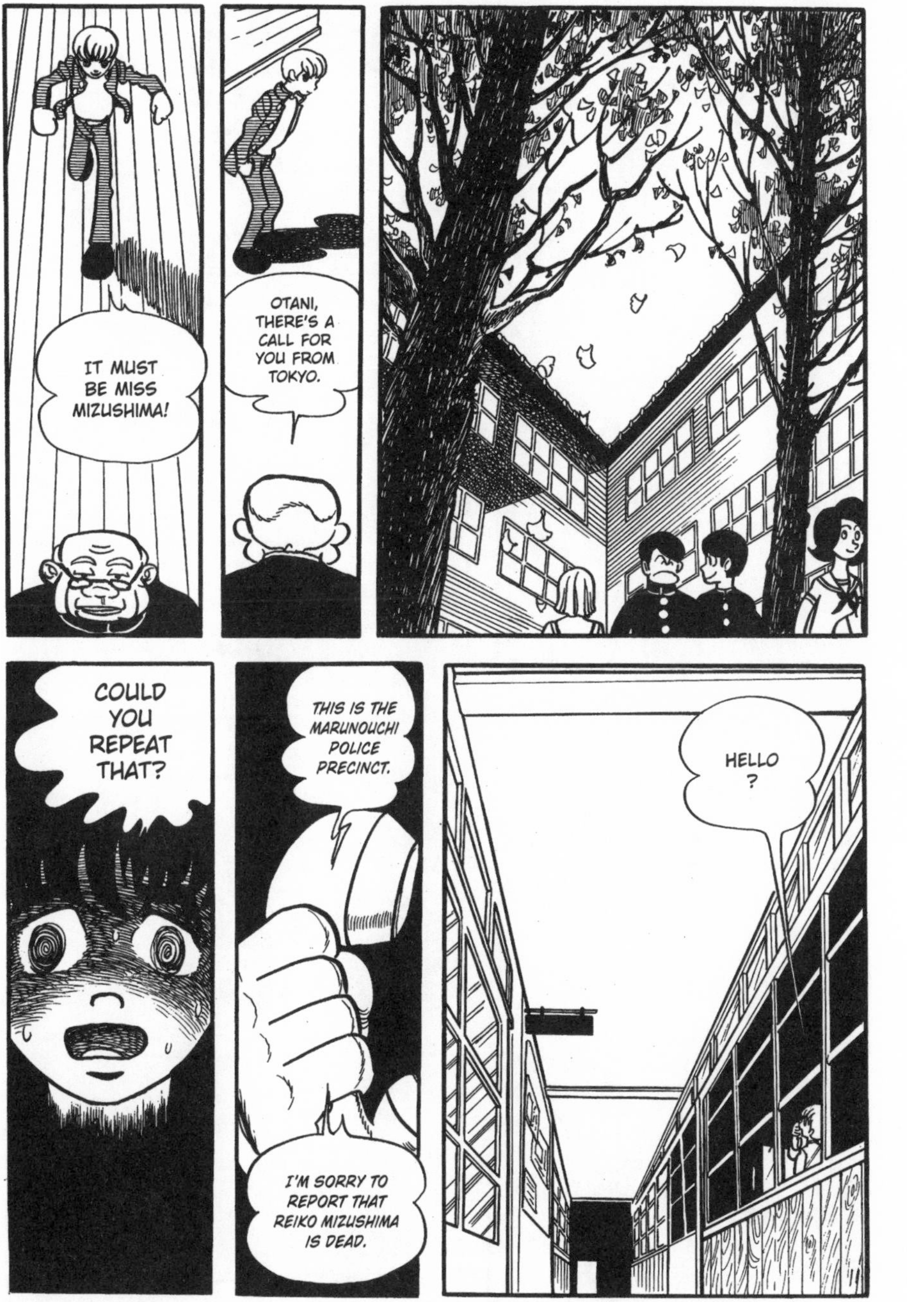
OTANI, THERE'S A CALL FOR YOU FROM TOKYO.
IT MUST BE MISS MIZUSHIMA!
HELLO ?
THIS IS THE MARUNOUCHI POLICE PRECINCT.
I'M SORRY TO REPORT THAT REIKO MIZUSHIMA IS DEAD.
COULD YOU REPEAT THAT?

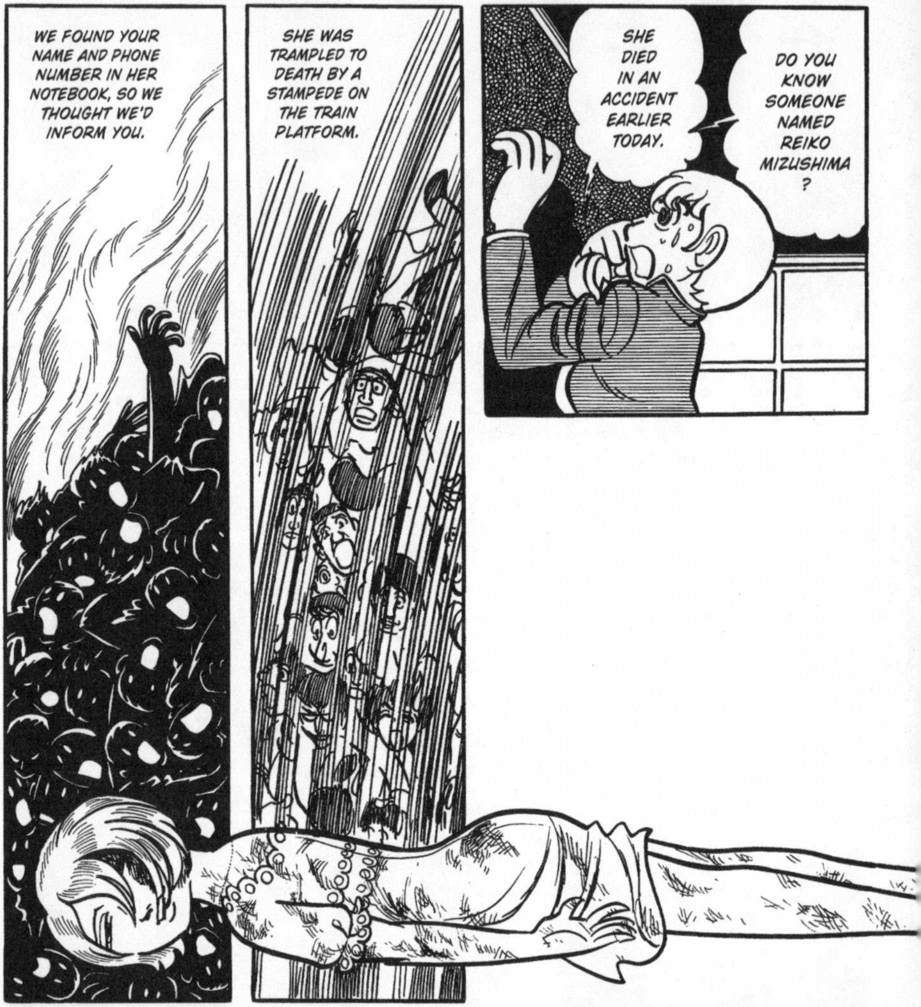
DO YOU KNOW SOMEONE NAMED REIKO MIZUSHIMA ?
SHE DIED IN AN ACCIDENT EARLIER TODAY.
SHE WAS TRAMPLED TO DEATH BY A STAMPEDE ON THE TRAIN PLATFORM.
WE FOUND YOUR NAME AND PHONE NUMBER IN HER NOTEBOOK, SO WE THOUGHT WE'D INFORM YOU.
MISS...
REIKO!

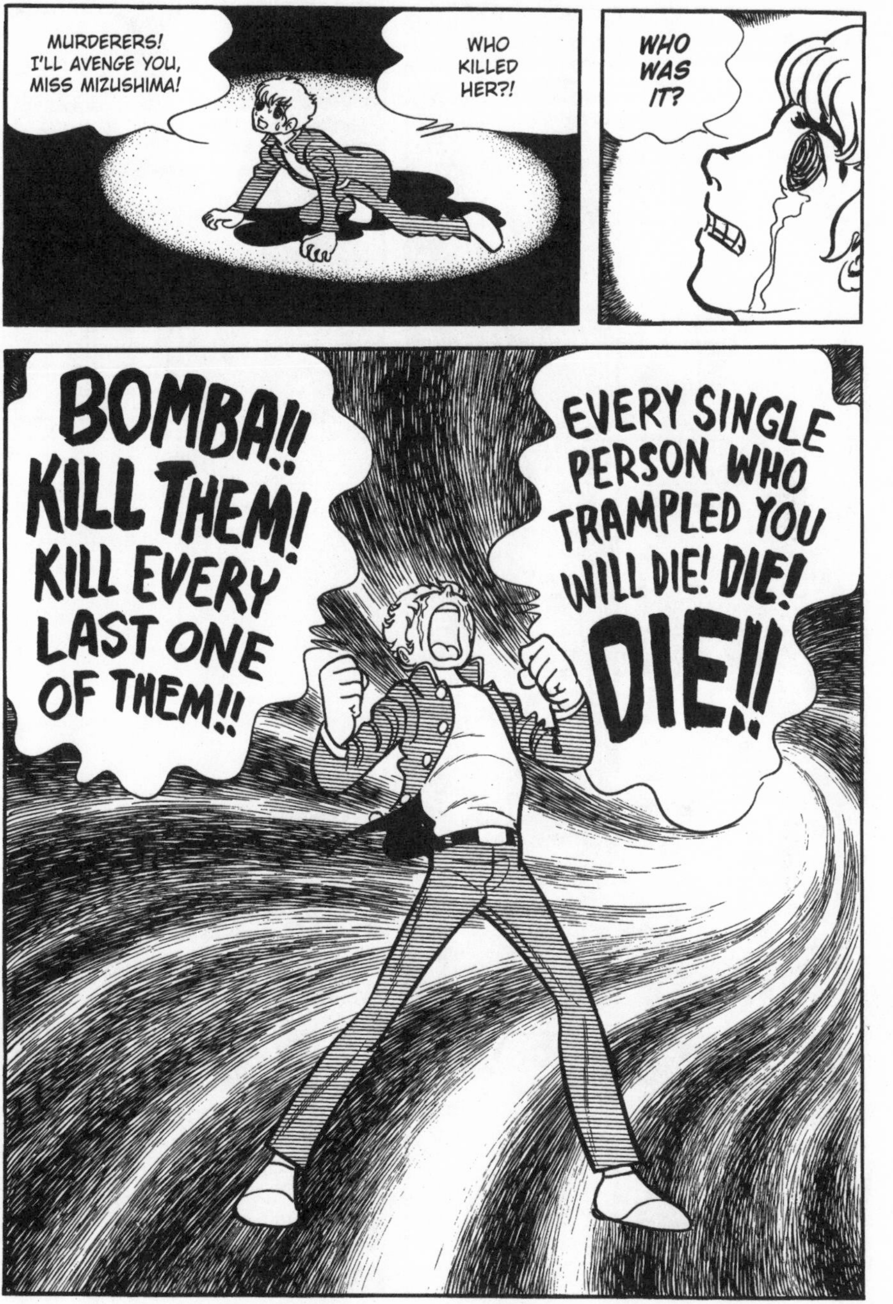

WHO WAS IT?
WHO KILLED HER?!
MURDERERS! I'LL AVENGE YOU, MISS MIZUSHIMA!
EVERY SINGLE PERSON WHO TRAMPLED YOU WILL DIE! DIE! DIE!!
BOMBA!! KILL THEM! KILL EVERY LAST ONE OF THEM!!

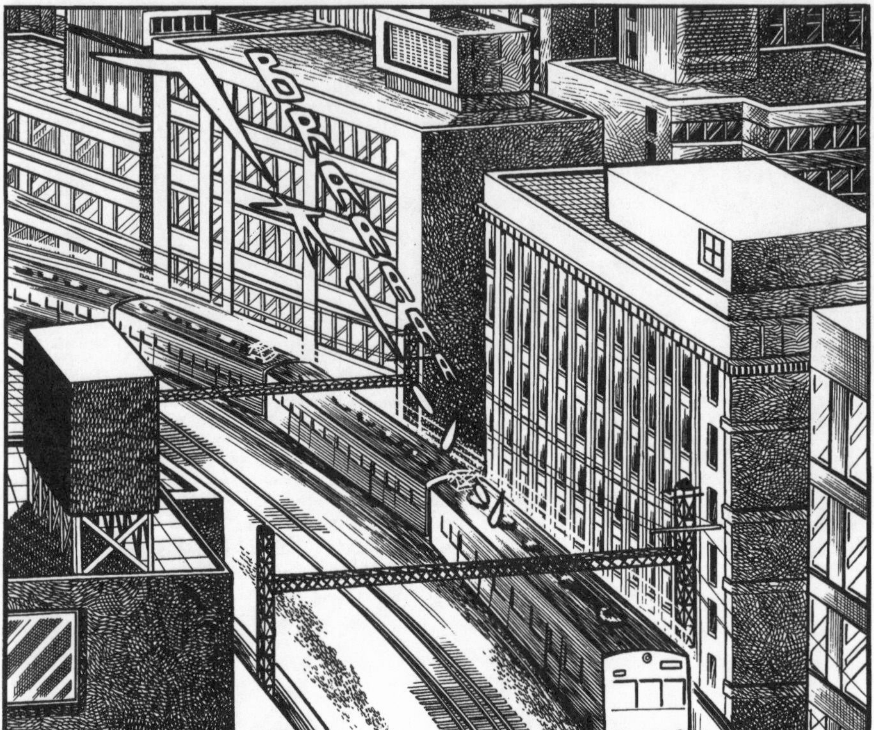

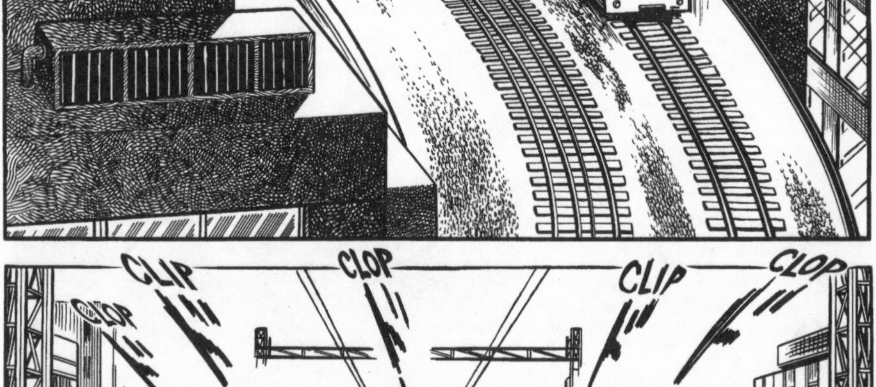
CLOP
CLIP
CLOP
CLIP
CLOP

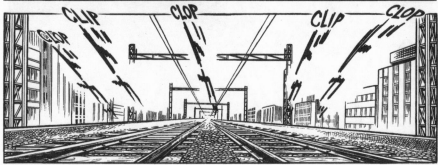

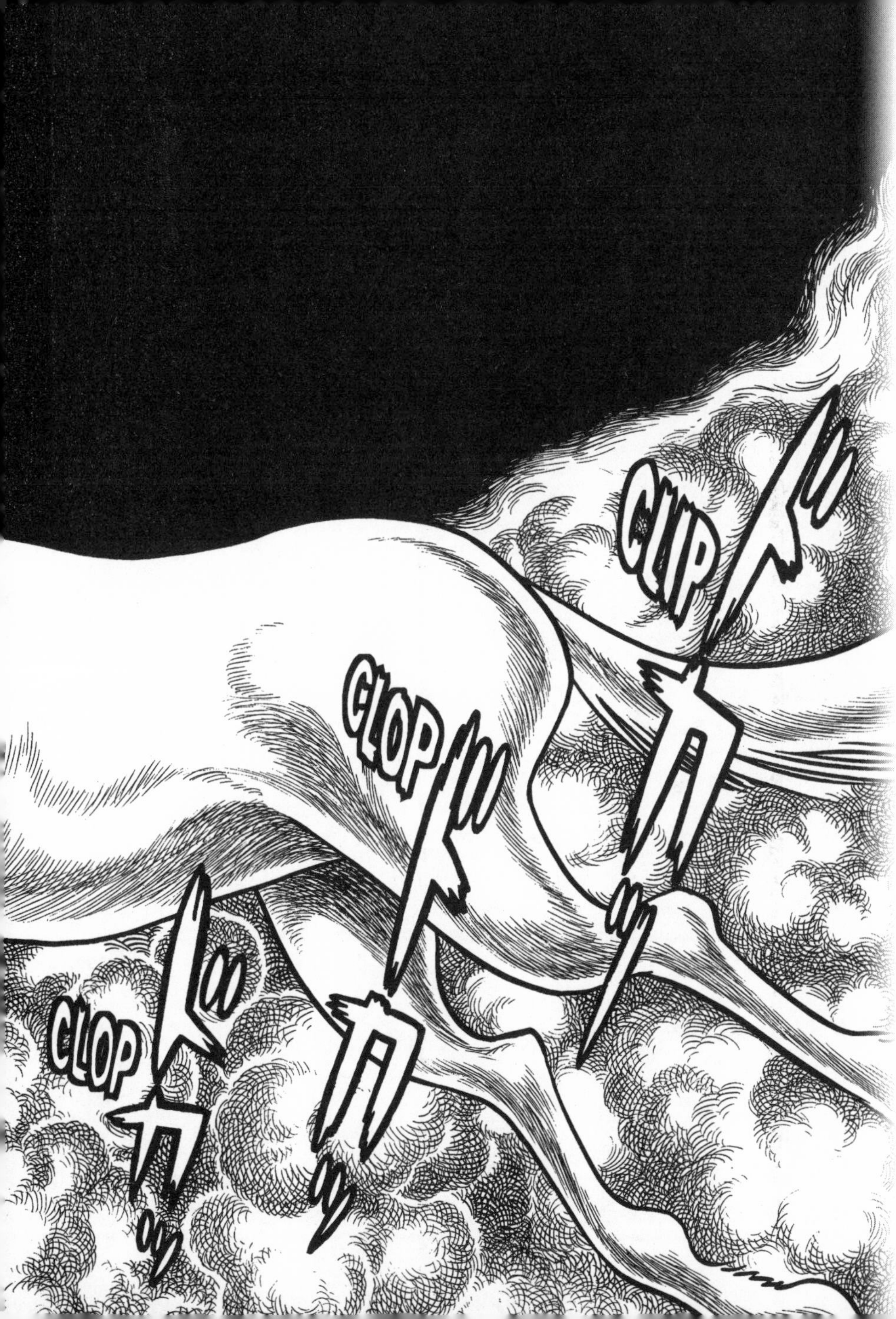
CLIP
CLOP
CLOP

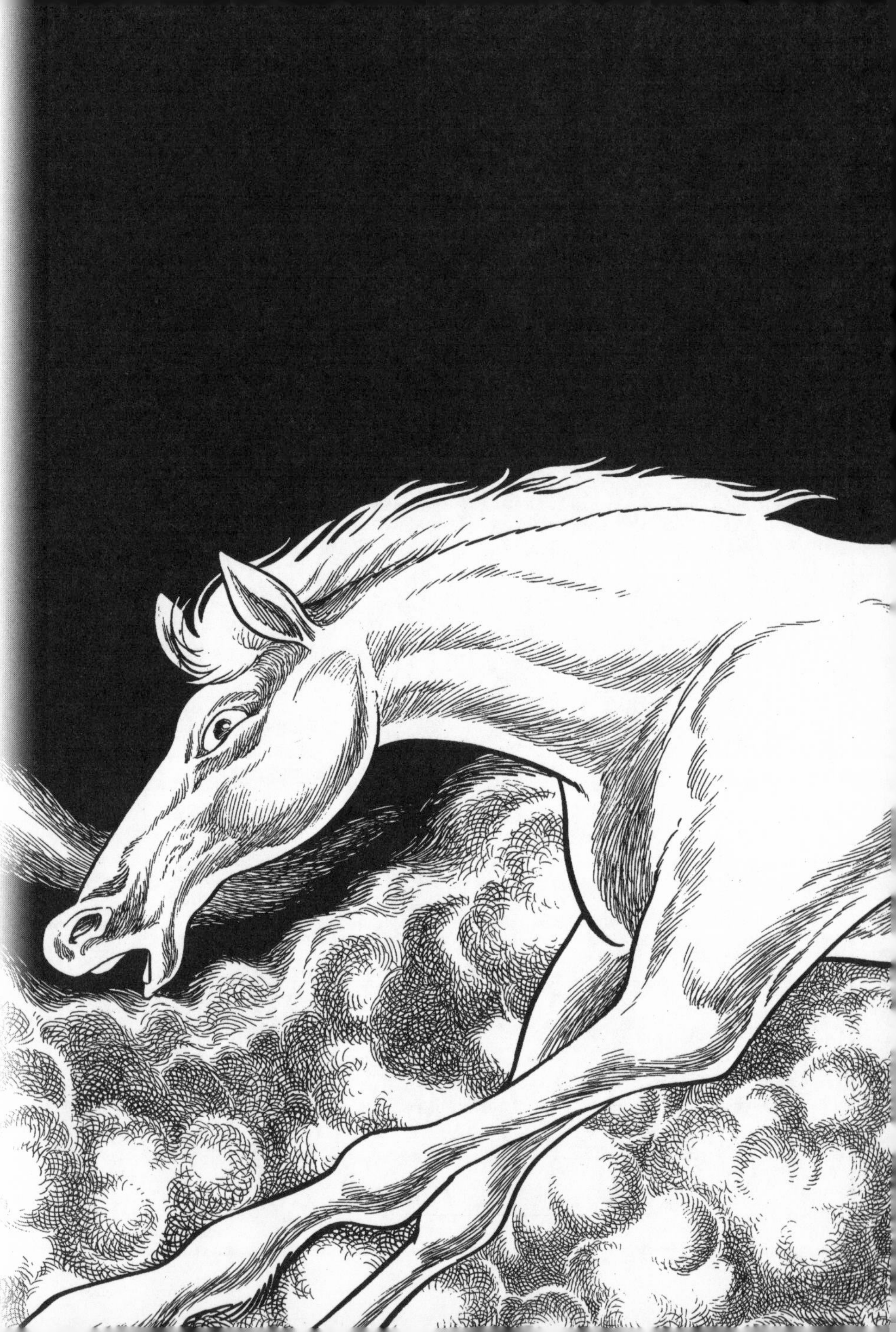

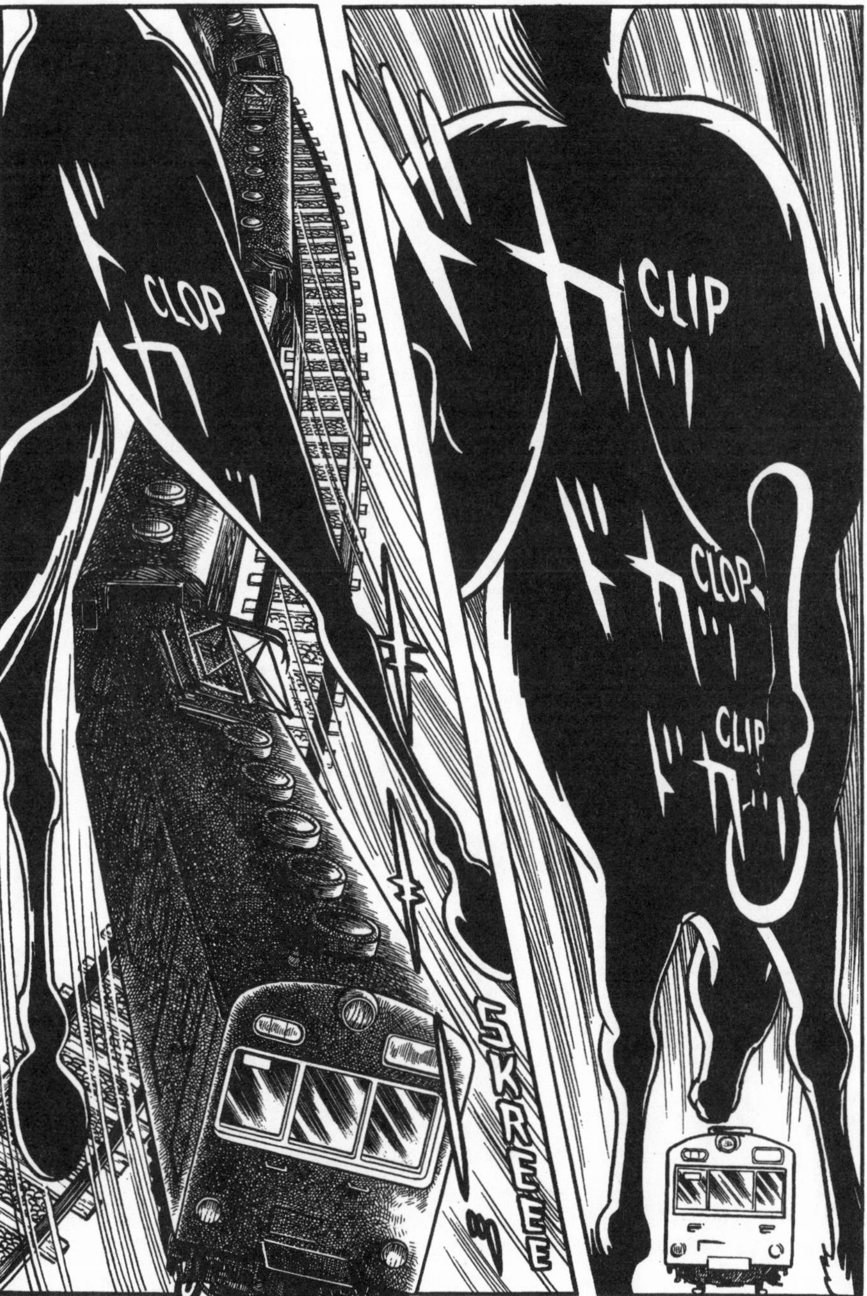
CLIP
CLOP
CLIP
CLOP
SKREEE

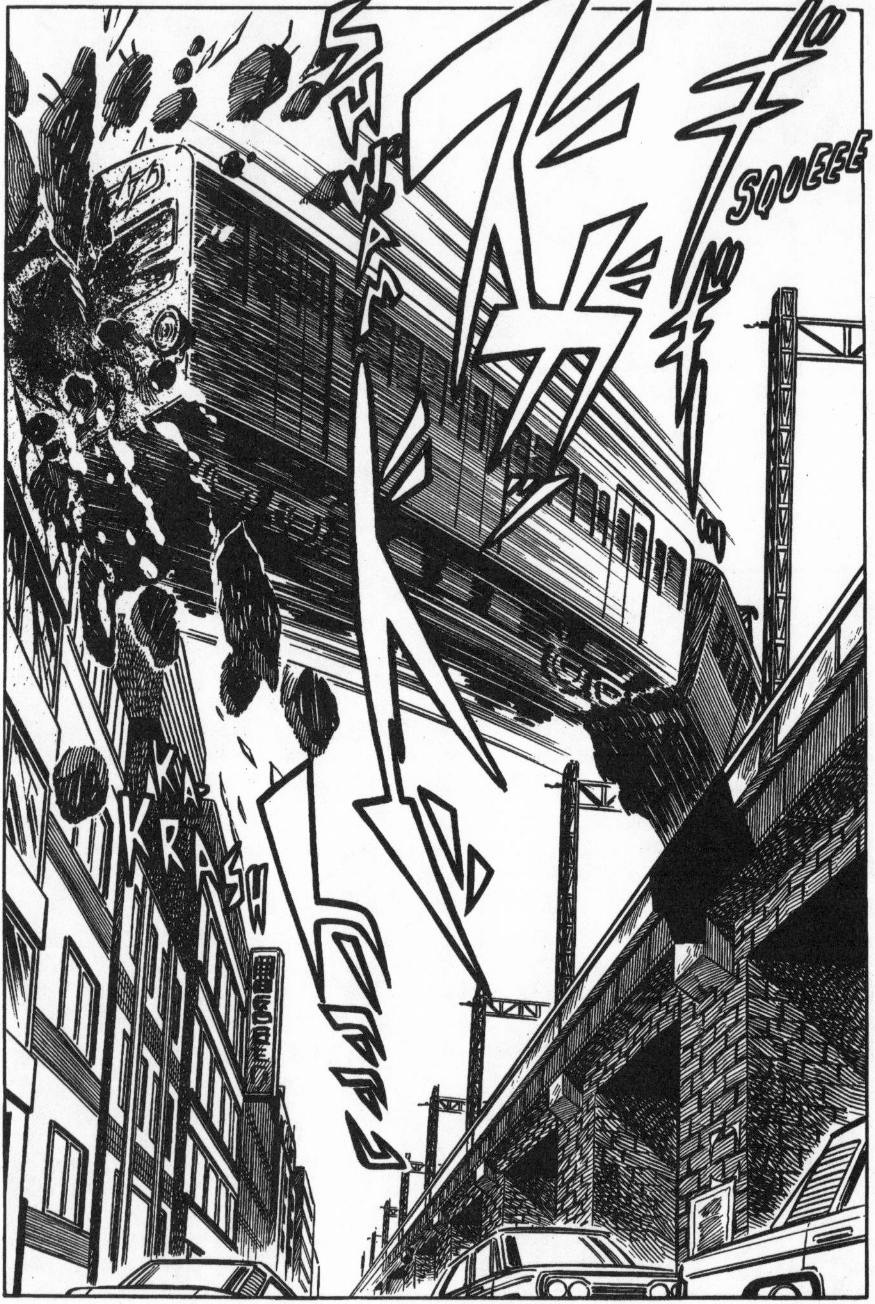
SQUEEEE
SHWAM
KA KRASH!

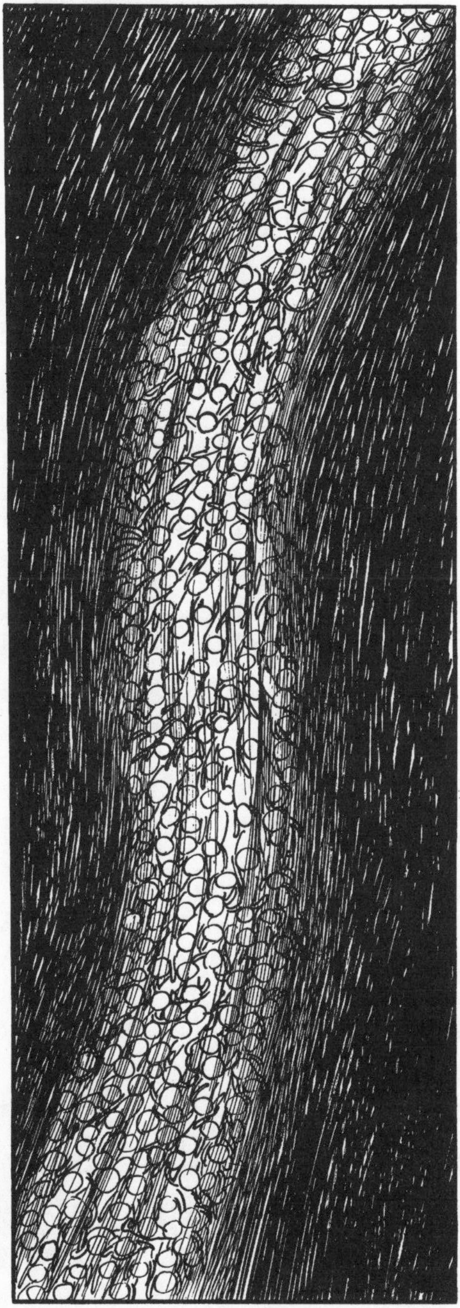

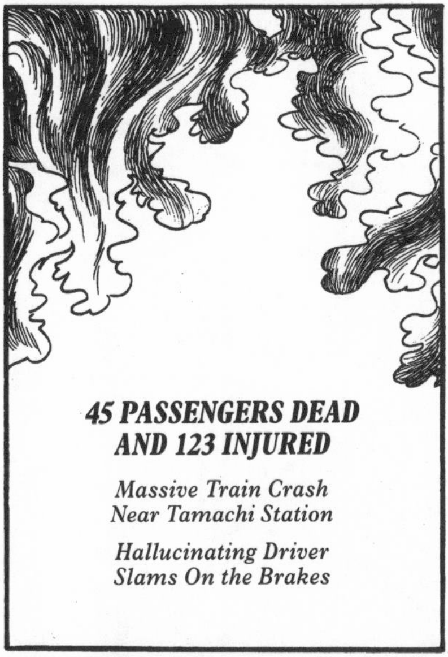
45 PASSENGERS DEAD AND 123 INJURED
Massive Train Crash Near Tamachi Station
Hallucinating Driver Slams On the Brakes

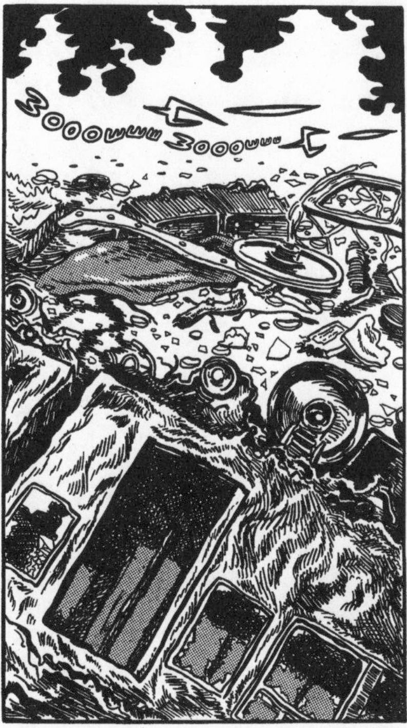

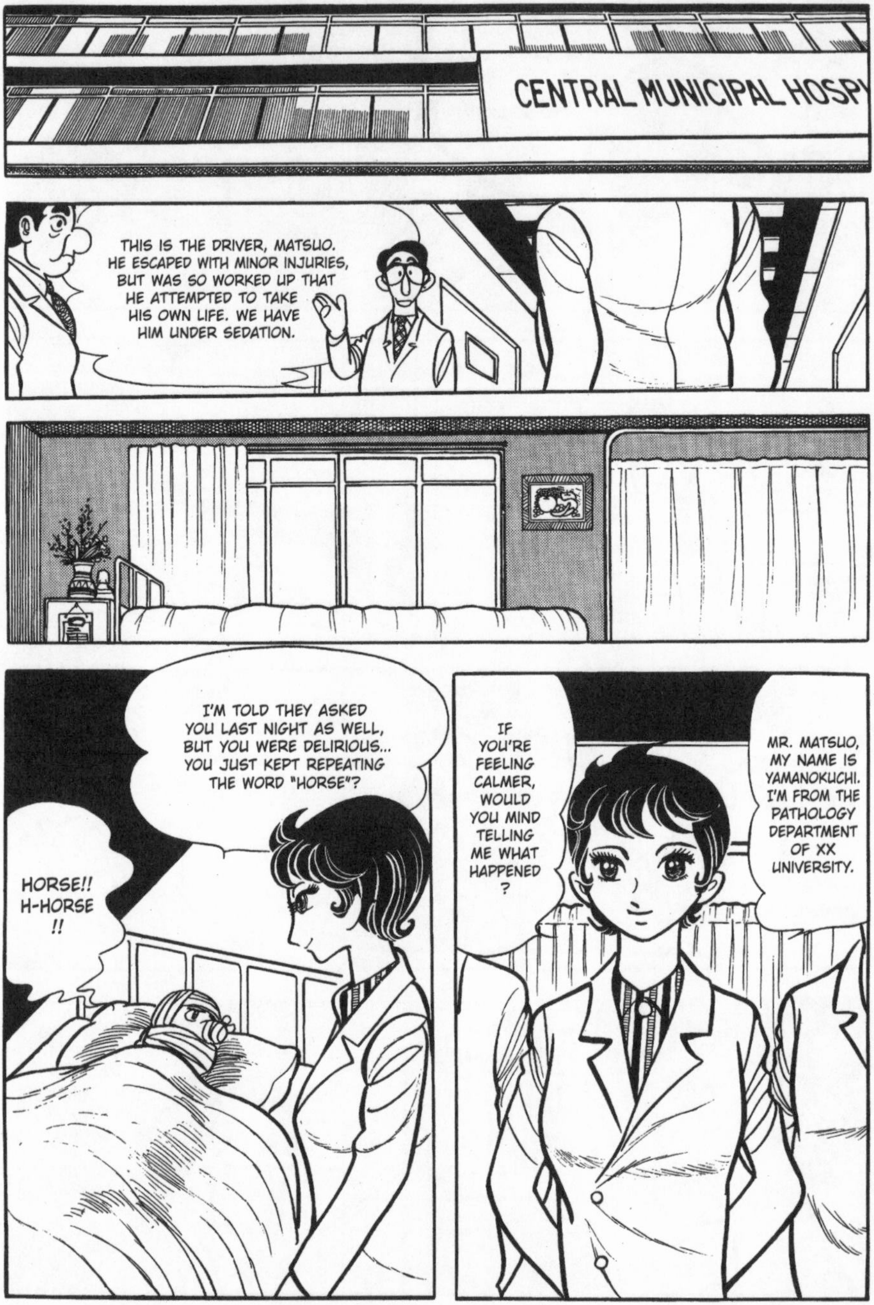
CENTRAL MUNICIPAL HOSPI
THIS IS THE DRIVER, MATSUO. HE ESCAPED WITH MINOR INJURIES, BUT WAS SO WORKED UP THAT HE ATTEMPTED TO TAKE HIS OWN LIFE. WE HAVE HIM UNDER SEDATION.
MR. MATSUO, MY NAME IS YAMANOKUCHI. I'M FROM THE PATHOLOGY DEPARTMENT OF XX UNIVERSITY.
IF YOU'RE FEELING CALMER, WOULD YOU MIND TELLING ME WHAT HAPPENED ?
I'M TOLD THEY ASKED YOU LAST NIGHT AS WELL, BUT YOU WERE DELIRIOUS... YOU JUST KEPT REPEATING THE WORD "HORSE"?
HORSE!! H-HORSE !!

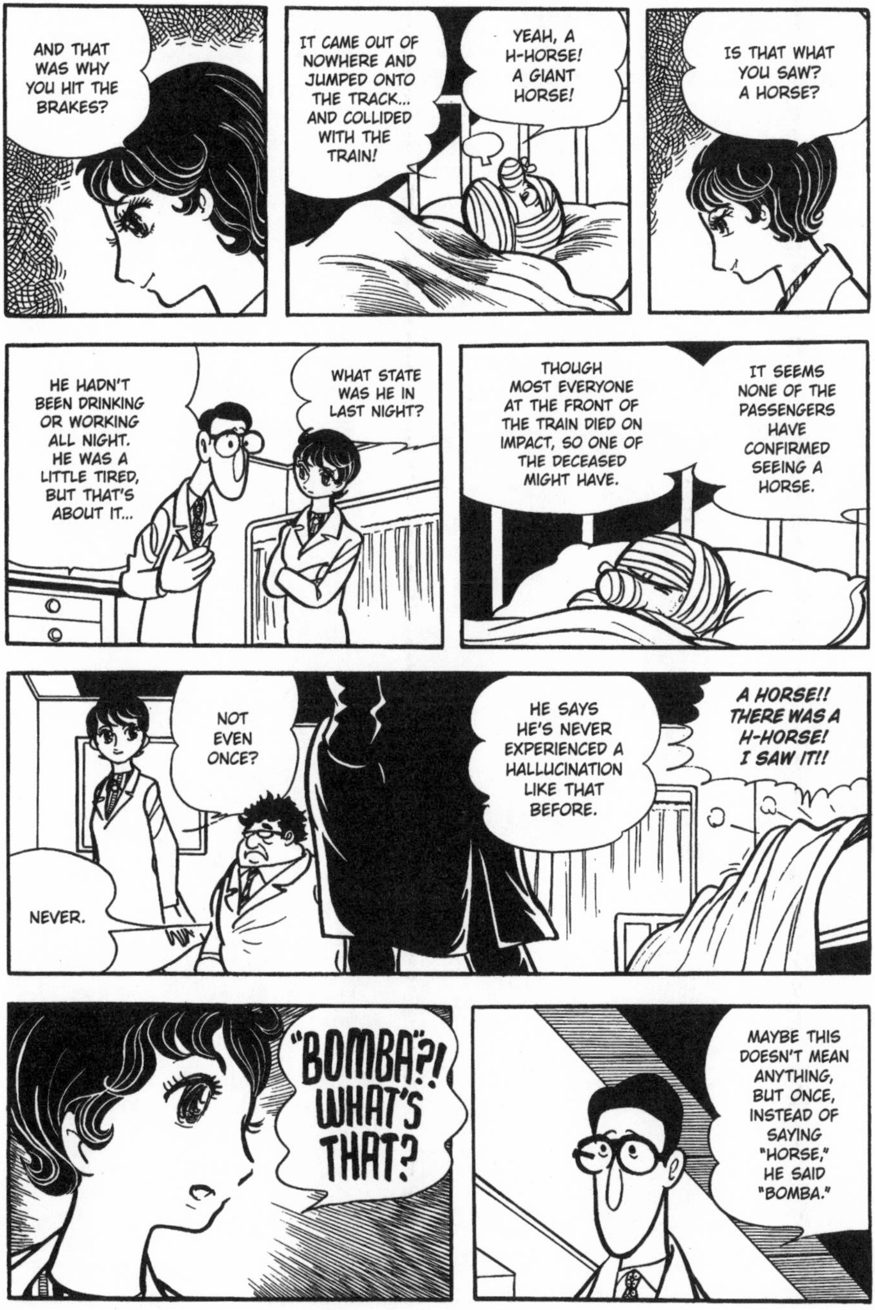
IS THAT WHAT YOU SAW? A HORSE?
YEAH, A H-HORSE! A GIANT HORSE!
IT CAME OUT OF NOWHERE AND JUMPED ONTO THE TRACK... AND COLLIDED WITH THE TRAIN!
AND THAT WAS WHY YOU HIT THE BRAKES?
IT SEEMS NONE OF THE PASSENGERS HAVE CONFIRMED SEEING A HORSE.
THOUGH MOST EVERYONE AT THE FRONT OF THE TRAIN DIED ON IMPACT, SO ONE OF THE DECEASED MIGHT HAVE.
WHAT STATE WAS HE IN LAST NIGHT?
HE HADN'T BEEN DRINKING OR WORKING ALL NIGHT. HE WAS A LITTLE TIRED, BUT THAT'S ABOUT IT...
A HORSE!! THERE WAS A H-HORSE! I SAW IT!!
HE SAYS HE'S NEVER EXPERIENCED A HALLUCINATION LIKE THAT BEFORE.
NOT EVEN ONCE?
NEVER.
MAYBE THIS DOESN'T MEAN ANYTHING, BUT ONCE, INSTEAD OF SAYING "HORSE," HE SAID "BOMBA."
"BOMBA"?! WHAT'S THAT?

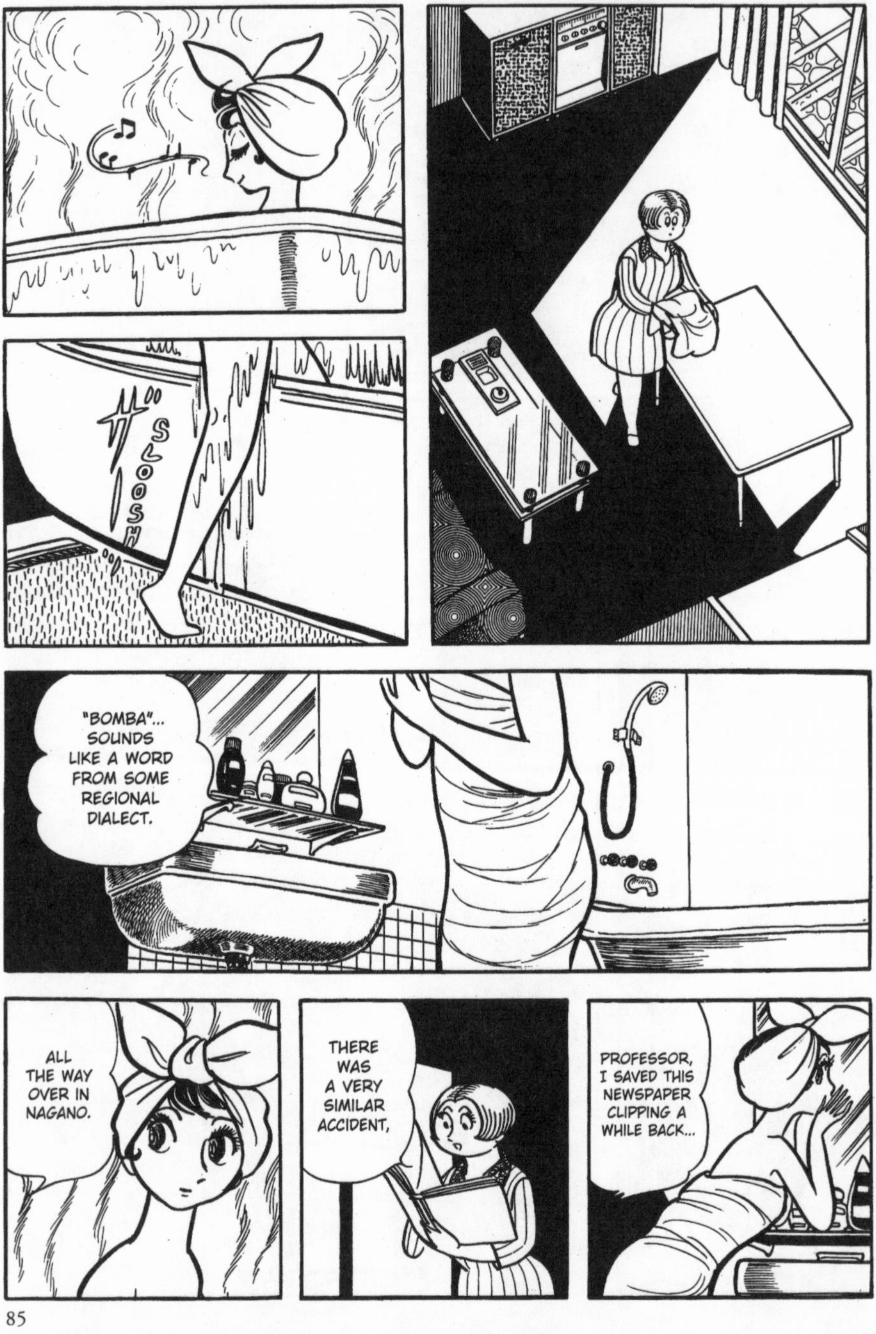
SLOOSH
"BOMBA"... SOUNDS LIKE A WORD FROM SOME REGIONAL DIALECT.
PROFESSOR, I SAVED THIS NEWSPAPER CLIPPING A WHILE BACK...
THERE WAS A VERY SIMILAR ACCIDENT,
ALL THE WAY OVER IN NAGANO.

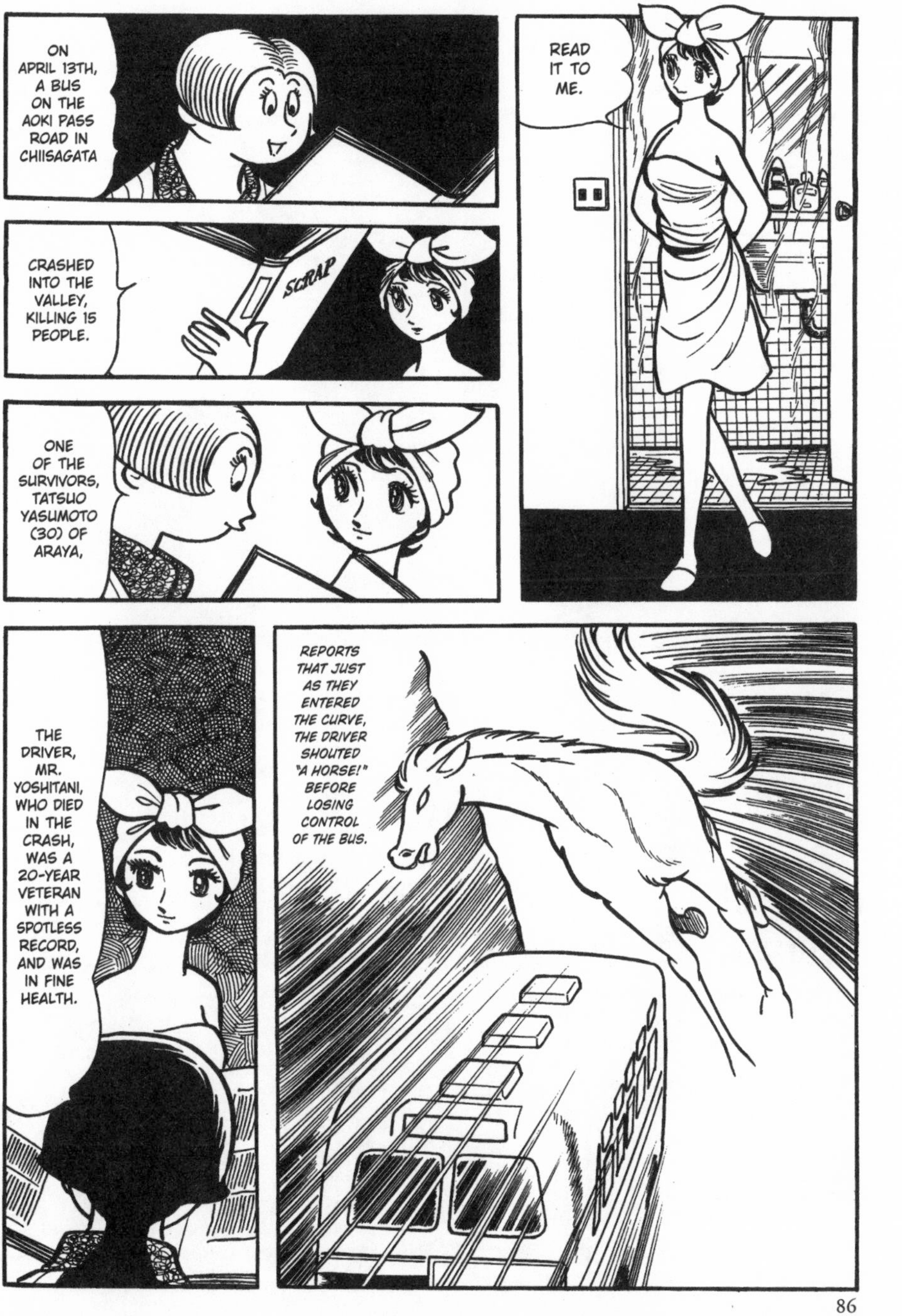
READ IT TO ME.
ON APRIL 13TH, A BUS ON THE AOKI PASS ROAD IN CHIISAGATA
SCRAP
CRASHED INTO THE VALLEY, KILLING 15 PEOPLE.
ONE OF THE SURVIVORS, TATSUO YASUMOTO (30) OF ARAYA,
REPORTS THAT JUST AS THEY ENTERED THE CURVE, THE DRIVER SHOUTED "A HORSE!" BEFORE LOSING CONTROL OF THE BUS.
THE DRIVER, MR. YOSHITANI, WHO DIED IN THE CRASH, WAS A 20-YEAR VETERAN WITH A SPOTLESS RECORD, AND WAS IN FINE HEALTH.

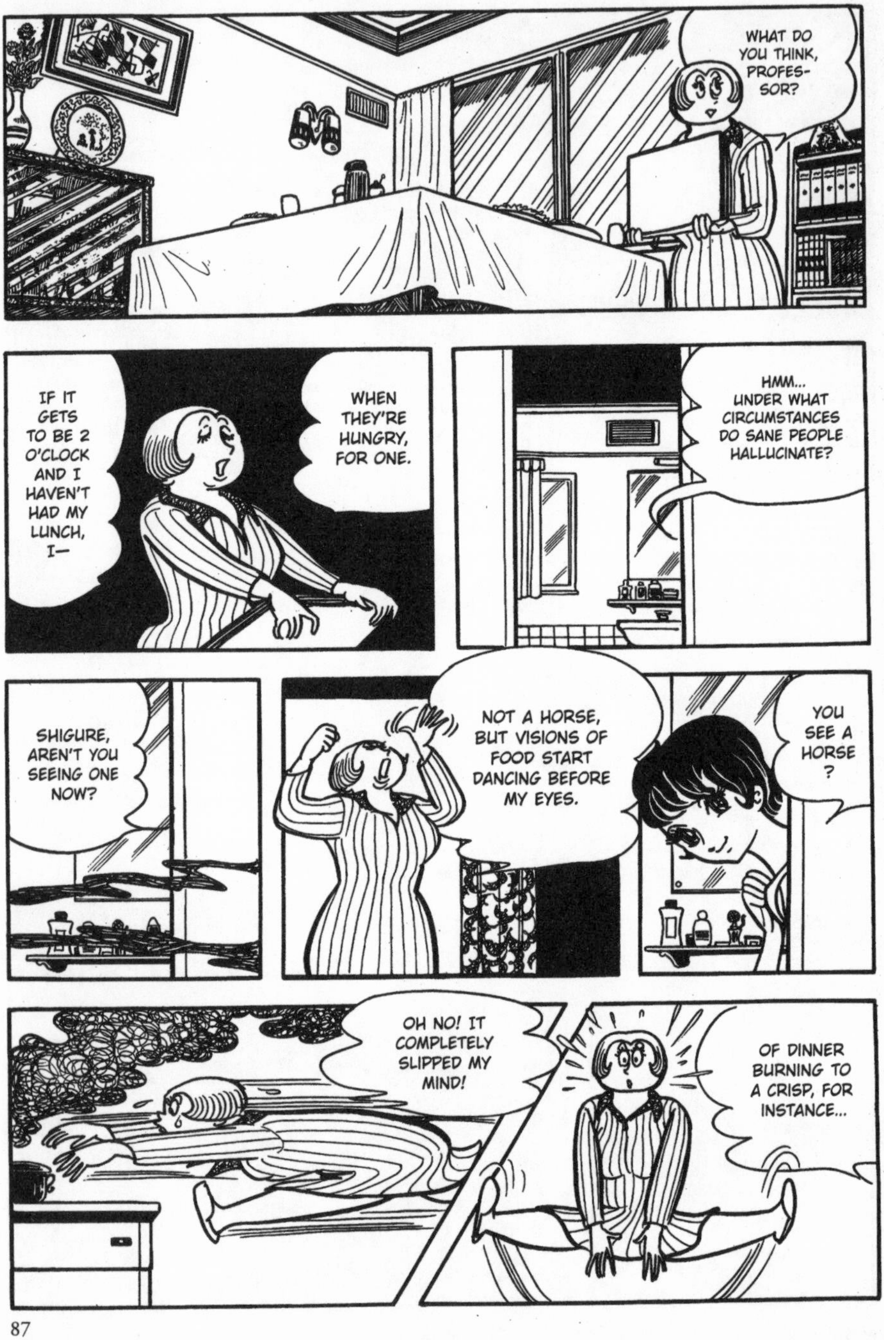
WHAT DO YOU THINK, PROFES-SOR?
HMM... UNDER WHAT CIRCUMSTANCES DO SANE PEOPLE HALLUCINATE?
WHEN THEY'RE HUNGRY, FOR ONE.
IF IT GETS TO BE 2 O'CLOCK AND I HAVEN'T HAD MY LUNCH, I—
YOU SEE A HORSE?
NOT A HORSE, BUT VISIONS OF FOOD START DANCING BEFORE MY EYES.
SHIGURE, AREN'T YOU SEEING ONE NOW?
OF DINNER BURNING TO A CRISP, FOR INSTANCE...
OH NO! IT COMPLETELY SLIPPED MY MIND!

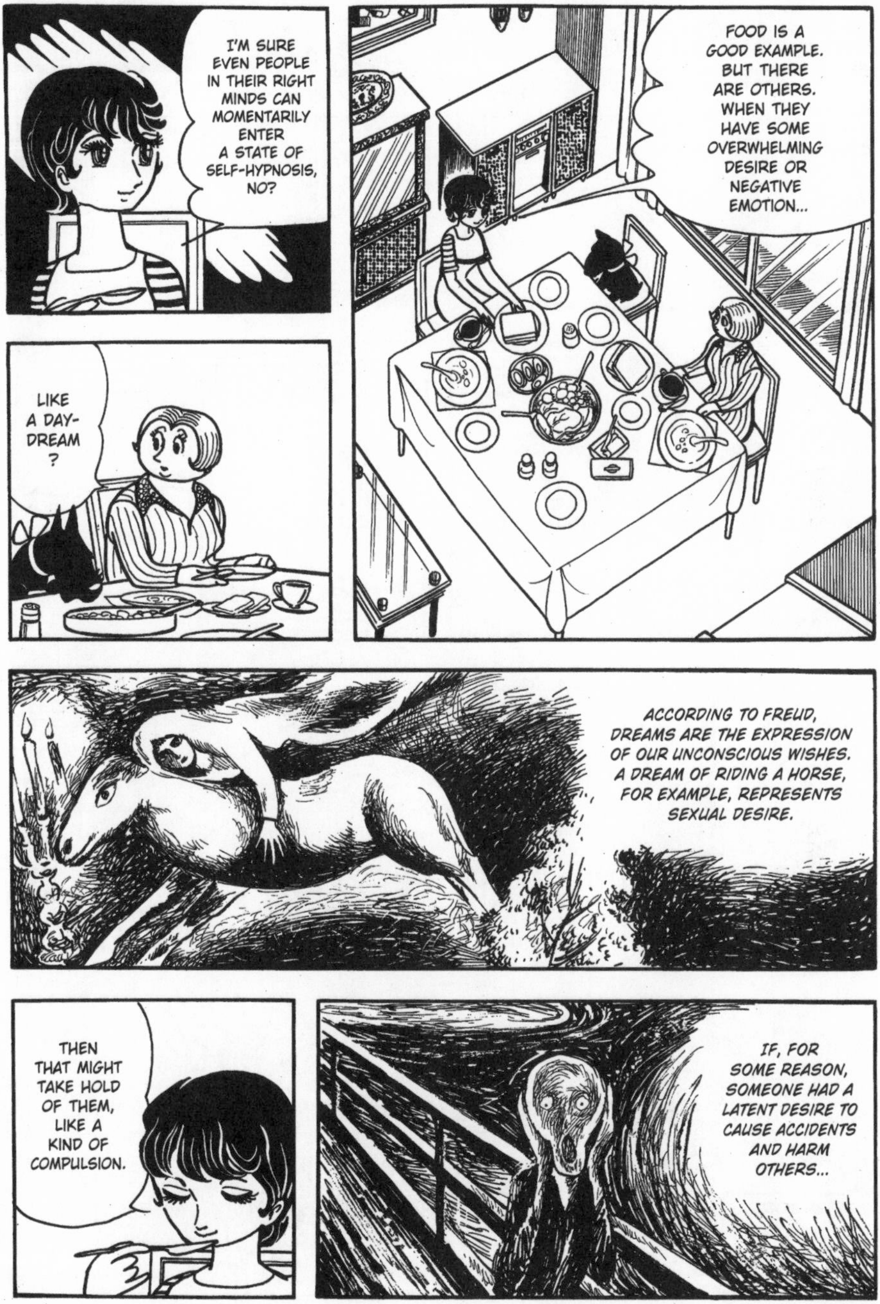
FOOD IS A GOOD EXAMPLE. BUT THERE ARE OTHERS. WHEN THEY HAVE SOME OVERWHELMING DESIRE OR NEGATIVE EMOTION...
I'M SURE EVEN PEOPLE IN THEIR RIGHT MINDS CAN MOMENTARILY ENTER A STATE OF SELF-HYPNOSIS, NO?
LIKE A DAY-DREAM?
ACCORDING TO FREUD, DREAMS ARE THE EXPRESSION OF OUR UNCONSCIOUS WISHES. A DREAM OF RIDING A HORSE, FOR EXAMPLE, REPRESENTS SEXUAL DESIRE.
IF, FOR SOME REASON, SOMEONE HAD A LATENT DESIRE TO CAUSE ACCIDENTS AND HARM OTHERS...
THEN THAT MIGHT TAKE HOLD OF THEM, LIKE A KIND OF COMPULSION.

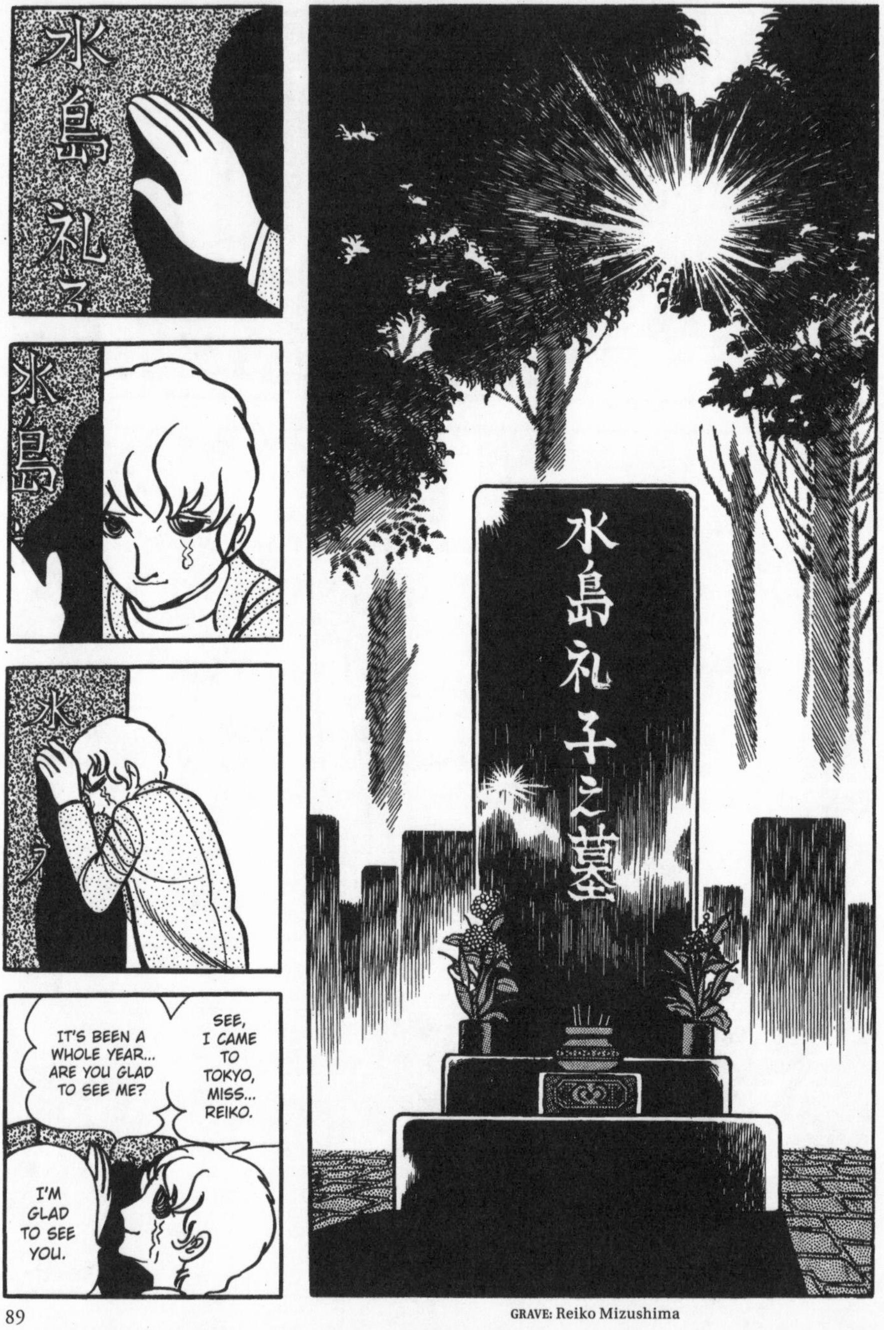
水島礼子之墓
SEE, I CAME TO TOKYO, MISS... REIKO.
IT'S BEEN A WHOLE YEAR... ARE YOU GLAD TO SEE ME?
I'M GLAD TO SEE YOU.

GRAVE: Reiko Mizushima

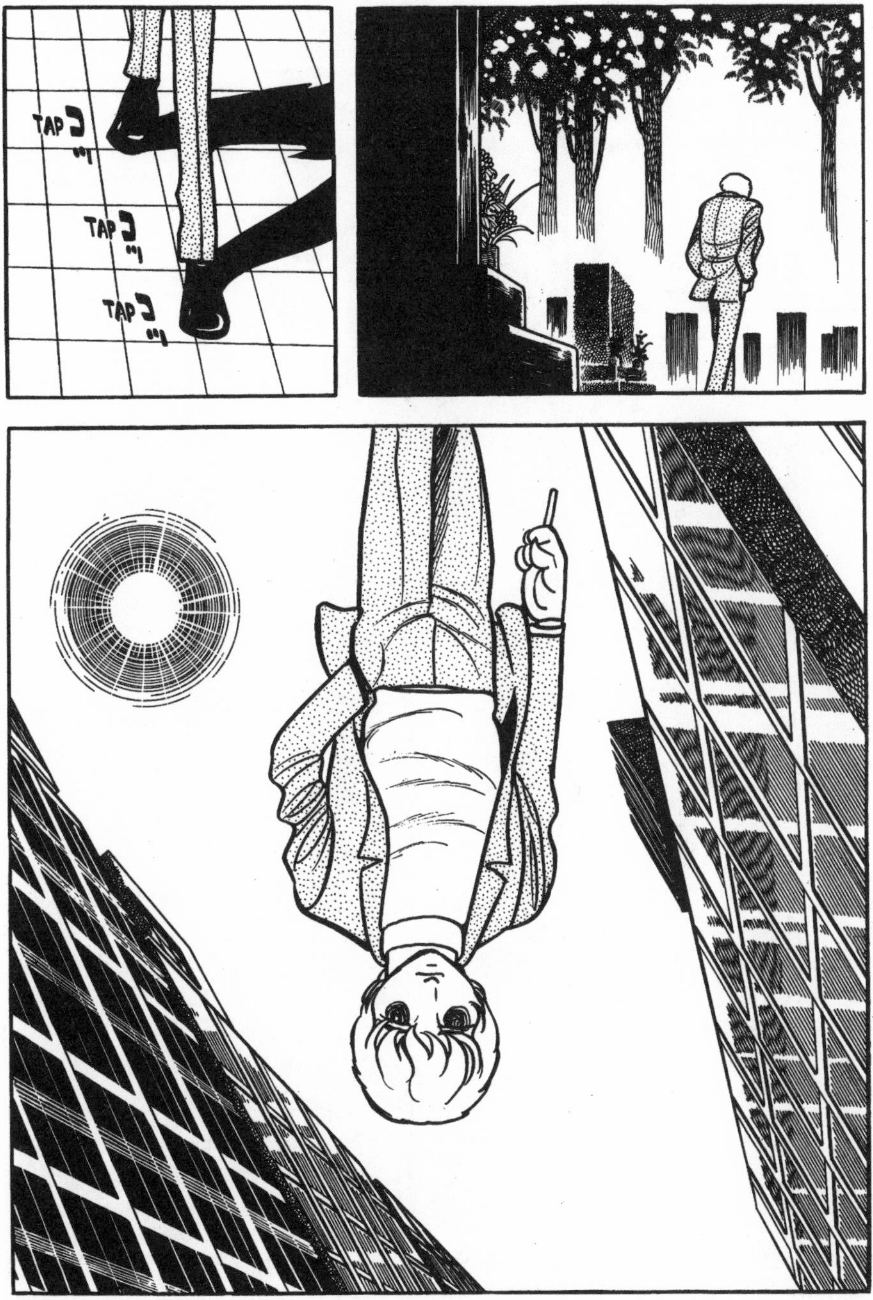
TAP
TAP
TAP

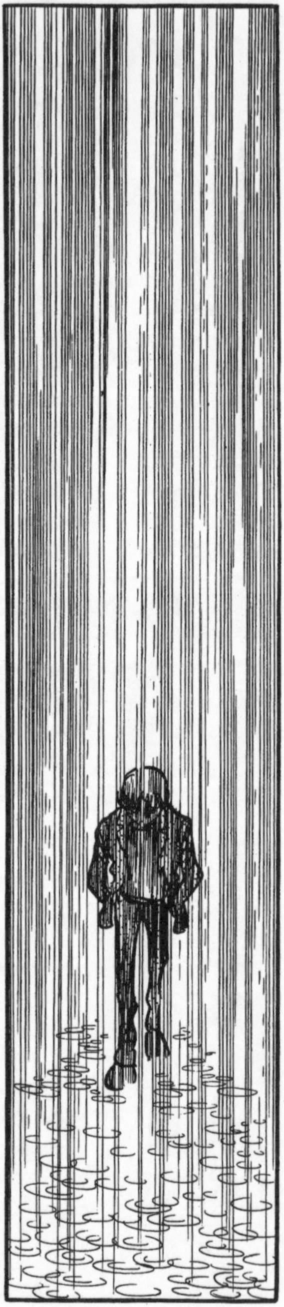

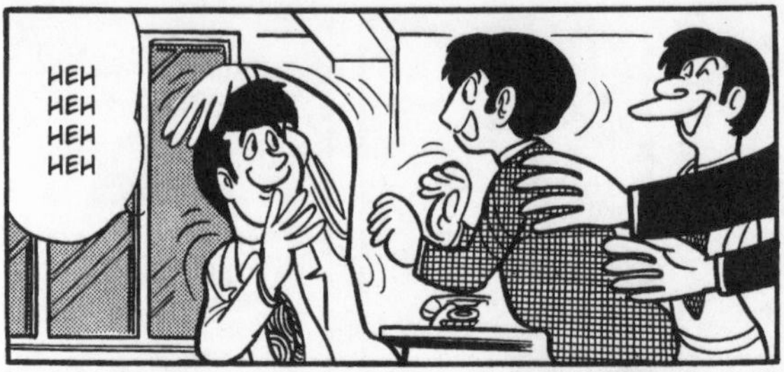
HEH
HEH
HEH
HEH

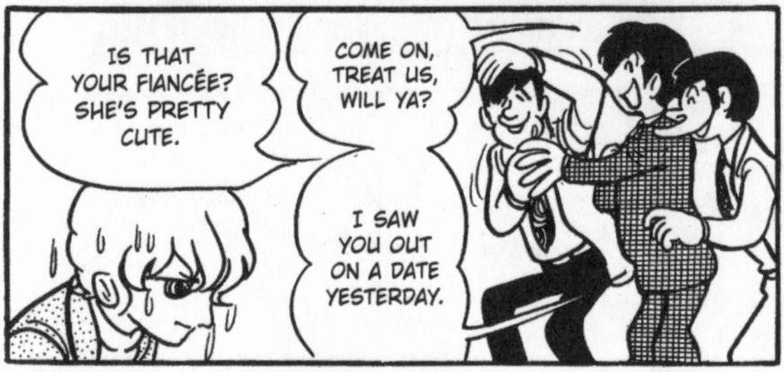
COME ON, TREAT US, WILL YA?
I SAW YOU OUT ON A DATE YESTERDAY.
IS THAT YOUR FIANCÉE? SHE'S PRETTY CUTE.

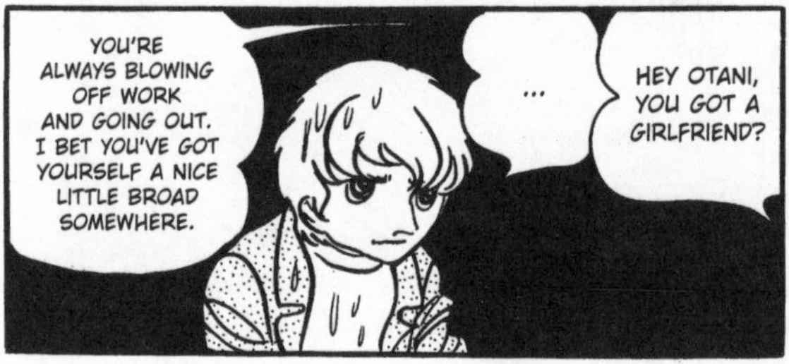
HEY OTANI, YOU GOT A GIRLFRIEND?
...
YOU'RE ALWAYS BLOWING OFF WORK AND GOING OUT. I BET YOU'VE GOT YOURSELF A NICE LITTLE BROAD SOMEWHERE.

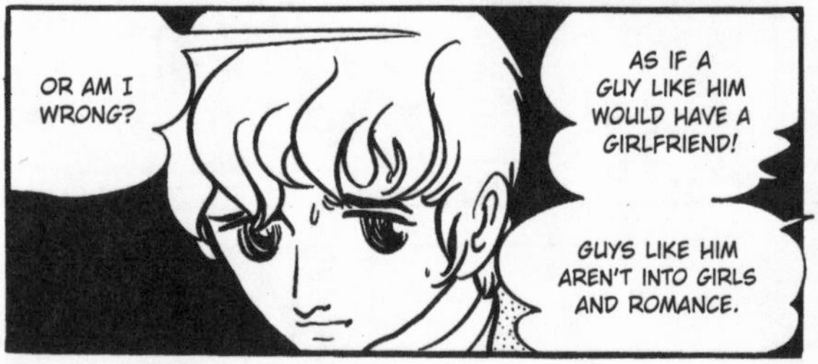
AS IF A GUY LIKE HIM WOULD HAVE A GIRLFRIEND!
GUYS LIKE HIM AREN'T INTO GIRLS AND ROMANCE.
OR AM I WRONG?

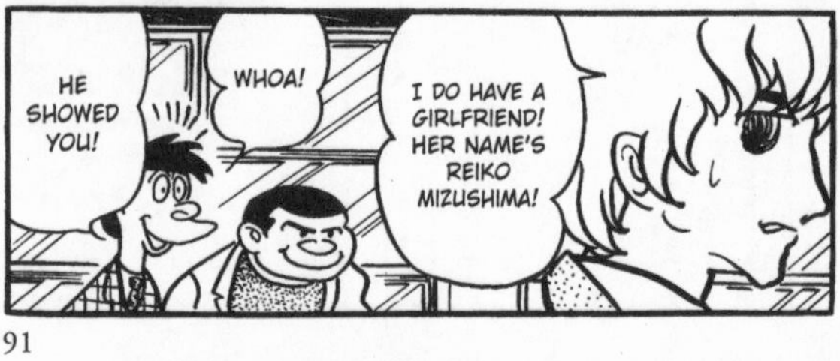
I DO HAVE A GIRLFRIEND! HER NAME'S REIKO MIZUSHIMA!
WHOA!
HE SHOWED YOU!

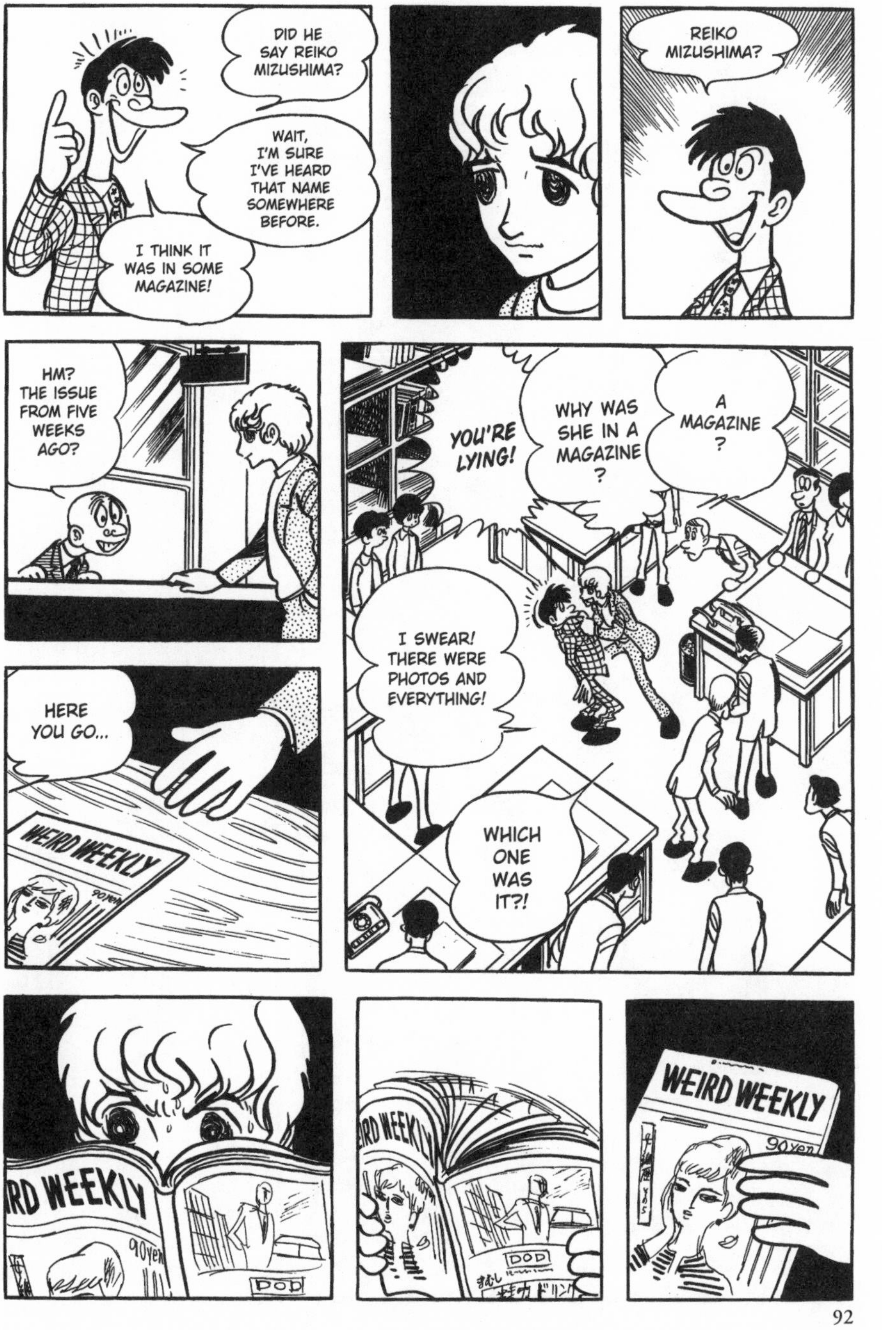
REIKO MIZUSHIMA?
DID HE SAY REIKO MIZUSHIMA?
WAIT, I'M SURE I'VE HEARD THAT NAME SOMEWHERE BEFORE.
I THINK IT WAS IN SOME MAGAZINE!
A MAGAZINE ?
WHY WAS SHE IN A MAGAZINE ?
YOU'RE LYING!
I SWEAR! THERE WERE PHOTOS AND EVERYTHING!
WHICH ONE WAS IT?!
HM? THE ISSUE FROM FIVE WEEKS AGO?
HERE YOU GO...
WEIRD WEEKLY
90 yen
WEIRD WEEKLY
90 yen
RD WEEKLY
DOD
IRD WEEKLY
90 yen
DOD

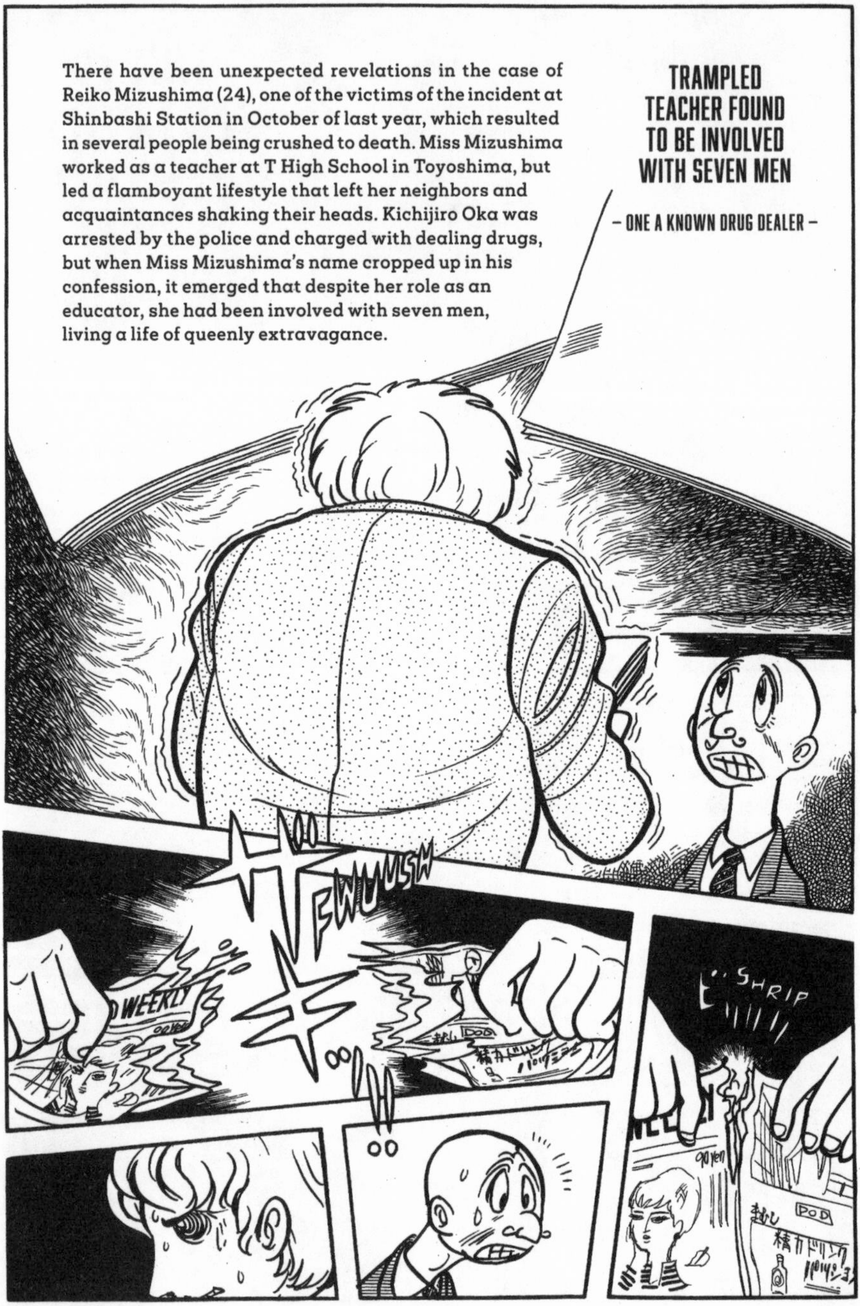
TRAMPLED TEACHER FOUND TO BE INVOLVED WITH SEVEN MEN
– ONE A KNOWN DRUG DEALER –
There have been unexpected revelations in the case of Reiko Mizushima (24), one of the victims of the incident at Shinbashi Station in October of last year, which resulted in several people being crushed to death. Miss Mizushima worked as a teacher at T High School in Toyoshima, but led a flamboyant lifestyle that left her neighbors and acquaintances shaking their heads. Kichijiro Oka was arrested by the police and charged with dealing drugs, but when Miss Mizushima's name cropped up in his confession, it emerged that despite her role as an educator, she had been involved with seven men, living a life of queenly extravagance.
SHRIP
POD
FWUUSH
WEEKLY
POD

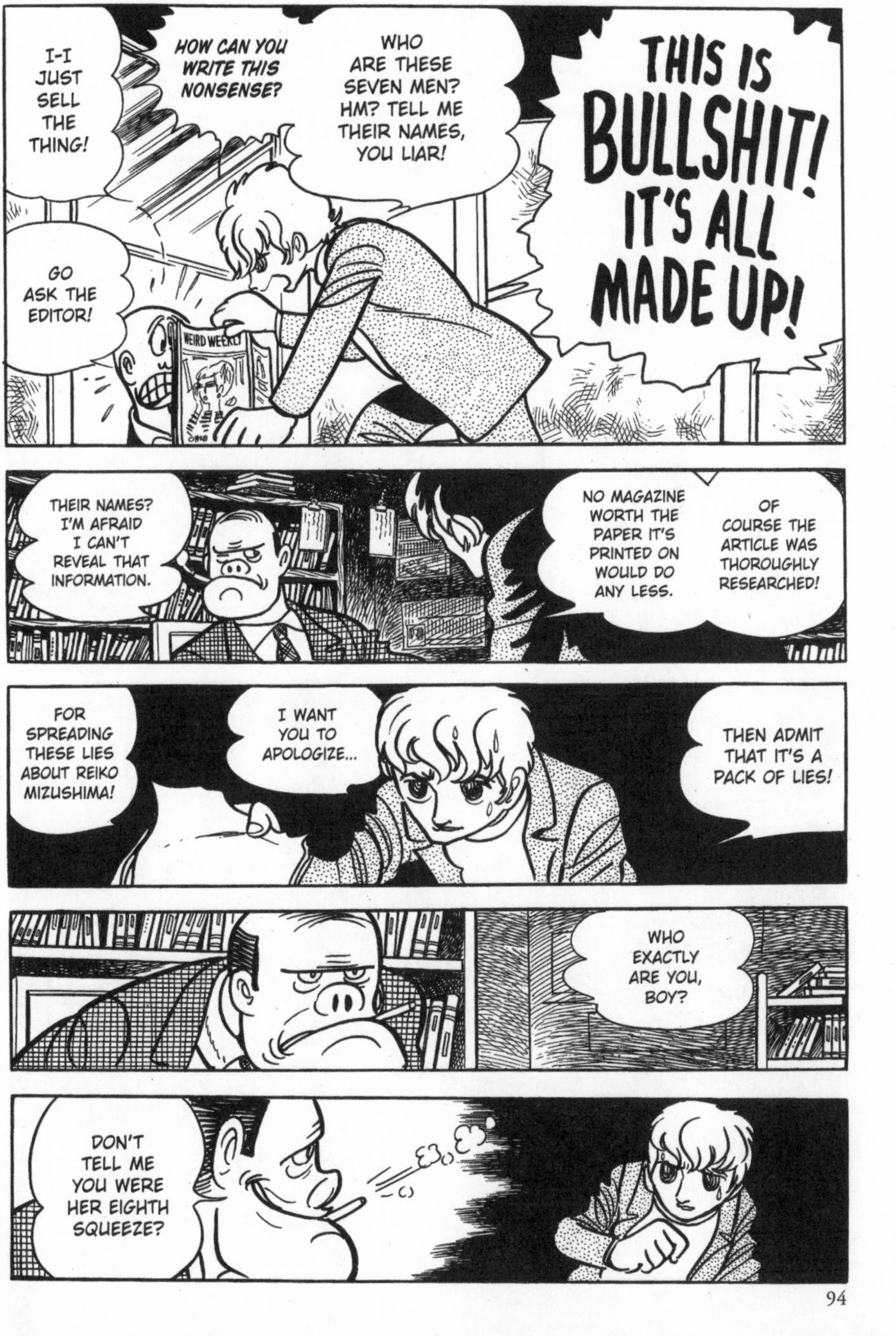
THIS IS BULLSHIT! IT'S ALL MADE UP!
WHO ARE THESE SEVEN MEN? HM? TELL ME THEIR NAMES, YOU LIAR!
HOW CAN YOU WRITE THIS NONSENSE?
I-I JUST SELL THE THING!
GO ASK THE EDITOR!
WEIRD WEEKLY
OF COURSE THE ARTICLE WAS THOROUGHLY RESEARCHED!
NO MAGAZINE WORTH THE PAPER IT'S PRINTED ON WOULD DO ANY LESS.
THEIR NAMES? I'M AFRAID I CAN'T REVEAL THAT INFORMATION.
THEN ADMIT THAT IT'S A PACK OF LIES!
I WANT YOU TO APOLOGIZE...
FOR SPREADING THESE LIES ABOUT REIKO MIZUSHIMA!
WHO EXACTLY ARE YOU, BOY?
DON'T TELL ME YOU WERE HER EIGHTH SQUEEZE?

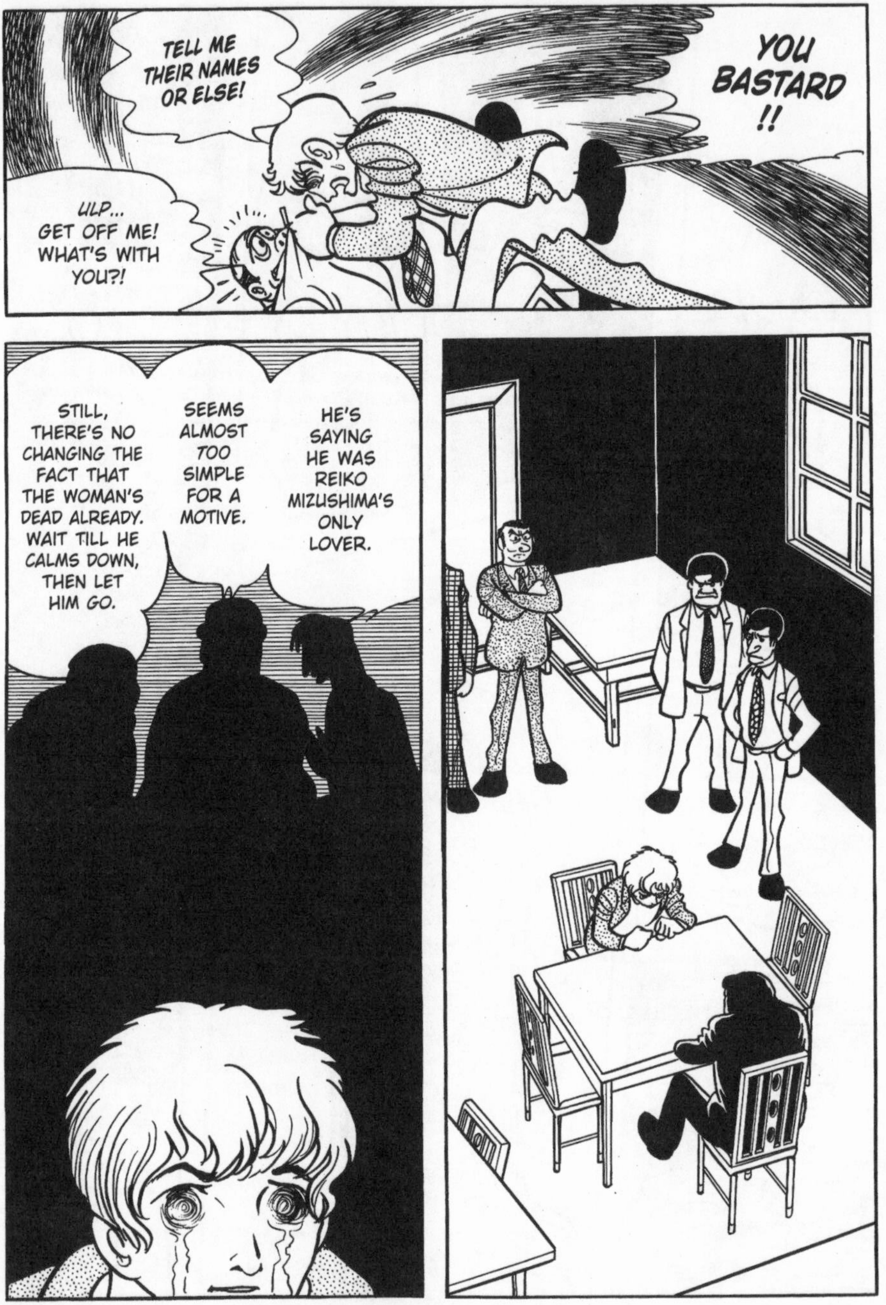
YOU BASTARD !!
TELL ME THEIR NAMES OR ELSE!
ULP... GET OFF ME! WHAT'S WITH YOU?!
HE'S SAYING HE WAS REIKO MIZUSHIMA'S ONLY LOVER.
SEEMS ALMOST *TOO* SIMPLE FOR A MOTIVE.
STILL, THERE'S NO CHANGING THE FACT THAT THE WOMAN'S DEAD ALREADY. WAIT TILL HE CALMS DOWN, THEN LET HIM GO.

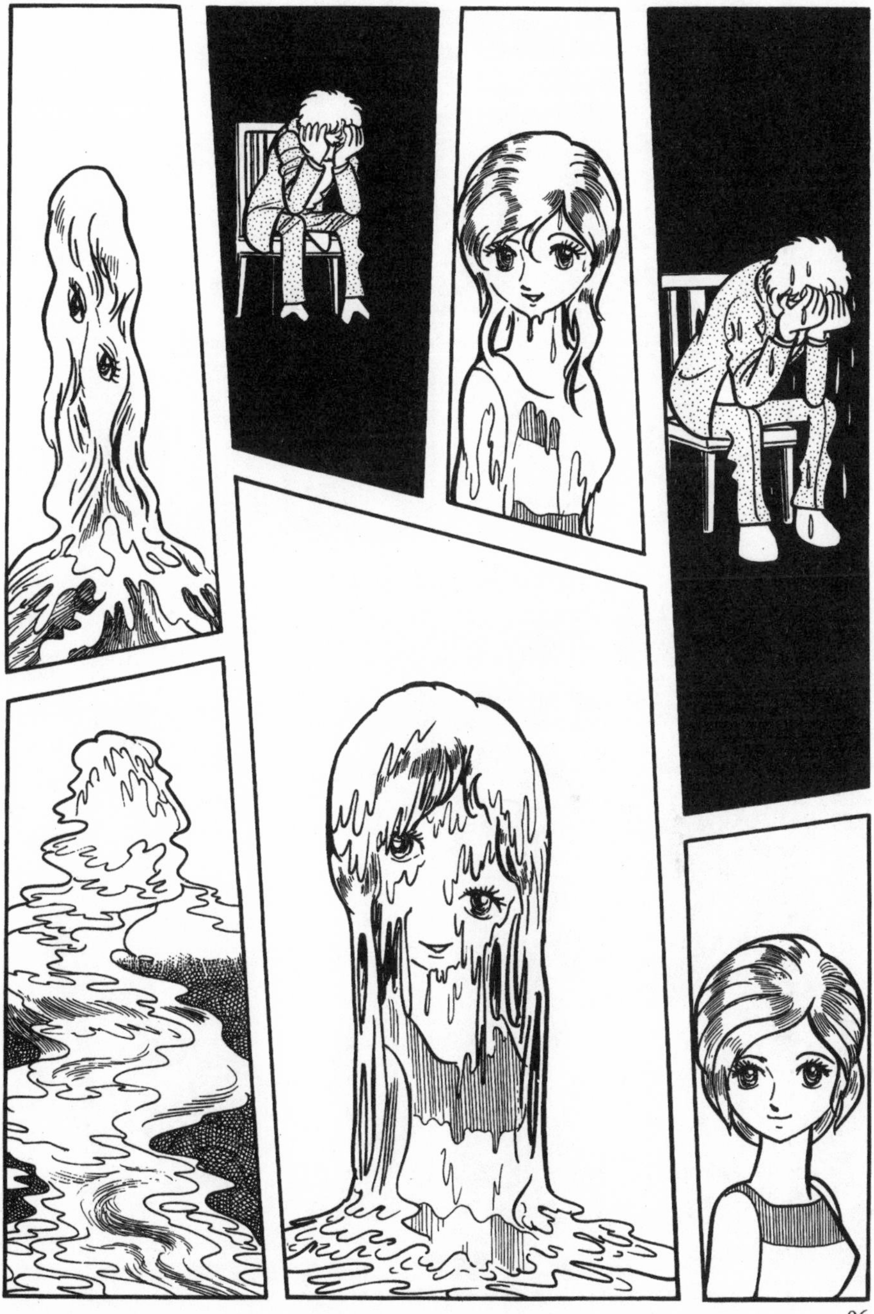

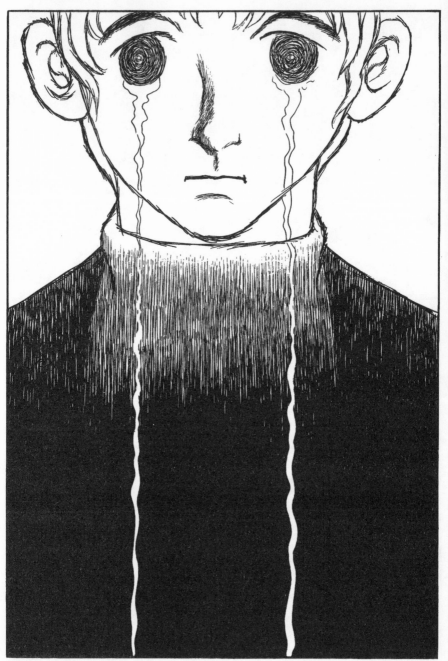

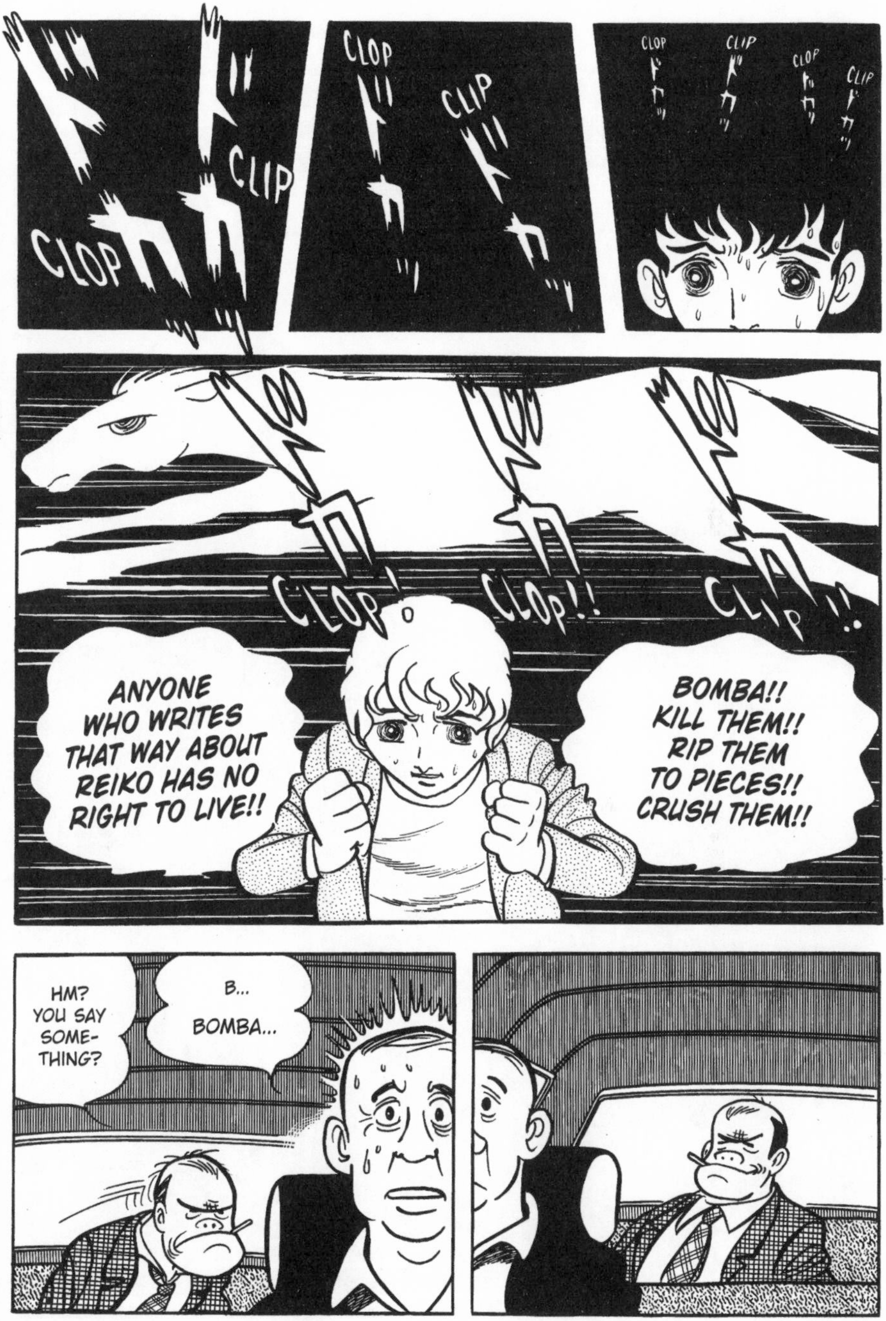
CLOP
CLIP
CLOP
CLIP
CLOP
CLIP
CLIP
CLOP
CLIP!!
CLOP!!
CLOP!
BOMBA!! KILL THEM!! RIP THEM TO PIECES!! CRUSH THEM!!
ANYONE WHO WRITES THAT WAY ABOUT REIKO HAS NO RIGHT TO LIVE!!
B... BOMBA...
HM? YOU SAY SOME-THING?

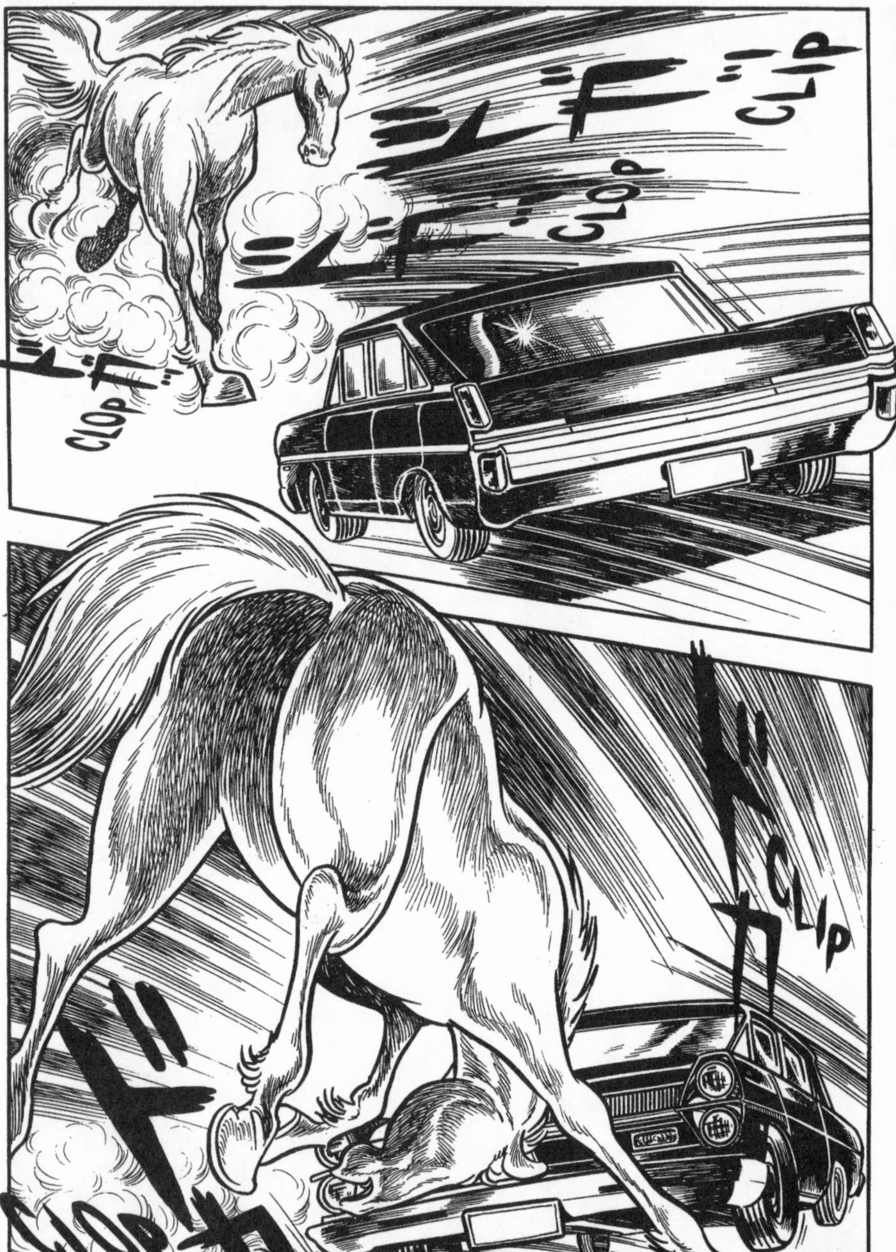
CLIP
CLOP
CLOP
CLIP
CLOP

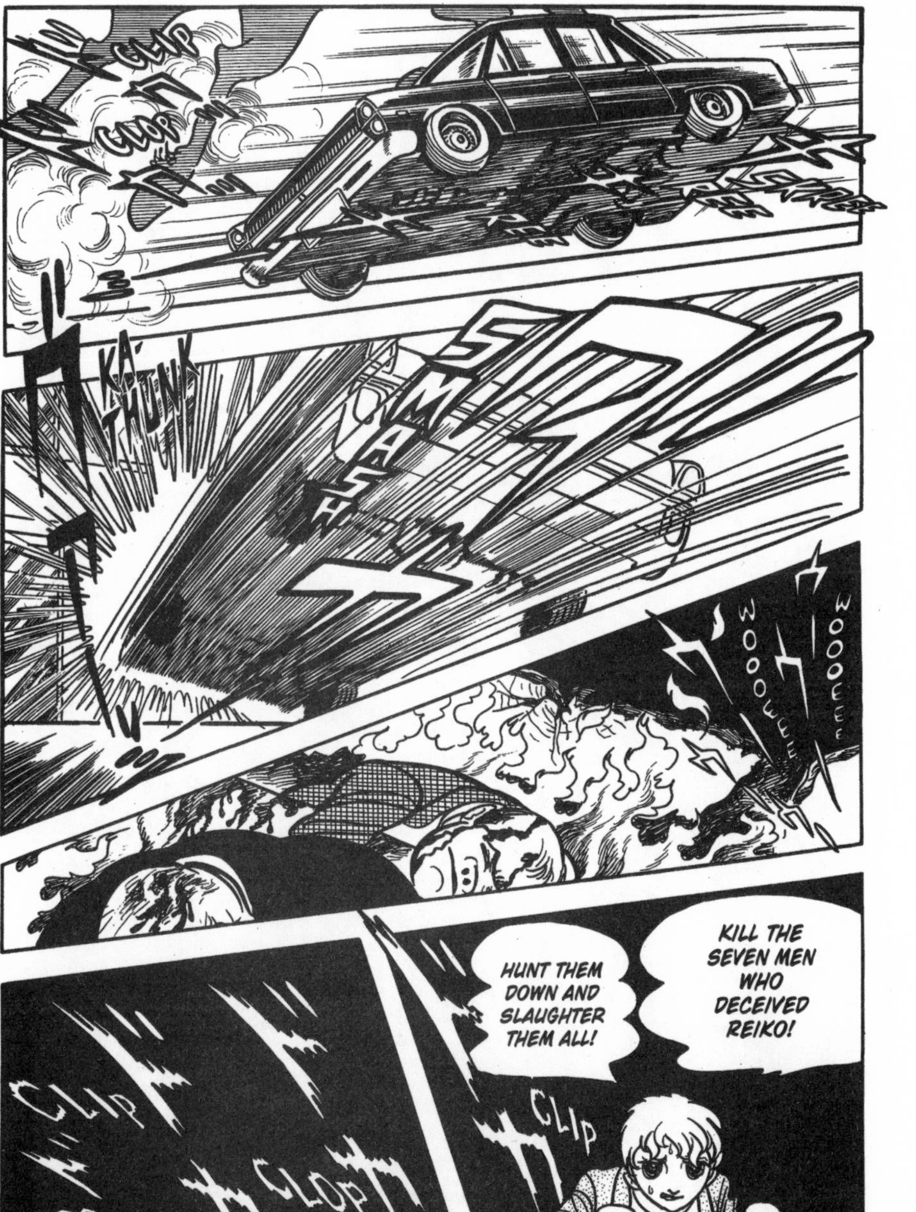
CLIP
CLOP
KA'THUNK
SMASH
WOOOWEEE
WOOOWEEE
KILL THE SEVEN MEN WHO DECEIVED REIKO!
HUNT THEM DOWN AND SLAUGHTER THEM ALL!
CLIP
CLIP
CLOP
CLOP

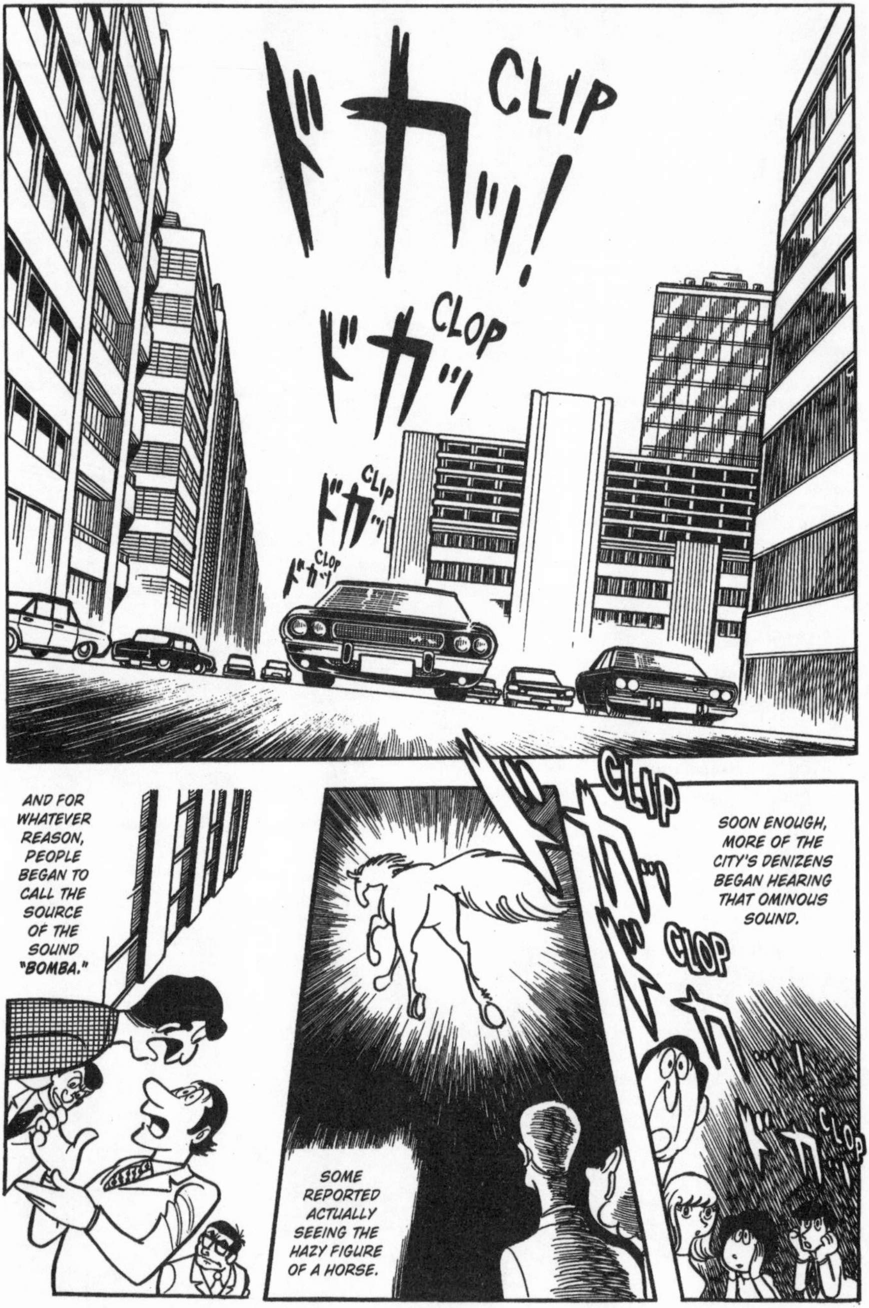
ドカッ!
CLIP
ドカッ
CLOP
ドカッ
CLIP
ドカッ
CLOP
SOON ENOUGH, MORE OF THE CITY'S DENIZENS BEGAN HEARING THAT OMINOUS SOUND.
CLIP
CLOP
CLOP
SOME REPORTED ACTUALLY SEEING THE HAZY FIGURE OF A HORSE.
AND FOR WHATEVER REASON, PEOPLE BEGAN TO CALL THE SOURCE OF THE SOUND "BOMBA."

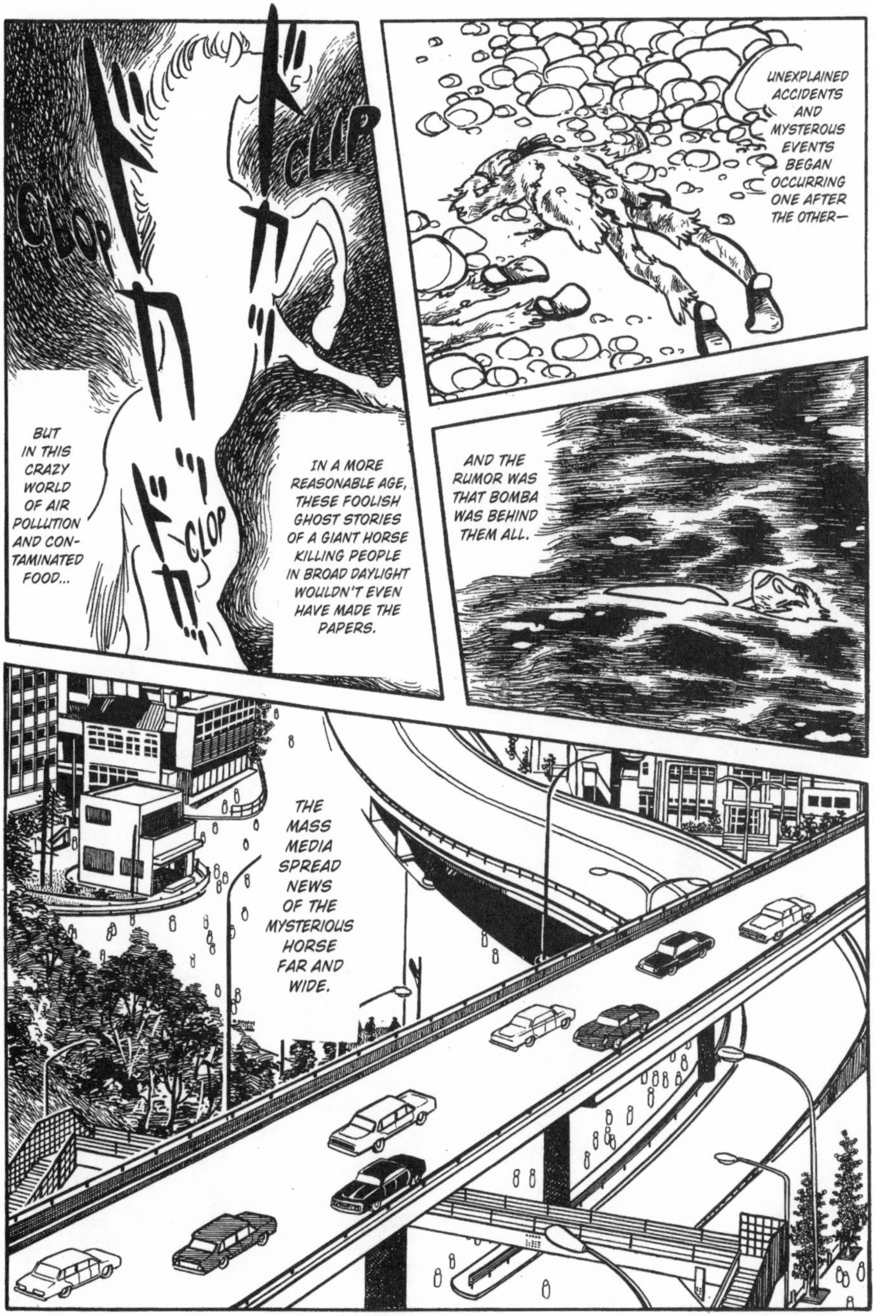
UNEXPLAINED ACCIDENTS AND MYSTEROUS EVENTS BEGAN OCCURRING ONE AFTER THE OTHER—
AND THE RUMOR WAS THAT BOMBA WAS BEHIND THEM ALL.
CLIP
CLOP
IN A MORE REASONABLE AGE, THESE FOOLISH GHOST STORIES OF A GIANT HORSE KILLING PEOPLE IN BROAD DAYLIGHT WOULDN'T EVEN HAVE MADE THE PAPERS.
CLOP
BUT IN THIS CRAZY WORLD OF AIR POLLUTION AND CONTAMINATED FOOD...
THE MASS MEDIA SPREAD NEWS OF THE MYSTERIOUS HORSE FAR AND WIDE.

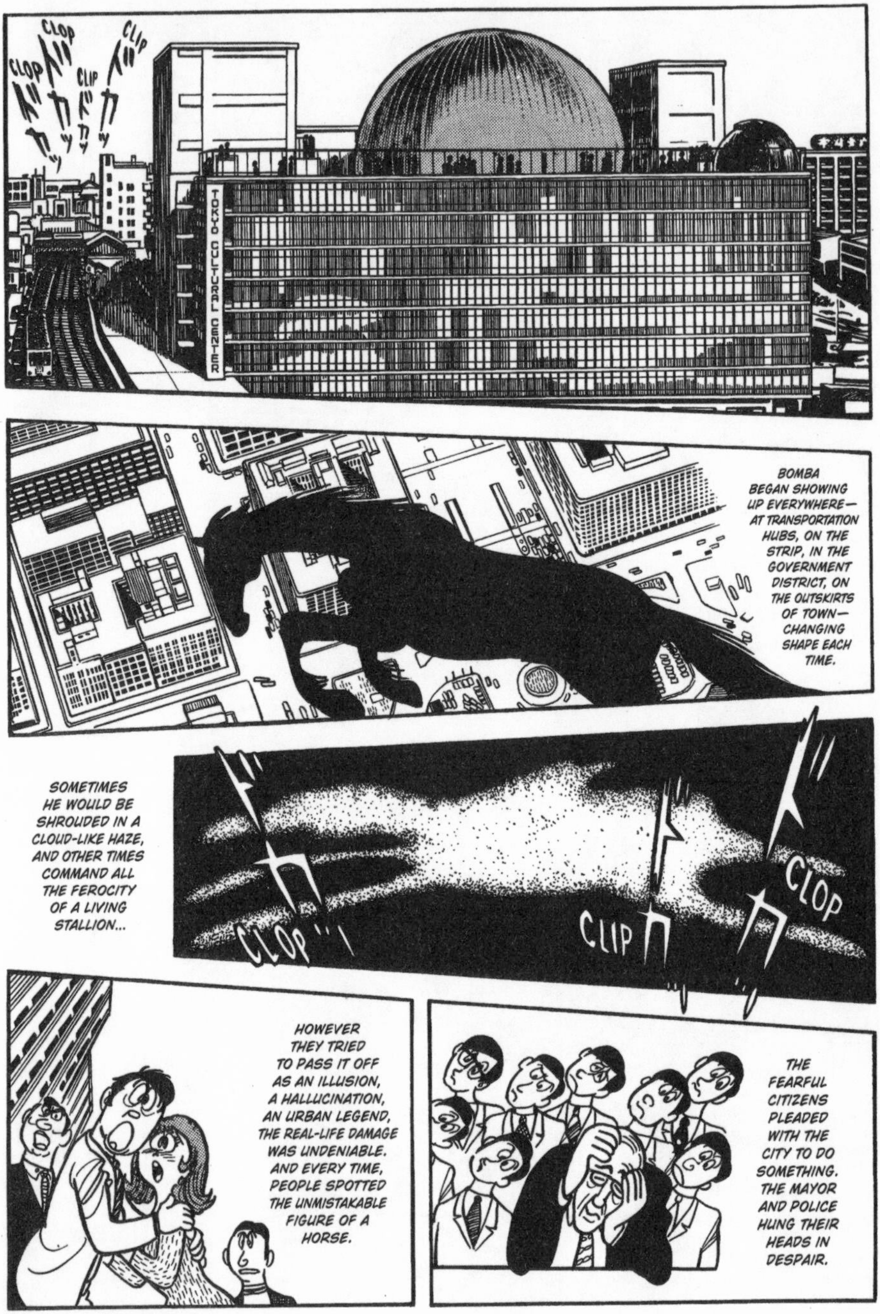
CLIP
CLIP
CLOP
CLOP
TOKYO CULTURAL CENTER
BOMBA BEGAN SHOWING UP EVERYWHERE—AT TRANSPORTATION HUBS, ON THE STRIP, IN THE GOVERNMENT DISTRICT, ON THE OUTSKIRTS OF TOWN—CHANGING SHAPE EACH TIME.
CLOP
CLIP
CLOP
SOMETIMES HE WOULD BE SHROUDED IN A CLOUD-LIKE HAZE, AND OTHER TIMES COMMAND ALL THE FEROCITY OF A LIVING STALLION...
THE FEARFUL CITIZENS PLEADED WITH THE CITY TO DO SOMETHING. THE MAYOR AND POLICE HUNG THEIR HEADS IN DESPAIR.
HOWEVER THEY TRIED TO PASS IT OFF AS AN ILLUSION, A HALLUCINATION, AN URBAN LEGEND, THE REAL-LIFE DAMAGE WAS UNDENIABLE. AND EVERY TIME, PEOPLE SPOTTED THE UNMISTAKABLE FIGURE OF A HORSE.

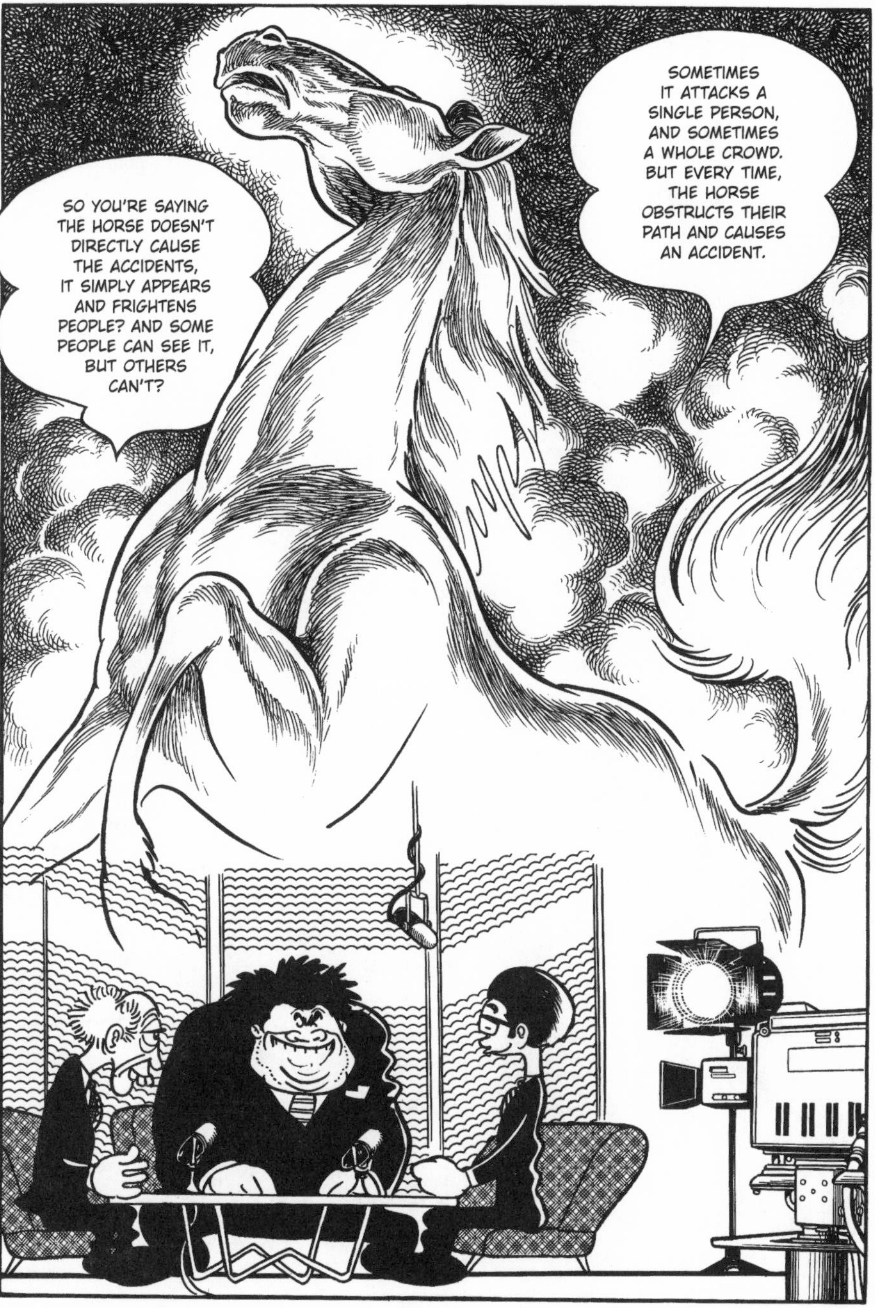
SOMETIMES IT ATTACKS A SINGLE PERSON, AND SOMETIMES A WHOLE CROWD. BUT EVERY TIME, THE HORSE OBSTRUCTS THEIR PATH AND CAUSES AN ACCIDENT.
SO YOU'RE SAYING THE HORSE DOESN'T DIRECTLY CAUSE THE ACCIDENTS, IT SIMPLY APPEARS AND FRIGHTENS PEOPLE? AND SOME PEOPLE CAN SEE IT, BUT OTHERS CAN'T?

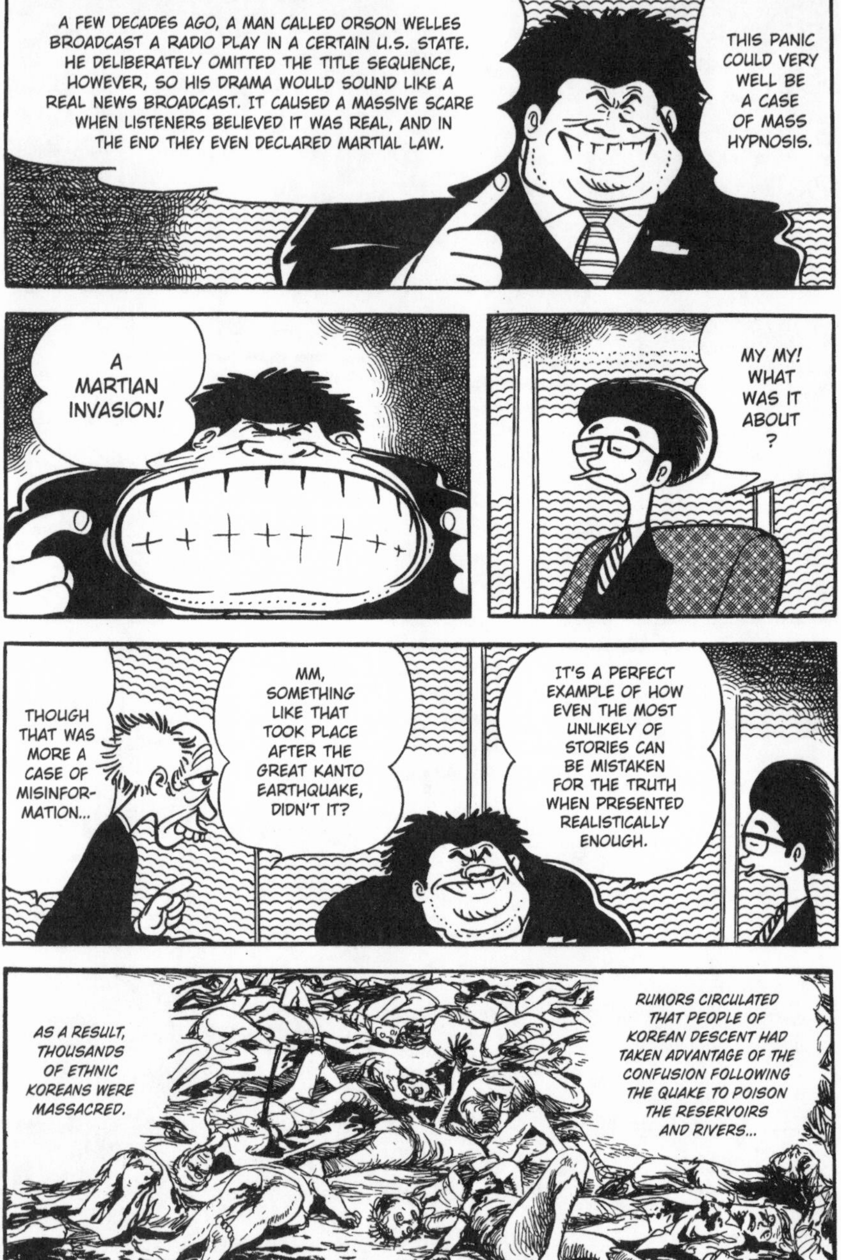
THIS PANIC COULD VERY WELL BE A CASE OF MASS HYPNOSIS.
A FEW DECADES AGO, A MAN CALLED ORSON WELLES BROADCAST A RADIO PLAY IN A CERTAIN U.S. STATE. HE DELIBERATELY OMITTED THE TITLE SEQUENCE, HOWEVER, SO HIS DRAMA WOULD SOUND LIKE A REAL NEWS BROADCAST. IT CAUSED A MASSIVE SCARE WHEN LISTENERS BELIEVED IT WAS REAL, AND IN THE END THEY EVEN DECLARED MARTIAL LAW.
MY MY! WHAT WAS IT ABOUT?
A MARTIAN INVASION!
IT'S A PERFECT EXAMPLE OF HOW EVEN THE MOST UNLIKELY OF STORIES CAN BE MISTAKEN FOR THE TRUTH WHEN PRESENTED REALISTICALLY ENOUGH.
MM, SOMETHING LIKE THAT TOOK PLACE AFTER THE GREAT KANTO EARTHQUAKE, DIDN'T IT?
THOUGH THAT WAS MORE A CASE OF MISINFORMATION...
RUMORS CIRCULATED THAT PEOPLE OF KOREAN DESCENT HAD TAKEN ADVANTAGE OF THE CONFUSION FOLLOWING THE QUAKE TO POISON THE RESERVOIRS AND RIVERS...
AS A RESULT, THOUSANDS OF ETHNIC KOREANS WERE MASSACRED.

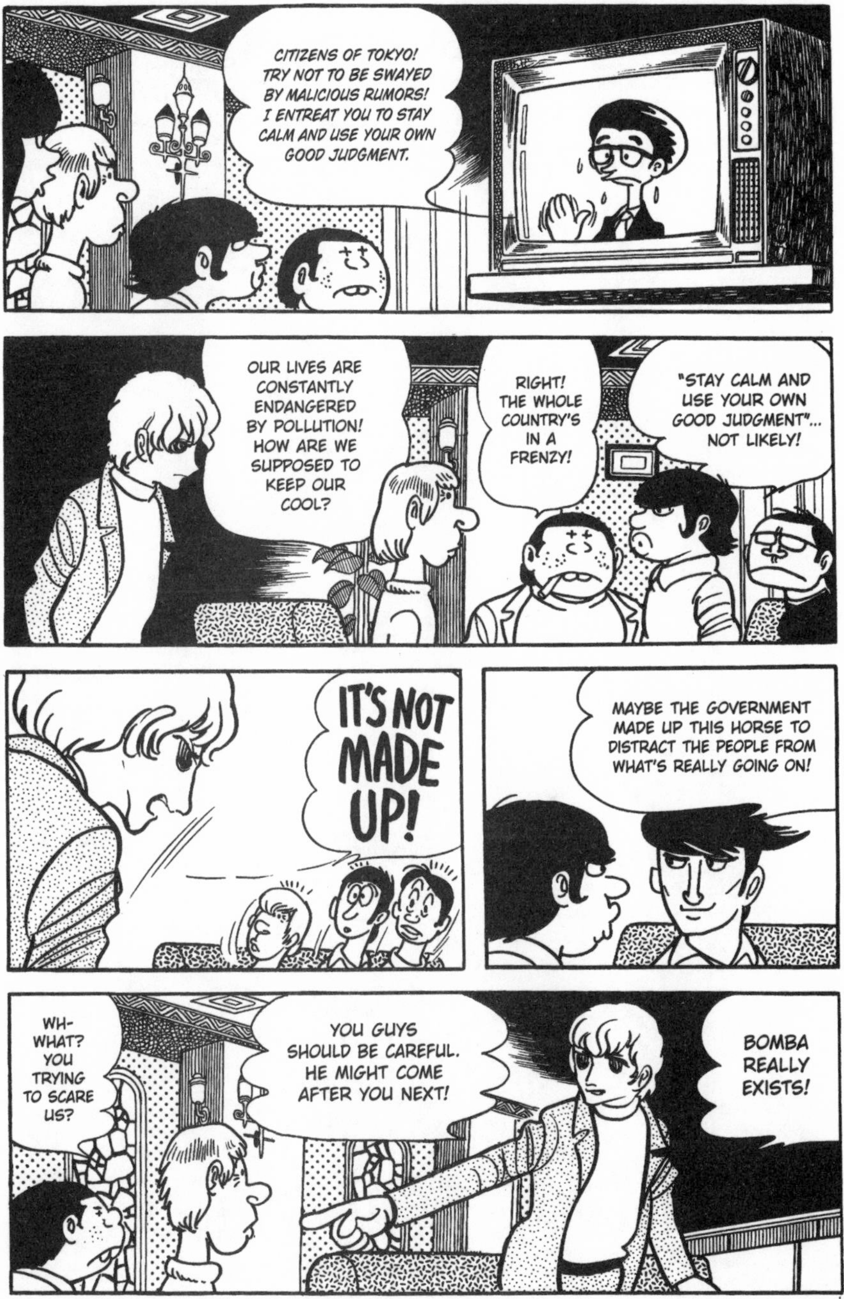
CITIZENS OF TOKYO! TRY NOT TO BE SWAYED BY MALICIOUS RUMORS! I ENTREAT YOU TO STAY CALM AND USE YOUR OWN GOOD JUDGMENT.
"STAY CALM AND USE YOUR OWN GOOD JUDGMENT"... NOT LIKELY!
RIGHT! THE WHOLE COUNTRY'S IN A FRENZY!
OUR LIVES ARE CONSTANTLY ENDANGERED BY POLLUTION! HOW ARE WE SUPPOSED TO KEEP OUR COOL?
MAYBE THE GOVERNMENT MADE UP THIS HORSE TO DISTRACT THE PEOPLE FROM WHAT'S REALLY GOING ON!
IT'S NOT MADE UP!
BOMBA REALLY EXISTS!
YOU GUYS SHOULD BE CAREFUL. HE MIGHT COME AFTER YOU NEXT!
WH-WHAT? YOU TRYING TO SCARE US?

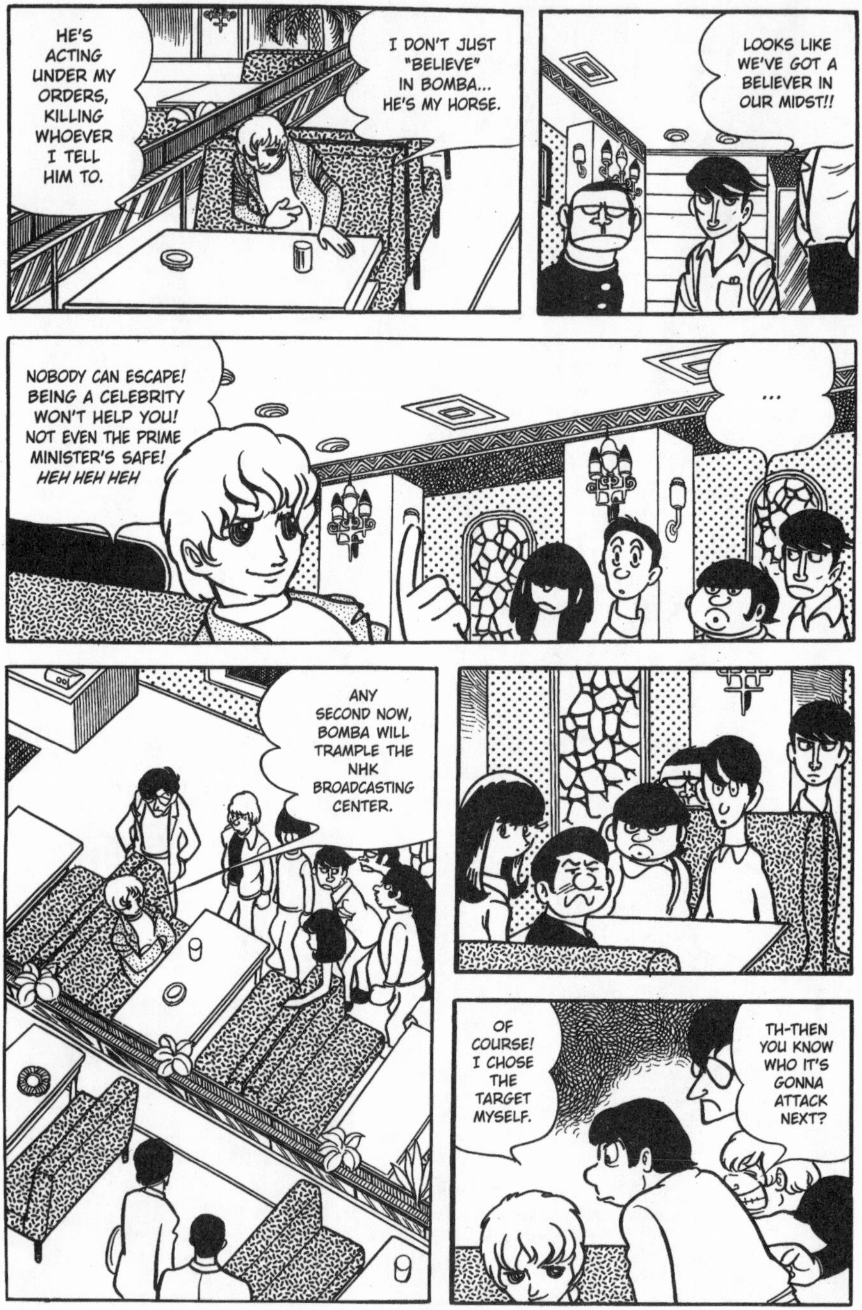
LOOKS LIKE WE'VE GOT A BELIEVER IN OUR MIDST!!
I DON'T JUST "BELIEVE" IN BOMBA... HE'S MY HORSE.
HE'S ACTING UNDER MY ORDERS, KILLING WHOEVER I TELL HIM TO.
...
NOBODY CAN ESCAPE! BEING A CELEBRITY WON'T HELP YOU! NOT EVEN THE PRIME MINISTER'S SAFE! *HEH HEH HEH*
TH-THEN YOU KNOW WHO IT'S GONNA ATTACK NEXT?
OF COURSE! I CHOSE THE TARGET MYSELF.
ANY SECOND NOW, BOMBA WILL TRAMPLE THE NHK BROADCASTING CENTER.

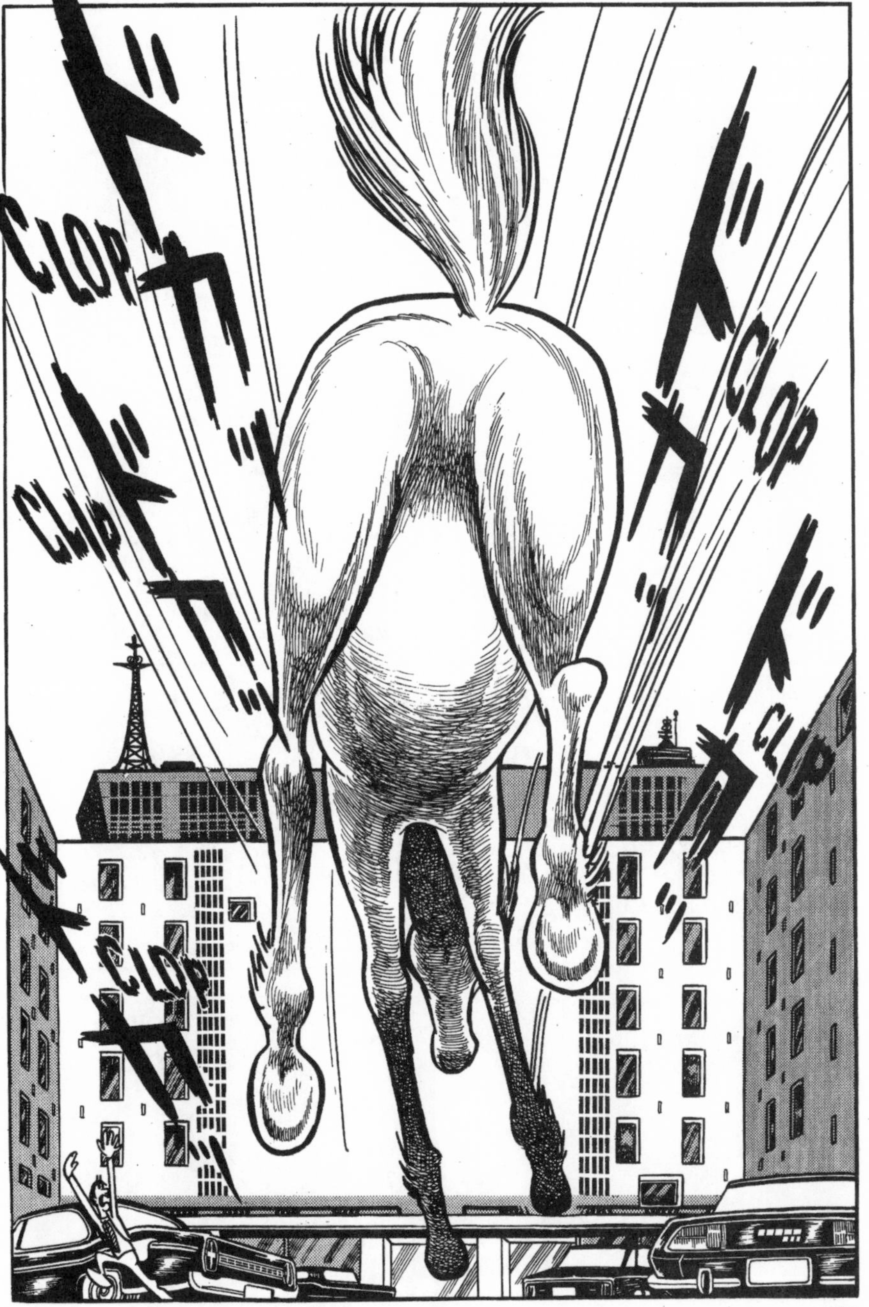
CLOP
CLIP
CLOP
CLIP
CLOP

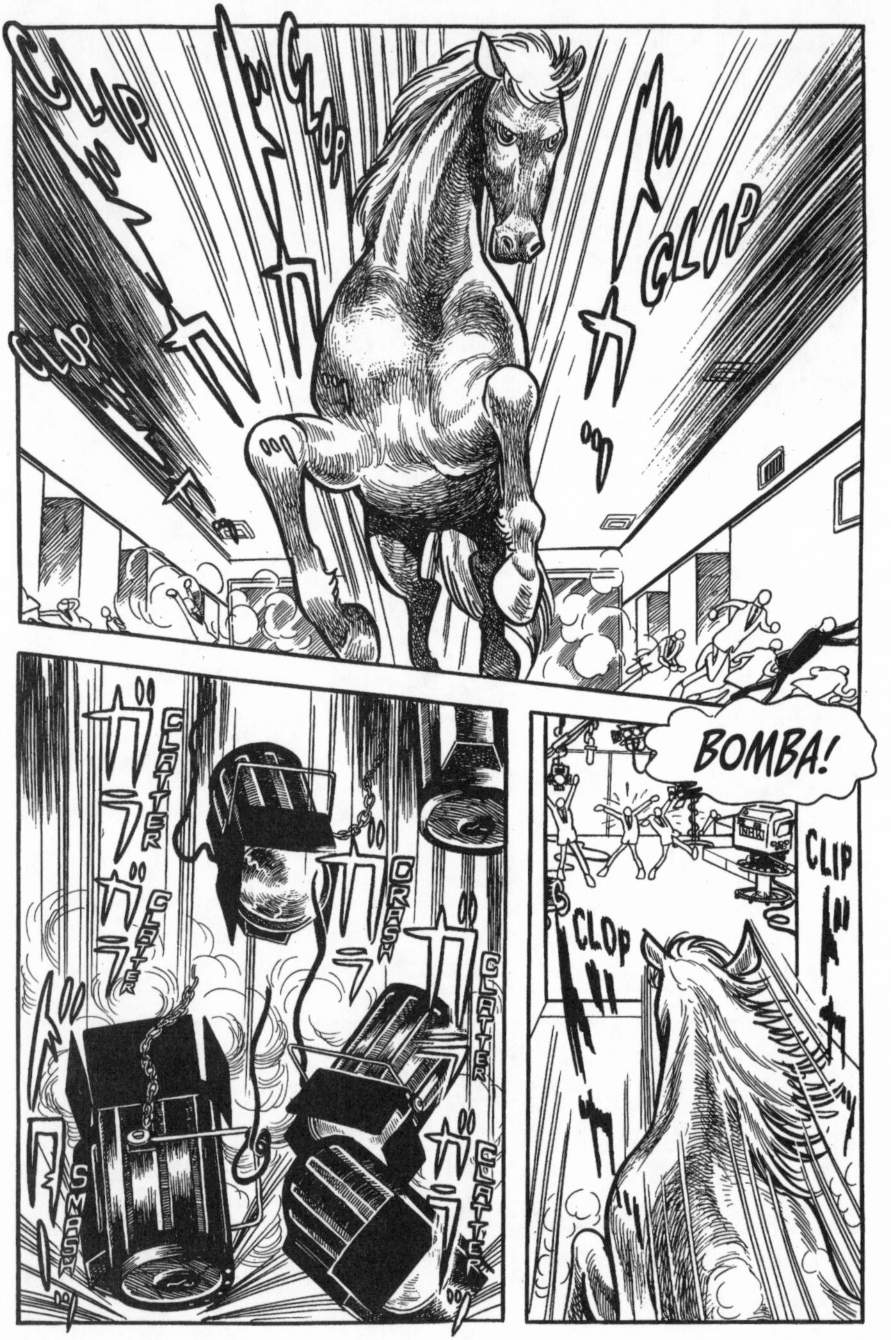
CLIP
CLOP
CLIP
CLOP
BOMBA!
CLIP
CLOP
CLATTER
CLATTER
CRASH
CLATTER
CLATTER
SMASH

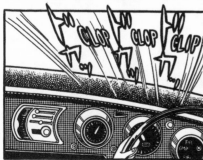

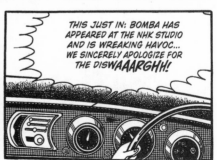

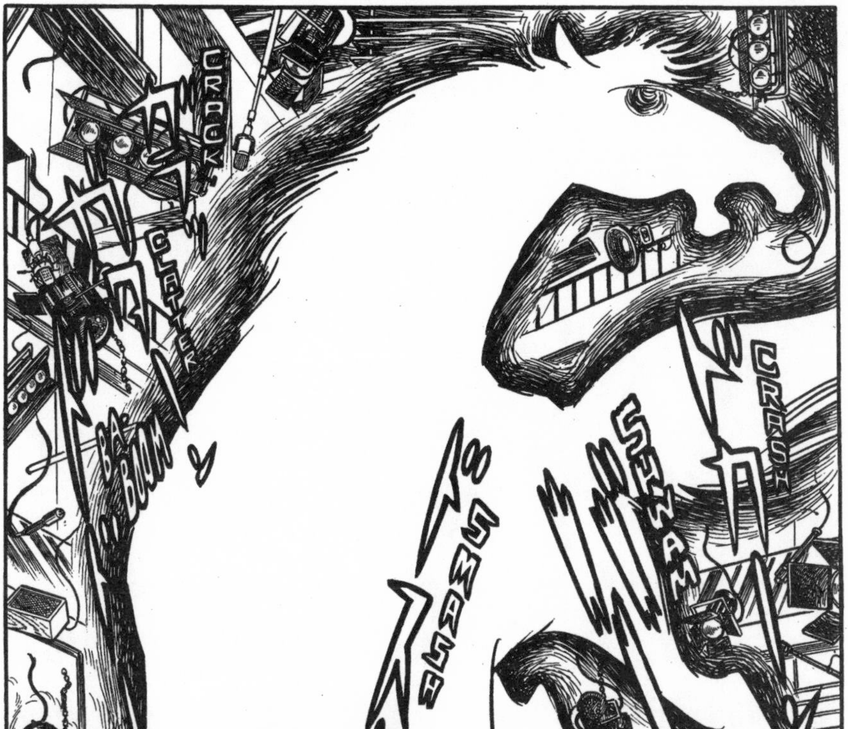
CRASH
SHWAM
SMASH
CRACK
CLATTER
BA-BOOM
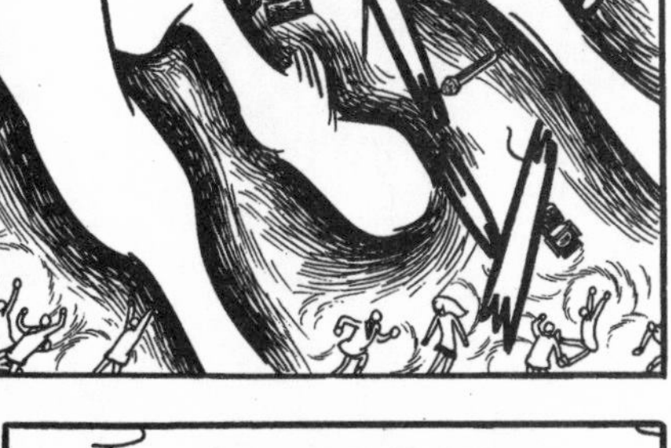
THIS JUST IN: BOMBA HAS APPEARED AT THE NHK STUDIO AND IS WREAKING HAVOC... WE SINCERELY APOLOGIZE FOR THE DISWAAARGHH!
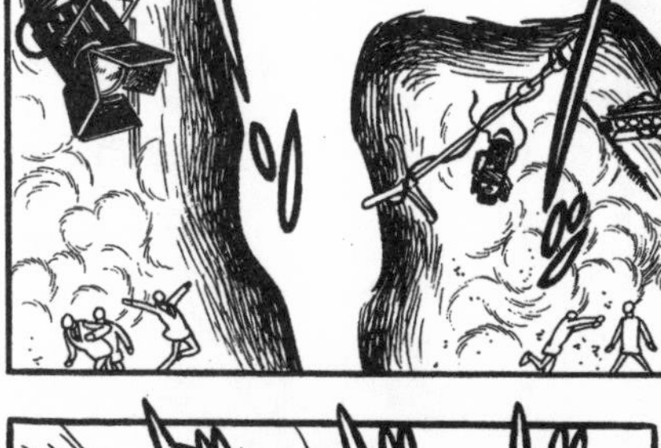
CLOP
CLOP
CLIP

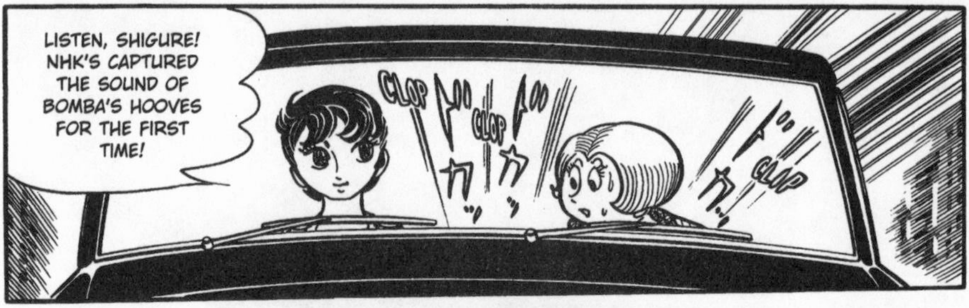
LISTEN, SHIGURE! NHK'S CAPTURED THE SOUND OF BOMBA'S HOOVES FOR THE FIRST TIME!
CLOP
CLOP
CLOP

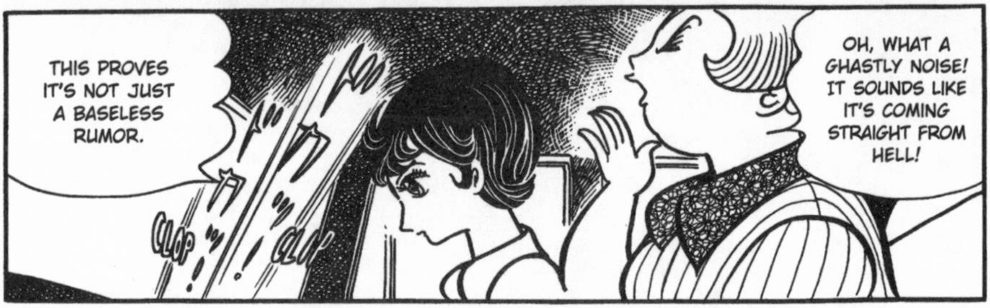
OH, WHAT A GHASTLY NOISE! IT SOUNDS LIKE IT'S COMING STRAIGHT FROM HELL!
THIS PROVES IT'S NOT JUST A BASELESS RUMOR.
CLOP
CLOP

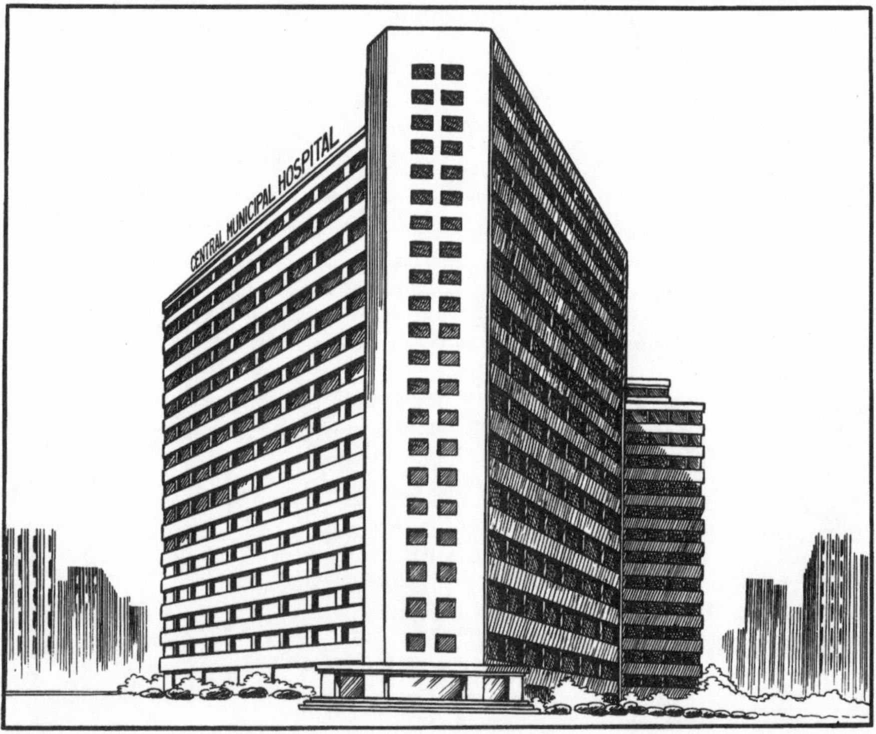
CENTRAL MUNICIPAL HOSPITAL

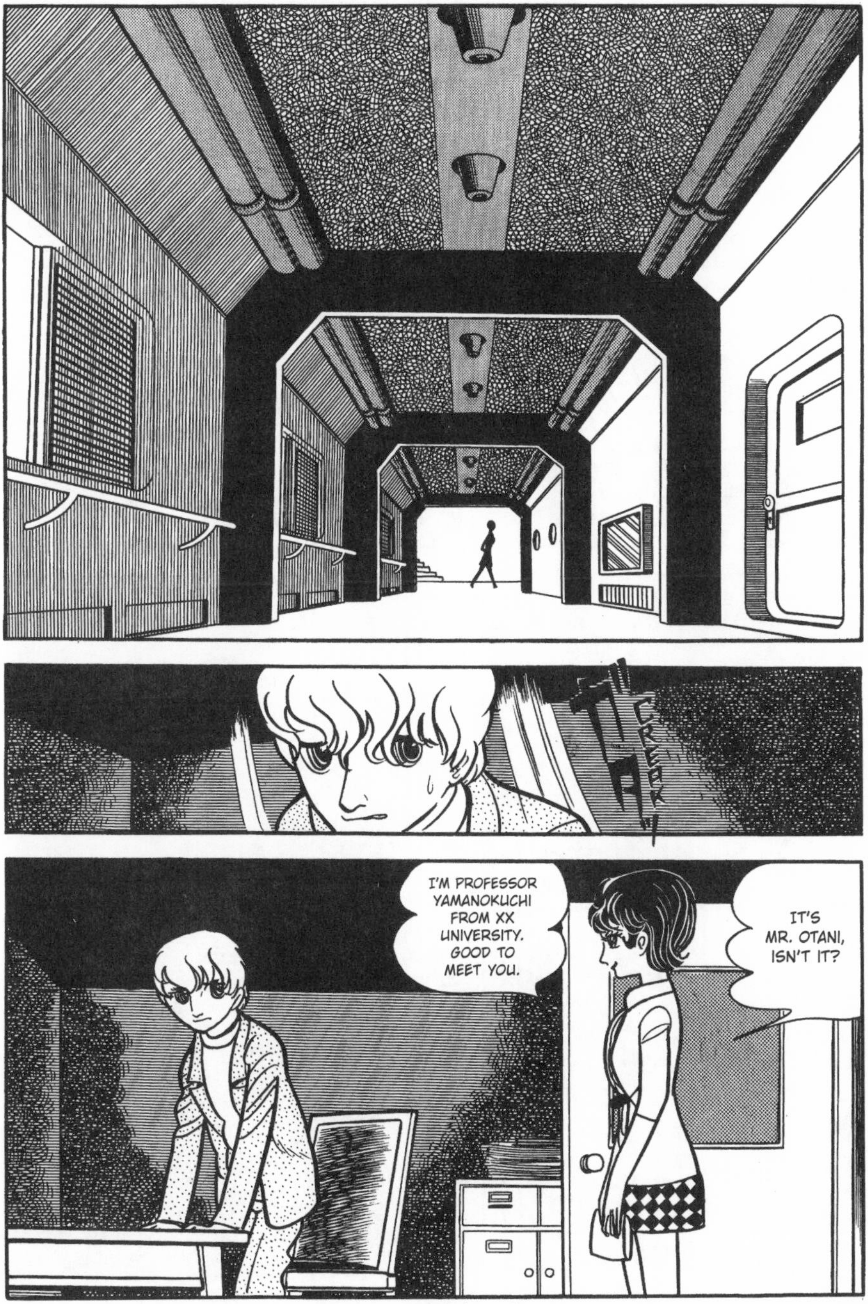
CREEEK!!
IT'S MR. OTANI, ISN'T IT?
I'M PROFESSOR YAMANOKUCHI FROM XX UNIVERSITY. GOOD TO MEET YOU.

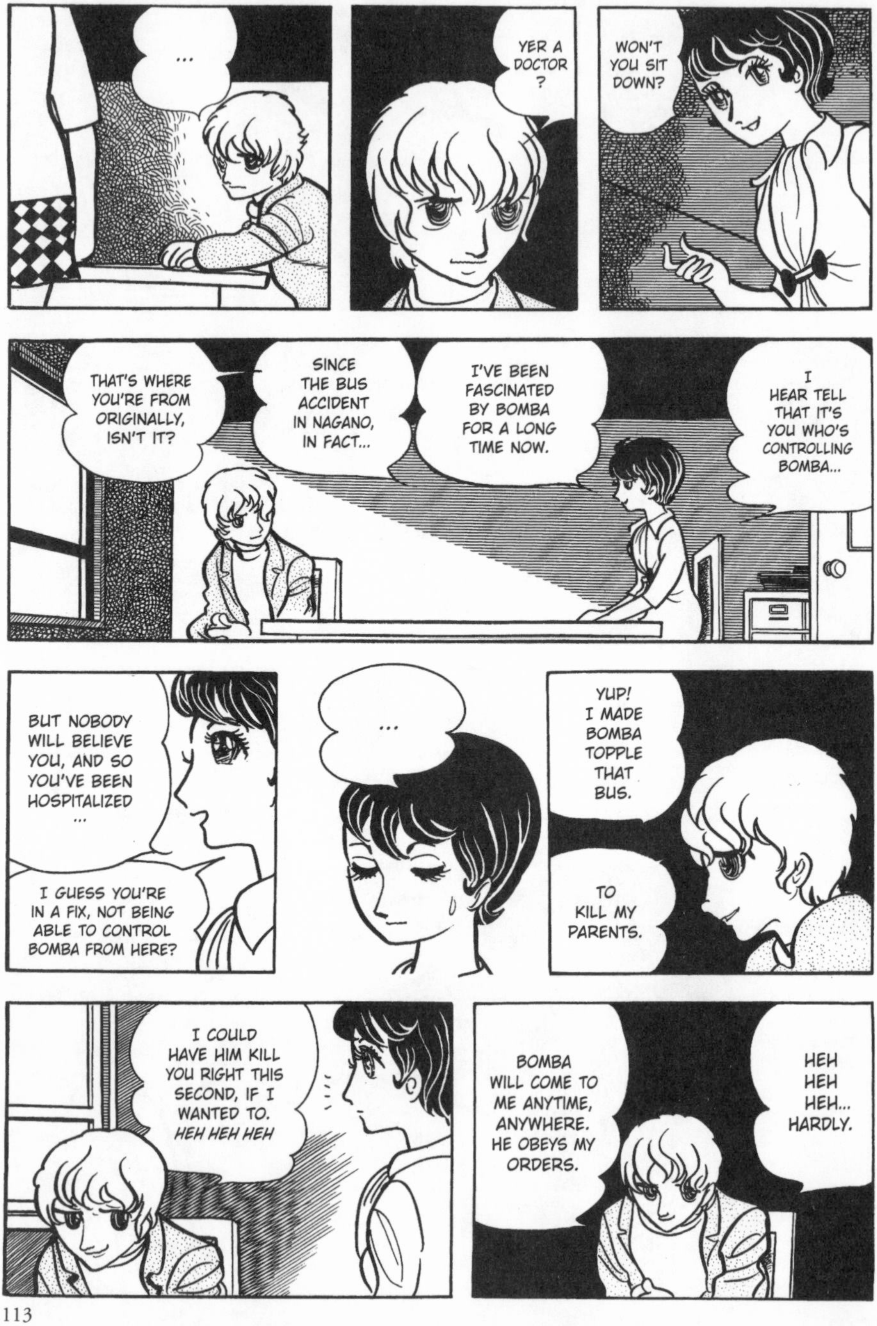
WON'T YOU SIT DOWN?
YER A DOCTOR ?
...
I HEAR TELL THAT IT'S YOU WHO'S CONTROLLING BOMBA...
I'VE BEEN FASCINATED BY BOMBA FOR A LONG TIME NOW.
SINCE THE BUS ACCIDENT IN NAGANO, IN FACT...
THAT'S WHERE YOU'RE FROM ORIGINALLY, ISN'T IT?
YUP! I MADE BOMBA TOPPLE THAT BUS.
TO KILL MY PARENTS.
...
BUT NOBODY WILL BELIEVE YOU, AND SO YOU'VE BEEN HOSPITALIZED ...
I GUESS YOU'RE IN A FIX, NOT BEING ABLE TO CONTROL BOMBA FROM HERE?
HEH HEH HEH... HARDLY.
BOMBA WILL COME TO ME ANYTIME, ANYWHERE. HE OBEYS MY ORDERS.
I COULD HAVE HIM KILL YOU RIGHT THIS SECOND, IF I WANTED TO. *HEH HEH HEH*

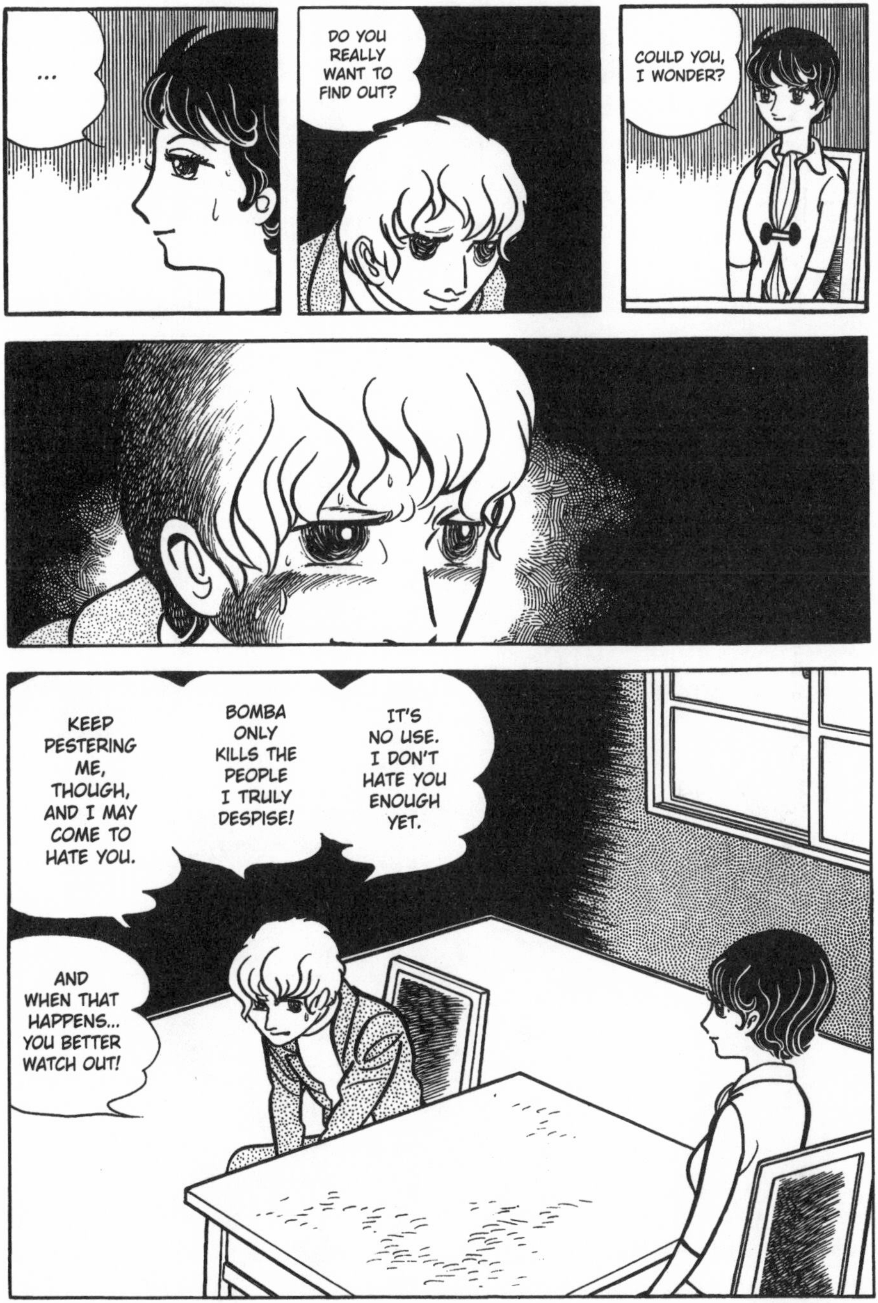
COULD YOU, I WONDER?
DO YOU REALLY WANT TO FIND OUT?
...
IT'S NO USE. I DON'T HATE YOU ENOUGH YET.
BOMBA ONLY KILLS THE PEOPLE I TRULY DESPISE!
KEEP PESTERING ME, THOUGH, AND I MAY COME TO HATE YOU.
AND WHEN THAT HAPPENS... YOU BETTER WATCH OUT!

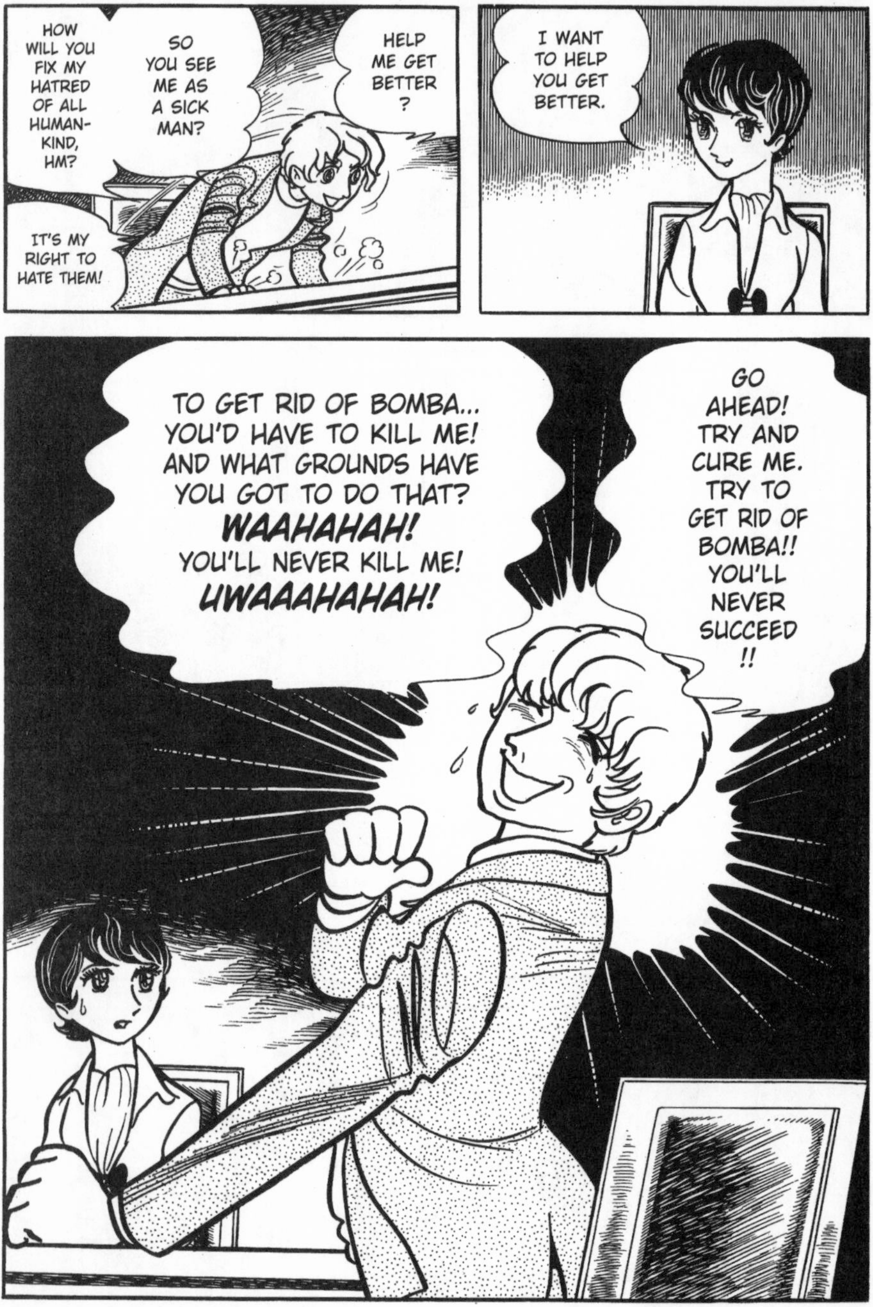
I WANT TO HELP YOU GET BETTER.
HELP ME GET BETTER?
SO YOU SEE ME AS A SICK MAN?
HOW WILL YOU FIX MY HATRED OF ALL HUMAN-KIND, HM?
IT'S MY RIGHT TO HATE THEM!
GO AHEAD! TRY AND CURE ME. TRY TO GET RID OF BOMBA!! YOU'LL NEVER SUCCEED!!
TO GET RID OF BOMBA... YOU'D HAVE TO KILL ME! AND WHAT GROUNDS HAVE YOU GOT TO DO THAT? WAAHAHAH! YOU'LL NEVER KILL ME! UWAAAHAHAH!

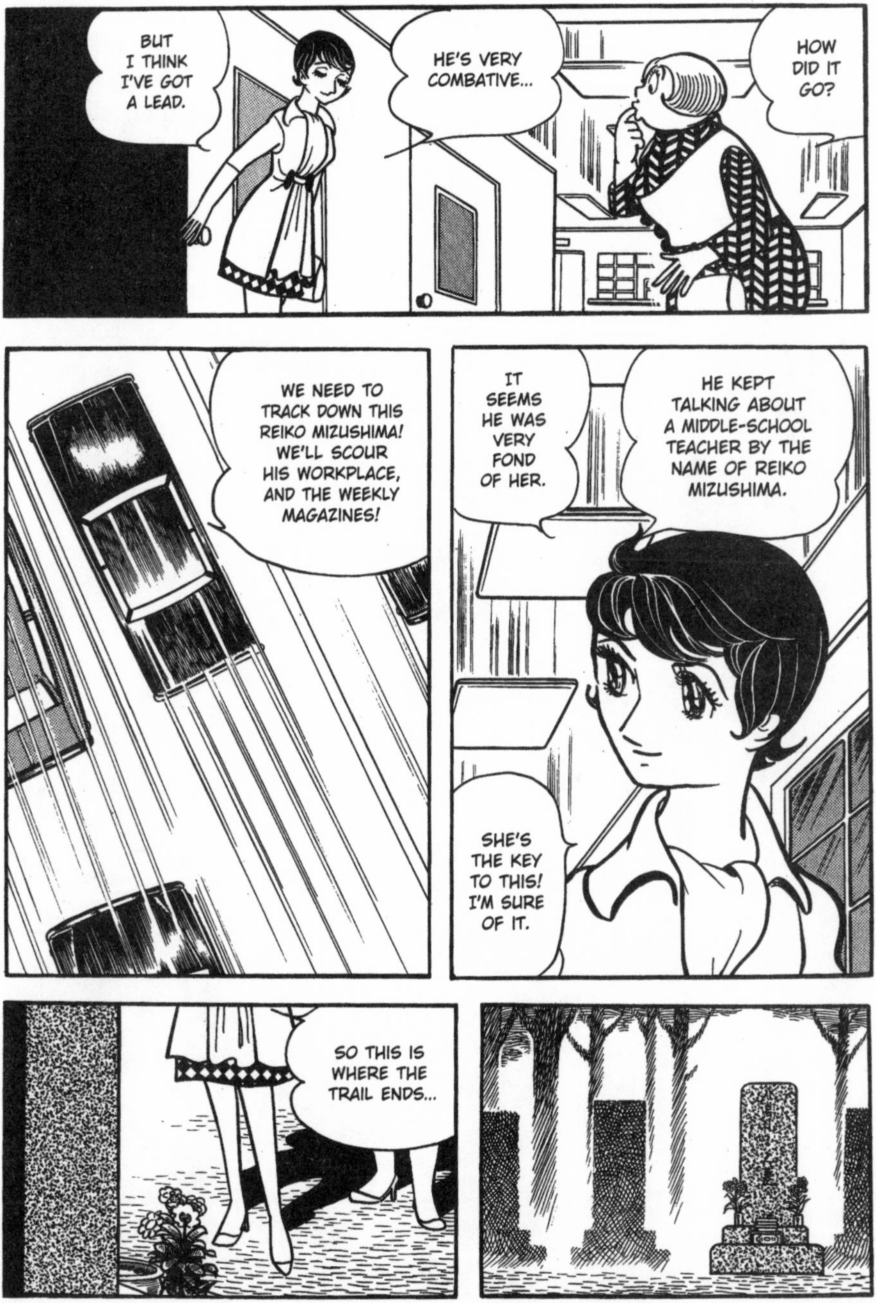
HOW DID IT GO?
HE'S VERY COMBATIVE...
BUT I THINK I'VE GOT A LEAD.
HE KEPT TALKING ABOUT A MIDDLE-SCHOOL TEACHER BY THE NAME OF REIKO MIZUSHIMA.
IT SEEMS HE WAS VERY FOND OF HER.
SHE'S THE KEY TO THIS! I'M SURE OF IT.
WE NEED TO TRACK DOWN THIS REIKO MIZUSHIMA! WE'LL SCOUR HIS WORKPLACE, AND THE WEEKLY MAGAZINES!
SO THIS IS WHERE THE TRAIL ENDS...

GRAVE: Reiko Mizushima

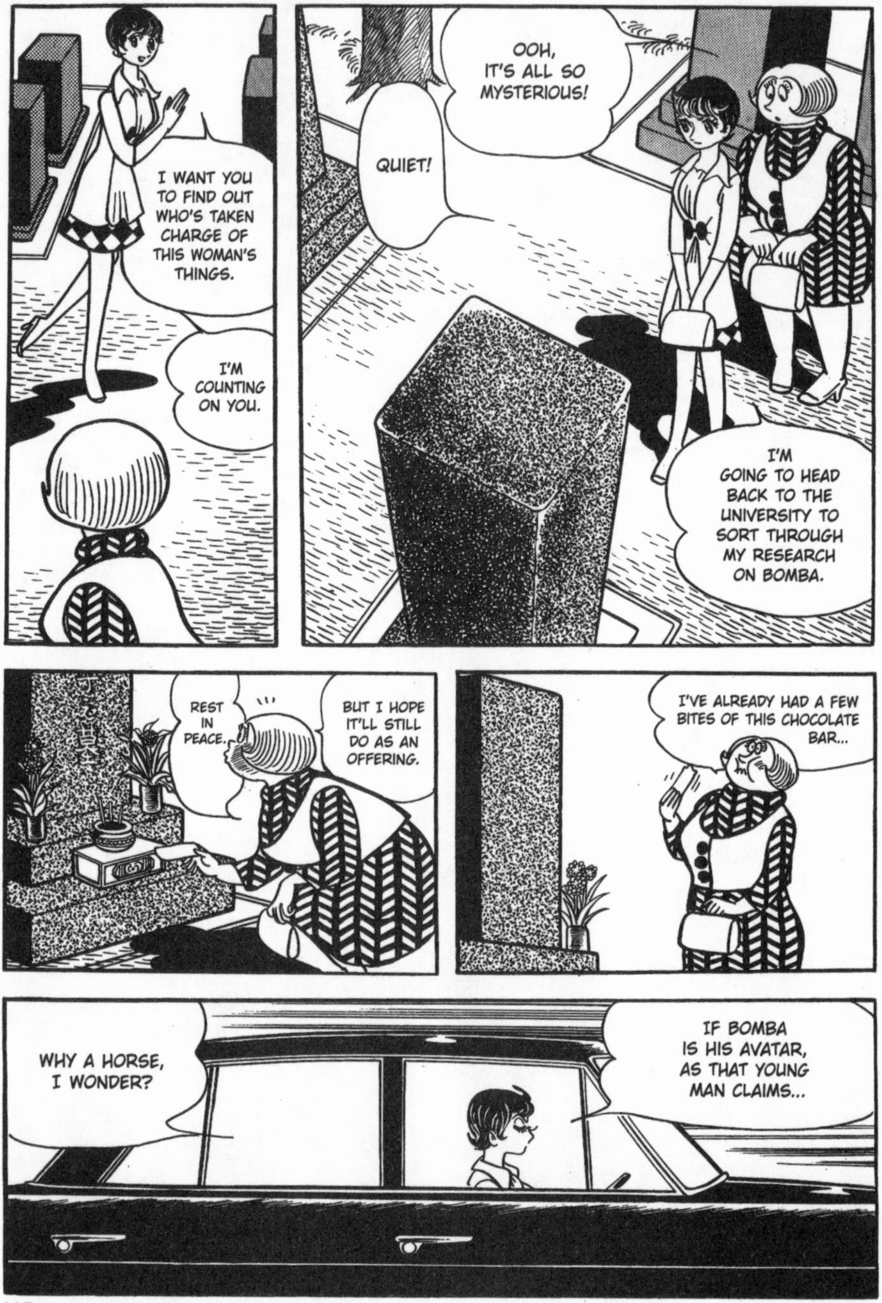
OOH, IT'S ALL SO MYSTERIOUS!
QUIET!
I'M GOING TO HEAD BACK TO THE UNIVERSITY TO SORT THROUGH MY RESEARCH ON BOMBA.
I WANT YOU TO FIND OUT WHO'S TAKEN CHARGE OF THIS WOMAN'S THINGS.
I'M COUNTING ON YOU.
I'VE ALREADY HAD A FEW BITES OF THIS CHOCOLATE BAR...
BUT I HOPE IT'LL STILL DO AS AN OFFERING.
REST IN PEACE.
IF BOMBA IS HIS AVATAR, AS THAT YOUNG MAN CLAIMS...
WHY A HORSE, I WONDER?

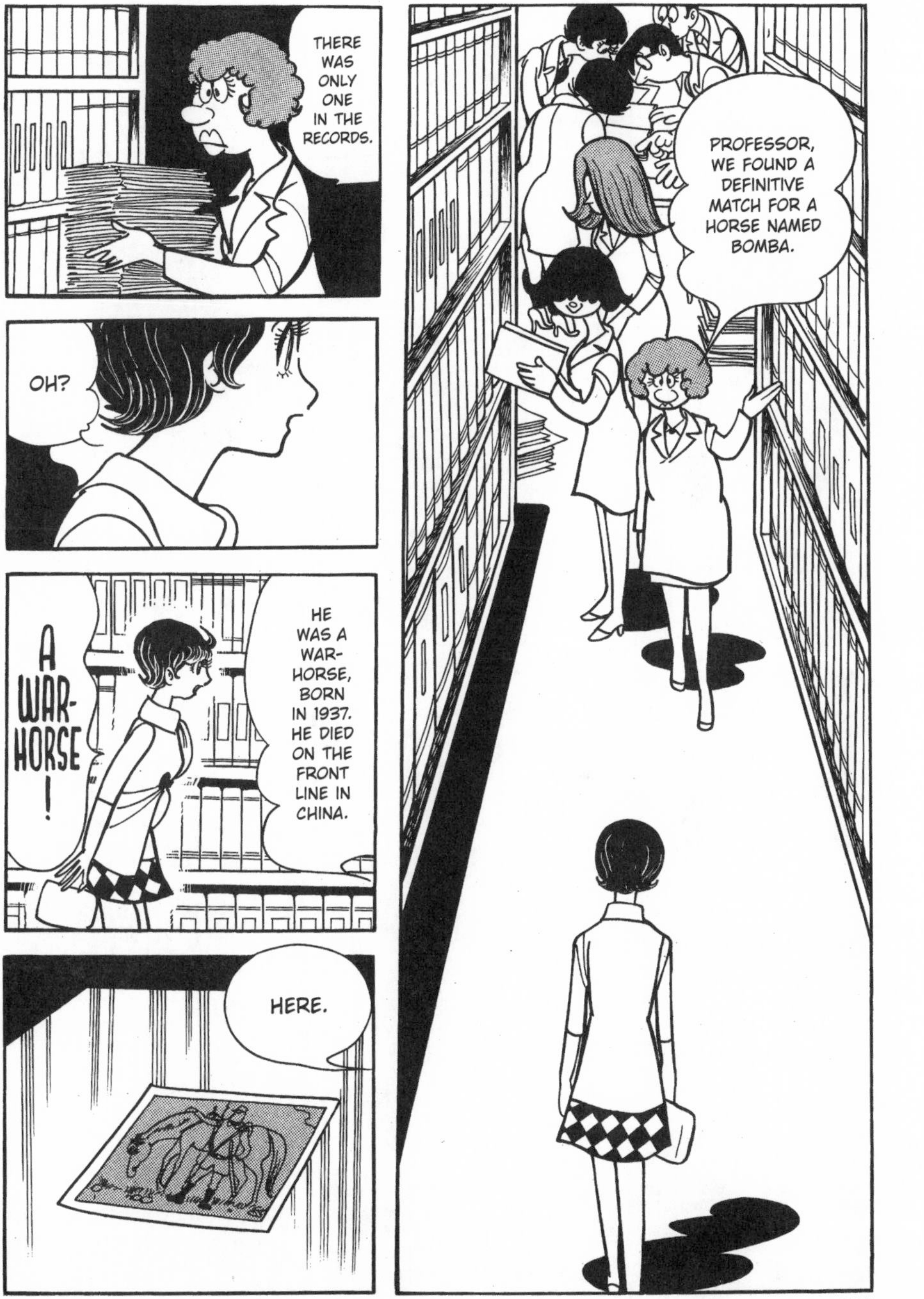
PROFESSOR, WE FOUND A DEFINITIVE MATCH FOR A HORSE NAMED BOMBA.
THERE WAS ONLY ONE IN THE RECORDS.
OH?
HE WAS A WAR-HORSE, BORN IN 1937. HE DIED ON THE FRONT LINE IN CHINA.
A WAR-HORSE!
HERE.

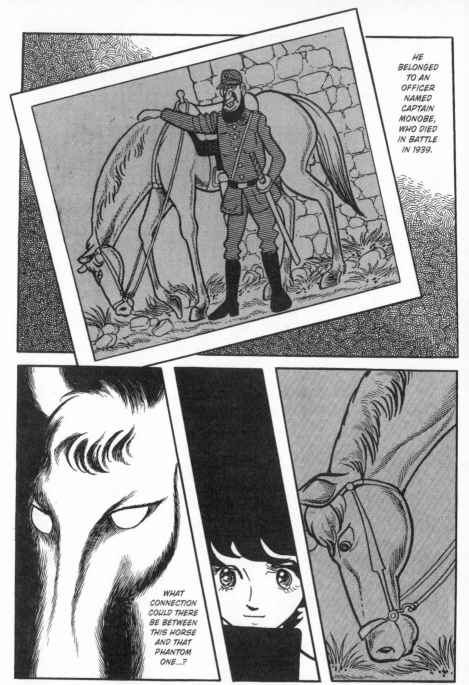

HE BELONGED TO AN OFFICER NAMED CAPTAIN MONOBE, WHO DIED IN BATTLE IN 1939.

WHAT CONNECTION COULD THERE BE BETWEEN THIS HORSE AND THAT PHANTOM ONE...?

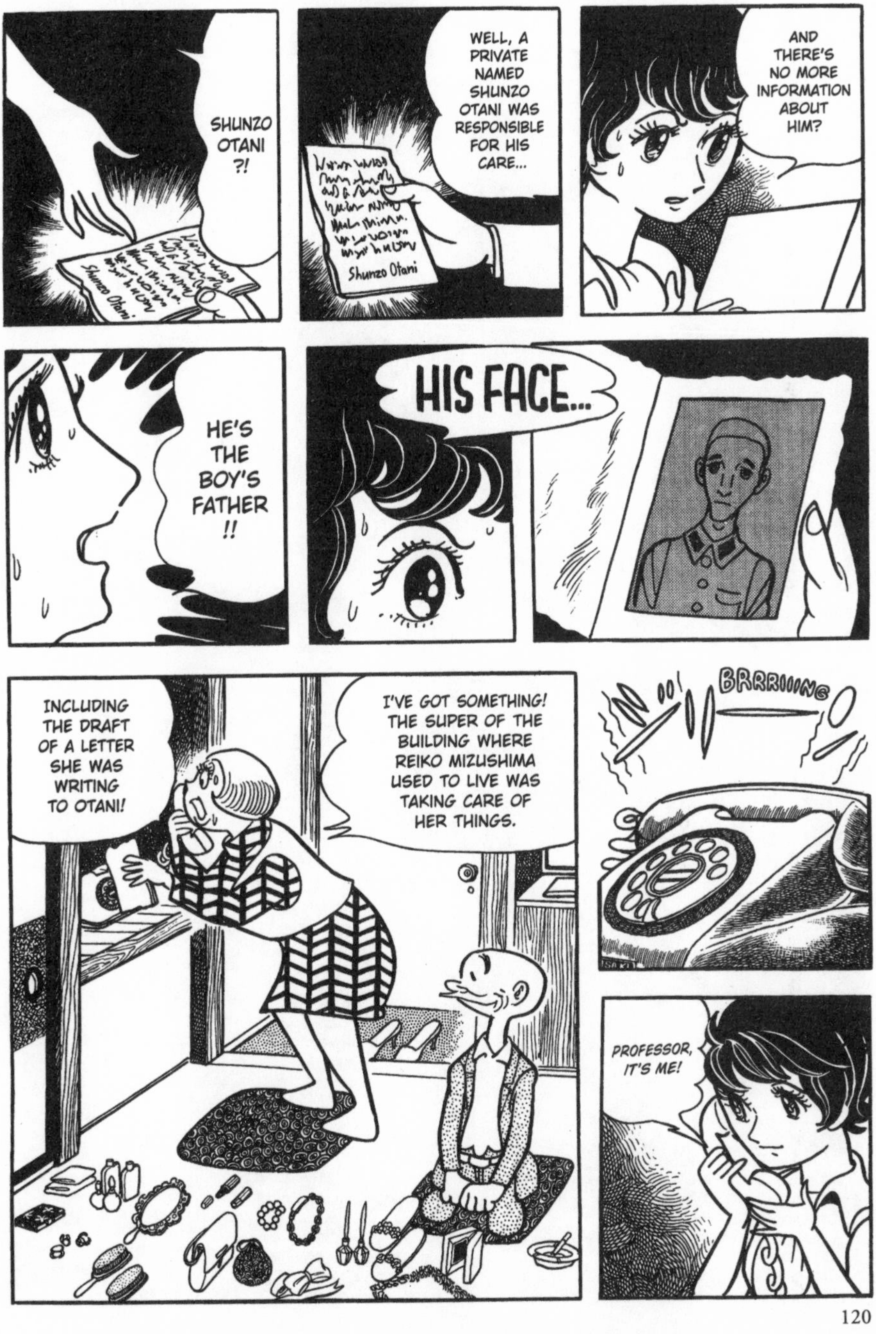
AND THERE'S NO MORE INFORMATION ABOUT HIM?
WELL, A PRIVATE NAMED SHUNZO OTANI WAS RESPONSIBLE FOR HIS CARE...
Shunzo Otani
SHUNZO OTANI ?!
Shunzo Otani
HIS FACE...
HE'S THE BOY'S FATHER !!
BRRRIIING
PROFESSOR, IT'S ME!
I'VE GOT SOMETHING! THE SUPER OF THE BUILDING WHERE REIKO MIZUSHIMA USED TO LIVE WAS TAKING CARE OF HER THINGS.
INCLUDING THE DRAFT OF A LETTER SHE WAS WRITING TO OTANI!

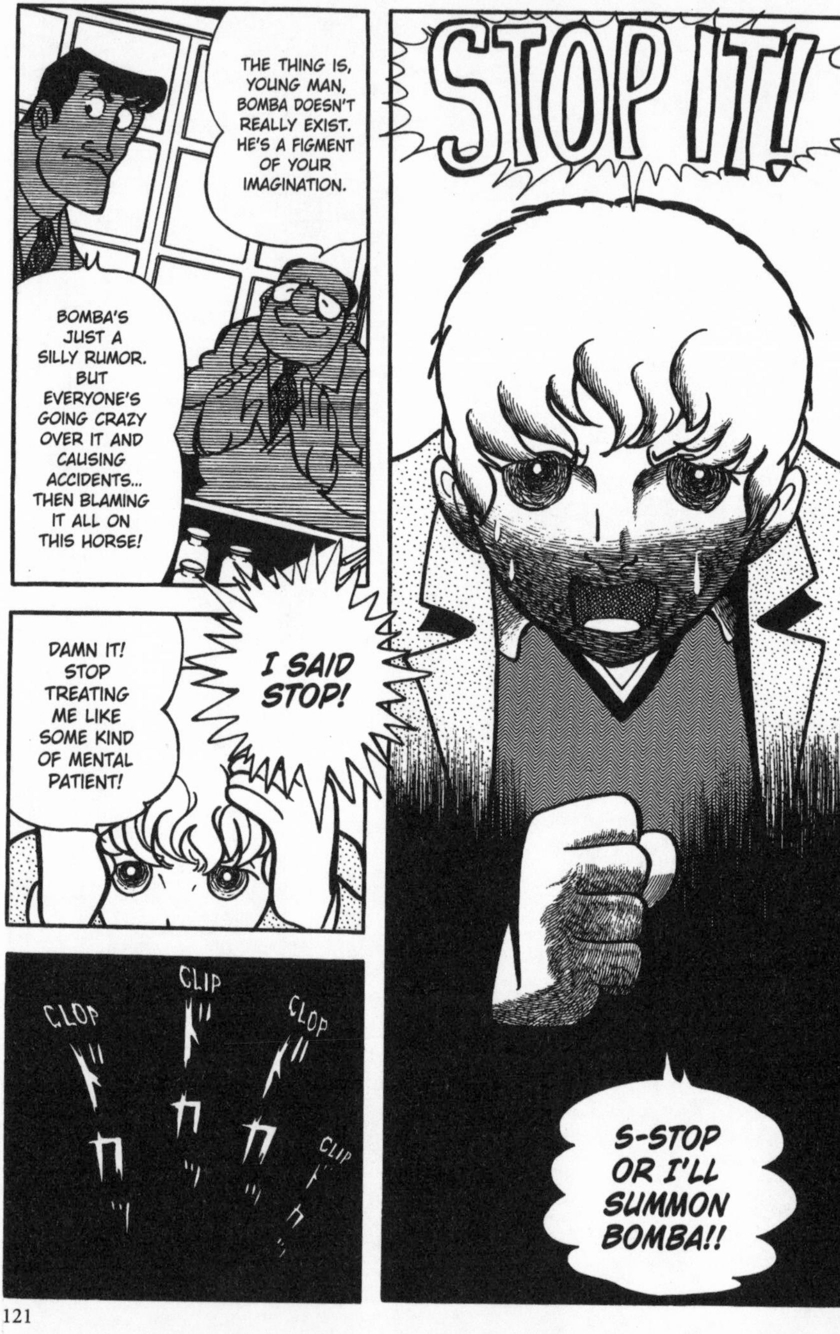
STOP IT!
S-STOP OR I'LL SUMMON BOMBA!!
THE THING IS, YOUNG MAN, BOMBA DOESN'T REALLY EXIST. HE'S A FIGMENT OF YOUR IMAGINATION.
BOMBA'S JUST A SILLY RUMOR. BUT EVERYONE'S GOING CRAZY OVER IT AND CAUSING ACCIDENTS... THEN BLAMING IT ALL ON THIS HORSE!
I SAID STOP!
DAMN IT! STOP TREATING ME LIKE SOME KIND OF MENTAL PATIENT!
CLOP
CLIP
CLOP
CLIP

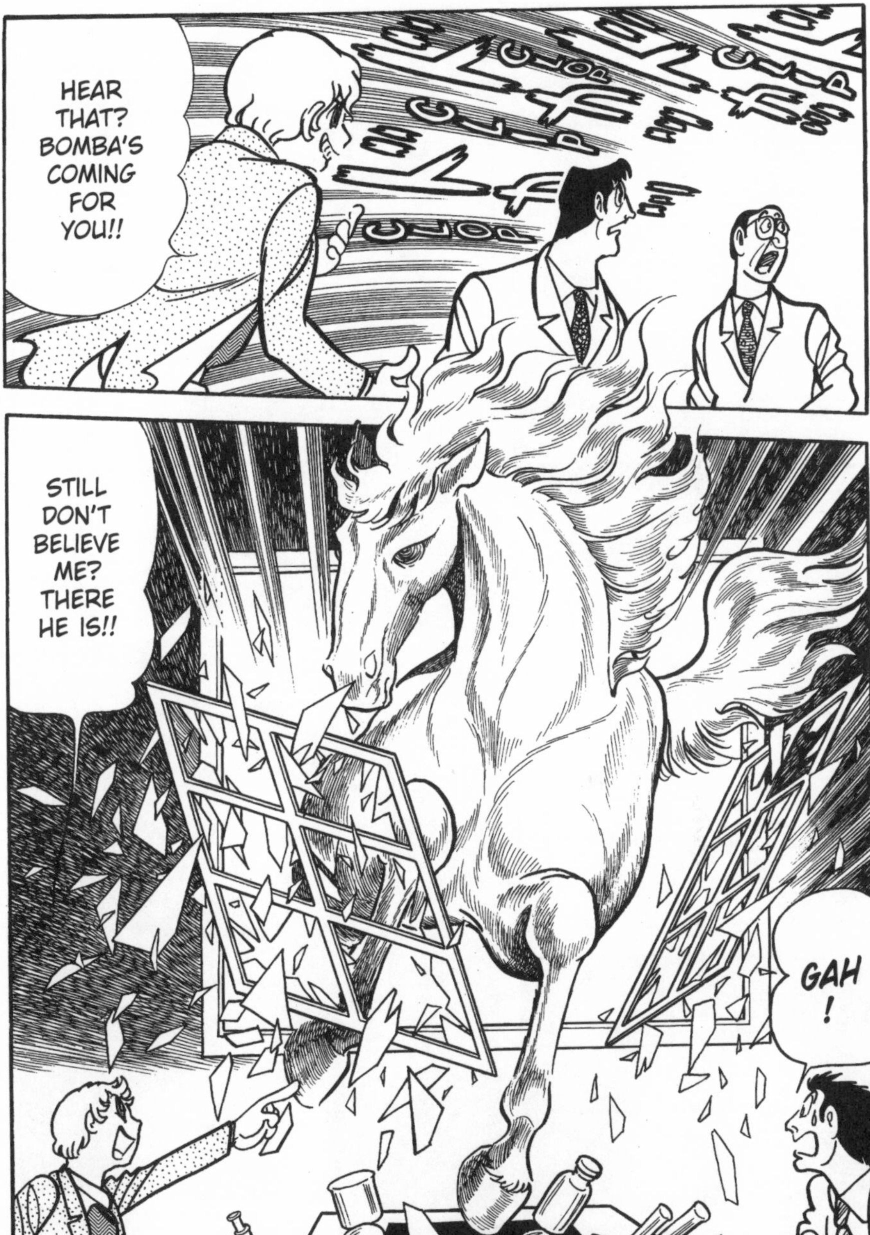
HEAR THAT? BOMBA'S COMING FOR YOU!!
STILL DON'T BELIEVE ME? THERE HE IS!!
GAH!

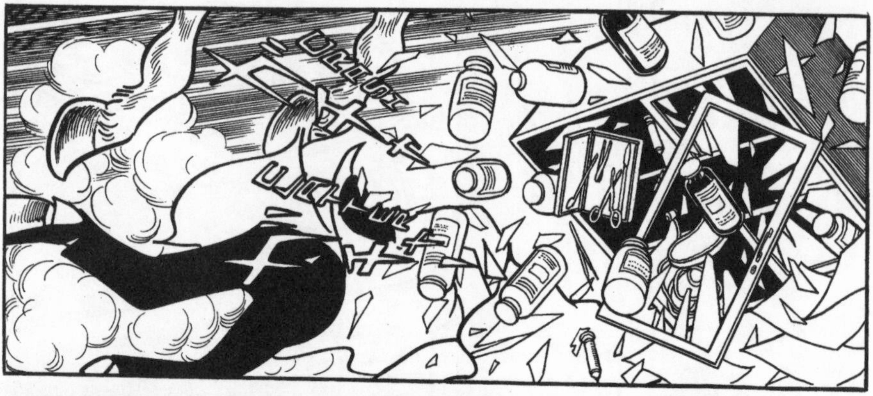

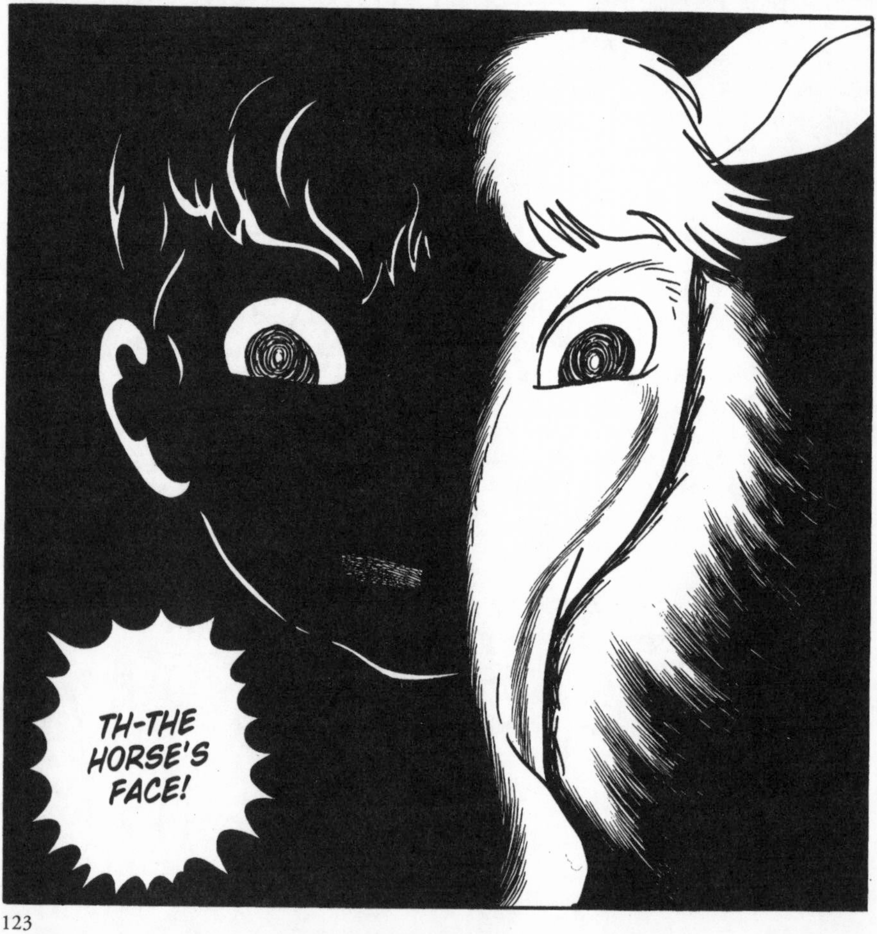
TH-THE HORSE'S FACE!

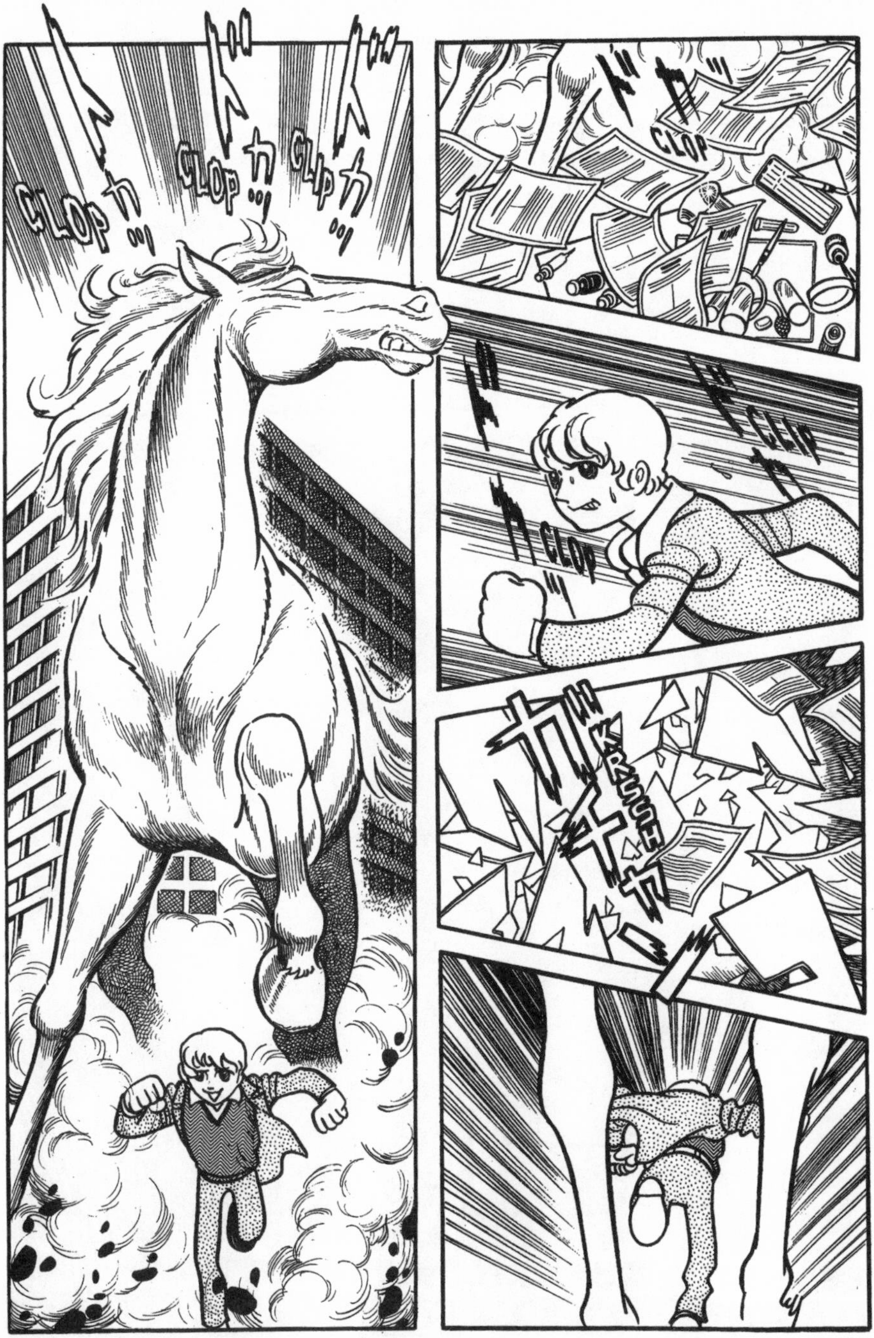
CLOP
CLIP
CLOP
KRUSCH
CLIP
CLOP
CLOP

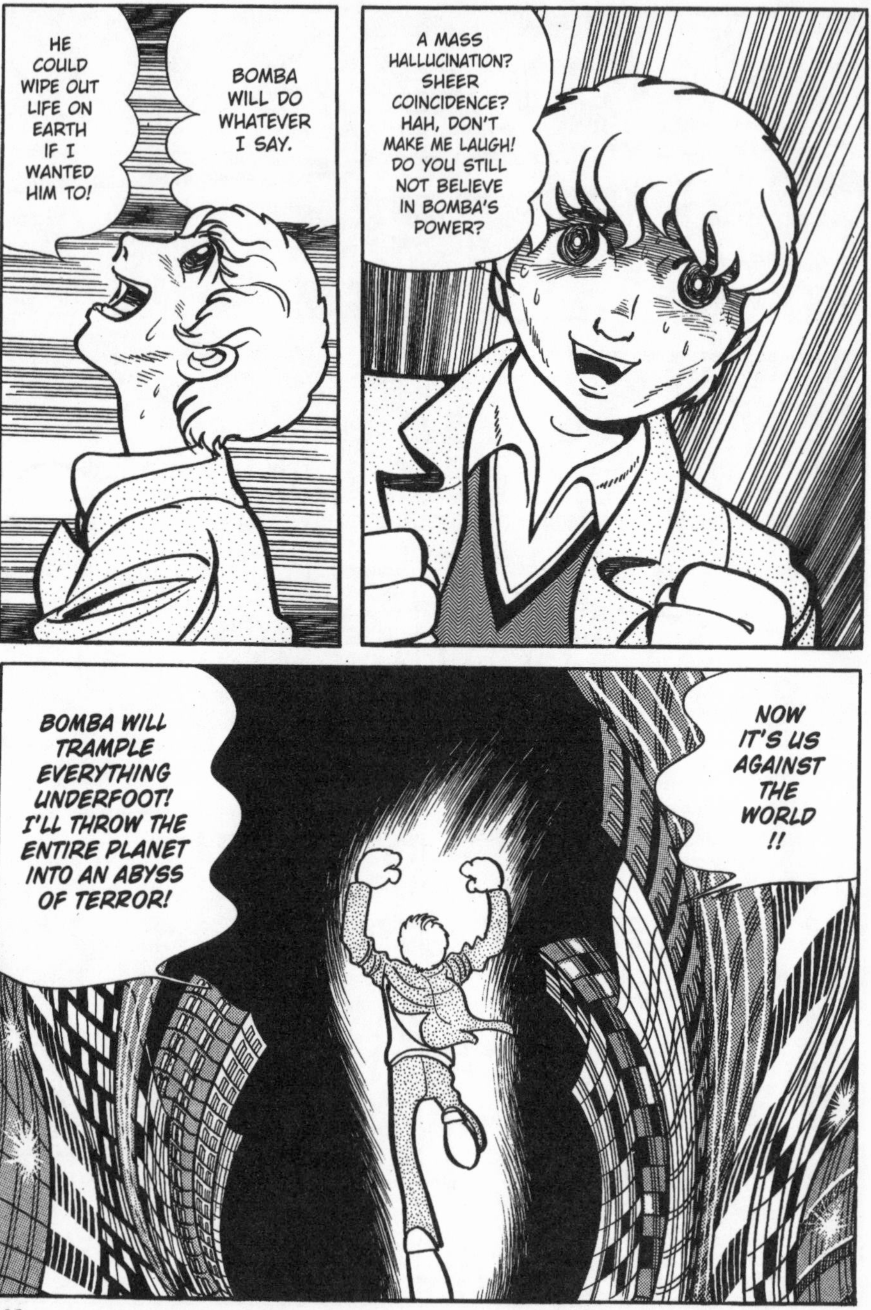
A MASS HALLUCINATION? SHEER COINCIDENCE? HAH, DON'T MAKE ME LAUGH! DO YOU STILL NOT BELIEVE IN BOMBA'S POWER?
BOMBA WILL DO WHATEVER I SAY.
HE COULD WIPE OUT LIFE ON EARTH IF I WANTED HIM TO!
NOW IT'S US AGAINST THE WORLD !!
BOMBA WILL TRAMPLE EVERYTHING UNDERFOOT! I'LL THROW THE ENTIRE PLANET INTO AN ABYSS OF TERROR!

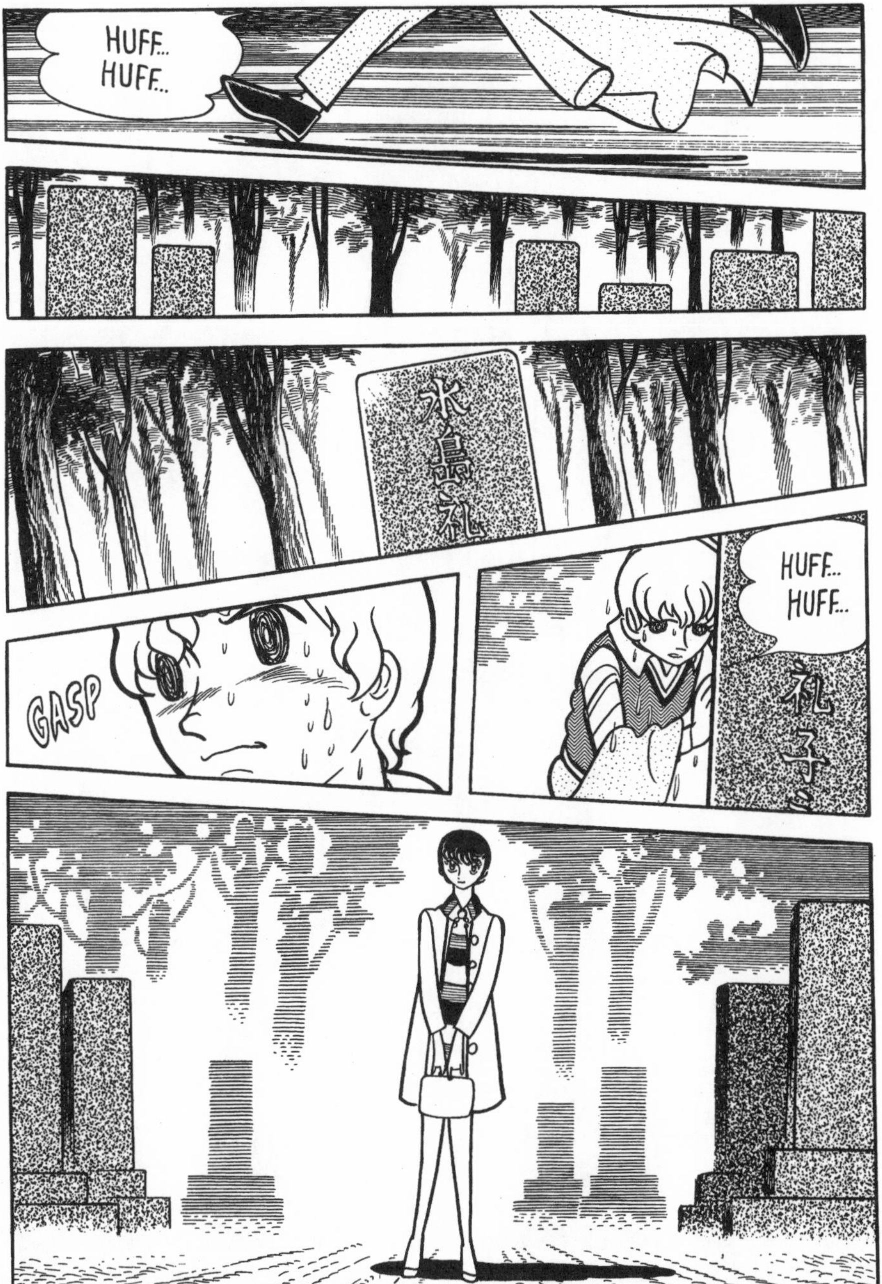
HUFF... HUFF...
水島礼
HUFF... HUFF...
礼子
GASP

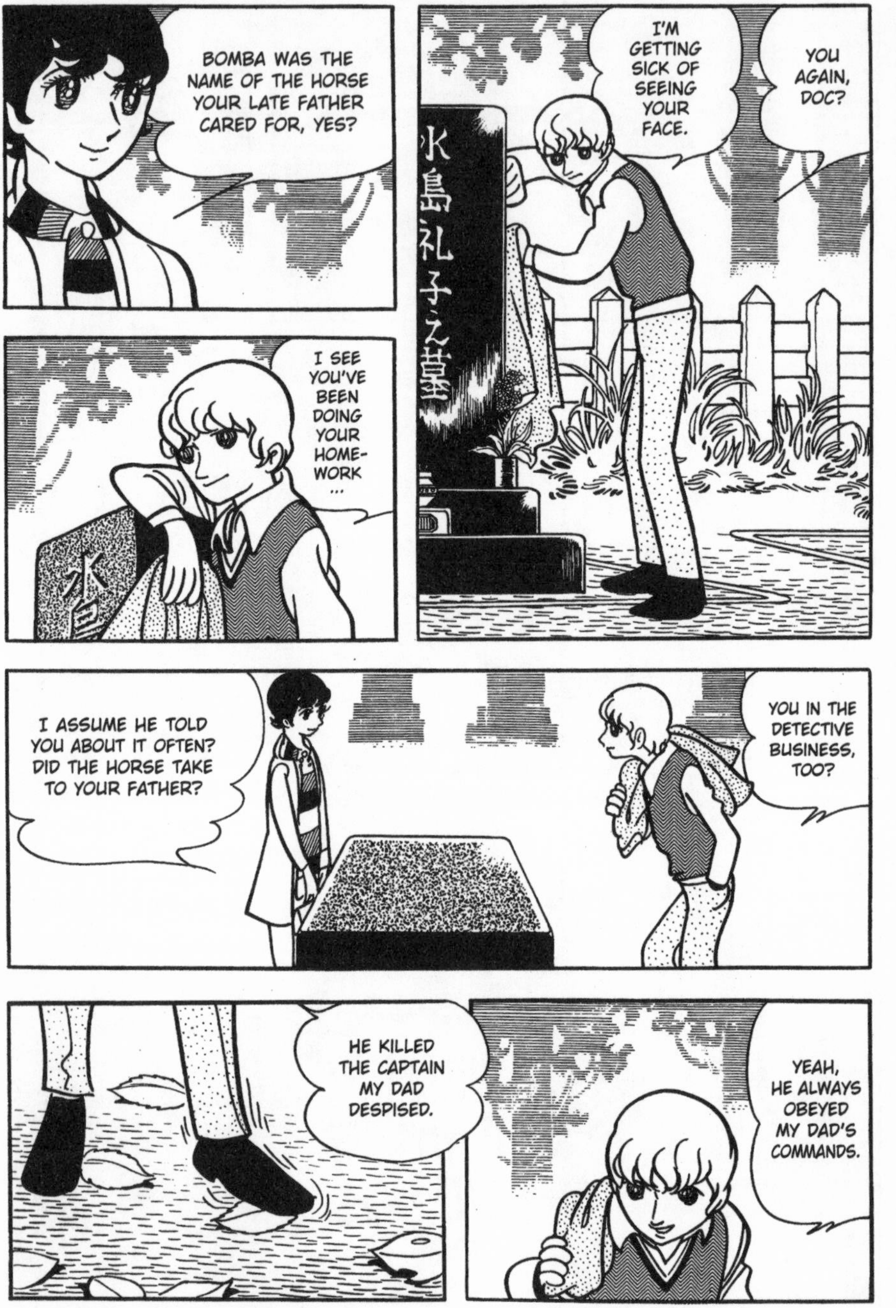
YOU AGAIN, DOC?
I'M GETTING SICK OF SEEING YOUR FACE.
水島礼子之墓
BOMBA WAS THE NAME OF THE HORSE YOUR LATE FATHER CARED FOR, YES?
I SEE YOU'VE BEEN DOING YOUR HOME-WORK ...
YOU IN THE DETECTIVE BUSINESS, TOO?
I ASSUME HE TOLD YOU ABOUT IT OFTEN? DID THE HORSE TAKE TO YOUR FATHER?
YEAH, HE ALWAYS OBEYED MY DAD'S COMMANDS.
HE KILLED THE CAPTAIN MY DAD DESPISED.

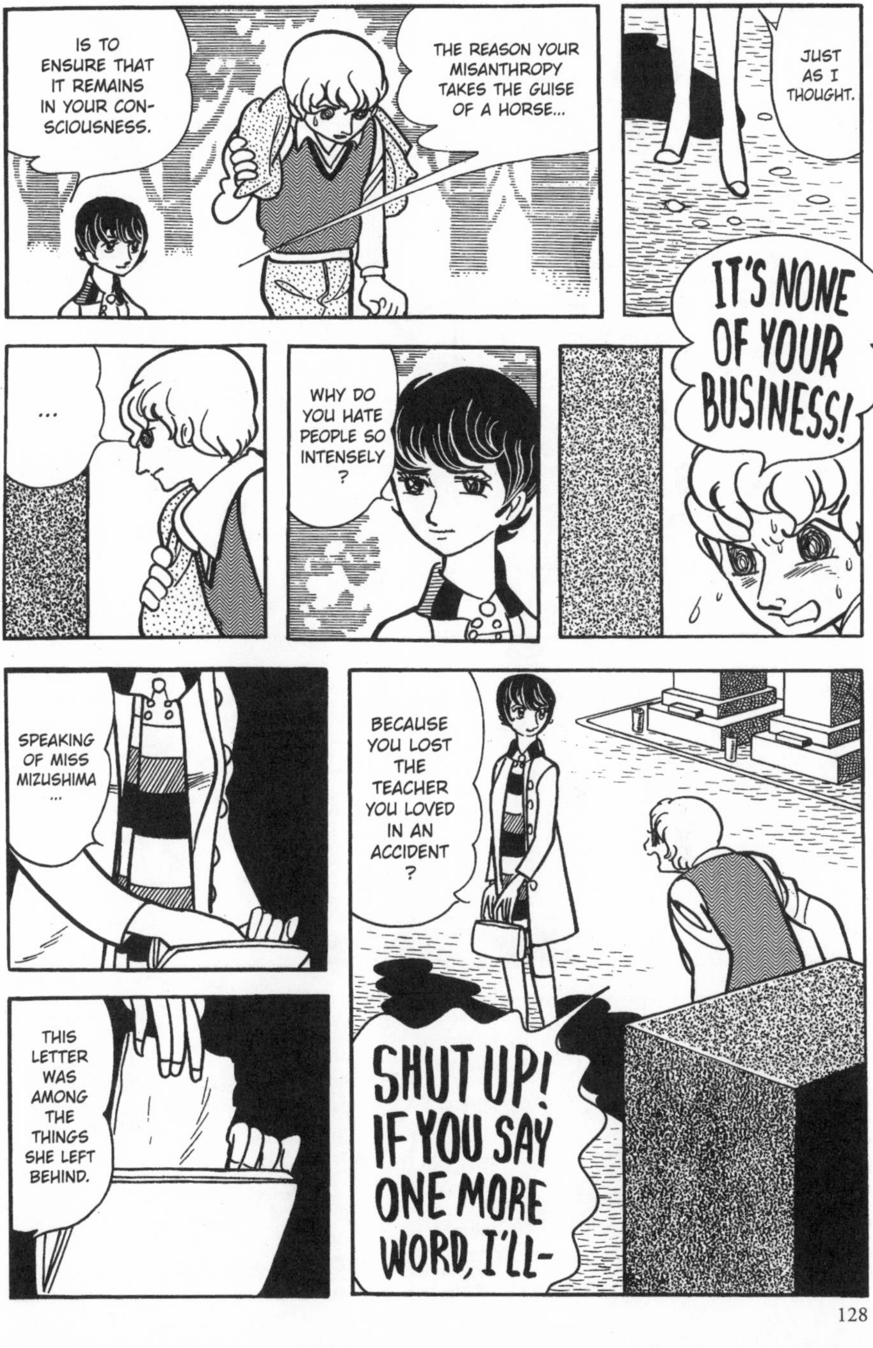
JUST AS I THOUGHT.
THE REASON YOUR MISANTHROPY TAKES THE GUISE OF A HORSE...
IS TO ENSURE THAT IT REMAINS IN YOUR CON-SCIOUSNESS.
IT'S NONE OF YOUR BUSINESS!
WHY DO YOU HATE PEOPLE SO INTENSELY?
...
BECAUSE YOU LOST THE TEACHER YOU LOVED IN AN ACCIDENT?
SHUT UP! IF YOU SAY ONE MORE WORD, I'LL-
SPEAKING OF MISS MIZUSHIMA...
THIS LETTER WAS AMONG THE THINGS SHE LEFT BEHIND.

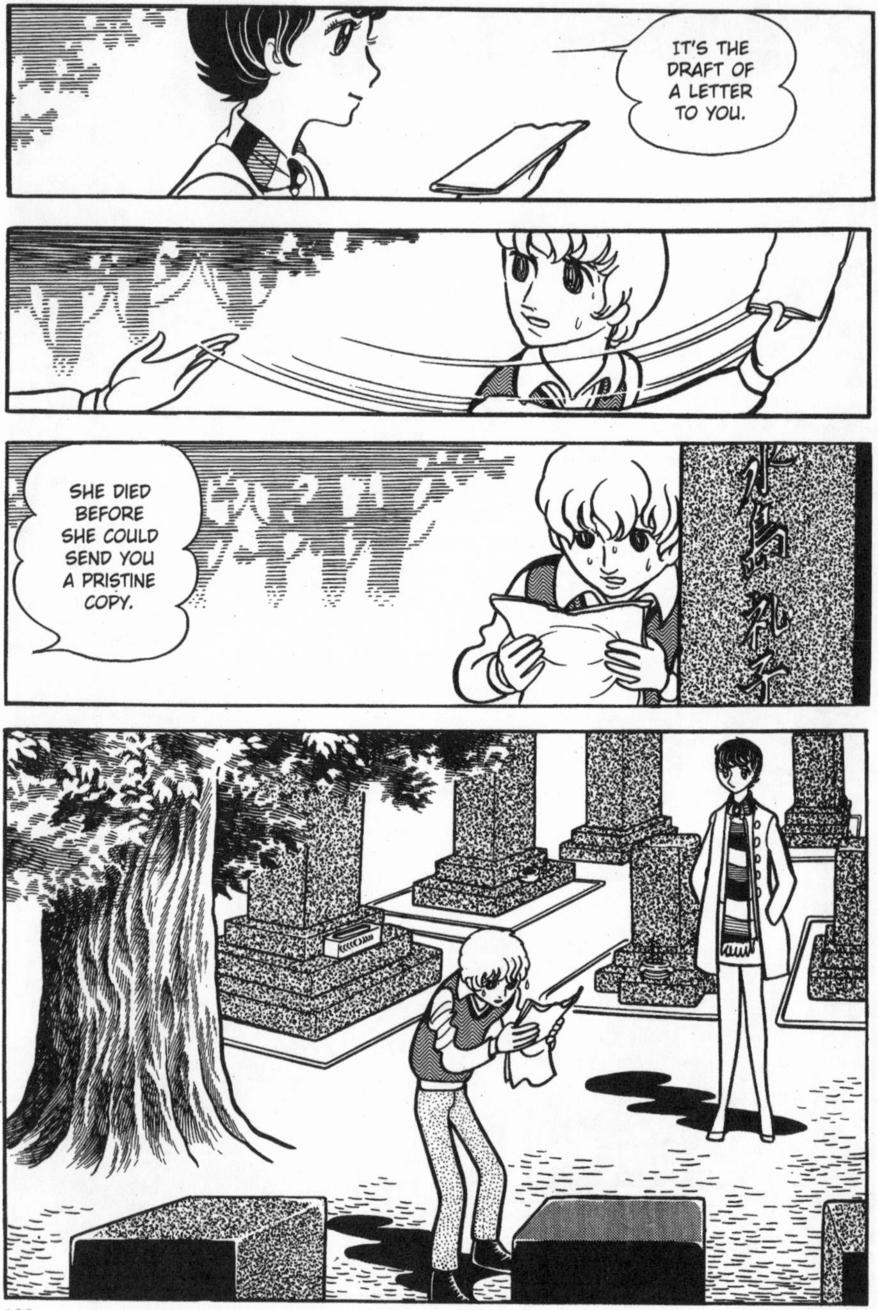
IT'S THE DRAFT OF A LETTER TO YOU.
SHE DIED BEFORE SHE COULD SEND YOU A PRISTINE COPY.

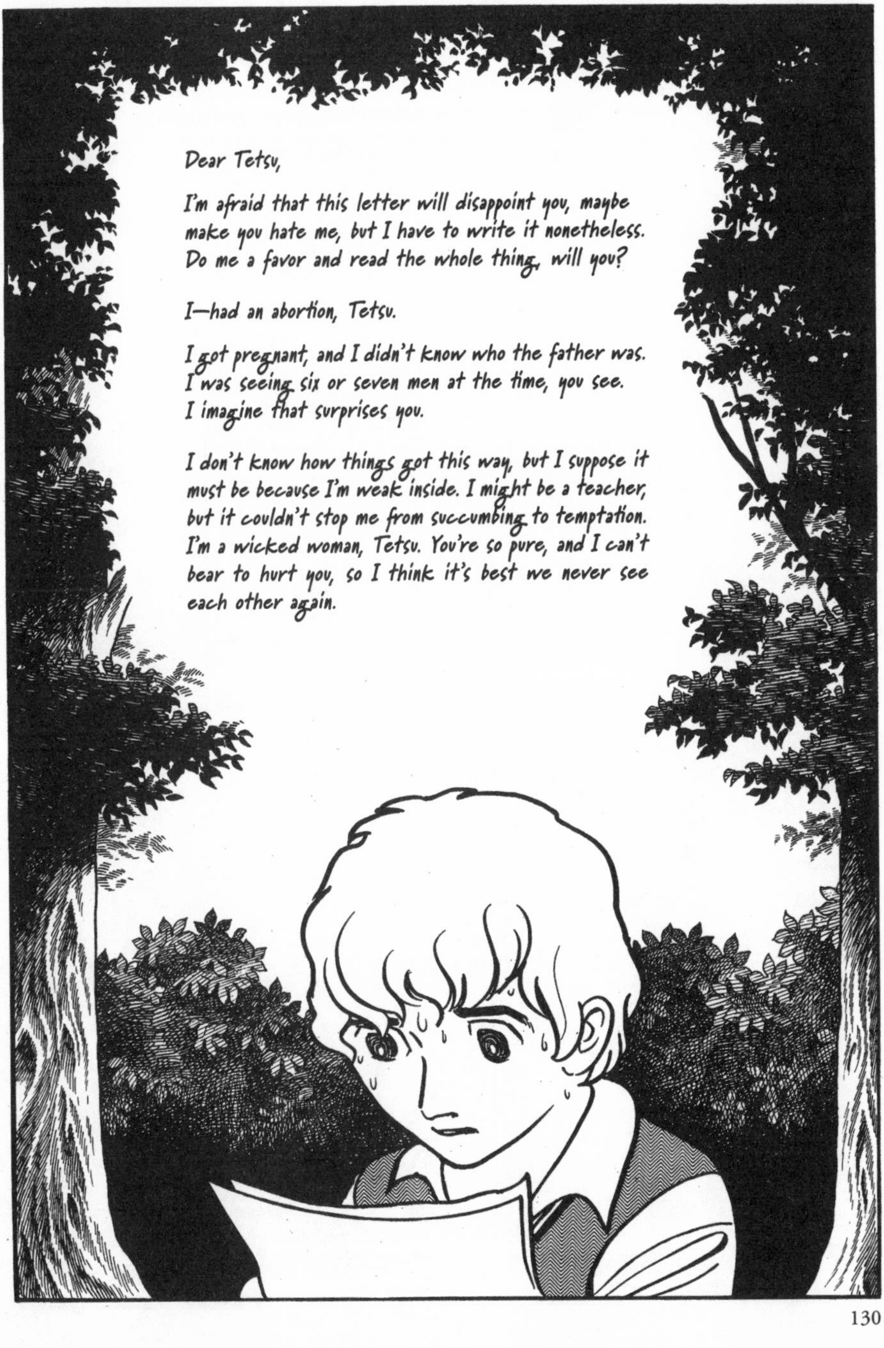
Dear Tetsu,
I'm afraid that this letter will disappoint you, maybe make you hate me, but I have to write it nonetheless. Do me a favor and read the whole thing, will you?
I—had an abortion, Tetsu.
I got pregnant, and I didn't know who the father was. I was seeing six or seven men at the time, you see. I imagine that surprises you.
I don't know how things got this way, but I suppose it must be because I'm weak inside. I might be a teacher, but it couldn't stop me from succumbing to temptation. I'm a wicked woman, Tetsu. You're so pure, and I can't bear to hurt you, so I think it's best we never see each other again.

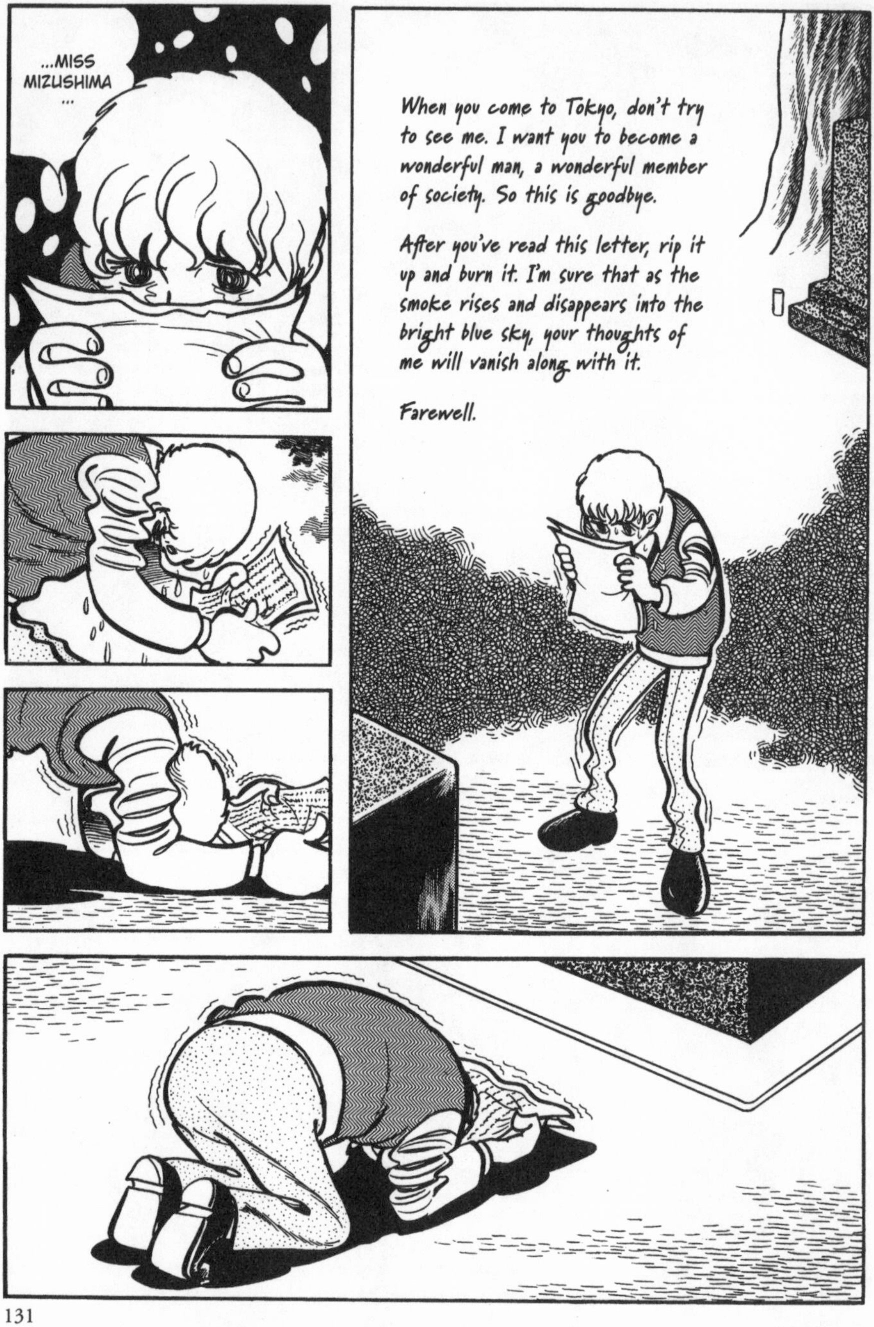
When you come to Tokyo, don't try to see me. I want you to become a wonderful man, a wonderful member of society. So this is goodbye.
After you've read this letter, rip it up and burn it. I'm sure that as the smoke rises and disappears into the bright blue sky, your thoughts of me will vanish along with it.
Farewell.
...MISS MIZUSHIMA ...

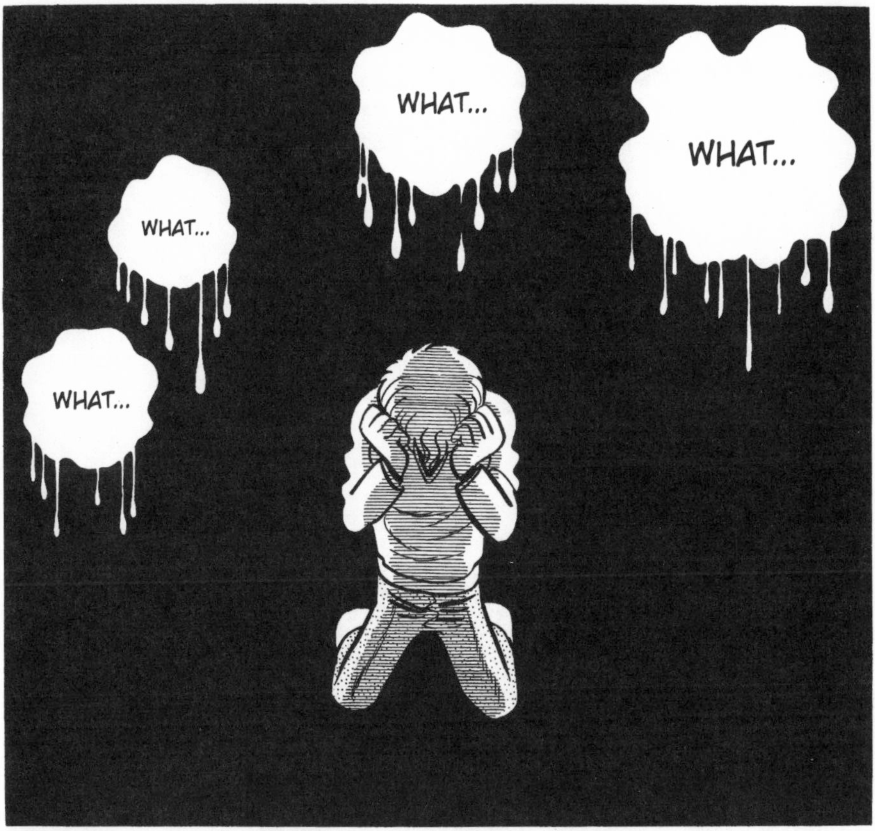
WHAT...
WHAT...
WHAT...
WHAT...
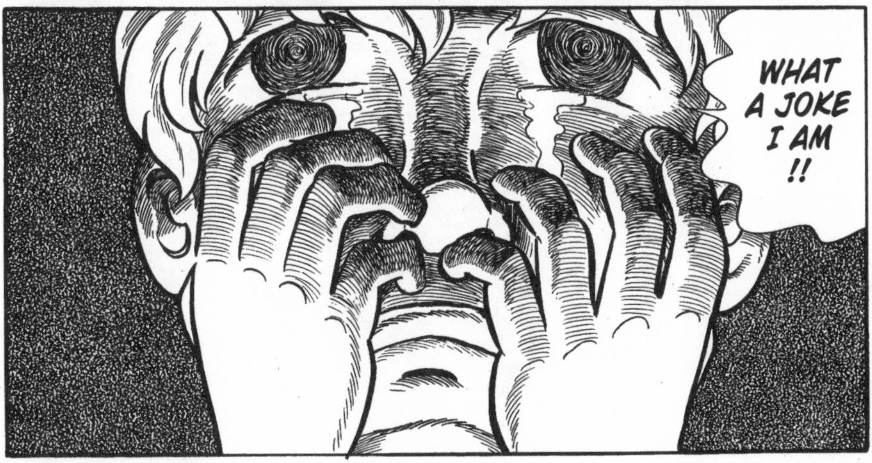
WHAT A JOKE I AM !!

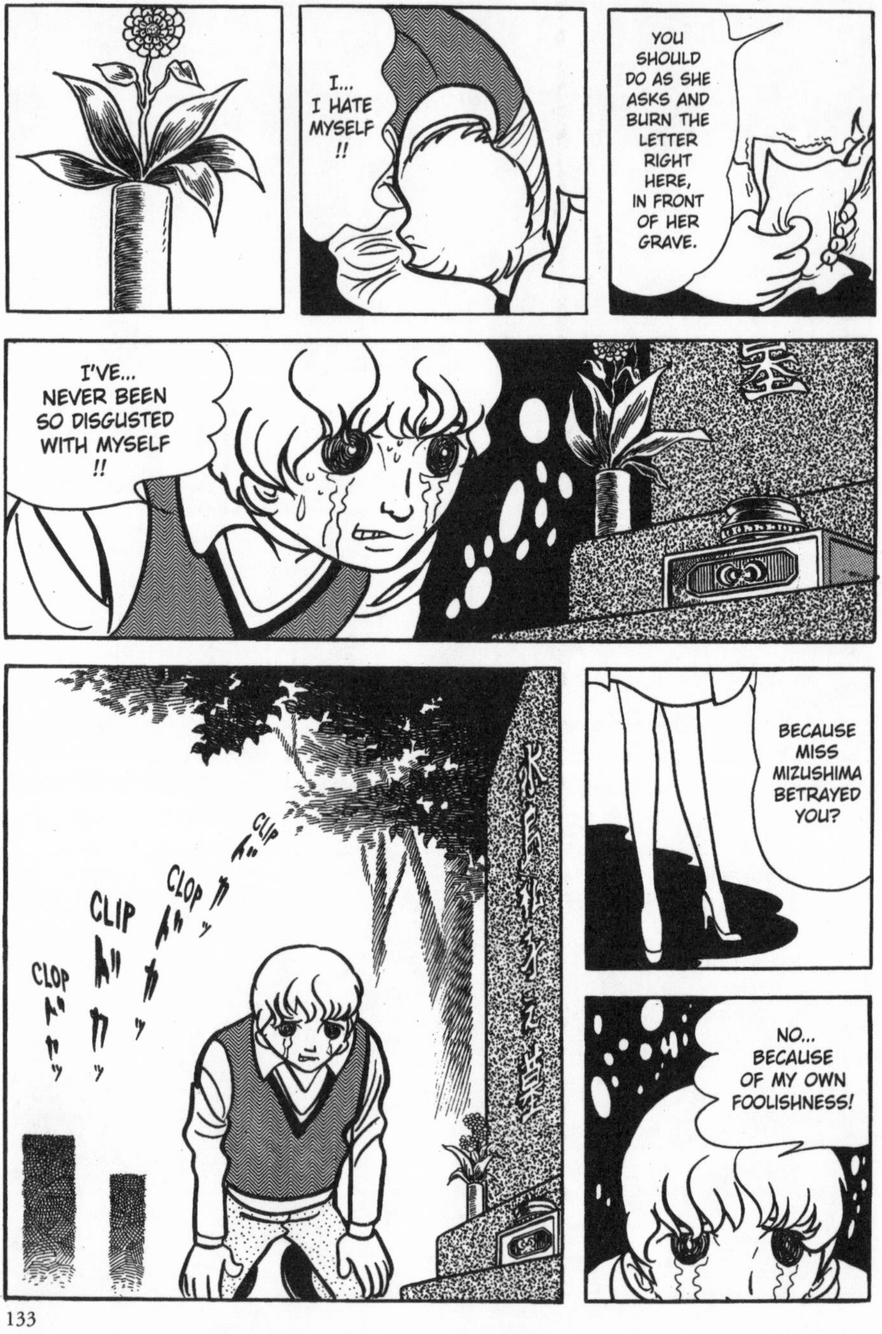
YOU SHOULD DO AS SHE ASKS AND BURN THE LETTER RIGHT HERE, IN FRONT OF HER GRAVE.
I... I HATE MYSELF!!
I'VE... NEVER BEEN SO DISGUSTED WITH MYSELF!!
BECAUSE MISS MIZUSHIMA BETRAYED YOU?
NO... BECAUSE OF MY OWN FOOLISHNESS!
CLIP
CLOP
CLIP
CLOP

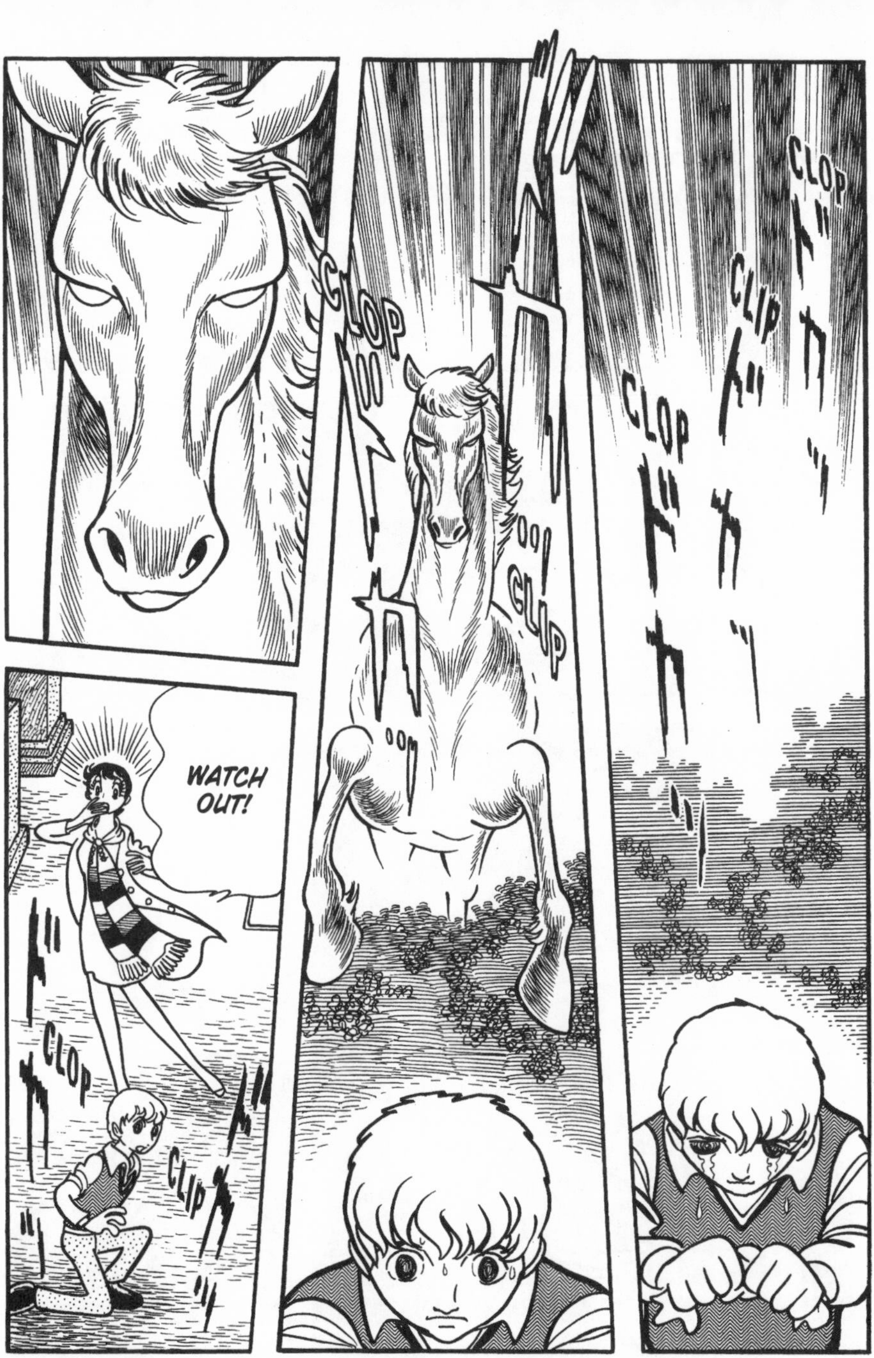
CLOP
CLIP
CLOP
CLOP
CLIP
WATCH OUT!
CLOP
CLIP

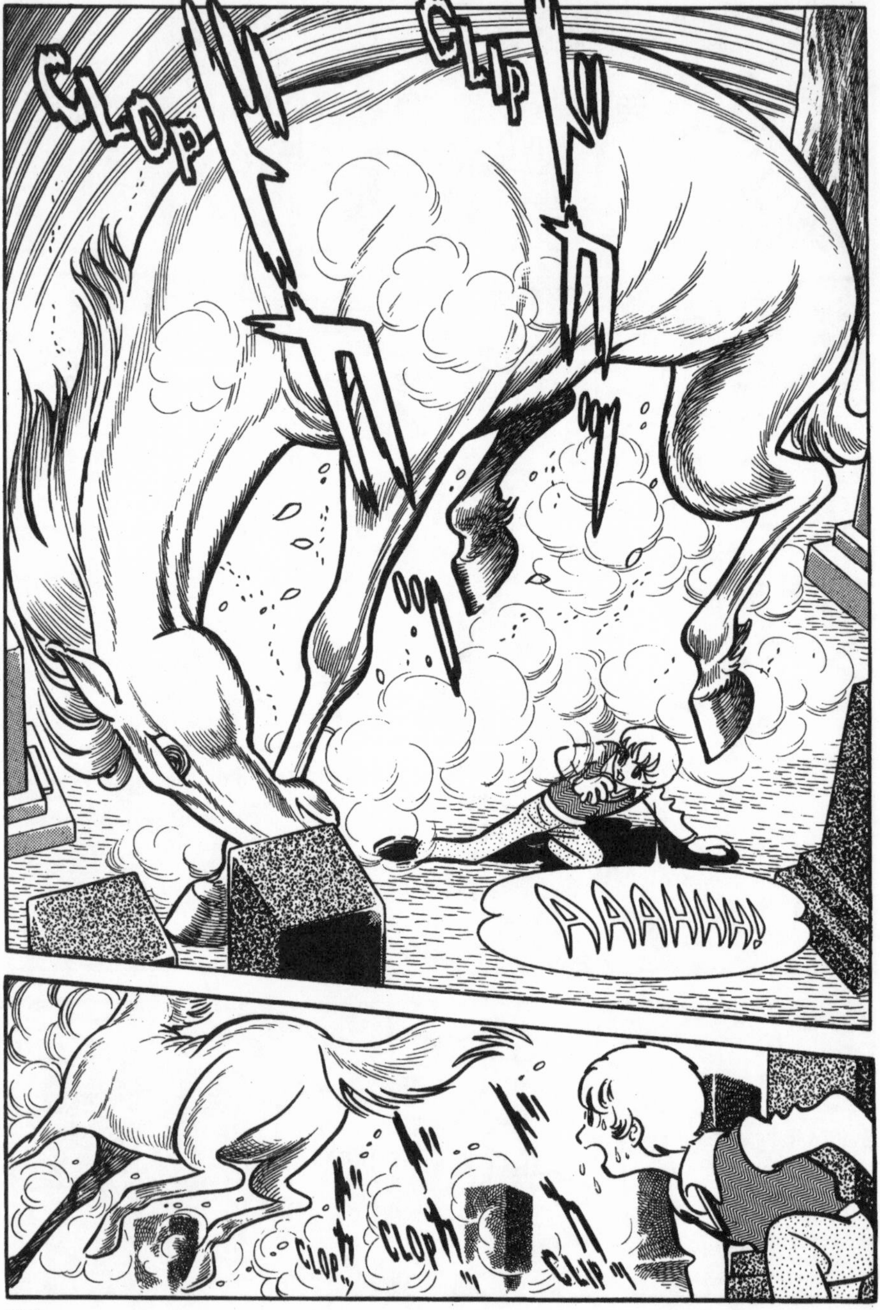
CLIP!!
CLOP!!
AAAHHH!
CLIP!!
CLOP!!
CLOP!!

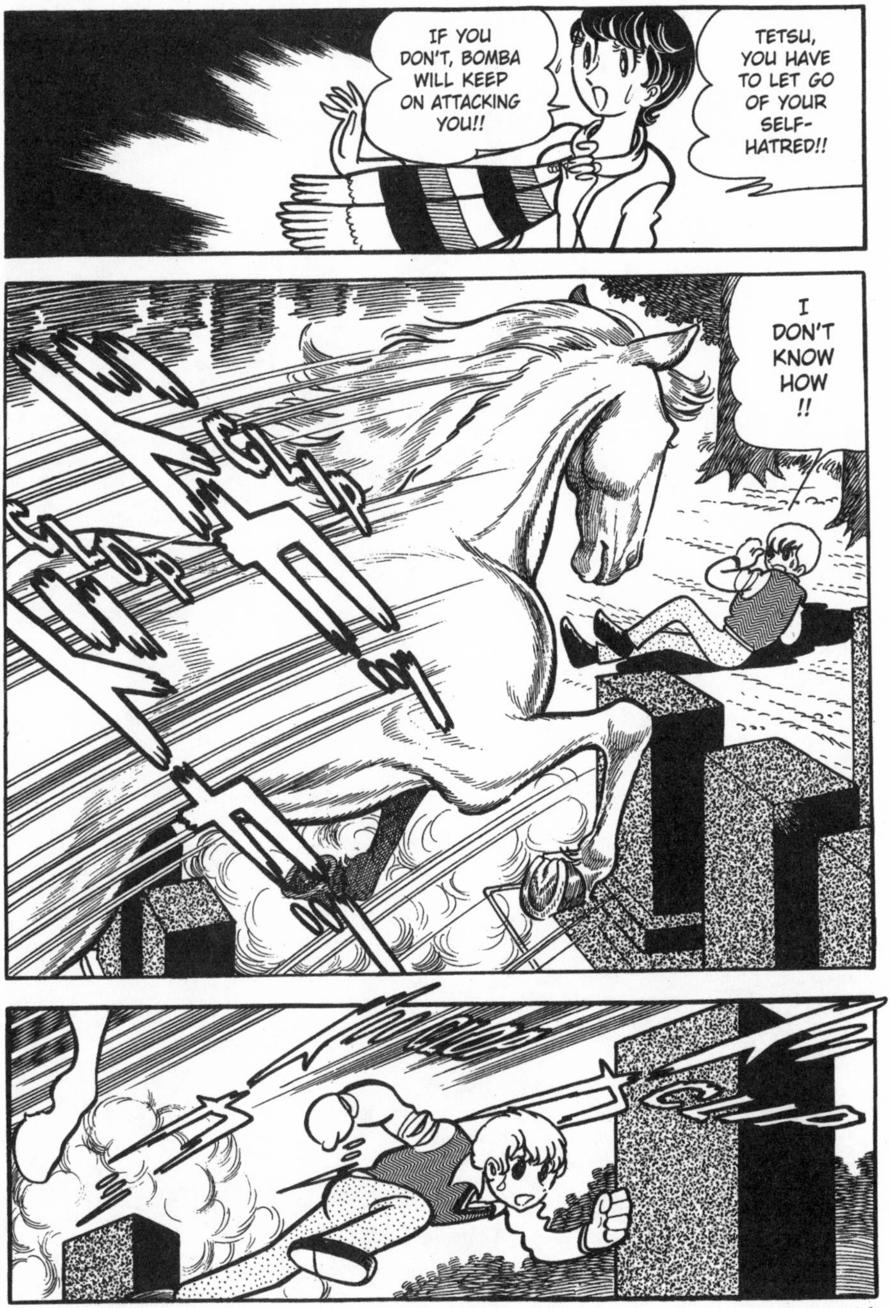
TETSU, YOU HAVE TO LET GO OF YOUR SELF-HATRED!!
IF YOU DON'T, BOMBA WILL KEEP ON ATTACKING YOU!!
I DON'T KNOW HOW !!

BELIEVE IN YOURSELF!! IF YOU CAN JUST BELIEVE IN YOURSELF AND SOCIETY, BOMBA WILL VANISH!!
CLOP
CLIP
CLOP
I CAN'T DO IT!
QUICK! GET IN!!

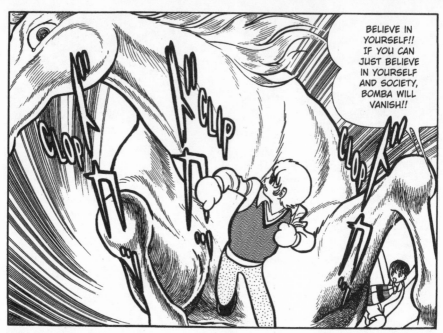

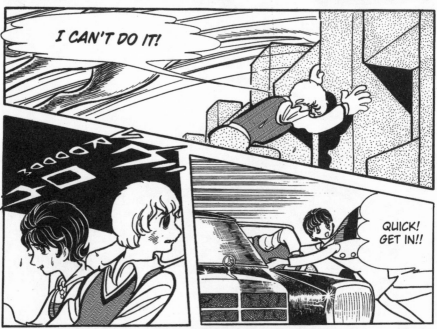

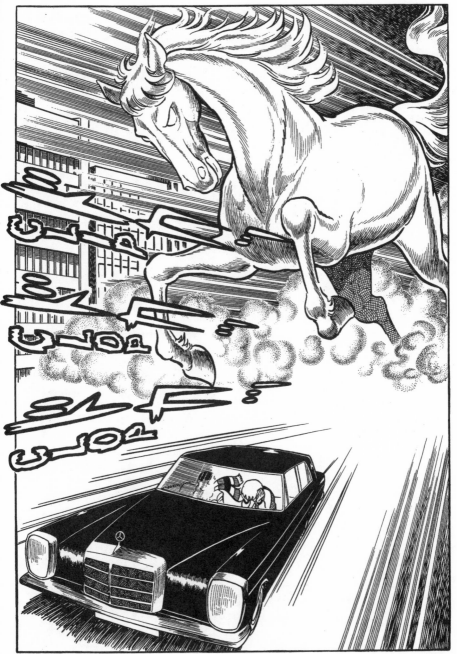

138

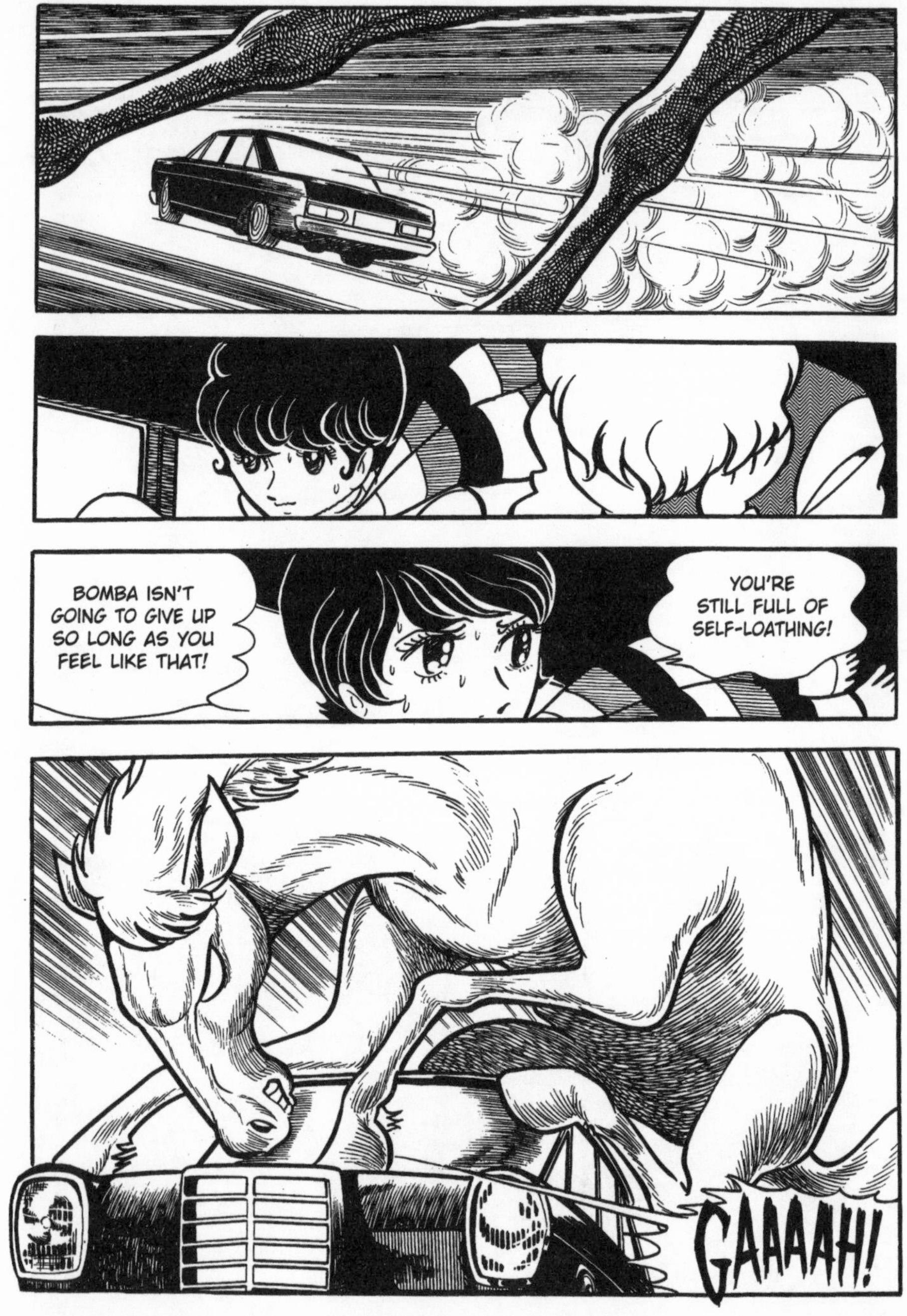
YOU'RE STILL FULL OF SELF-LOATHING!
BOMBA ISN'T GOING TO GIVE UP SO LONG AS YOU FEEL LIKE THAT!
GAAAAH!

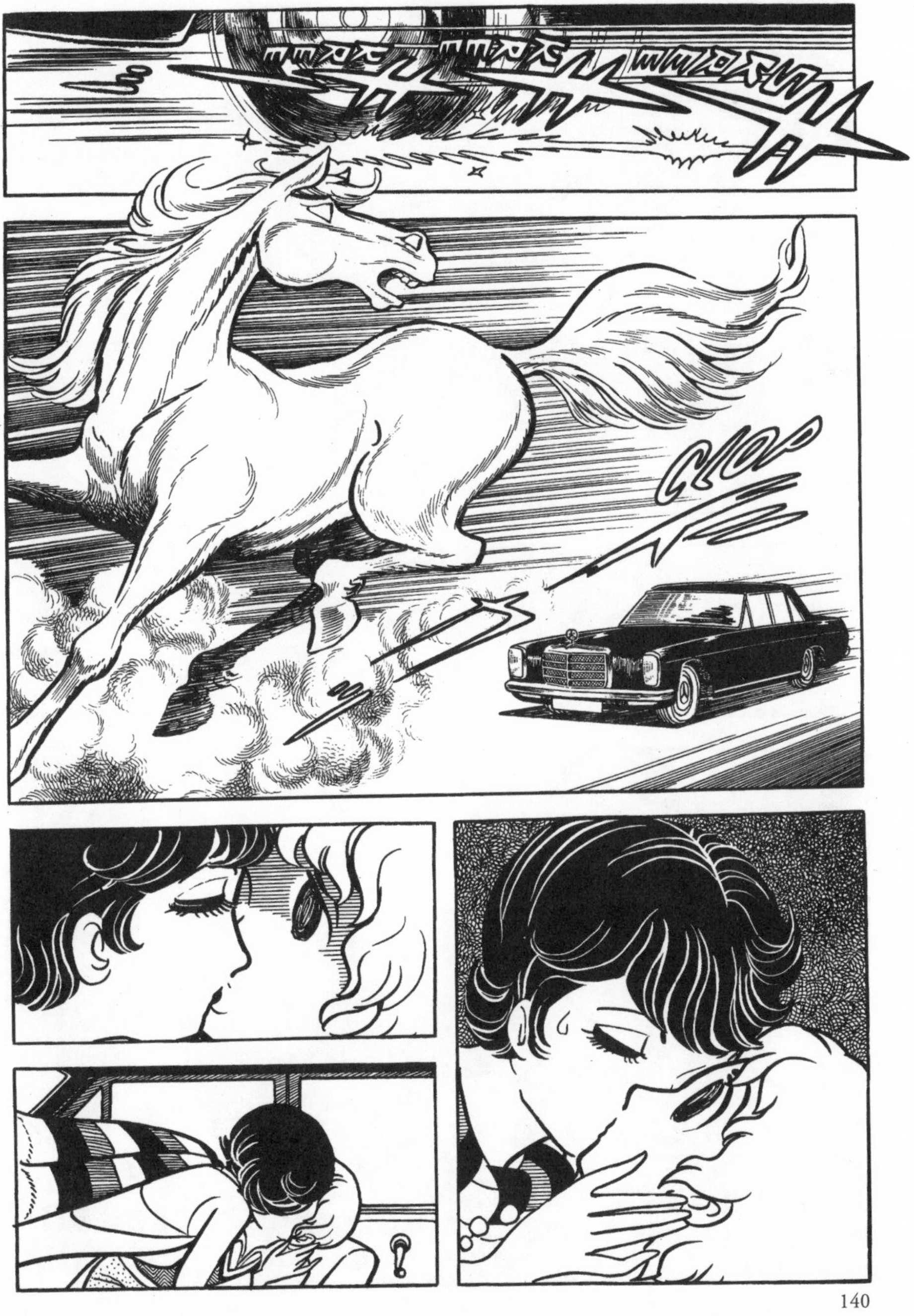
CLOP

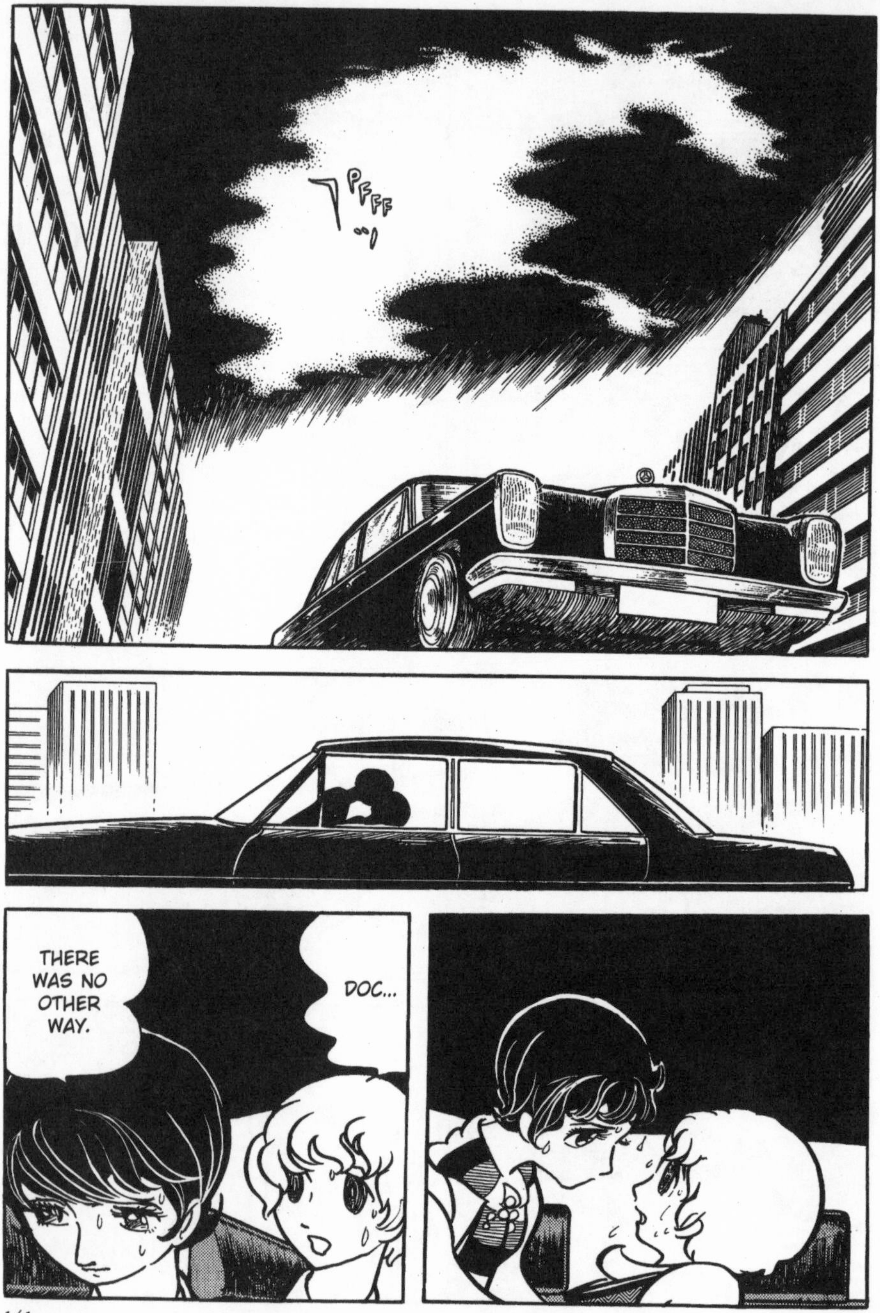
PFFFF..!
DOC...
THERE WAS NO OTHER WAY.

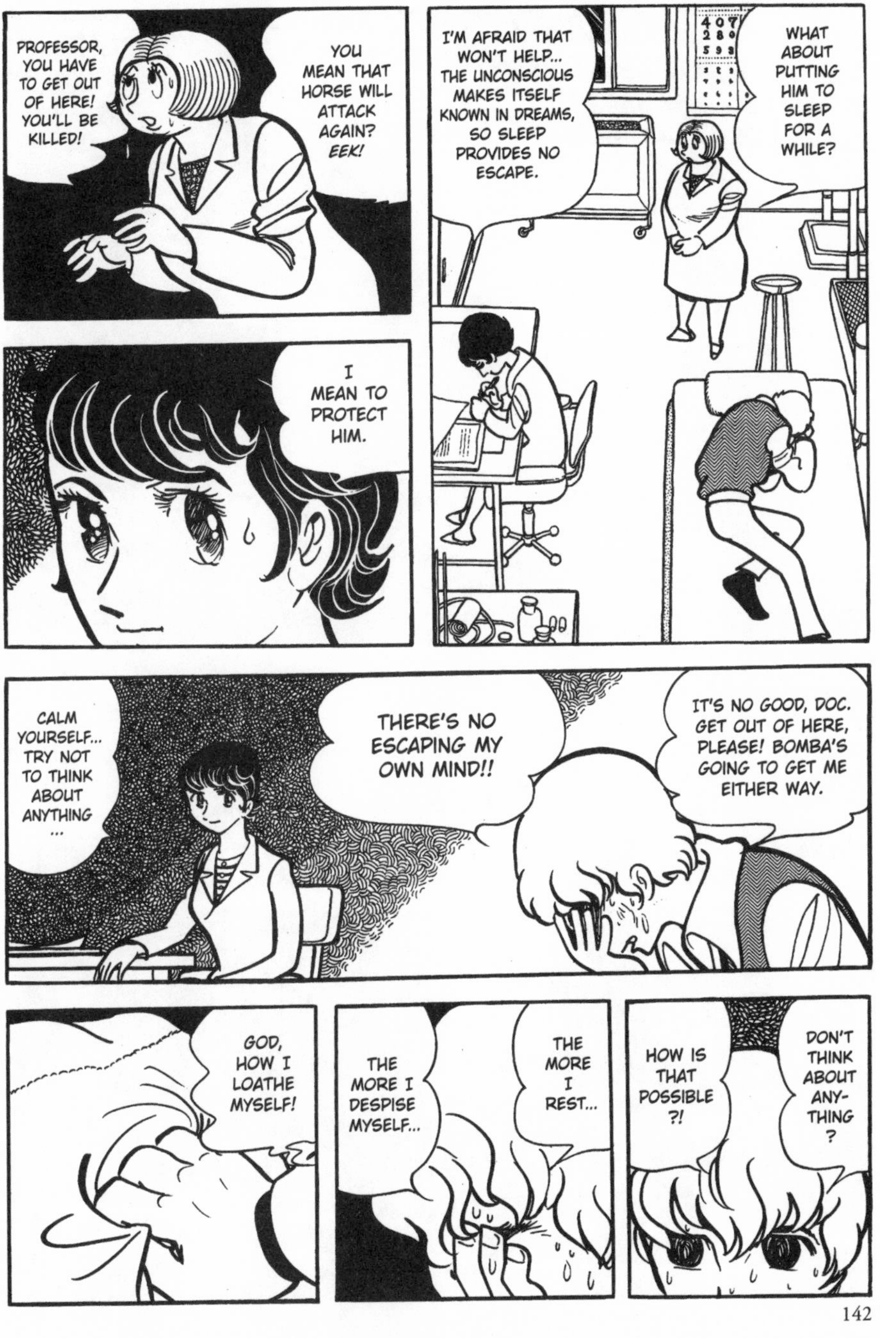
WHAT ABOUT PUTTING HIM TO SLEEP FOR A WHILE?
I'M AFRAID THAT WON'T HELP... THE UNCONSCIOUS MAKES ITSELF KNOWN IN DREAMS, SO SLEEP PROVIDES NO ESCAPE.
YOU MEAN THAT HORSE WILL ATTACK AGAIN? EEK!
PROFESSOR, YOU HAVE TO GET OUT OF HERE! YOU'LL BE KILLED!
I MEAN TO PROTECT HIM.
IT'S NO GOOD, DOC. GET OUT OF HERE, PLEASE! BOMBA'S GOING TO GET ME EITHER WAY.
THERE'S NO ESCAPING MY OWN MIND!!
CALM YOURSELF... TRY NOT TO THINK ABOUT ANYTHING ...
DON'T THINK ABOUT ANY-THING ?
HOW IS THAT POSSIBLE ?!
THE MORE I REST...
THE MORE I DESPISE MYSELF...
GOD, HOW I LOATHE MYSELF!

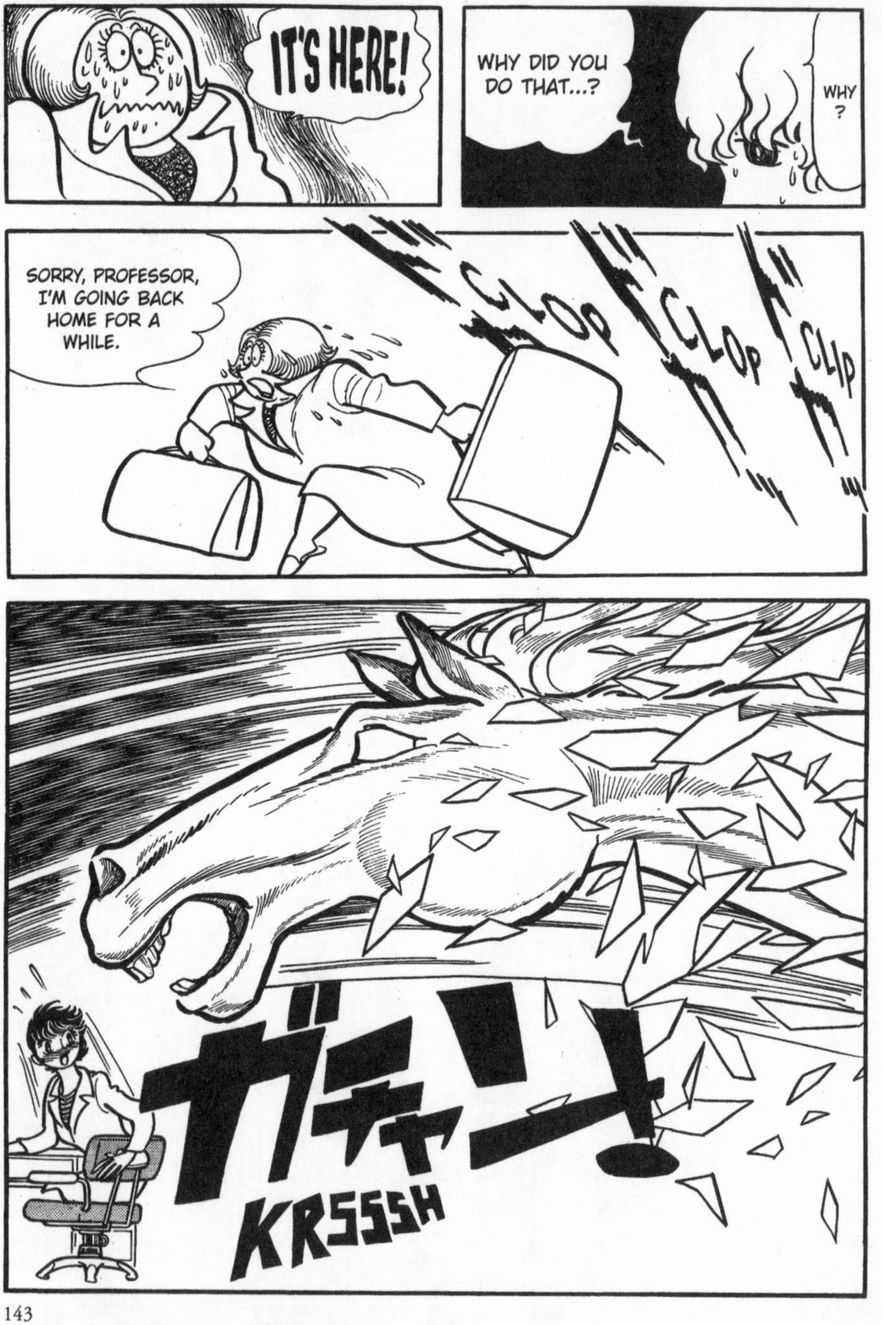

WHY ?
WHY DID YOU DO THAT...?
IT'S HERE!
CLIP
CLOP
CLOP
SORRY, PROFESSOR, I'M GOING BACK HOME FOR A WHILE.
ガチャーン!
KRSSSH

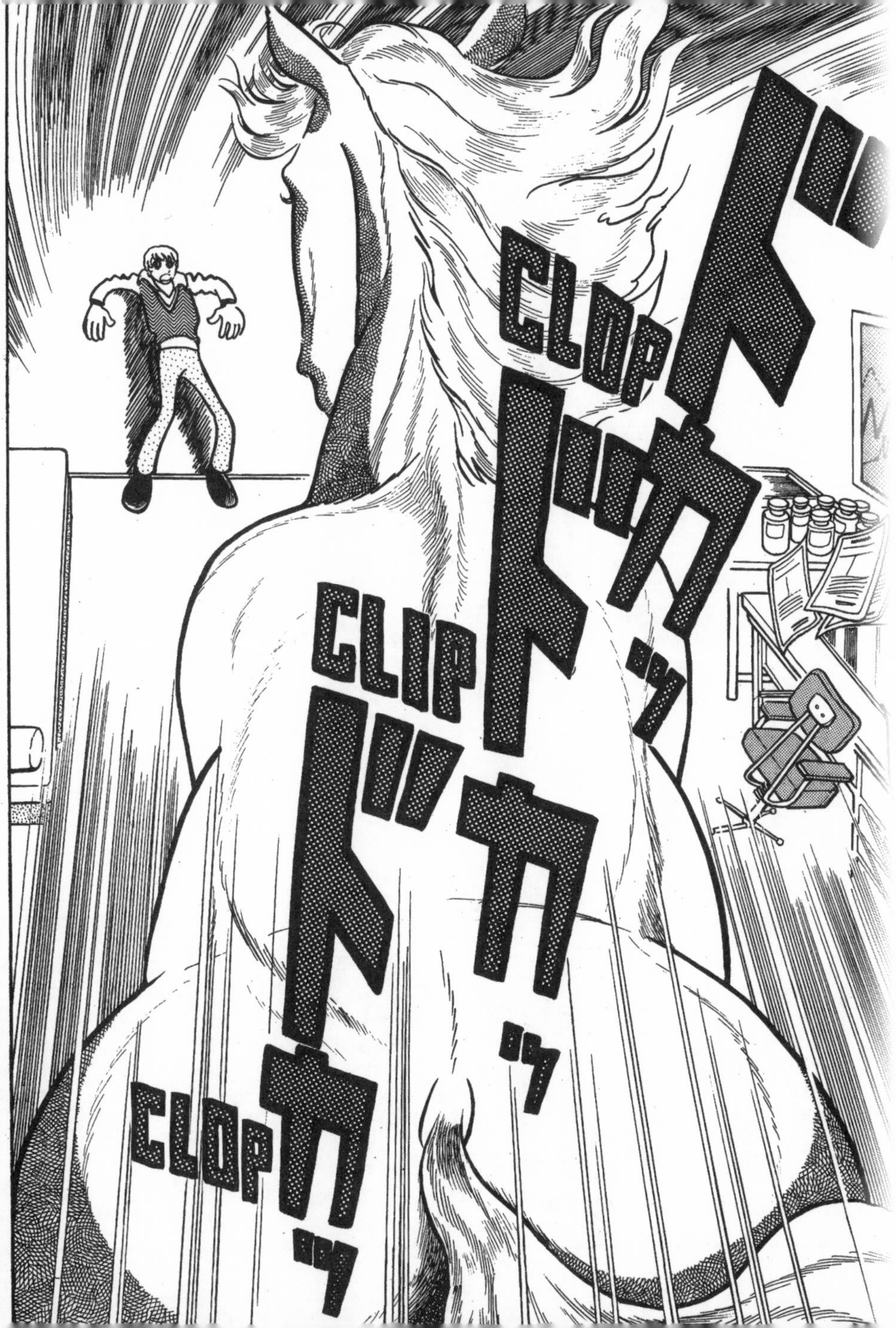

ド
CLOP
ドカッ
CLIP
ドカッ
CLOP
カッ

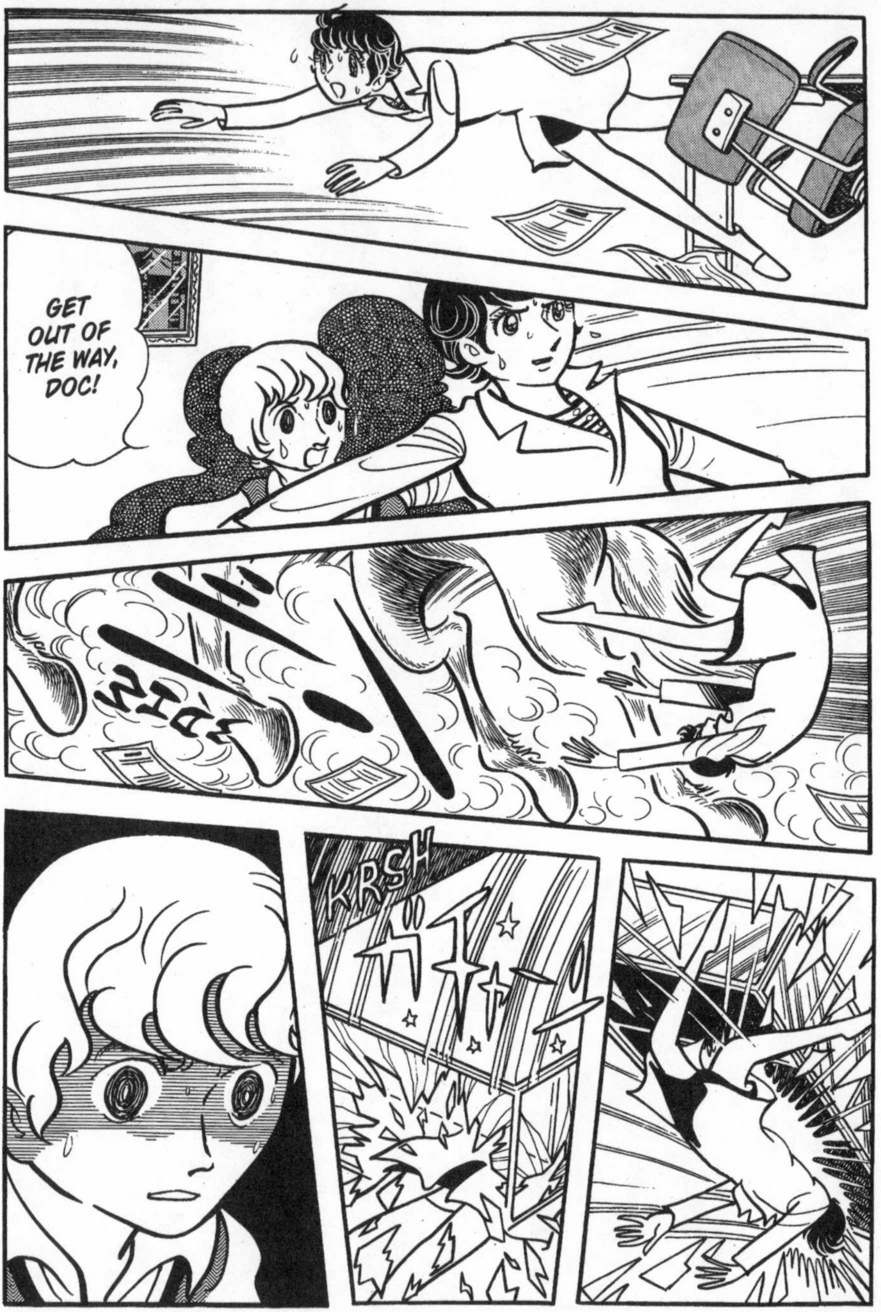
GET OUT OF THE WAY, DOC!
KRSH

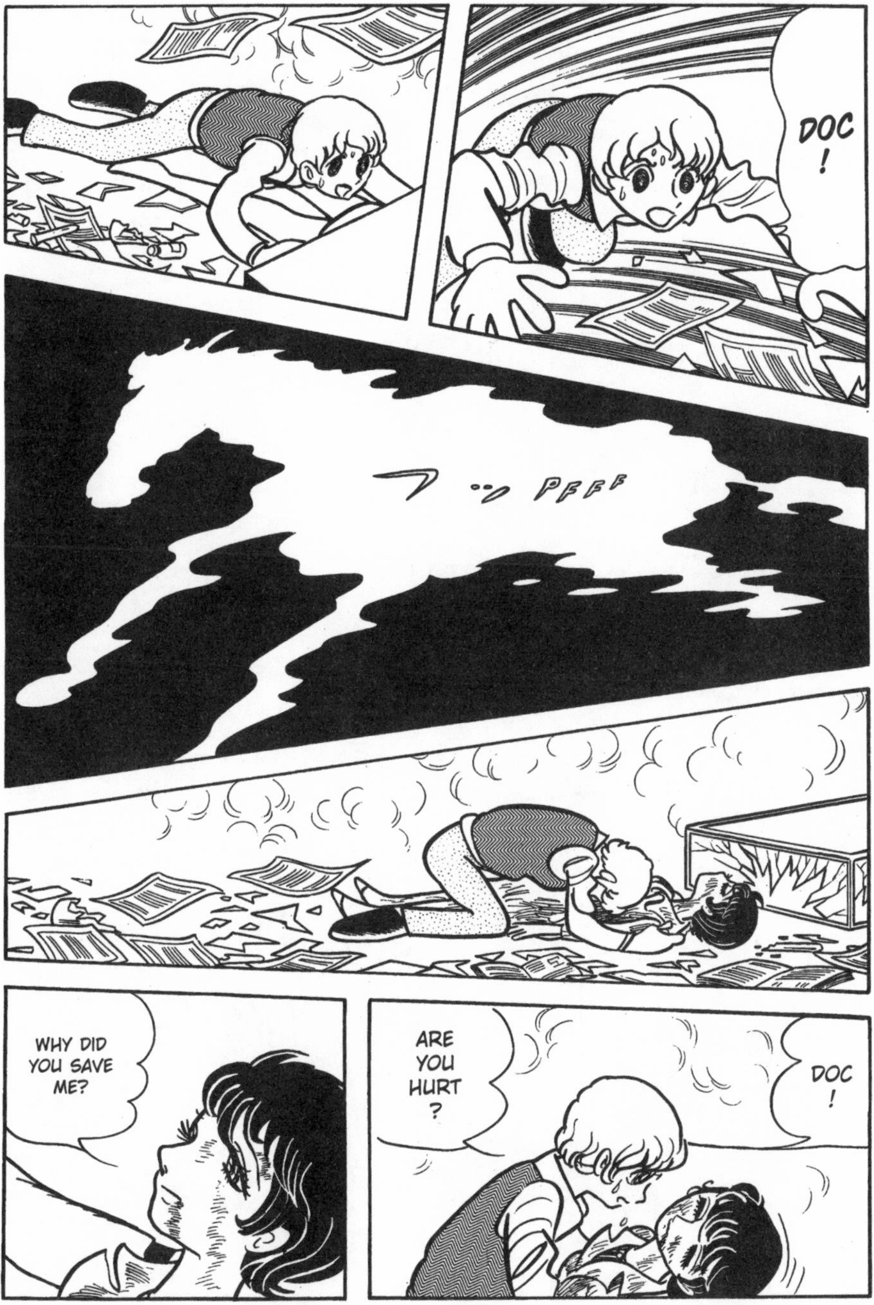
DOC!
PFFF
DOC!
ARE YOU HURT?
WHY DID YOU SAVE ME?

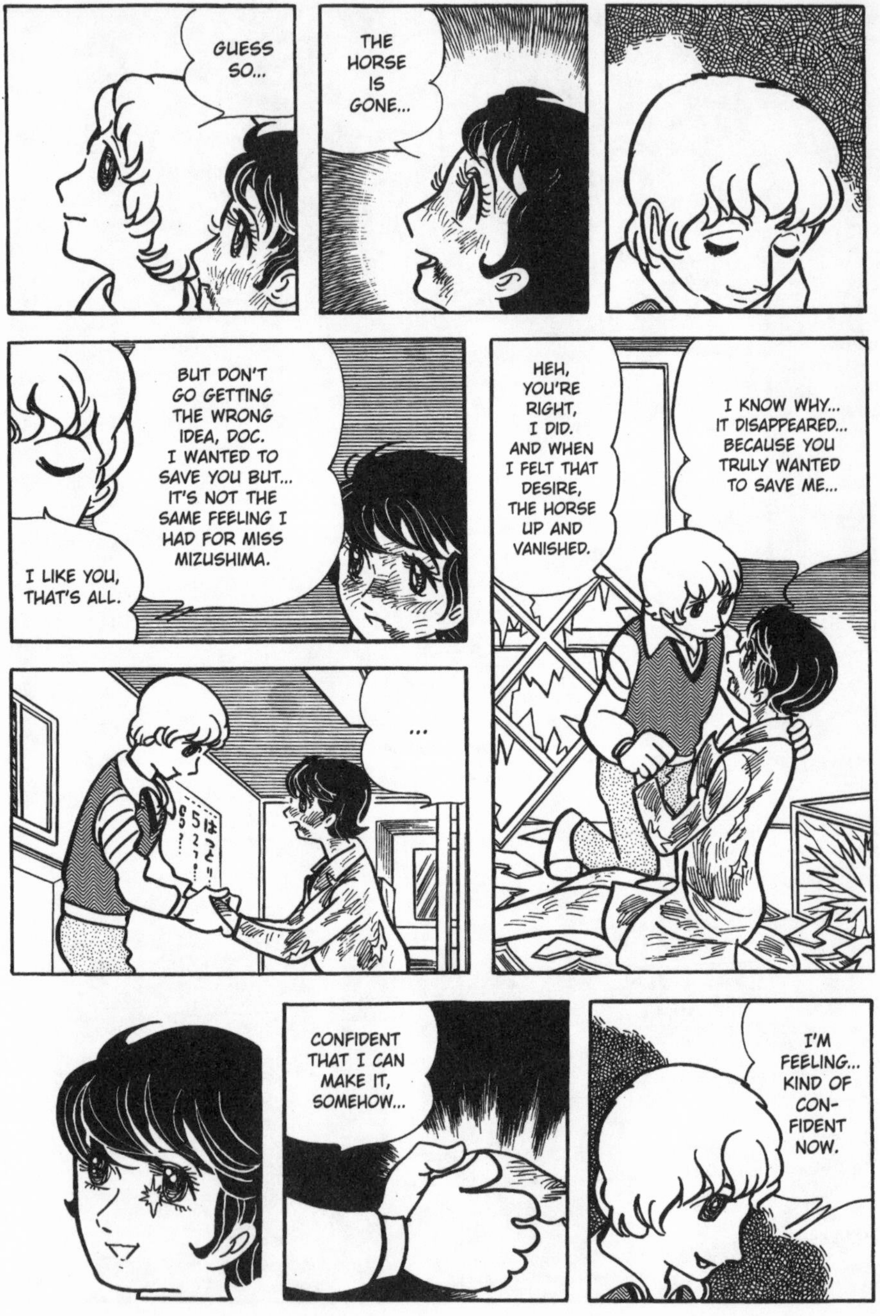
THE HORSE IS GONE...
GUESS SO...
I KNOW WHY... IT DISAPPEARED... BECAUSE YOU TRULY WANTED TO SAVE ME...
HEH, YOU'RE RIGHT, I DID. AND WHEN I FELT THAT DESIRE, THE HORSE UP AND VANISHED.
BUT DON'T GO GETTING THE WRONG IDEA, DOC. I WANTED TO SAVE YOU BUT... IT'S NOT THE SAME FEELING I HAD FOR MISS MIZUSHIMA.
I LIKE YOU, THAT'S ALL.
...
I'M FEELING... KIND OF CON-FIDENT NOW.
CONFIDENT THAT I CAN MAKE IT, SOMEHOW...

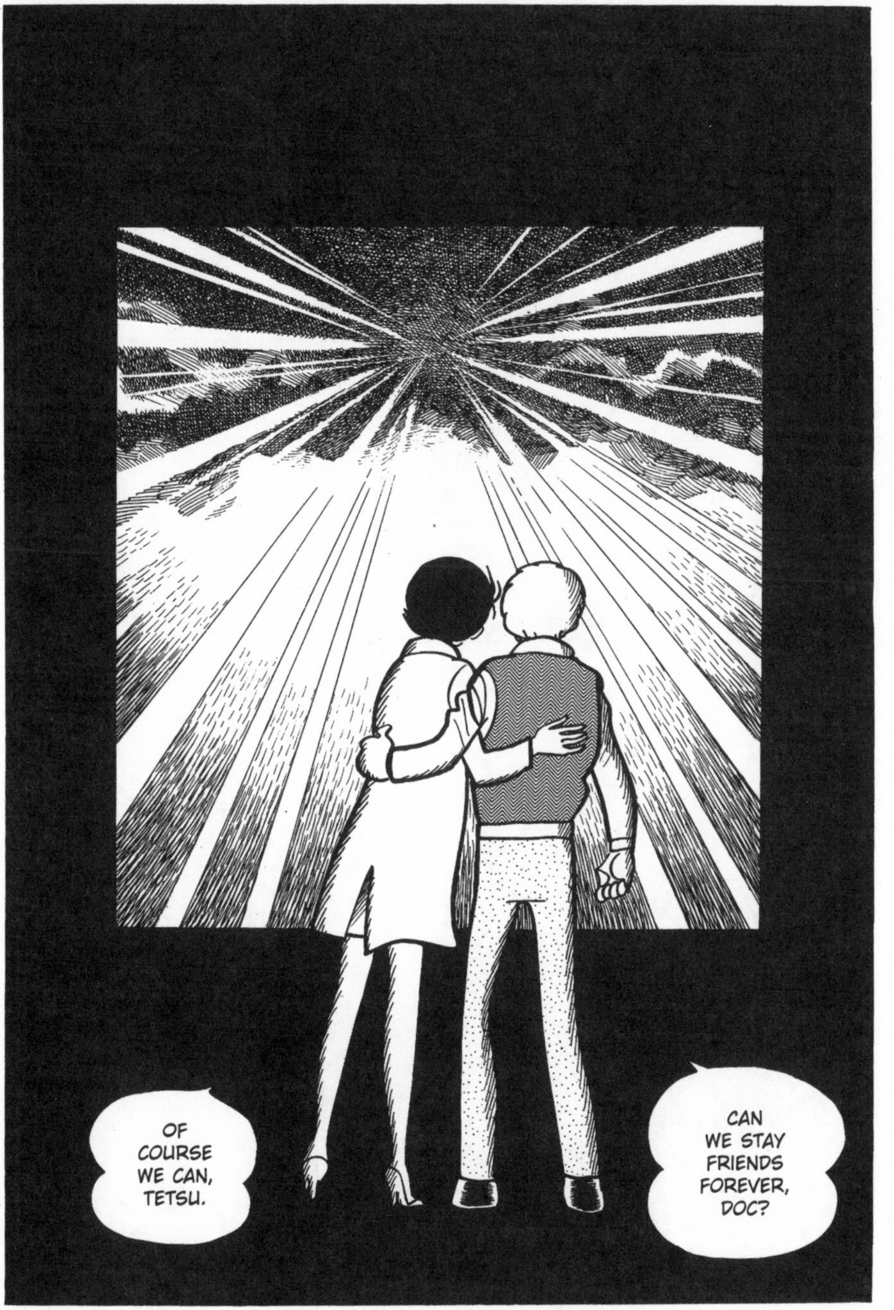
CAN WE STAY FRIENDS FOREVER, DOC?
OF COURSE WE CAN, TETSU.

THE END

PRINCESS KNIGHT

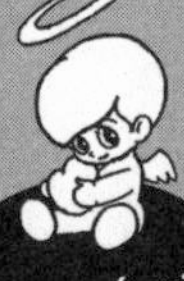

More classic Osamu Tezuka from Vertical!

omnibus edition preview

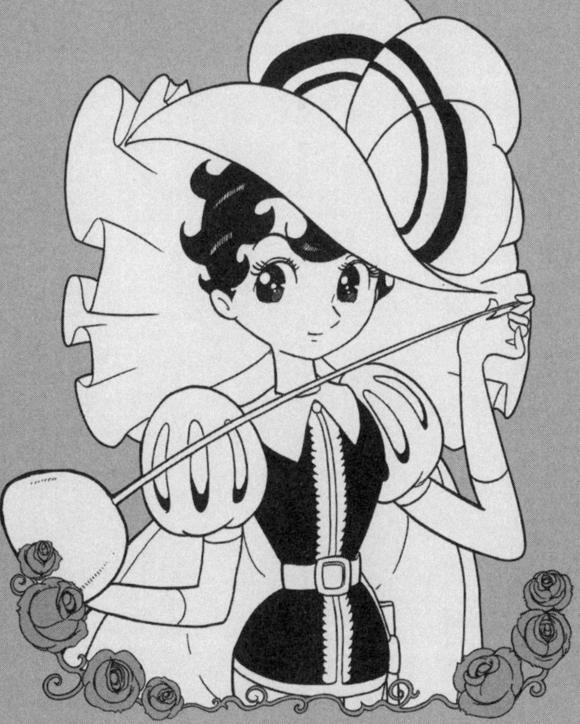

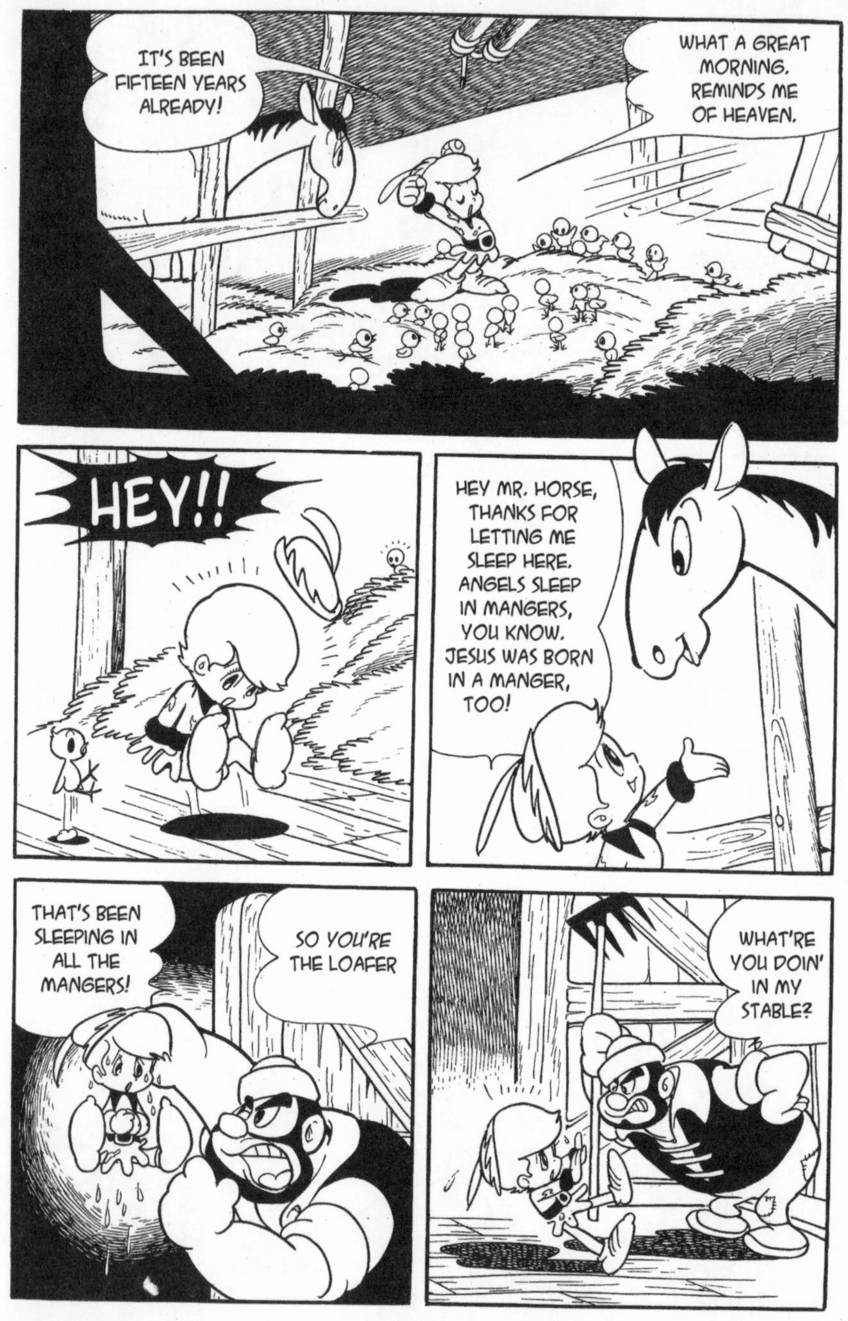
WHAT A GREAT MORNING. REMINDS ME OF HEAVEN.
IT'S BEEN FIFTEEN YEARS ALREADY!
HEY MR. HORSE, THANKS FOR LETTING ME SLEEP HERE. ANGELS SLEEP IN MANGERS, YOU KNOW. JESUS WAS BORN IN A MANGER, TOO!
HEY!!
WHAT'RE YOU DOIN' IN MY STABLE?
SO YOU'RE THE LOAFER
THAT'S BEEN SLEEPING IN ALL THE MANGERS!

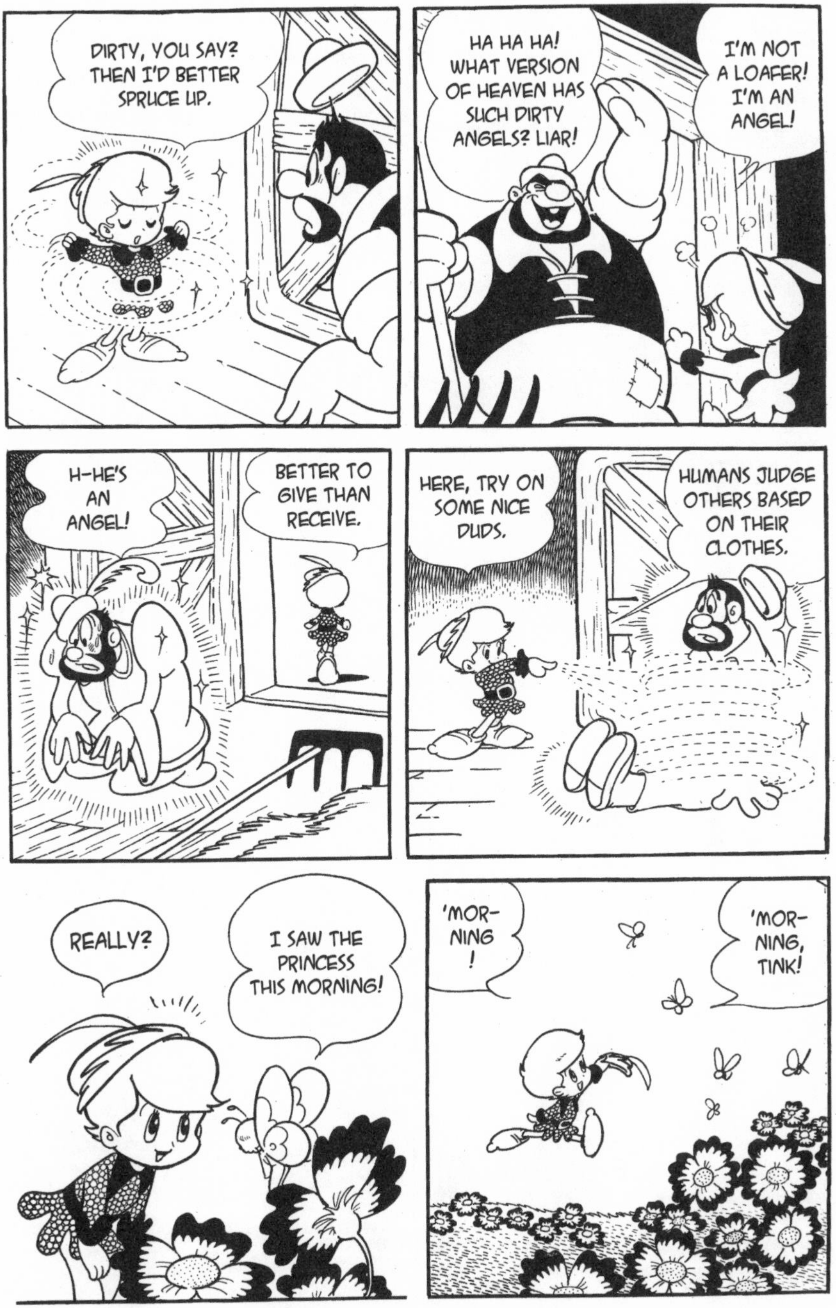
I'M NOT A LOAFER! I'M AN ANGEL!
HA HA HA! WHAT VERSION OF HEAVEN HAS SUCH DIRTY ANGELS? LIAR!
DIRTY, YOU SAY? THEN I'D BETTER SPRUCE UP.
HUMANS JUDGE OTHERS BASED ON THEIR CLOTHES.
HERE, TRY ON SOME NICE DUDS.
BETTER TO GIVE THAN RECEIVE.
H-HE'S AN ANGEL!
'MORNING, TINK!
'MOR-NING!
I SAW THE PRINCESS THIS MORNING!
REALLY?

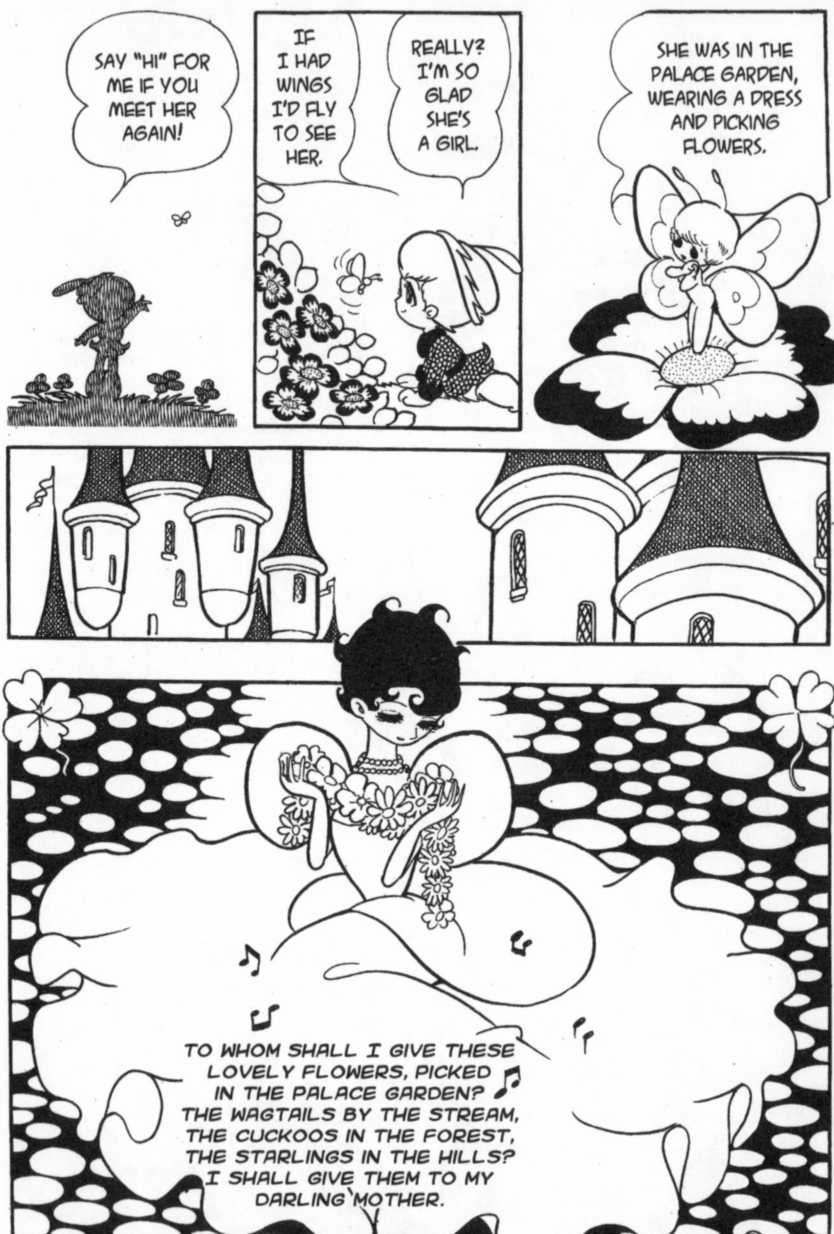
SHE WAS IN THE PALACE GARDEN, WEARING A DRESS AND PICKING FLOWERS.
REALLY? I'M SO GLAD SHE'S A GIRL.
IF I HAD WINGS I'D FLY TO SEE HER.
SAY "HI" FOR ME IF YOU MEET HER AGAIN!
TO WHOM SHALL I GIVE THESE LOVELY FLOWERS, PICKED IN THE PALACE GARDEN? THE WAGTAILS BY THE STREAM, THE CUCKOOS IN THE FOREST, THE STARLINGS IN THE HILLS? I SHALL GIVE THEM TO MY DARLING MOTHER.

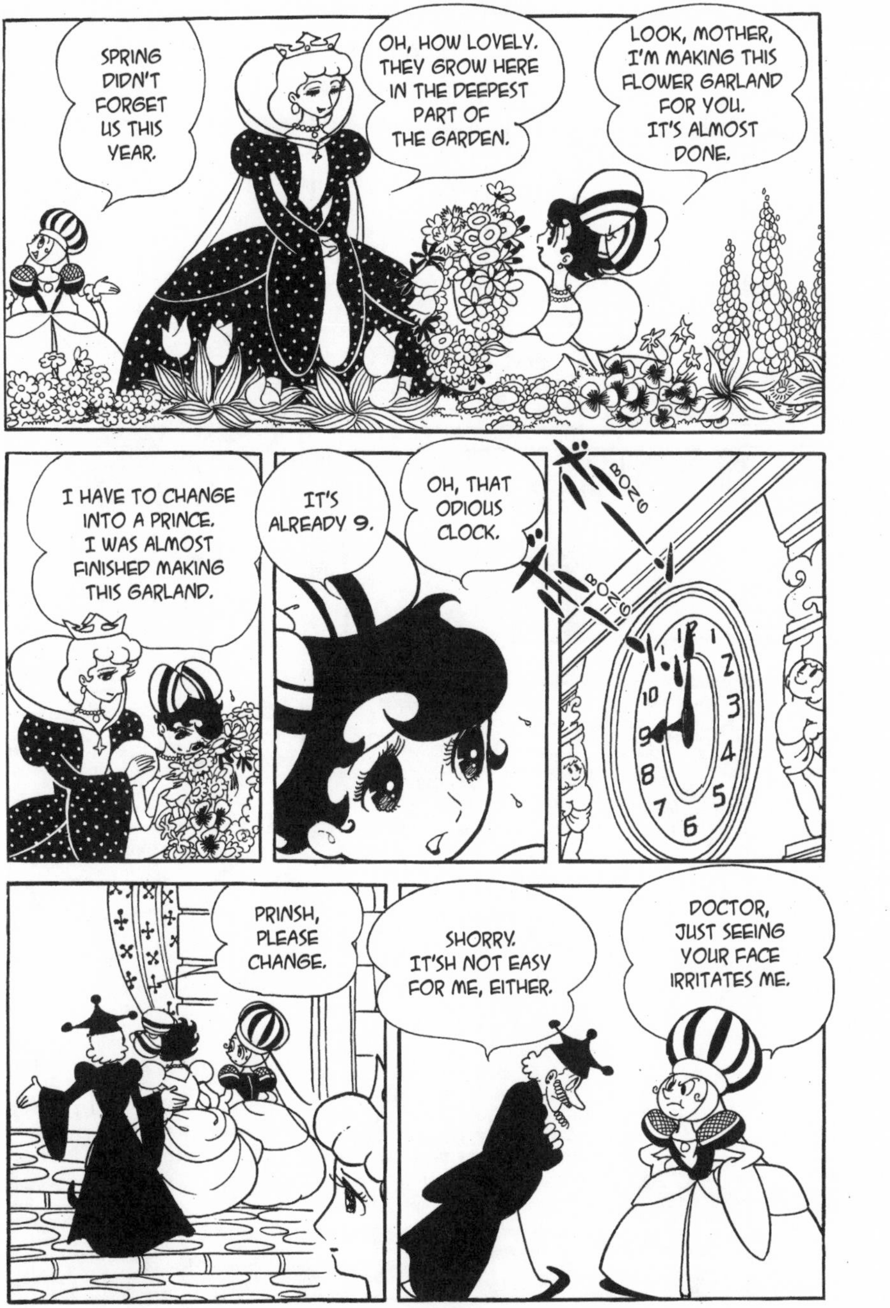
LOOK, MOTHER, I'M MAKING THIS FLOWER GARLAND FOR YOU. IT'S ALMOST DONE.
OH, HOW LOVELY. THEY GROW HERE IN THE DEEPEST PART OF THE GARDEN.
SPRING DIDN'T FORGET US THIS YEAR.
BONG
BONG
OH, THAT ODIOUS CLOCK.
IT'S ALREADY 9.
I HAVE TO CHANGE INTO A PRINCE. I WAS ALMOST FINISHED MAKING THIS GARLAND.
DOCTOR, JUST SEEING YOUR FACE IRRITATES ME.
SHORRY. IT'SH NOT EASY FOR ME, EITHER.
PRINSH, PLEASE CHANGE.

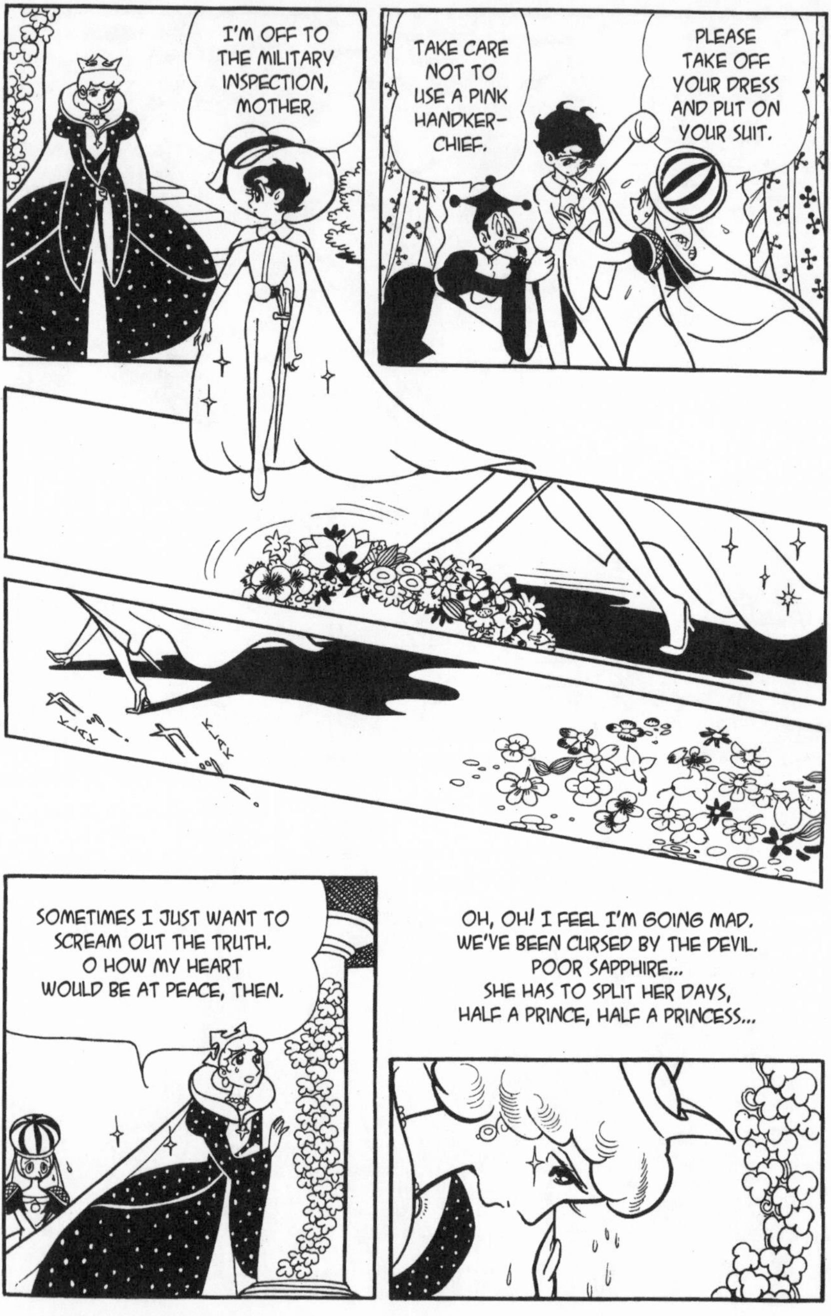
PLEASE TAKE OFF YOUR DRESS AND PUT ON YOUR SUIT.
TAKE CARE NOT TO USE A PINK HANDKERCHIEF.
I'M OFF TO THE MILITARY INSPECTION, MOTHER.
KLAK
KLAK
OH, OH! I FEEL I'M GOING MAD. WE'VE BEEN CURSED BY THE DEVIL. POOR SAPPHIRE... SHE HAS TO SPLIT HER DAYS, HALF A PRINCE, HALF A PRINCESS...
SOMETIMES I JUST WANT TO SCREAM OUT THE TRUTH. O HOW MY HEART WOULD BE AT PEACE, THEN.

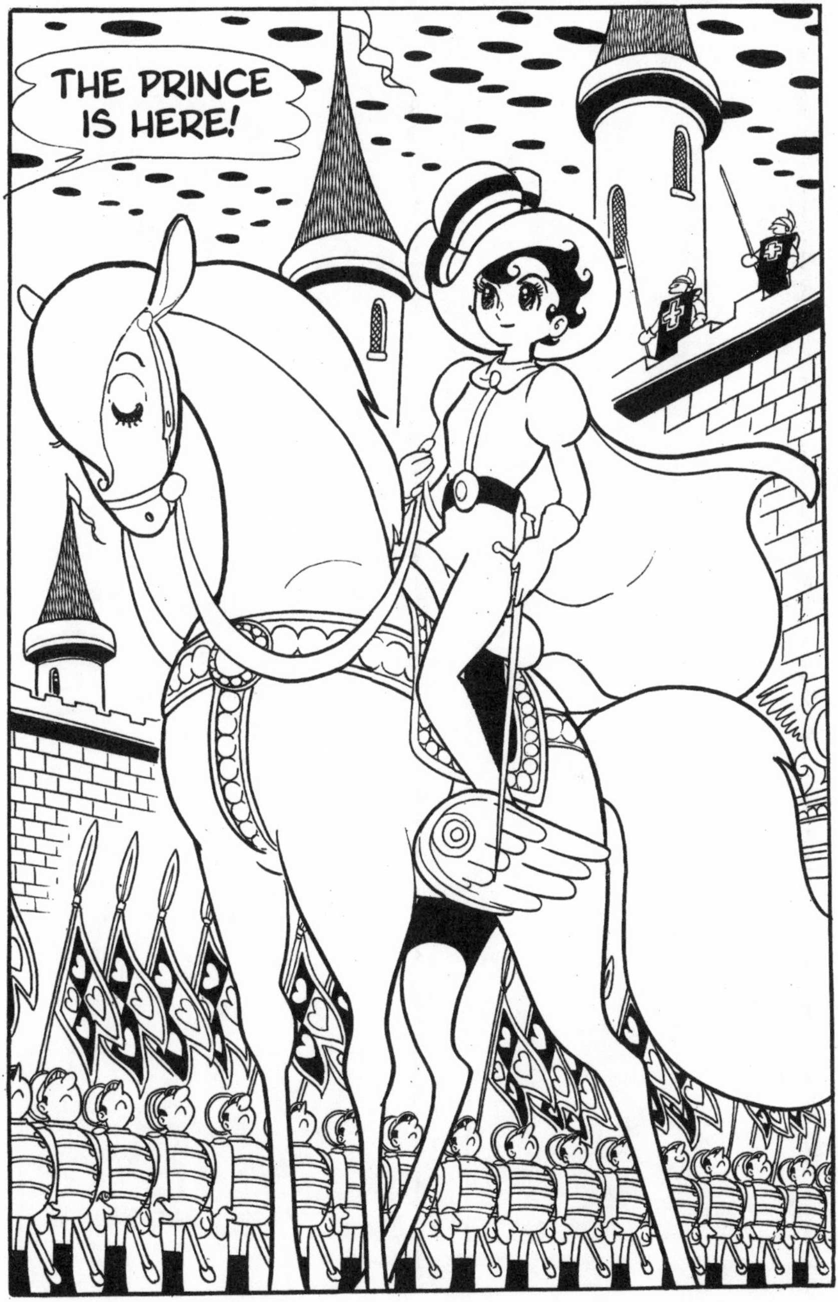
THE PRINCE IS HERE!

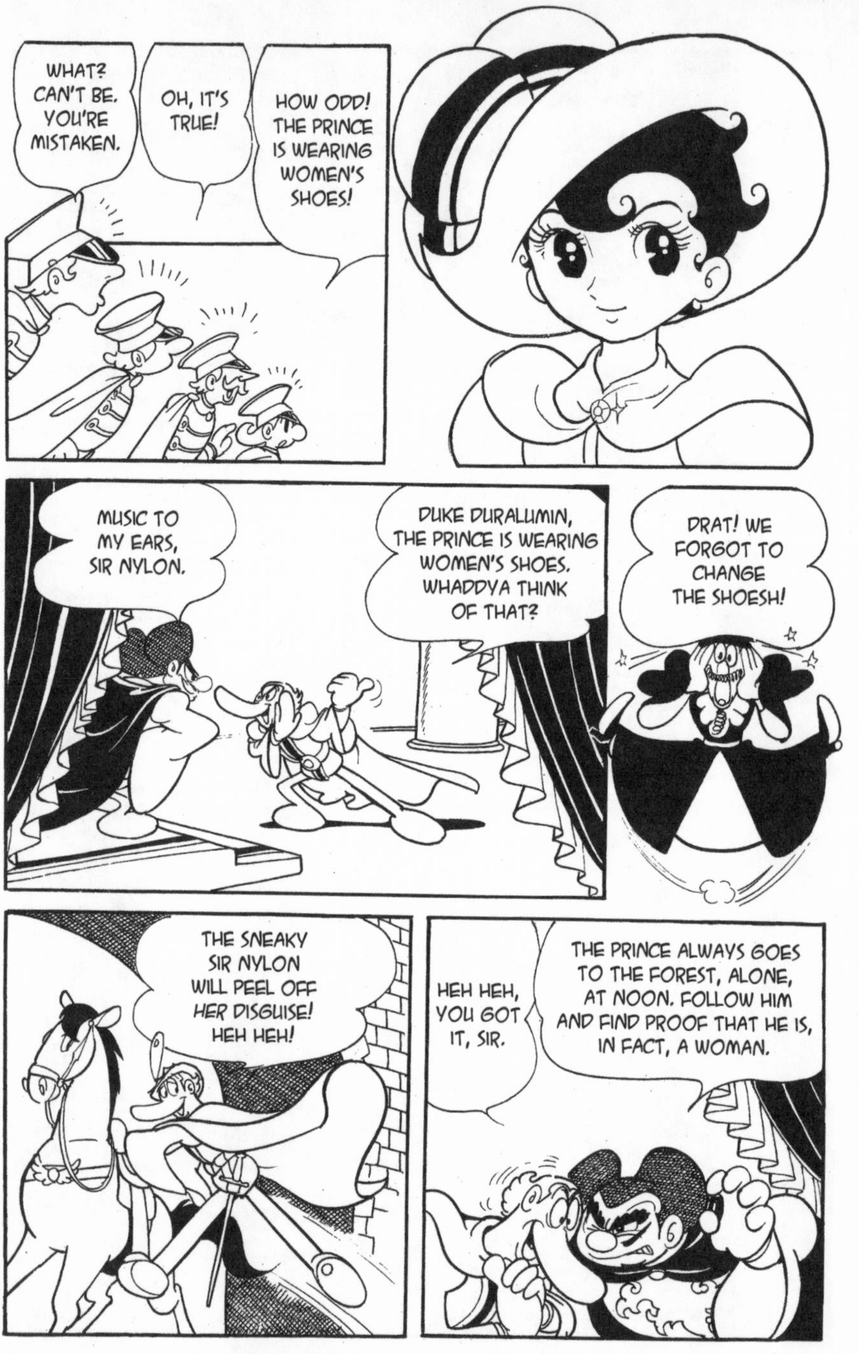
HOW ODD! THE PRINCE IS WEARING WOMEN'S SHOES!
OH, IT'S TRUE!
WHAT? CAN'T BE. YOU'RE MISTAKEN.
DRAT! WE FORGOT TO CHANGE THE SHOESH!
DUKE DURALUMIN, THE PRINCE IS WEARING WOMEN'S SHOES. WHADDYA THINK OF THAT?
MUSIC TO MY EARS, SIR NYLON.
THE PRINCE ALWAYS GOES TO THE FOREST, ALONE, AT NOON. FOLLOW HIM AND FIND PROOF THAT HE IS, IN FACT, A WOMAN.
HEH HEH, YOU GOT IT, SIR.
THE SNEAKY SIR NYLON WILL PEEL OFF HER DISGUISE! HEH HEH!

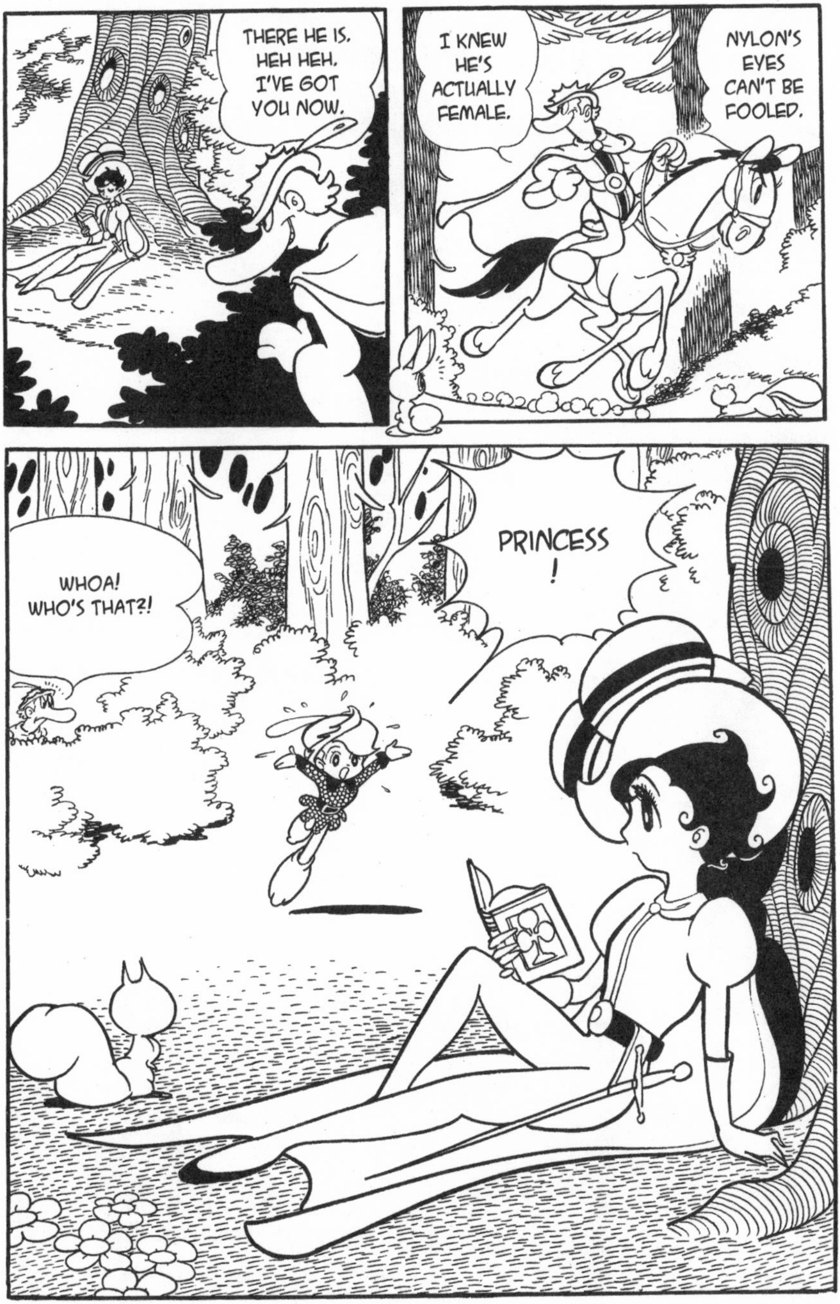
NYLON'S EYES CAN'T BE FOOLED.
I KNEW HE'S ACTUALLY FEMALE.
THERE HE IS. HEH HEH. I'VE GOT YOU NOW.
PRINCESS!
WHOA! WHO'S THAT?!

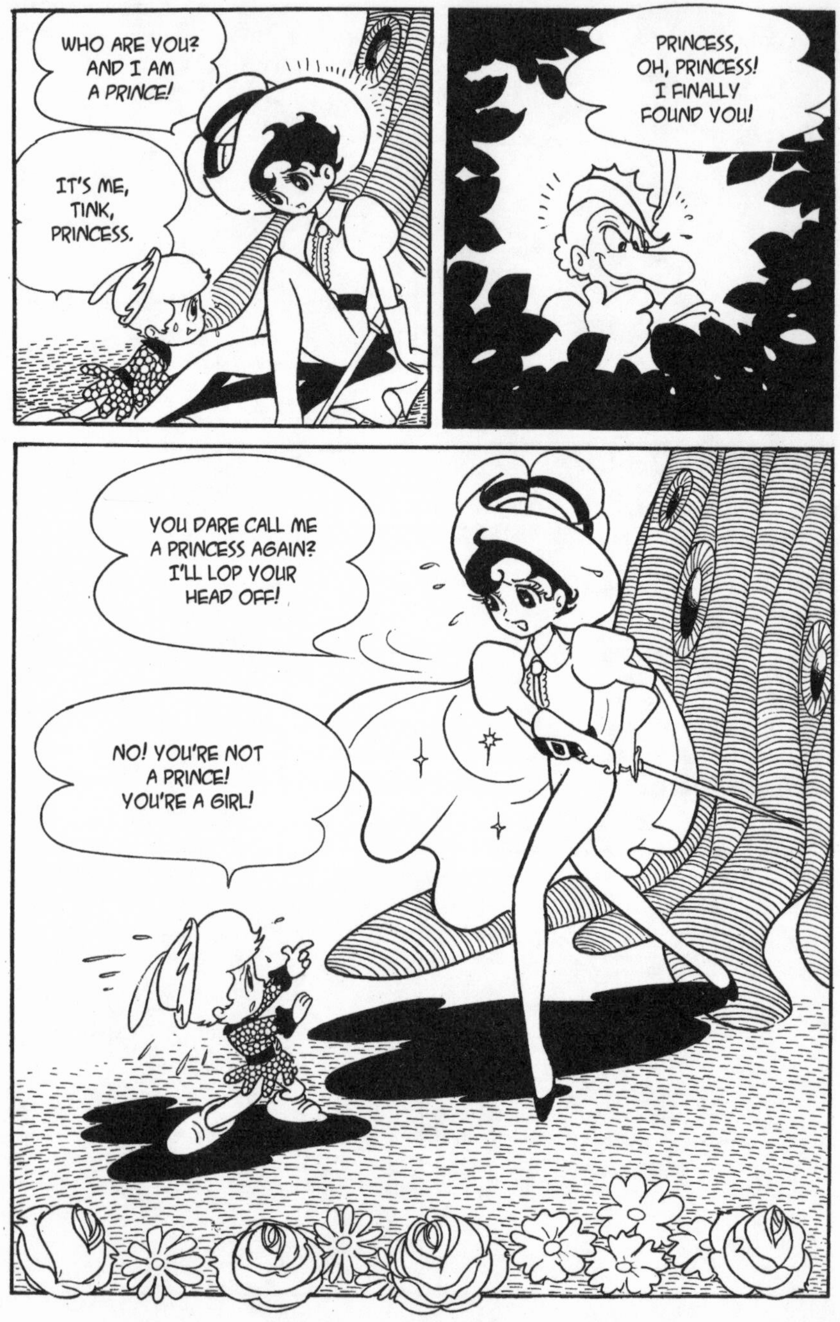
PRINCESS, OH, PRINCESS! I FINALLY FOUND YOU!
WHO ARE YOU? AND I AM A PRINCE!
IT'S ME, TINK, PRINCESS.
YOU DARE CALL ME A PRINCESS AGAIN? I'LL LOP YOUR HEAD OFF!
NO! YOU'RE NOT A PRINCE! YOU'RE A GIRL!

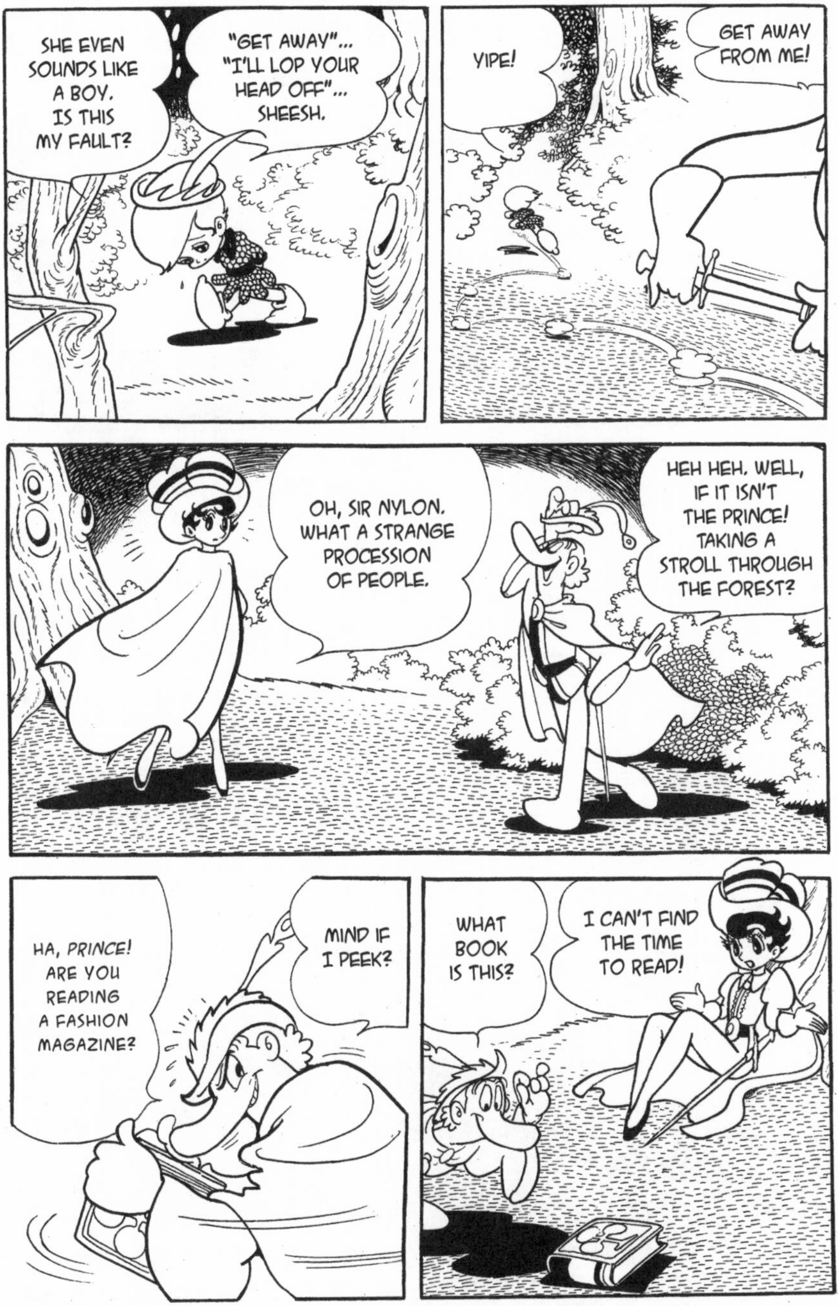
GET AWAY FROM ME!
YIPE!
"GET AWAY"... "I'LL LOP YOUR HEAD OFF"... SHEESH.
SHE EVEN SOUNDS LIKE A BOY. IS THIS MY FAULT?
HEH HEH. WELL, IF IT ISN'T THE PRINCE! TAKING A STROLL THROUGH THE FOREST?
OH, SIR NYLON. WHAT A STRANGE PROCESSION OF PEOPLE.
I CAN'T FIND THE TIME TO READ!
WHAT BOOK IS THIS?
MIND IF I PEEK?
HA, *PRINCE*! ARE YOU READING A FASHION MAGAZINE?

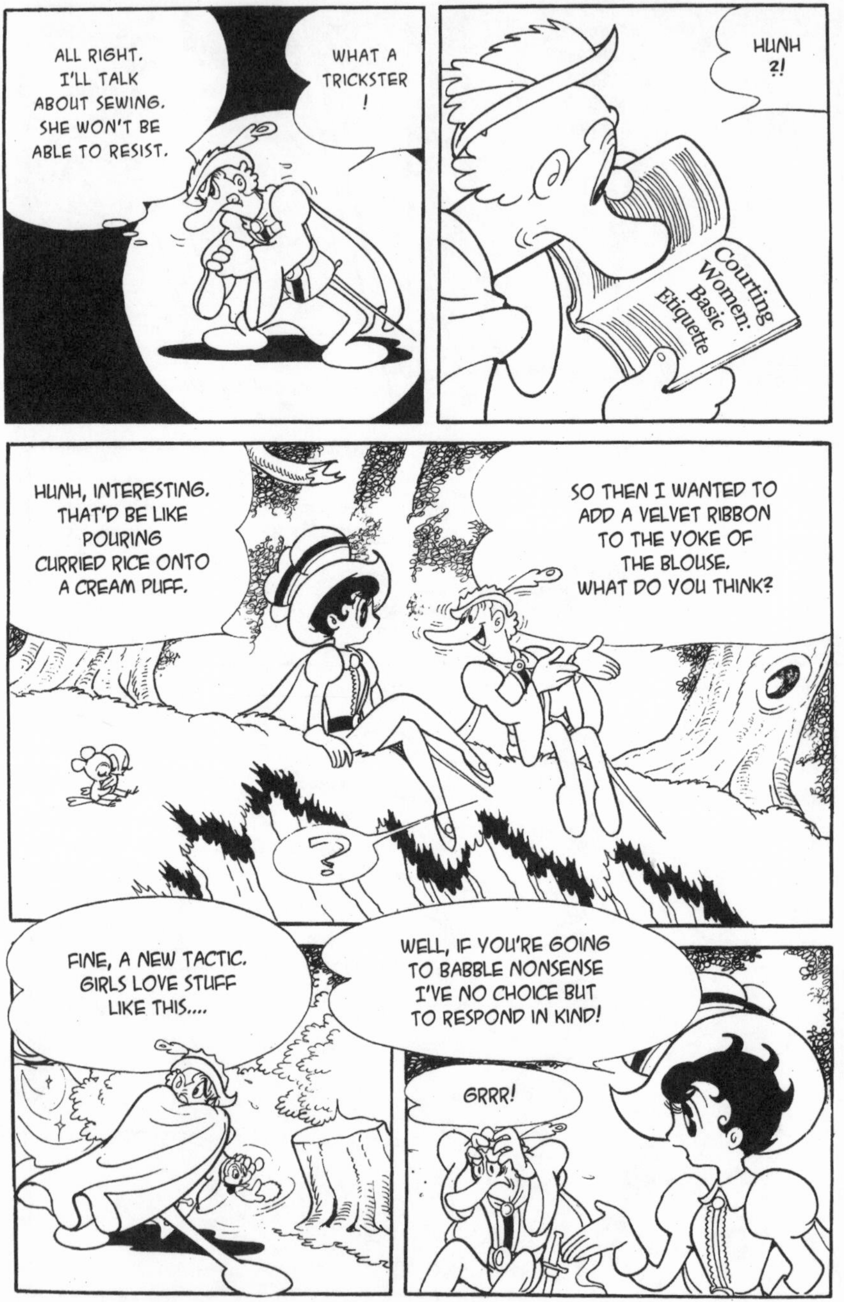
HUNH ?!
Courting Women: Basic Etiquette
WHAT A TRICKSTER !
ALL RIGHT. I'LL TALK ABOUT SEWING. SHE WON'T BE ABLE TO RESIST.
SO THEN I WANTED TO ADD A VELVET RIBBON TO THE YOKE OF THE BLOUSE. WHAT DO YOU THINK?
HUNH, INTERESTING. THAT'D BE LIKE POURING CURRIED RICE ONTO A CREAM PUFF.
?
WELL, IF YOU'RE GOING TO BABBLE NONSENSE I'VE NO CHOICE BUT TO RESPOND IN KIND!
GRRR!
FINE, A NEW TACTIC. GIRLS LOVE STUFF LIKE THIS....

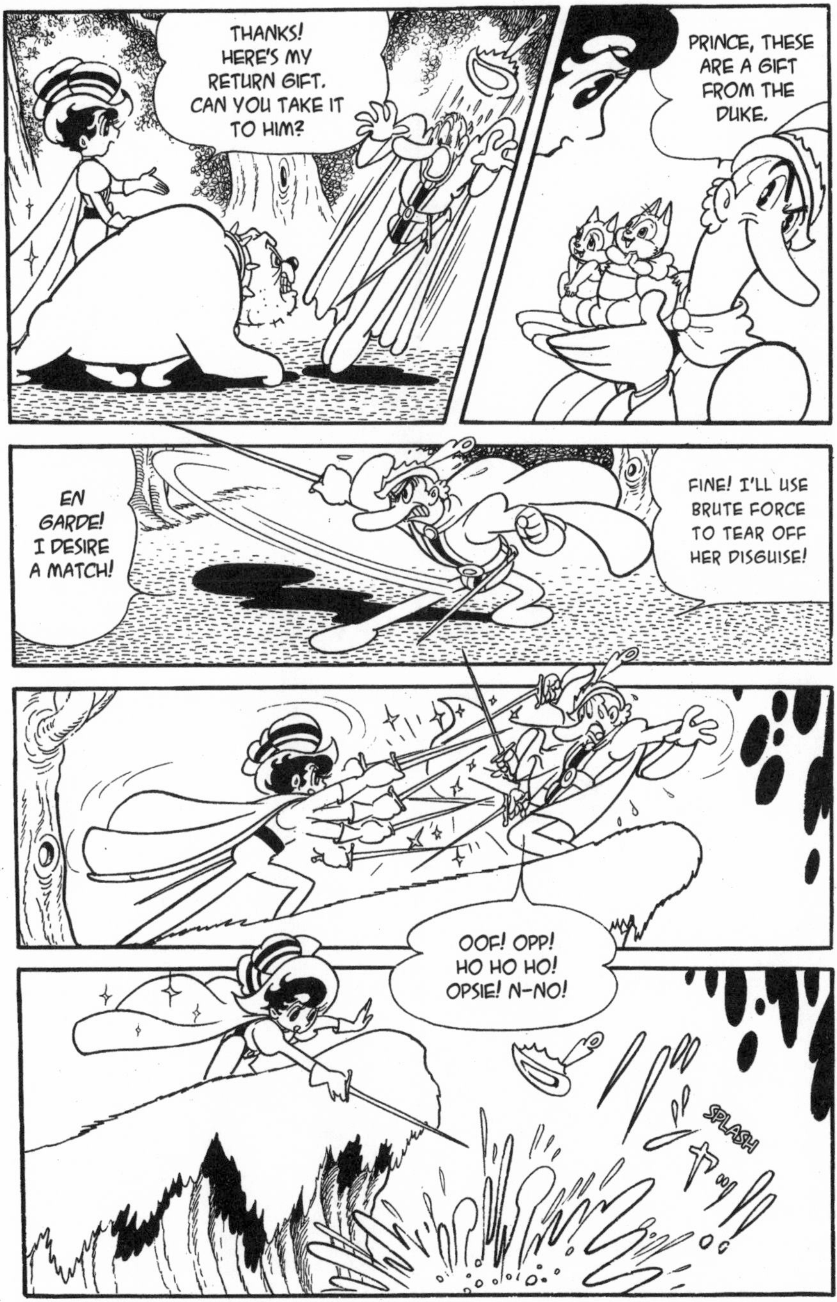
PRINCE, THESE ARE A GIFT FROM THE DUKE.
THANKS! HERE'S MY RETURN GIFT. CAN YOU TAKE IT TO HIM?
FINE! I'LL USE BRUTE FORCE TO TEAR OFF HER DISGUISE!
EN GARDE! I DESIRE A MATCH!
OOF! OPP! HO HO HO! OPSIE! N-NO!
SPLASH

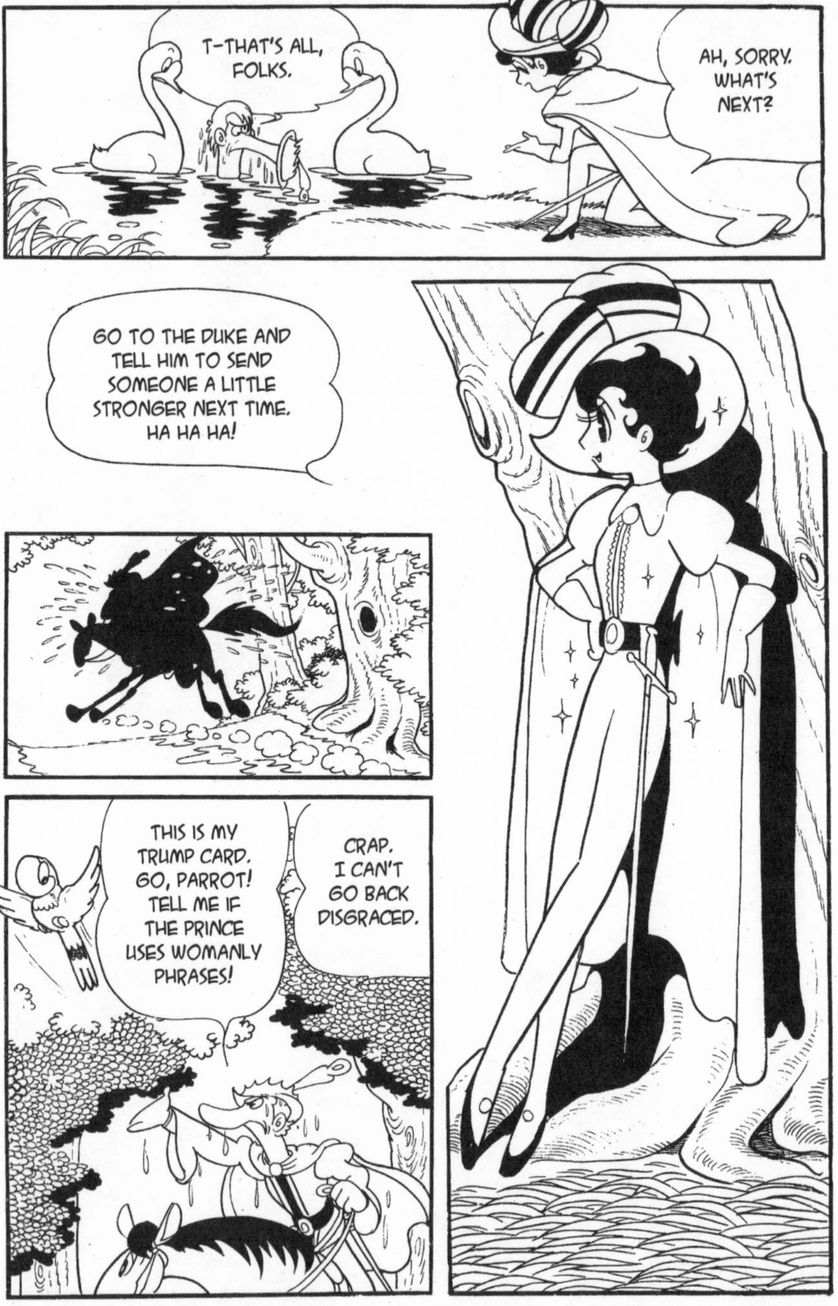
AH, SORRY. WHAT'S NEXT?
T-THAT'S ALL, FOLKS.
GO TO THE DUKE AND TELL HIM TO SEND SOMEONE A LITTLE STRONGER NEXT TIME. HA HA HA!
CRAP. I CAN'T GO BACK DISGRACED.
THIS IS MY TRUMP CARD. GO, PARROT! TELL ME IF THE PRINCE USES WOMANLY PHRASES!

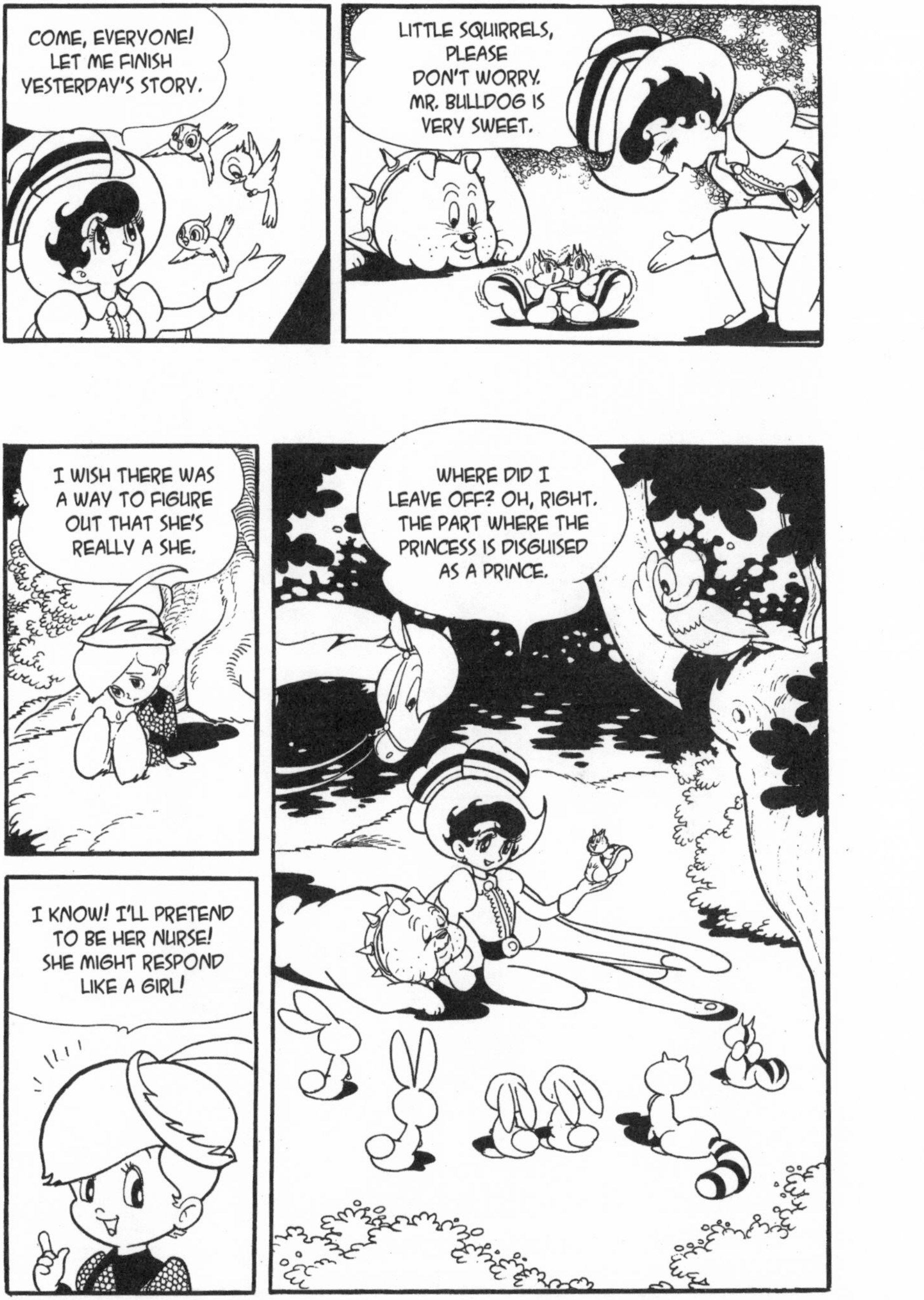
LITTLE SQUIRRELS, PLEASE DON'T WORRY. MR. BULLDOG IS VERY SWEET.
COME, EVERYONE! LET ME FINISH YESTERDAY'S STORY.
WHERE DID I LEAVE OFF? OH, RIGHT. THE PART WHERE THE PRINCESS IS DISGUISED AS A PRINCE.
I WISH THERE WAS A WAY TO FIGURE OUT THAT SHE'S REALLY A SHE.
I KNOW! I'LL PRETEND TO BE HER NURSE! SHE MIGHT RESPOND LIKE A GIRL!

A mischief-making angel's prank goes too far when the new-born princess of Silverland ends up with two hearts—one male and one female. But since the laws of Silverland only allow a male heir to ascend the throne, Princess Sapphire is raised as a prince...

Princess Knight is the fast-paced tale of a heroic princess who can best any man at fencing, yet is delicate and graceful enough to catch the eye of Prince Charming. Filled with narrow escapes, treacherous courtiers, dashing pirates, meddlesome witches, magical transformations and cinema-worthy displays of derring-do, you'll be swept along as Sapphire tackles one challenge after another. *Princess Knight* mixes themes of gender identity and politics with classic shojo-style illustration to create a charming proto-feminist masterpiece by the "Godfather of Manga," one which has captured the hearts of generations of readers.

"An irresistible fantasy" —*The Manga Critic*

PRINCESS KNIGHT

by

Osamu Tezuka

Omnibus Edition coming 2022!

Translation: Maya Rosewood
Production: Grace Lu, Hiroko Mizuno, Jill Rittymanee, Tomoe Tsutsumi

PRINCESS KNIGHT

Princess Knight is a fast-paced tale of a heroic princess who can best any man at fencing, yet is delicate and graceful enough to catch the eye of Prince Charming. Filled with narrow escapes, treacherous courtiers, dashing pirates, meddlesome witches, magical transformations and cinema-worthy displays of derring-do, you'll be swept right along as Sapphire tackles one challenge after another.

ODE TO KIRIHITO

A promising young doctor visits a remote Japanese mountain village to investigate the source of the latest medical mystery. While he ends up traveling the world to discover what it takes to be cured of such a disease, a conspiracy back home attempts to explain away his absence.

APOLLO'S SONG

Apollo's Song follows the tragic journey of Shogo, a young man whose abusive childhood has instilled in him a loathing for love so profound he finds himself compelled to acts of violence when he witnesses any act of intimacy or affection—whether by human or beast. His hate is such that the gods intervene, cursing Shogo to experience love throughout the ages, only to have it ripped from his heart every time.

COMING 2022!

MORE FROM OSAMU TEZUKA

Classic Osamu Tezuka titles are back in print in an all-new format!

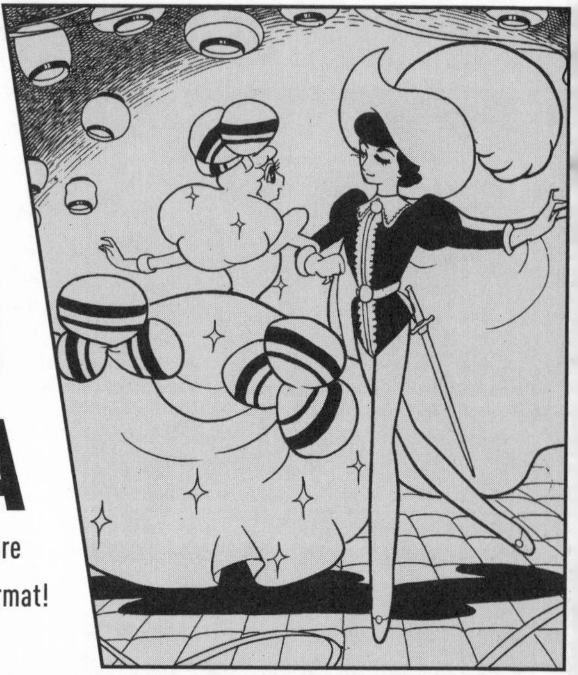

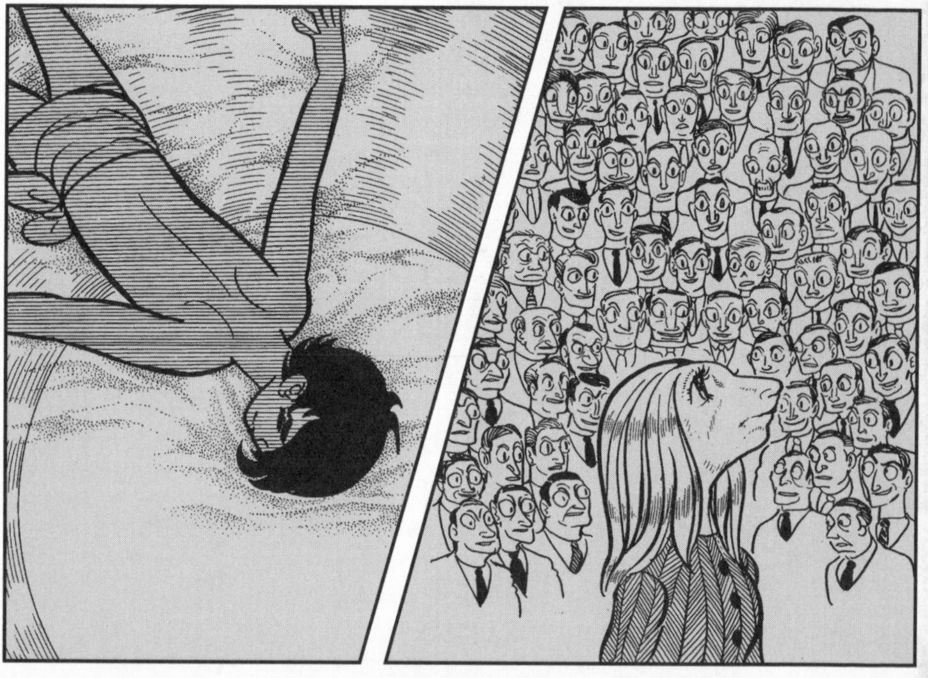

MORE FROM OSAMU TEZUKA

MW

Comics god Osamu Tezuka's darkest work, *MW* is a chilling picaresque of evil. The willfully "anti-Tezuka" achievement from the master's own pen neverthless pulsates with his unique genius.

DORORO

A samurai lord has bartered away his newborn's organs to forty-eight demons in exchange for dominance on the battlefield. Yet, the abandoned infant survives thanks to a medicine man who equips him with prosthetics—lethal ones with which the wronged son will hunt down the multitude of demons to reclaim his body one piece at a time and confront his father.

AYAKO

A Naturalist masterpiece that portrays postwar Japan through the decline of a landowning family and its ill-fated daughter.